Elevated Realms – An Anatomy of Mina Loy

For Po Ruby

Elevated Realms – An Anatomy of Mina Loy

Sara Crangle

Edinburgh University Press is one of the leading university presses in the UK. We publish academic books and journals in our selected subject areas across the humanities and social sciences, combining cutting-edge scholarship with high editorial and production values to produce academic works of lasting importance. For more information visit our website: edinburghuniversitypress.com

© Sara Crangle 2024, 2025

Edinburgh University Press Ltd
13 Infirmary Street
Edinburgh EH1 1LT

First published in hardback by Edinburgh University Press 2024

Typeset in 11/13pt Adobe Sabon
by Cheshire Typesetting Ltd, Cuddington, Cheshire

A CIP record for this book is available from the British Library

ISBN 978 1 3995 2432 2 (hardback)
ISBN 978 1 3995 2433 9 (paperback)
ISBN 978 1 3995 2434 6 (webready PDF)
ISBN 978 1 3995 2435 3 (epub)

The right of Sara Crangle to be identified as the author of this work has been asserted in accordance with the Copyright, Designs and Patents Act 1988, and the Copyright and Related Rights Regulations 2003 (SI No. 2498).

Contents

List of Figures vi
Acknowledgements viii
Abbreviations x
Preface. "[T]hat uncircumscribed entity, an Infinitarian":
  Loy the Esotericist xii

PART I

1. **Hearts Absented and Newborn: Loy's Esoteric Eros** 3
   Loy the Initiate: Esotericism and Avant-Gardism 12
   Loy the Adept: Esoteric Eros 27
   Ancient and Atomic Eros 59

PART II

   Introduction. Backs, Nerves, Eyes: From Proneness to
     Visionary Transcendence 93

2. **"The Supine Event"** 101
   Spinal Irritations and Nerviness: Feminised Lunacy 105
   Decadent Languor, Somnolence, and Male Violence 111
   Enchantment, Supinity, and the Hypnotic Gaze:
     Mesmerism and Spiritualism 119
   Telepathy, Voices, and Visions 132

3. **The Blind Back** 154
   Blindsiding Dorsality 154
   Backing and Forthing: Pineal Eye, Fourth Dimension 185

Bibliography 237
Index 258

Figures

0.1 Mina Loy, *Untitled (Surreal Scene)* (c. 1935). Gouache with collage on panel, 20 3/4 × 16 3/4 inches (52.71 × 42.55 cm). Collection of Roger Conover.   xxiv

1.1 Mina Loy, *Untitled (Surreal Scene)* (c. 1935), detail. Gouache with collage on panel, 20 3/4 × 16 3/4 inches (52.71 × 42.55 cm). Collection of Roger Conover.   6

1.2 Mina Loy, *Portrait of Freud* (1921). Carolyn Burke Collection on Mina Loy and Lee Miller. Yale Collection of American Literature, Beinecke Rare Book and Manuscript Library. Permission granted by Roger Conover.   41

2.1 Giacomo Balla, *La pazza* (1905). National Gallery of Modern and Contemporary Art of Rome. By kind concession of the Ministry of Cultural Heritage, Activities, and Tourism. ©ADAGP, Paris and DACS, London 2016.   109

3.1 Peter Paul Rubens, *Venus in Front of the Mirror* (1613–15). Liechtenstein Museum, Wenen.   180

3.2 René Magritte, *Les Liaisons dangereuses* (1936). Musée Toulouse-Lautrec; 2016©Photo SCALA, Florence/©ADAGP, Paris and DACS, London 2016.   181

3.3 René Magritte, *Not to be Reproduced* (1937). Museum Boijmans van Beuningan; 2016©Photo SCALA, Florence/©ADAGP, Paris and DACS, London 2016.   182

3.4 "Evolution of Root Races in the Fourth Round", Helena Blavatsky, *The Secret Doctrine*, Volume 2 (1888).   196

3.5 Mina Loy, *Untitled (Surreal Scene)* (c. 1935), detail. Gouache with collage on panel, 20 3/4 × 16 3/4 inches (52.71 × 42.55 cm). Collection of Roger Conover.   201

3.6 Marcel Duchamp, *Five-Way Portrait* (1917).
©Succession Marcel Duchamp/ADAGP, Paris and
DACS, London 2016; courtesy of Francis M. Naumann
Fine Art, LLC, New York. 215

Acknowledgements

The lengthy acknowledgements for the first volume are a direct reflection of my oceanic intellectual indebtedness. These acknowledgements are of a more personal nature, and should by all rights include gestures to my partner for the care that opened up the time to finish this *Anatomy of Mina Loy*, and the constancy that motivated me through too many setbacks to name. In addition, I consider myself incredibly lucky to have a circle of mainstays in my world who make all endeavours worthwhile. These books irrefutably exist because of those mainstays, even as they are not, in this specific instance, for them.

These two volumes are dedicated respectively to Val Raworth and Po Ruby. Although their dates of birth are nearly sixty years apart, Val and Po share many qualities: intelligence, discernment, excellent laughs. They are both unflagging moral compasses; in my home, Val is known as True North. Both are terrific readers: of character and circumstance, of ideology and culture.

In the nearly twenty years that it was my privilege to know her, Val told me many times that she liked the work of Mina Loy. This affinity makes sense. Val lived boldly, forthrightly, shrewdly, beautifully, seeking pleasure in all its guises. Her feminism was as integral as it was complex. While it is not self-evidently complimentary to be the dedicatee of a volume on abjected body parts, Val was rare among octogenarians (and septuagenarians, and people of any age) in completely lacking squeamishness. She was frank about sexuality and fabulously open-minded about human desire in general. Her gifts to me were time, stories, unparalleled loyalty and love. I was never bored in her company, always elated to come round for lunch and stay until midnight. Val amplified my life and thinking in all the best ways.

Po Ruby: from the very first, you opened your eyes to scrutinise, to think, to bring a canniness that disarms and motivates. There's a touch of greatness about Po, a friend once said, and I continue to look forward to how that greatness emerges in your creative, smart world, one to which you bring graft, tenacity, exactingness, righteousness, passion. Val admired you immeasurably. Through you I have learned that the body is not all-determining; through you I have learned to set aside my scepticism about what exceeds us. So the second volume of this *Anatomy*, on mystical feminism, on the self as a portal to transcendence, and on love above all, is for you.

Abbreviations

Mina Loy

B 6: 12	*Brontolivido* (c. 1913–20)
	Folders 1–9; pagination as prescribed by Beinecke PDFs
CP 19: 6	*The Child and the Parent* (c. 1932–6)
	Folders 10–20; Loy's pagination where extant
EP 21, EP 23: 2	*Esau Penfold* (c. 1910s/20s)
	Folders 21–6; only 23 is paginated
G32 7	*Goy Israels: A Play of Consciousness* or *Goy 32* (1932)
	Pages 1–39
GI 28: 127	*Goy Israels* (1925–30+)
	Folders 27–9
I	*Insel* (1933–6)
IA 69: 142	*Islands in the Air* (c. 1940s–50s)
	Folders 58–71; Loy's pagination
LaLB	*The Last Lunar Baedeker*
LoLB	*The Lost Lunar Baedeker*
SE	*Stories and Essays of Mina Loy*

Georges Bataille

AS1	*The Accursed Share* Vol. 1
AS2	*The Accursed Share* Vol. 2
AS3	*The Accursed Share* Vol. 3
BR	*Bataille Reader*
E	*Erotism*
G	*Guilty*
IE	*Inner Experience*
LE	*Literature and Evil*
TR	*Theory of Religion*

Henri Bergson
CE *Creative Evolution*

Carolyn Burke
BM *Becoming Modern*

Preface

"[T]hat uncircumscribed entity, an Infinitarian": Loy the Esotericist

The back cover of Mina Loy's second, final collection of poetry, *Lunar Baedeker and Time-Tables* (1958), reads: "An interplanetary voice whose subtle vibrations only faintly pierce our smug-laden atmosphere." In celebrating Loy's otherworldliness, the American novelist Henry Miller takes his place in a long lineage. Loy's cosmic proclivities were often commented upon by the modernist writers, publishers, and artists with whom she associated. Loy was said to speak as though she occupied an oneiric, alternate realm, to poetise "perception[s] of a fourth dimension", and write in a manner "'mediumistic, as if spoken from another world'"; her brilliant conversation was imbued with "cerebral fantasies" that beguilingly, artistically evaded "sense or reality or logic"; memorably, she conveyed an unshaken belief "that there was something in life that wasn't there."[1] These leanings arise in the earliest print valuations of Loy's writing. Reviewing the anthology released in 1919 by the small magazine *Others*, the English writer and publisher John Rodker asserts: "Mina Loy appears to be the only poet in this bag who is really preoccupied with that curious object THE SOUL", noting more prosaically that her otherwise "distinguished" poetry appears to have "lost grip" ("'Others'" 55).[2]

Rodker's language is emblematic: however esoterically directed, estimations of Loy consistently admit of the material and somatic, the grippable and grasping.[3] Accolades betray this fascination with Loy's simultaneously embodied and disembodied presence. American art patron and writer Mabel Dodge Luhan maintained that Loy's "'roots [were] in the universe'" (*Movers* 319). By this reading, Loy originated in the cosmos, remaining tentacularly embedded in the same. Likewise, the Italian Futurist leader F. T. Marinetti evidently chastised Loy for being a "'busy little mystic'"; unduly preoccupied by this world and the next, Loy is elevated and diminished by Marinetti's canny epithet (*B* 8: 6). And in a story featuring a version of Loy as protagonist, Djuna Barnes writes:

> All people gave her their attention, stroking her, and calling her pet or beast, according to their feelings. They touched her as if she were an idol, and she stood tall, or sat down to drink, unheeding, absent. You felt that you must talk to [her], tell her everything, because all her beauty was there, but uninhabited, like a church . . . . Only she was not holy, she was very mortal, and sometimes vulgar, a ferocious and oblivious vulgarity. (77–8)

For Barnes's narrator, Loy is object or place of worship, distant and divine, yet Loy is grounded by the abject, by her bestiality, her tactility, her coarseness.

Loy was a thinker who devoted herself to alternate realms whilst ceaselessly validating – desirously, blissfully, reluctantly, uncomfortably – their inextricability from the constrained third-dimensional world. This truth is the substance of a 1923 presentation of Loy's authorial persona written by the then-editor of *Poetry* magazine, Harriet Monroe:

> If, having experienced, whether actively or imaginatively, too much of life to endure it, one can't be a saint like Teresa of exalted memory, it may be that this lady's cynical acceptance of flitting inexplicable pains and raptures is but the shadowed under-side of the saint's ecstatic sensuality. (102)

By Monroe's account, a beleaguered Loy aspires to, yet never attains, a canonised beatification. Yet Loy's ambition is sufficient to the cause of situating her sensory highs and lows within the realm of the ecstatic mysticism for which the Catholic visionary Teresa of Ávila (1515–82) was renowned. So close to Loy's preoccupations and process is Monroe that she inadvertently paraphrases a key maxim of Loy's unpublished essay "Conversion" (c. 1920s): "The aim of the artist is to miss the absolute" (*SE* 228). Recognising Loy as an artist-mystic, Monroe posits a truth central to Loy's work and this volume, namely that, throughout her life, Loy prioritises and theorises a carnal, transcendental Eros. This Eros is the foundation and requisite counterpoint to Loy's Thanatos, or the aggressive, combative drive that is so magnificently deployed in her feminist satires.

Scottish poet Edwin Muir encapsulates this central argument still more poignantly in his 1924 review of Loy's first book, *Lunar Baedecker* (*sic*):

> She is a mystic of a very peculiar kind, a negative mystic, the chief fruit of whose mysticism is an acridly intimate awareness of the flesh. She is perplexed, she is disconcerted painfully, by the senses; and her poetry is a protest against them, expressed in a photographic, relentless portrayal of their antics. Even when she is moved by pity, the sense of metaphysical obscenity is not far away; but that obscenity is the complement of her subconscious, helpless mysticism. This deep-set and unresolved conflict gives her work intensity, but, naturally, gives it only in flashes; and she never attains the serenity out of which great poetry comes. Given her limits, however, she is so genuine that her utterance arrests us. (223)

Time and shifts in political consciousness have done much to correct Muir's rote underestimation of Loy's abilities, his claims of her feminised overwhelm, unawareness, and inconstancy, a misogyny extended by the jarring racism of his insistence, later in the same review, that she writes "Babu English" (223). These offences notwithstanding, Muir remains astute about Loy's gnostic leanings, which are grounded in the soma entire, a soma pungent, exposable, adamantly present. Contrarily, given the passivity and negativity of the above quotation, Muir also positions Loy as fearlessly aware of the worst abuses a body can suffer, noting that, in her writing, an "awful intimacy" emerges from "act[s] of mutilation . . . rendered" to generate "cosmic meaning" (223).

As I argue in the first volume of this *Anatomy of Mina Loy*, Loy is a writer who attacks her enemies to bring them closer rather than to assert a distance between herself and the violent or repugnant, which is the traditional aim of satire. Directing our attention toward the potentially generative interdependence of aggression and intimacy is the novel ground of Loy's feminist satire. Her verbal assaults expose the inextricability of satire and sacrifice, and highlight the emphasis upon women within the sacrificial economy. In the process, Loy demonstrates that abjection is a universal condition, one not ascribable to the marginalised alone, and likewise expresses an omnipresent, ungendered, and liberating need for proximity and affective vulnerability. In this second volume, I turn to Loy's esoteric theorisations of Eros as a foundation of her artistry. For Loy, Eros offers a transcendental generativity that remains resolutely of the body as a flawed, sensory material object, a proudly "metaphysical obscenity" that celebrates corporeality at its most orgasmic and uncontained. Or, as Loy asserts: "There is no understanding of the metaphysical except through participation" ("Notes on Metaphysics").

Raised in a North London household that adhered to her English mother's evangelical Protestantism whilst remaining conscious of her Hungarian father's Jewish heritage, Mina Loy (1882–1966) is widely understood to have converted to Christian Science in 1909 and to have remained an adherent to this sect for the remainder of her life.[4] But while Science endured as a mainstay of the adult Loy's daily consciousness, the story of her esoteric proclivities is far more complicated than these facts suggest, involving as it does the mesmeric, telepathic, and spiritualist; the enchanted and visionary; Freudian and post-Freudian psychoanalysis, including psychosynthesis; philosophies Platonic and phenomenological; Blavatsky's Theosophy and Joel S. Goldsmith's *The Infinite Way* (1947); atomic physics and fourth dimensionality, as well as the occasional session of numerology. In turn, these occult methodologies and aims fed their way back into Loy's approach to Christian Science, which she often treated as a form of sympathetic magic. These myriad influences on Loy's esoteric Eros – an Eros situated and represented through Loy's writerly emphases on bodily positioning and anatomy – are examined in this volume. Ecumenically heterodox, what remained constant in Loy's belief system was her strong resistance toward orthodoxies. She contended that her parents' mixed marriage made her "'a wanderer infinitely more haunted than the eternal Jew'", her mind constantly seeking "'orbits'" beyond Torah or catechism (qtd. in *BM* 375).[5] Or, as she succinctly put it in 1930: "I have a different Cosmos every week" (Undated letter, Loy to Julien and Joella Levy, Box 30, Folder 10, 1930). Loy's spiritual quest never fully abated: in the 1940s, as she entered her sixties, she could regularly be found at New York's legendary Gotham Book Mart, whiling away her time in the occult section (*BM* 399).

This is the first book devoted to the process of situating Loy's esotericism within a range of beliefs that encompasses ancient thinking and post-eighteenth-century modernity, a process daunting and assuredly damned to incompletion.[6] What is more, this book uniquely aspires to a comprehensive consideration of Loy's writings, meaning evidence is drawn from her published poems, essays, and short fictions, and from her archived scraps and orts in Philadelphia and New Haven, among the latter essayistic fragments that may have been intended as parts of a longer, unrealised work. I also attend closely to the full range of Loy's drafts, both manuscript and typescript, of interrelated and often incomplete autobiographical writings, writings I label her romans à clef, and accordingly treat as representations of her self and life.[7] In this latter category, the eight texts to which I refer are: *Brontolivido* (c. 1913–20), *Esau Penfold* (c. 1910s/20s), *Goy Israels* (1925–30+), *Goy Israels: A Play of Consciousness* (1932), *Insel* (1933–6), *The Child and the Parent* (c. 1932–6), *Islands in the Air* (c. 1940s–50s), and *Colossus*, Loy's biography of her relationship with Arthur Cravan that was partially published by Roger Conover in 1985.[8] Within these texts are two distinct autobiographical lineages: the early career dialogic – in which a female protagonist spars with a male associate of a vanguard movement – and the late life künstlerromans that articulate Loy's development as an artist and as a feminist theorist of a sex-positive esoteric love or Eros. Loy oxymoronically described these later works as a form of "thwarted activity". Conflicted sites laboured over lovingly and intensively, they were also, in a phrasing that echoes Muir, the place where Loy claimed to do "battl[e] with the preposterous negativism of [her] fractured destiny" ("Promised Land"). This battle grew harder as Loy aged: to her son-in-law Julien Levy, whose editorial insights she habitually pursued, she likened writing these works to the experience of a fly trapped in flypaper, to inhibition and constipation, and to being mocked by the English language itself (Undated letter, Loy to Julien and Joella Levy, Box 30, Folder 13, 1933).

In their earliest guises, Loy considered the künstlerromans a tracking out of "psychological evolution" that pitted "Jewish brain" against "Christian credulity", a process underpinned by the awareness that no resolution or "absolute conclusion" could be attained. In a lengthy letter from 1933, Loy suggested that what emerges from this conflict is "the <u>seer</u>" who is "composed of racial – primeval cosmic memory or awareness" and "also the <u>memory</u> of the future." Historical examples of Loy's seer include Christ, Freud, and herself, or she who continues and betters Freud's attempt to balance "the sacred & profane scission in the human mind." As seer, Loy is always "'in' on the most vitally significant manifestation of the signs of the times"; as seer, Loy's ideal mate – her second husband Cravan is expressly named – appears as a pagan god, akin to Mercury; as seer, Loy interweaves her book with "the white magic theme of the materialisation of thought", and attends closely to women's association with materiality of life, its "detritus . . . cosmic dust & erosion" (Letter dated Easter Eve, Loy to Julien and Joella Levy, Box 30,

Folder 13, 1933). Loy acknowledged that her epistolary essay was a garbled, partial summary of her aims, yet these coordinates are discernibly reoriented and expanded in the numerous manifestations of Loy's encyclopaedic text that follow.

Pivotally, this letter affirms Loy's lifelong determination to tussle with and replace orthodoxies with esotericisms that include supernatural prophetic powers, enchantment, and the primeval. These esotericisms are undergirded by an attentiveness to the sexual awakening for which Loy consistently celebrates Freud whilst labouring to correct his failure to attend sufficiently to women's socio-sexual positioning. Loy's youngest daughter considered the late prose her mother's "book about her Dimension" – a space singular and ethereal – and feared that Loy might lose her mind in her attempts to bring it to realisation (Letter dated 24 April 1930, Fabienne Lloyd to Julien and Joella Levy, Box 30, Folder 6, 1929–74). While Loy's künstlerromans can be as uniquely otherworldly as her daughter suggests, they draw from discernible heterodox influences that are the focus of this volume, and move implicitly and explicitly toward the feminist vision of Eros subtending Loy's self-proclaimed oracularity. This oracularity notably aligns Loy with the satiric tradition at which she excelled; as is discussed in the first volume, since its inception, maledictive, judgemental satire has always been associated with the prophetic.

To some degree, attending to the broad array of Loy's esoteric affiliations resolves a recurrent problem in Loy criticism: her readers have often struggled to locate direct allegiances between Loy's embodied, unabashedly sexual writings and her ties to Christian Science, a religion that aspires to a pure spirituality by refusing to acknowledge any truth in bodily materiality, need, or longing.[9] For founder Mary Baker Eddy (1821–1910), illness or mental distress are indications that an individual has strayed too far from what should be an all-encompassing relationship with God. Christian Scientists uphold the view that with sufficient faith and correct religious practice, third-dimensional limitations can always be transcended. But as Tim Armstrong coherently argues, there exists an unacknowledged inextricability of errant corpus and perfectible soul in these tenets: "paradoxically, despite the denial of the importance of physical life in Christian Science, the body is the ground where its power must be proved". Armstong maintains: "in its return to health, [the body must] testify to the primacy of Spirit", meaning that "its materiality is both transcended and returns as evidence" (210).

While Armstrong's insight resonates, the body is persistently shunned and shamed in Baker Eddy's writings in ways wholly inconsistent with Loy's artistic and intellectual valuation of the corporeal, her foregrounding of anatomical parts, desires, affects, gestures, and postures at every turn. Loy recognises and mobilises these inconstancies to her advantage, praising Baker Eddy as "the first person to put the higher intellectual facts to a practical use" and encouraging Science practitioners – her daughter among them – "to benefit by its exoteric power over the traditions of matter" whenever convenient (Undated letter, Loy to Julien and Joella Levy, Box 30, Folder 8, 1928; 15 December 1927, Loy to Julien and Joella Levy, Box 30, Folder 7, 1927). As I will discuss in Chapter 1, Loy has a remarkable capacity to separate out the aspects of Science that do not accord with her own thinking – its diminishment of sexual ecstasy in particular – thereby cannily locating within its tenets ways of "hav[ing her] cake and eat[ing] it too" (Undated letter, Loy to Julien and Joella Levy, Box 30, Folder 8, 1928).

With the above in view, this volume follows a lead established by Maeera Shreiber during the late 1990s critical reclamation of Loy:

> Instead of placing Loy's work within the context of a specific brand of religious practice, I want to make a broader claim about a life-long spiritual quest that informed not only her poetry, but her prose writings [and visual art]; taken as a whole, these works constitute an act of devotion in the service of the corporeality of God (469).

Akin to Loy's earliest critics and associates, Shreiber identifies Loy as a mystic in perpetual search of a direct, immediate, and intimate relationship with the divine. While Loy's valuation of somatic sensation and gratification is so great that it might well threaten her claims to the mystical, Shreiber identifies her as operating within the bounds of a tradition that "licenses certain proclivities for sensual experience as central to knowledge of God" (470).[10] So it is that Loy perpetually attends to the nethered human parts that were the focus of the first volume of this *Anatomy* – feet, legs, genitals, bellies, wombs – whilst giving equal shrift to the elevated realms that demand our attention in this second text, the heart, spine, and eyes. These realms are literally elevated in belonging to the upper body, and because these same body parts are the physical launching grounds and centres of Loy's resolutely transcendent Eros, an Eros that propels us heavenward. Loy's Eros is spiritual, philosophical, aesthetic; it is also expressly figured as orgasmic precisely because it operates in necessary tandem with debased anatomical regions.

"The sign of the true mystic will ever be his declaration of the 'impossible'", argues Loy, and her balancing act between corpus and cosmos may well exemplify this unattainability ("Notes on Religion" 15). But on the inextricability of this binary Loy insists, as does her erotically and gnomically oriented peer, the French philosopher Georges Bataille (1897–1962). As Loy optimistically postulates: "in illumination the mystic abstractly perceived our impossible to blossom forth as *the* POSSIBLE", an illumination facilitated by an "ECSTASY" that offers access to "THE CREATIONAL OVERTURE" that reveals beauty, music, and climactic pleasures in their nascent, universalised states (*SE* 243). Bataille concurs: "The mystic is fundamentally a man for whom tortures become delights" ("Surrealist Religion" 89). Materiality and the sensory are integral to Loy's mysticism, which, particularly in her early writings, flies in the face of tradition in venerating bodies that are broken rather than aspiring to wholeness, holiness. As Schreiber avers, these anatomisations and fragmentations are feminist in validating "a theology of lack" that draws upon the mystical by way of "destabiliz[ing] psychoanalytic accounts of sexual difference" through which women are presented as partial, devoid of the phallus that would make them a subject entire (470, 477).

Deploying Luce Irigaray, Shreiber's brilliant argument justifies the coordinates of my own *Anatomy*, but hers is also an unstintingly celebratory recovery of what remained a deep wound in Loy's psyche. For while it is true that Loy emphasises human "brokenness" throughout her oeuvre, her late autobiographical and essayistic writings reveal that this was not, for her, "an ultimate state of being" but one that she restlessly, sometimes agonisingly, strove to overcome from adolescence to senescence (Shreiber 475). As I will discuss, this very longing for wholeness feeds Loy's ambivalence toward Freud, whose psyche she found too riven, too anatomised, and in dire need of spiritual coherence. In emphasising divination, Loy is a typical mystic, seeking a unification that she knows can only ever be fleetingly accessed by mere mortals. Recognising its limitations, this same coalescing pursuit drives Loy's lifelong theorisations of an esoteric Eros.

How, if at all, might we characterise the immensely variegated "continuum of idealisms" to which the mystical Loy ascribed? (Cook 458). Two interrelated, broad traits cohere Loy's mystical leanings. Firstly, like any esotericist, she seeks articulations of the divine that promise direct access to infinitude. But more specifically, Loy is drawn to doctrines that actively minimise or eradicate the threat posed by bodily harm and death whilst providing her with the means to contact an unrestrained cosmological beyond. These needs are as all-consuming as they are all-defining, as Loy affirms at the outset of her undated, late story "Street Sister":

> Being that uncircumscribed entity, an infinitarian, traditionless, almost conditionless, I have been privileged, but so seldom, to slip over the psychological frontier of that unvisited region where those others withhold the confidences of their deprivation, and see the light that lingers in the shadow of mankind. (41)

Loy's narrator is oxymoronically without limits or affiliation, but is also tethered to knowable existence, bounded by mode and being. Hers is a beneficent, omniscient presence who easily straddles this world and the next; as her story continues, she continues to position herself as an unquestionable arbiter of all that ails society.[11] While the narrative command of this "infinitarian" is formidable, a little scratching at the surface of Loy's thinking exposes her tone as a feint to stave off deeply human apprehensions. In refusing the putrescent, fragile body, Christian Science propagated a religious will so strong that it not only promised to eliminate disease and discomfort, but opened the possibility of eschewing death itself (Bloom 132, 144). For Loy, this capacity was foundational to its appeal.

In her archive, Loy asserts: "'Mary Eddy's revelation was of the safeguarding aspect of the infinite Power—a homey, comforting antidote to the anxiety of raising a family'" (qtd. in Shreiber 470). Not God, but a protective "infinite Power". This same need to be saved from mortal constraints assuredly drew Loy to Frederic W. H. Myers's *Human Personality and its Survival of Bodily Death* (1903). It also motivates Loy's lifelong belief in reincarnation, which aligns her with Theosophy and, notably, runs expressly counter to Christian Science teachings, which restrict followers to a single earthly manifestation. In her correspondence, Loy occasionally articulates returning to Christian Science after a lapse in faith; in the 1940s, this cyclical disenchantment saw her turn to the teachings of Joel S. Goldsmith. A former Science practitioner, Goldsmith emphasised that ageing is inevitable but is ultimately as irrelevant as bodily health, given that "the power of immortality is in the Spirit" (*Living* 75). Goldsmith promised to strengthen the spirit through a meditative prayer methodology that aspired to near-constant access to the deific. Tellingly, members of Goldsmith's global following do not die, but "transition". In like spirit, when responding to a questionnaire circulated by the Surrealist magazine *View* in 1942, Loy envisions a future where the "unpleasant process of death will give place to an instantaneous dissolution, a painless disappearance" (*LaLB* 307).

Secondly, Loy gravitates toward spiritual or occult leaders who validate the exceptional individual. These leaders follow in the wake of Nietzsche's *Übermensch* or Overman in celebrating the artist, philosopher, saint, or genius, figures who set themselves apart from the masses by surpassing subjective limitations and traditional modes of thinking. In Jesus, Loy admires a Nietzschean distinctness from the herd, one she claims he preached to his disciples. Loy's contortion of Christian humility is as brash as it is unsustainable, yet she avers: "Jesus saw through us far better than Freud—in seeing that our real dilemma was [not instinctual], but our desperate determination to establish our identity apart from the general mass." Regularly conflating artists with the deific, Loy argues that the full depth of Jesus's biblical teachings is most accessible to "the more out-reaching intellect" shared by herself and her avant-garde peers, intellects who recognise him as "a synopsis of the future" and "an antidote to extinction" ("Notes on Religion" 14–15). Reading the New Testament through this self-affirming lens, Loy consistently admires thinkers who likewise validate her uniqueness as a highly cerebral artist: Myers promotes the genius as having exceptional access to subliminal uprushes of inspiration; his peer, the French philosopher Henri Bergson, similarly believed artists were in possession of an intuition that can commune, if fleetingly, with a universal consciousness. When she grew restless with these writers, Loy sought variations on their themes, turning, for instance, to Italian psychiatrist Roberto Assagioli's psychosynthesis as a methodology that reassuringly cohered the self, affirmed introspective creativity, and presented genius as cosmic connectivity. As the first line of her poem "Apology of Genius" (1922) asserts, Loy was immensely reassured to consider herself among the select and brilliant few "[o]stracized . . . with God" (*LoLB* 77).

In sum, Loy's broadly ecumenical infinitarianism oscillated vertiginously between debilitating mortal consternations and a vaingloriousness by which she approximates Christ. From this vexed perspective, the body provides much-needed ground. Consistent with what I defined in the first volume as Loy's atavistic avant-gardism, her somatic mysticism looks backward and forward simultaneously. In seventeenth-century Europe, the body was inextricable from a cosmological context; only recently has Western liberal modernity insisted upon "an atomistic view" of subject, corpus, social world, and universe (Birke 53, 171). As readily, Loy is a precursor to twenty-first-century feminisms that posit material, fleshy human corporeality as inextricable from its immediate environment and from a broadly defined "more-than-human world" (Alaimo 238). Loy's demarcation of an Eros defined by "[s]exual and emotional inclination" that eschews moral, religious, and gendered tradition reinforces Loy's anticipation of this contemporary framework (Cavarero 3).

Immensely sex positive, Loy's mysticism proves capable of orgasms amorous, spiritual, aesthetic, and humanitarian (*IA* 63: 41–2). No stranger to imposed restraint, Loy rejects asceticism as a path to enlightenment, instead foregrounding a deeply visceral, pleasurable love as its source. Having reached this state of illumination through her second husband, Loy felt it was her duty to impart "the electric incitement of Eros" to the uninitiated (*SE* 247–8). Loy's proselytising prioritises a female need so often absent from the teachings of her occult and intellectual peers, attending closely to how women remain dependent upon and constrained by male interpretations of their anatomies and longings. By this typically gendered state of affairs, women are left "entirely void" even after the brief resuscitation of the sex Loy elevates to the status of sacrament (*CP* 18: 65). Loy's summation of this situation is as succinct as it is apt: "WOMAN – – the big Review – – still inconsummate" (*CP* 18: 69). For Loy, as for her peer Bataille, "The erotic moment is . . . the zenith of this life", but so important is women's desire to Loy that she refrains, as Bataille does not, from tying transcendence to procreation (Bataille, *Tears* 33).[12] For Loy, women's satiation is legacy enough.

Central to Loy's spiritual quest is a problem recognised by Irigaray in the 1970s, namely that women continue to be imbued with guilt and anxiety about sexual desire, and struggle for recognition or affirmation in this regard that does not simply prove self-sacrificing (30–2). As a direct consequence of these difficulties, Irigaray argues:

> Feminine pleasure has to remain inarticulate in language, in its own language, if it is not to threaten the underpinnings of logical operations. And so what is most strictly forbidden to women today is that they should attempt to express their own pleasure. (77)

Judith Butler takes umbrage with Irigaray's formulation, asking: "is specifically feminine pleasure 'outside' of culture as its prehistory or as its utopian future?" If the answer to either option is yes, Butler wonders: "of what use is such a notion for negotiating the contemporary struggles of sexuality within the terms of its construction?" (*Gender* 41). For Butler, Irigaray cannot have it both ways: to argue simultaneously for the social construction of female pleasure and for its place outside of society is "a cultural impossibility and a politically impracticable dream" (*Gender* 42).

Perhaps too conveniently, Loy's esotericism precludes the need for the logic and pragmatism Butler understandably seeks. Whilst recognising, as do Irigaray and Butler, that women's sexuality has been historically defined by a phallic economy, Loy is a mystic continually in pursuit of ideas and experience that exceed her own cultural confines; the belief that she can surpass the status quo defines her spirituality as much as it does her avant-gardism.[13] By sanctifying female pleasure, Loy elevates women's satiation to orgasmically transcendent heights, transposing it into a gnomic, unrealised utopia available to a feminist elect and anyone open-minded and driven enough to join their company. The as-yet-unsolved riddle of women's pleasure is as old as, and often personified by, the prehistoric Sphinx in Loy's imaginary. Loy's *Untitled (Surreal Scene)* (c. 1935) diagrams this belief: a collage supernatural and anatomical, this work gestures to the demonic, the angelic, the saved and the damned, autonomous body parts and partial yet functioning bodies domestic, human, spectral, and artistic.[14] The left-hand side of this painting is dominated by a near-naked white woman whose breasts and exposed reproductive system are represented by fecund flowers in full bloom and foundational Christian symbology (Fig. 0.1). Her womb is a chalice of wine, merging menstrual flow with Christ's blood; her ovaries, the wheat signifying Christ's body, or the Eucharist; in combination, her reproductive organs are readied for an ecstatic resurrection.[15]

Placidly impractical, Loy's esoteric Eros resolutely addresses the impossibilities of easeful or coherent self-identification within long-established and marginalising power structures, difficulties that continue to determine the direction of contemporary feminist discourse.[16] Loy is forward-thinking in privileging not only the pursuit of women's pleasure, but also in articulating a right to satiation. The unresolved need to interrogate, affirm, and meet female longing has been at the forefront of generations of feminist thinking. In 1918, British women's rights campaigner Marie Stopes caused a sensation by extolling the unexamined particularities of women's sexuality and the need to correct aggressive, "prudish or careless husbands" who, "content with their own satisfaction, little know the pent-up aching, or even resentment, which may eat into a wife's heart, and ultimately may affect her whole health" (39). Remarkably, dispiritingly, predictably, contemporary feminist thinkers continue to articulate sexual needs met and unmet with similar all-consuming trepidation and frustration.[17] Throughout

Fig. 0.1 Mina Loy, *Untitled (Surreal Scene)* (c. 1935). Gouache with collage on panel, 20 3/4 × 16 3/4 inches (52.71 × 42.55 cm). Collection of Roger Conover.

the twentieth and twenty-first centuries, the value and complexity of women's sexuality has been cyclically jettisoned and newly "discovered": while Stopes's pioneering work was internationally recognised, come 1976, *The Hite Report* on female sexuality was touted as the first to ask women directly about their own desire (Wolf 162).

While these agendas are troublingly competing and/or partial, the urgency at stake has remained consistent for well over a century.

Loy's terms and approach to a celebratory, gnomic Eros are readily discerned within this feminist trajectory. In the late 1970s, Audre Lorde reclaims the erotic "as a resource within each of us that lies in a deeply female and spiritual plane, firmly rooted in the power of our unexpressed or unrecognized feeling" (53). More recently, Jennifer C. Nash recovers black women's ecstasy as a transcendence of self-limitation, imposed or material, and as a means of capturing inarticulable bliss (2). This thinking is similarly locatable in José Muñoz's assertion that queerness remains unknown or, in Loy's terms, "inconsummate" (22). Muñoz articulates the need for an ecstasy that "can only exist as a critique of the dominant order", by which he means the powerful heteronormativity that has fuelled rigorous reappraisal and abiding despair within queer studies (22, 39). For Muñoz, ecstasy is refreshingly, positively utopian, an embodied transcendence he likens to the religious rapture of Saint Teresa (185). This drive to reinvigorate and politicise an esoteric ecstasy potentially holds open a space for a different kind of identity politics, one that abandons the model of the body as totalising material constraint, and instead moves toward what Riki Lane describes as a universal, dynamic transformativity of bodies in perpetual flux, a "bodily becoming" less inhibited because less bound to category or systematised strictures. Lane speaks to what Amelia Jones characterises as "the nascent but growing sense that identity must be understood as multiple, fluid, intersectional, performative, contingent" (148). A product of her Victorian upbringing, Loy can cleave to gendered distinction and heteronormativity in her writings. But little was static about Loy's thinking, which habitually dismantled binaries and unexamined norms. Oscillating between identifying as an Anglo-Jewish "mongrel" and a "mystic", Loy was a feminist who knew that identity eschewed ready category, who gravitated toward individuals queer, racialised, impoverished, and disabled whilst writing near-didactically of the universal right to a spiritual ecstasy grounded in a body constrained yet uncontainable.[18]

While ecstasy is readily seen as a liberator of the self, pain is rarely interpreted as a like catalyst. The intellectual history of transcendence has long been critiqued for adhering to a masculine fear of merging with the material, feminised corpus. But as Susan Wendell argues, feminist theory has been slow to recognise that the same desire to exceed subjective confines can be rooted in the rational pursuit of "independen[ce from] illness, pain, weakness, exhaustion, and accident" (165–6). Wendell's arguments are reinforced by Loy's contemporary influence, the sexologist Havelock Ellis, who argues that it is normal for men to dominate and women to submit, meaning that courtship between men and women is interlaced with a cruelty that presumes that "the idea of pain" is innately "pleasurable to women" (*Studies* I 688). In Loy, liberation from the chronic trauma of domination turned abuse is a catalyst for her mystical proclivities, a trauma that no doubt fed into an adulthood marked by depressive periods and, in her later years, an incapacitating stomach ulcer (*BM* 390).

It is well known that Loy's childhood home was combative: throughout her romans à clefs, as in "Anglo-Mongrels and the Rose" (1923–5), Loy repeatedly discusses how her father – an ambitious Jewish tailor – migrated from Eastern Europe, ultimately becoming a middle-class business owner who nevertheless remained anxious, at times crassly boastful, about his success (*GI* 28: 88–9). As Loy observes, her father valued social propriety and position over domestic harmony, "shar[ing], with an almost total majority of men at the time, a somehow subtly obscene aversion" toward any encouragement to "cut his marriage in half" (*IA* 67: 99). This marriage Loy considered "an invisible acid" that "sprea[d] and erod[ed]" her family entire (*GI* 28: 115). Loy's mother was tempestuous and dominating, behaviours Loy associates with the worst excesses of English imperialism. Her working-class maternal heritage is only belatedly and derogatorily relayed in Loy's last roman à clef, where her mother's perpetually harsh language is attributed to her having been raised by those who lack "superficial graces as amenity, the expression of affection or the tempered rebuke" (*IA* 65: 63).[19] Attempting "every conceivable conduct" to mitigate her mother's insatiable, unpredictable, and contrary expectations, Loy finds nothing succeeds; in response, guilt defines and overtakes her existence. Loy's romans à clef often read as disquisitions of the parent with whom she spent the majority of her childhood days. But while Loy's mother is singularly blamed for the pain that defined Loy's upbringing – a brunt emphasised by Loy and replicated by her critics – her father bears responsibility for the truth that "[a]n everlasting anger is all the love" that the child Loy "ever encountered" (*GI* 28: 115).

Loy tends to mention fatherly indiscretions in passing, as when she articulates her parents' concerns about her marriageability that lead to "the accustomed dual opposition" to behaviour deemed unfeminine (*IA* 67: 11–12). But this resistance is not her parents' only alignment, as their humiliating tactics are often shared: Loy is dressed in ill-fitting, cheap clothing that exposes her body to view, a situation her tailor father permits; and, while her mother accuses her of sin, slyness, narcissism, greed, and disrespect, her father "catches" her in a lie in which he conspired by way of testing her honesty (*GI* 29: 146; *IA* 65: 64–5; 55–6). "[D]efenceless, abject with shame", Loy narrates her thinly fictionalised self as so relentlessly well-intentioned and spotlessly innocent that she may well spark the reader's incredulity (*IA* 65: 6). But the surfeit of evidence on offer is irrefutable and distressing: Loy's mother clearly chastised her daughter out of a racist distaste for her part-Jewish origins and out of envious loathing toward her burgeoning sexuality; what is more, her incessant verbal abuse spills over into the physical.[20] These memories explain why Loy's mind "conform[ed] automatically to a rhythm of recurrent culpability", sparking a survivalist if "precocious introspection", skills upon which she no doubt drew again in her first, abusive marriage (*IA* 65: 61). Taken together, this trauma and subsequent inward turn are catalysts for the artist and mystic Loy will become, an individual attuned from youth to meditation and aesthetic ruminations by which she escaped and reconfigured her daily life. As is exemplified by the satires directed at her domineering male vanguard associates and lovers, Loy became adept, from lived necessity, at strategically combating her most intimate enemies, a category that can include herself. As a direct corollary, Loy devoted intellectual energy toward articulating an esoteric Eros that affirms her "infinitarian" place both in and beyond this world, a place maligned and uncertain through her formative years.

These are the coordinates by which Loy's adult life was defined.[21] Continually accused of imposture, Loy generates creative and spiritual postulations. The romans à clef map out how Loy develops her own version of what Iris Marion Young theorises as a "female comportment" through which women around the world navigate their respective societies, both physically and in their purposiveness, aspiring toward individual aims. For Young, female embodiment is defined by contradiction: like any human being, a woman knows herself to be a lived subject capable of overcoming her lived reality. But as a woman, she is continually witness to her own objectification, and is thereby forced to see herself as autonomously positional and co-optatively positioned ("Throwing" 144). As a result, women develop what Young calls an "*ambivalent transcendence,* a transcendence that is at the same time laden with [an] immanence" that becomes an undue burden, that prevents women moving through the world with ease and openness, bereft of a masculinised, confident "unbroken directedness" in taking up space or position ("Throwing" 148). It is this ambivalence that Loy meets with an enabling esoteric Eros.

Loy's Eros is the counter to the supinity expected of the passive female, the woman idealised as shrinking and prone, the woman presumed to inhabit the tipping point of hysteria.[22] As this book argues, Loy elevates this abject, feminised posturing into a dorsality with the potential to access the cosmos, to become a utopian portal into the universal ether from which she believes all humans emerge, and to which artists and geniuses retain the strongest connection. Elevates, rather than erects: the human spine appeals to Loy because of its flexibility, its deviant curves, its refusal of straight lines. By her vision of the "blind back" – a back that incorporates the legacy of the all-seeing third eye – Loy seeks out a future free of the impositions of biological origin, one that validates her artistic access to the unlimited creativity offered by the fourth dimension. Loy's visionary journey is not a consistent forward march. As Sandeep Parmar attests: "although the promise of modernity for Loy was a continual psychic rebirth, her actual engagement with the process of becoming modern engages with a past, real or imagined, and expresses the dilemma of being both at once in the present moment and rooted in the pervading influence of memory on perception" (46). Ecstatic retroversion is the guiding motif of this volume, through which I will show Loy repeatedly embracing dorsality and backwardness to circumvent the confines of progressivist, rationalised Enlightenment subjectivity.

My first chapter, "Hearts Absented and Newborn: Loy's Esoteric Eros", is unique within this *Anatomy* in prioritising an ethereal heartscape rather than a living organ; its terms are demarcated by what Loy calls "the percussion of Eros" (*CP* 17: 54). While critics have long recognised Loy's brilliantly exercised "caustic scrutiny" upon intimacy, I redirect the Loy reader toward her fidelity to what she performatively eschewed, namely "'that meaning, value, hope, and even transcendence can be found through love'" (Selinger 23, 19). Mocking romance, Loy nevertheless consistently turns to the affairs of the heart, to a multivalent love itself, for the unrivalled coherence and insight that this affect promises. Part proselytiser, part feminist advocate, Loy proffers a resolutely physical love: she believes that we can right the historical wrongs of Western socio-sexual morality by authenticating lust as a "sane *impulse*", thereby rescuing lust from exoteric vilification (*SE* 283–4). Against critics who have categorised Loy as a satirist in her early years, a mystic in her late, I argue that Loy's esoteric Eros and satire exist interdependently from the outset of her authorial career. Loy's quest for a liberating "heartsease" is ecstatic, sexualised, intimate, but also familial, artistic, and spiritual, the requisite Eros to her satiric Thanatos (*LoLB* 129). For Loy, its symbolic touchstone is Arthur Cravan, or he "who made euphonious / our esoteric universe" (*LoLB* 129).

In establishing Loy's Eros, this chapter presents esotericism and avant-gardism as discourses aligned in rejecting the status quo and embracing a pursuit of the gnomic by an elect few. Although Yeats has long been touted as the pre-eminent modernist mystic, evidence drawn from Loy's entire oeuvre illustrates that she is a thoroughgoing, emblematic, and innovative esotericist in her own right. Having established the strong foundations of Loy's heterodoxy, I demarcate Loy's theory of Eros, which works with and opposes key tenets of psychoanalysis, occult practice, the philosophy of Georges Bataille, and Surrealism. An adherent to the liberating power of the Freudian libido, Loy believes that psychoanalysis is too masculinist and can only do its work when it foregrounds, rather than represses, the occult leanings from which it originated; consequently, I trace out evident connections between Loy's thought and Frederic Myers, as well as second-generation psychoanalysts Karen Horney, Roberto Assagioli, and Sandor Rado.

While Loy and Bataille are alike in theorising an intellectual awareness that ascends to orgasmic and spiritual overwhelm, Bataille's philosophy is a cypher for a phallocentric sexual mysticism that Loy redirects, and finds egregiously ever-present in Surrealism. This chapter locates clearer lines of influence upon Loy in spiritual leaders who foreground gender, among them the nineteenth-century sex-positive American Rosicrucian Paschal Beverly Randolph, the English utopian socialist Edward Carpenter, the American writer and propagator of "womb or love-vision" H. D., and Baker Eddy at her most feminist (H. D., *Notes* 20–1). While this chapter strives to lay cogent ground, it is also a provocation: there remains work to be done on the modernist pursuit of feminist mysticisms.[23] Reaching back still further, I examine Loy's debt to classical thought, and specifically Plato's *Symposium* (c. 385–370 BCE), which presents philosophy as "the translation of eros into logos", an Eros that like Loy's incorporates both the pursuit of beauty and carnality (Han 52–3). Rocketing forward in time, the chapter concludes with a turn to the "atomic emotion" by which Loy is torn asunder after Cravan's disappearance (*LoLB* 131). Atomic physics mattered to Loy, and her esoteric Eros gains traction alongside the growing threat of nuclear extinction. While occultist practice often grounds itself in the scientific, Loy's sourcing of love in a totalising, destructive illumination is a singular alchemy of near-unimaginable dimensions. Crucially, this incursion exemplifies how Loy's sardonic Thanatos coexists alongside her esoteric Eros.

Chapter 2 marks a turn to the dorsality central to the second part of this volume, which is introduced under the heading "Backs, Nerves, Eyes: From Proneness to Visionary Transcendence". As thematic, backwardness and replications define the two genres of Loy romans à clef, dialogic and künstlerroman. In the dialogic, Loy presents scabrous banter between an artist and her male vanguard associates, a tension rooted in the female protagonist's continual expectation of men's "insatiate leave-takings & deferred returns" (*B* 8: 4). In her portraits of herself as a young artist, Loy returns to origins, interrogating her points of departure as woman, creator, and visionary (*B* 8: 4). Predicated on a dialectics of reversal, both genres challenge the female experimenter's rearguard status, affirming the possibility that what is deemed arrière-garde can metamorphose into avant. Furthermore, Loy's backs extend the inclinatory Eros of Chapter 1, underscoring how digressions from "forward linearity mak[e] reference to what is behind", evoke "a decelerating [rearward] pull" (Wills 5). Love is Loy's counter to rectilinearity; love actively, generatively decentres the supposedly autonomous self.

Entitled "The Supine Event", Chapter 2 shows how Loy utilises the inclinations of the spine to satirise the unexamined rectitude of the Italian Futurists. Against the movement's individual male affiliates, Loy positions female protagonists that are supplicant, prone, yet passively resistant. Through very close readings of Loy's *Brontolivido* (c. 1913–20) and its companion text, the short story "Pazzarella" (c. 1914–16), this chapter considers the complex origins of the supine emphases in these early works. Loy actively draws upon influences that run from the Victorian bed-ridden female hysteric or neurasthenic to the hypnotic, feminised patient popularised by Franz Mesmer in the eighteenth century, a mediumistic legacy discernible in nineteenth-century spiritualism, telepathy, and psychoanalysis. This intellectual and heterodox history is conscientiously, chronologically traced out in Loy's earliest writings. Along the way, Loy further twists her knife into the Futurist loathing of all things homosocial or feminised by ensuring that her women protagonists patently embody degenerative Decadent aesthetics and, more specifically, that movement's love of an all-consuming, somnambulistic languor. Loy's narrative *coup de grâce* is her subtle demonstration – anatomical, gestural, silent yet visible – of how the Futurists unwittingly come to embody the inactive supinity that is anathema to their insomniac-touting, forward-propelling diktats.

In short, Loy ensures that the Futurists become mediums to their unexamined misogynist and reactionary anxieties, technophilic vassals subdued by women's occultist control. A penetrating, enchanted, but consenting gaze is key to this transfer of power. Loy's emphasis on oracular mutuality implicitly and pervasively undermines the aggressions of the paternalistic scopic regime by which women remain systematically objectified. Her contagious, feminised supinity thus becomes a conduit to a liberating feminist vision that works symbiotically with Loy's theorisation of a metaphoric and anatomical blind back, or the dorsal portal to alternate realms that is my final focus.

Chapter 3, "The Blind Back", begins with an examination of Loy's manifold dorsality, a construction thus far only glancingly considered by critics. Where the phrase "the blind back" is presumed to be a late Loy manifestation, this chapter shows that its coordinates emerge in Loy's earliest writings. In its polyvalence, the blind back emblematises the inextricability of Loy's spiritual and anatomical truths by which the body, when coherently structured, can link us to the universe entire. Loy's blind back is both prosaic reality – we can never see what lies behind us – and mystical paradox. Dorsality signals our lived myopia, our too-great attachment to a dead, material past, yet is simultaneously figured by Loy as a gateway to the beyond, to an idealised cosmos in league with Loy's infinitarian expansivity. A multivalent threshold, the blind back is posited as atavistic, as the domain of the intellectually deficient, those unduly tied to what Henri Bergson calls the *"already-made"*; to innovate, we must move away from the past toward the *"being-made"*, a skill exhibited by the genius (*CE* 35; 117; 136). While Loy admires Bergson, it is to Frederic Myers that she turns to formulate retrocognition, or the paranormally acquired knowledge of the past, the subliminal uprush by which the creative intellect accesses a harmonious relationship with past and universe alike. What binds Myers's integrated psyche, self, and cosmos? The love Loy prizes above all. Against this embodied spiritual ideal, Loy defines women's dorsality as a lived drudgery tantamount to disablement. But in her consistently paradoxical fashion, Loy ensures that female posteriority contains its opposite, stressing how the "invisible ligament in the woman's land of our blind backs" effects the torsion requisite to Loy's esoteric Eros, the intimate inclinations toward which her writings aspire (*CP* 20: 14).

The second section of this last chapter, "Backing and Forthing: Pineal Eye, Fourth Dimension", extends the coordinates of Loy's blind back to Theosophy. Both Loy and founder of the Theosophical Society Helena Blavatsky move through Cartesian postulations about the pineal gland to develop theories about the dorsal third eye. For Blavatsky, the third eye is temporarily dormant due to human overindulgence in materiality, but will be reinvigorated when humanity sufficiently re-embraces spiritual wisdom. Loy concurs, presenting the pineal eye as a conduit to the cosmos, one that facilitates a heightened internal vision. Like Blavatsky, Loy engages with this organ to pit an atavistic past against a utopian future; furthermore, Loy's writings on this subject are attended by a theory of reincarnation that is wholly consistent with Theosophical tenets. The major distinction between Loy and Blavatsky, however, is that for the latter, the pineal eye retreats due to overindulgence in the sensuality Loy valorises. For Loy, physical intimacy enhances rather than forecloses the cerebral "orb of consciousness" (*GI* 28: 113).

In celebrating pineality and sexuality, Loy is in fuller accord with Bataille's ecstatically explosive, wilfully self-sacrificing cranial eye that is in contact with a universal electricity. For both Loy and Bataille, the parietal is a means of endorsing a fabulously deviant rearward spiritual vision and an orgasmically convulsive body, an effective challenge to epistemological and religious rectitudes alike. This chapter concludes with a consideration of the motivations behind Loy's blind yet oracular back. Via this transcendent, visionary portal, Loy aims to access the fourth dimension, or the spine upon which her nerval irrationalities of longing and belief coalesce; as such, the blind back structures Loy's drive for coherency. Like many of her modernist peers – her lifelong friend Marcel Duchamp in particular – Loy posited the fourth dimension as a realm of endless possibility. For Loy, atavistic avant-gardist, obscene metaphysician, anatomised mystic, the fourth dimension held out the promise of converting her third-dimensional, past traumas into a recognised creative genius that embraced the aggressions and intimacies of her experimental, satiric feminist vision. As this volume attests, she maps that vision through the beating heart and twisting spine, through nerves shattered but obdurate, and through eyes that penetrate the body and the beyond.

Notes

1. In order of appearance, these comments are attributable to the writer Natalie Barney (1896–1956); writer and artist Charles Henri Ford (1908–2002); publisher and author Robert McAlmon (1876–1972);

and the artist Man Ray, as quoted in an interview by Loy's eldest daughter Joella Bayer (Barney 160; qtd. in *BM* 402; McAlmon 37; Bayer, "Interview, Burke and Bayer").
2. Rodker's assessment was published in *The Little Review*, which subsequently facilitated a dialogue between Rodker and Loy in which both affirm a descent from the metaphysical to its counterpart: the resolutely anatomical. In her riposte, Loy sidesteps the question of soulfulness, preferring to tease Rodker for preferring writing that exhibits "guts" ("John Rodker's Frog" 57). Following her lead, Rodker replies with the claim that she threatens his "more delicate anatomy" ("To Mina Loy" 45). If indirectly, throughout this exchange, Loy asserts her fundamental belief in the necessary interdependence of metaphysical soul and abjectified body.
3. Loy's associates yield often and stereotypically to descriptions of Loy's beauty and palpable charisma. For some, such as Robert McAlmon, these qualities reassuringly counterbalanced the pervasive sense that Loy was not always firmly situated or situatable on this planet.
4. Mary Ann Caws provides a good example of the pervasiveness of this view: in 2022, she characterises Loy's late writing as "the mental-metaphysical Christian Science texts" (*Mina* 13).
5. Loy's father was a non-practising Jew who refrained from attending Protestant church with Loy, her two sisters, and her mother (*BM* 31). Loy remembered him as an "'unbeliever'" who boasted of his intelligent-to-aristocratic Hebraic "'pedigree'" (*BM* 375). Burke details how Loy's similar mingling of anxiety and pride about her Jewish origins led to her occasionally expressing anti-Semitic views (*BM* 400, 411). A like masochistic self-hatred is common to many individuals with marginalised identities. Compellingly if disconcertingly, Burke's reportage suggests that Loy's vocalised anti-Semitism arises in the aftermath of the Holocaust (*BM* 400, 411).
6. My work is notably directed toward the Westernised sources upon which Loy most evidentially relies, even as, in their respective Loy studies, Lara Vetter and Carolyn Burke assert that Loy explored "New Thought and Eastern religions before settling on Christian Science" (*BM* 440).

By Burke's account, Loy's immersion in Eastern religious thinking was brief. In 1912, Mabel Dodge Luhan brought Swami Paramananda to Italy. While both Loy and her first husband received his Vedanta teachings, only Haweis appears to have actively studied the philosophical origins of Hinduism. Aiming to establish a religious centre in Italy, Swami Paramananda quickly returned to the United States when he discovered he could not maintain his Florence outpost alongside his Boston temple (*BM* 132–3).

Loy has not yet been credited with reading Eastern religious tenets first-hand. But as I will discuss in Chapter 3 of this volume, Loy shows clear lines of affiliation with Theosophy, a religion widely understood to have brought an Eastern perspective to Western mysticism. Theosophy was studied by many Loy associates, Dodge Luhan included. It is my sense that it is this reworked Eastern thinking that reaches Loy, even as I welcome the possibility that this may be a lacuna in Loy studies that will be addressed by future scholarship and/or archival discoveries.

7. Many Loy articles or monographs understandably focus on specific portions of Loy's unwieldy oeuvre, much of which remains unpublished; this problem was partly resolved by the welcome digitisation of her Yale archive in 2017. Identifiable gaps remain within deservedly influential Loy criticism. Sarah Hayden's fantastic *Curious Disciplines: Mina Loy and Avant-Garde Artisthood* (2018), for instance, does not address *Stories and Essays of Mina Loy* (2011). An example more germane to the topic of this volume is Lara Vetter's *Modernist Writings and Religio-Scientific Discourse* (2010), a wonderful incursion into Loy's esoteric proclivities that attends to two of Loy's eight romans à clef.

In 2022, Mary Ann Caws described herself as "[w]andering a bit lost among [Loy's] last late and heavy fragments" that, at their best, make her appreciate Loy the poet first and foremost (*Mina* 75). Caws's perplexed dismissal of the material that forms the basis of this volume is true to many readers' experience. This book aims to draw formal lines of coherence through these later works not only because they contain valuable intellectual and aesthetic content, but because they are importantly related to the Loy writings more generally prioritised by readers and scholars.

In the Preface to *Nethered Regions*, I discuss at length my rationale for treating Loy's fictionalised accounts of her upbringing autobiographically.

8. *Colossus* remains undated. Pages of this work surface erratically throughout Loy's Yale archive (for instance, in the manuscripts of *Esau Penfold*) and can also be located in the Carolyn Burke Collection on Mina Loy and Lee Miller. Both archives are held at the Beinecke Rare Book and Manuscript Library.

9. Foregrounding Loy's practice of Christian Science, Lara Vetter argues that, in her late life, Loy came to see the material world as illusory, and located religiosity in a spirituality that denied the bodily whilst turning to science writ large for the recovery of the material (*Modernist* 1, 16, 160–1). While I appreciate the sophistication of Vetter's claim, significant evidence suggests that Loy's faith is never divorced from an intensely embodied Eros, as this book will discuss at length.

Maeera Shreiber offers a refreshingly unresolved, openly conflicted account of Loy's relationship to Christian Science:

> Loy's reverence for the sexual body may be understood as an interpretation of Christian Science's view of the spiritual value of the physical.

> And perhaps with its concern for suffering on earth, Christian Science helps license and gives focus to Loy's concern for the human (as opposed to the holy) family. But such readings are at best suggestive, at worst reductive. (469)

On this same perplexing irresolvability, see also Cook 462; Ayers 223; and Armstrong, "Loy and Cornell" 205–7.

10. With regards to the threat Loy's sexual leanings pose to her own mysticism, I take my cue from Denis Saurat's influential *Literature and Occult Tradition* (1930). Eros is Loy's demiurge, arguably akin to Milton's Son, Shelley's world soul, or Blake's universal man; for Saurat, these poets foregrounded pleasure and the sensory to such an extent that they cannot properly be called mystics (17, 56).
11. I am making a similar argument here to Richard Cook, whose essay prompted my attention to Loy as "infinitarian" and my return to the quotation from "Street Sister" (see Cook 459–61).
12. Resolutely heteronormative and homophobic throughout his writings, Bataille argues that "the greatest force and the greatest intensity are revealed whenever two beings are attracted to each other, mate, and perpetuate life"; for Bataille, "in its reproduction, life overflows, and in overflowing it reaches the most extreme frenzy" (*Tears* 33). While Loy often normalises pregnancy and childrearing as inevitable female experiences – see her "Feminist Manifesto" (1914) in *The Lost Lunar Baedeker* for cogent evidence – her esoteric Eros is not expressly tied to human procreation. That said, as discussed above, Loy's Eros has generative qualities: it produces art, beauty, kindness, as well as intimacies cosmic and physical.
13. As Irigaray compellingly states: "Woman lives her own desire only as the expectation that she may at last come to possess an equivalent of the male organ" (24). Similarly, Butler expressly discusses how the very materiality of the body is constructed by power at the outset of *Bodies That Matter: On the Discursive Limits of "Sex"* (1993).
14. Loy's *Untitled (Surreal Scene)* may be collaged in substance and gestation: as Jennifer R. Gross argues, the painting "has long been attributed to [Loy] yet remains an anomaly in her oeuvre and new research strongly indicates many of the details are in keeping with [her daughter] Fabi's drawing techniques" (78). Gross proposes that the work could be attributable to both members of the family.
15. Loy returns to this feminised Christian symbology in *Househunting* (c. 1940s/50s), an artwork made of refuse dominated by a woman's upper body and face. The central figure's crowned head supports a platelike halo filled with domestic detritus: a ball of yarn impaled by knitting needles; laundry strung on a clothesline; a severely cracked teapot. This woman grasps two sheaves of wheat to her sternum; each hangs downwards from either side of the clasped hands, fecundly positioned in the regions of her breasts. An excellent image of this Loy

16. Persuasive examples of this ongoing debate include Linda Martín Alcoff's *Visible Identities: Race, Gender, and the Self* (2006), which presents identity "as an epistemically salient and ontologically real identity" (5). Alcoff's defence is directed against left- and right-wing opponents: the former can deride identity politics as a temporary necessity that capitulates unduly to the very power structures that catalyse marginalisation; the latter can perceive the same as a self-victimising, conformist, and unnecessary balkanisation of national boundary or greater cultural affiliation. For Alcoff, identity is often visibly worn on the individual body and perpetuates lived, specific consequences; when organised and recognised, identity is a sustaining association and a necessary challenge to the supposedly autonomous, homogeneous subject venerated by the much-critiqued European Enlightenment. In sum, Alcoff argues that we cannot and will not "overcome" identity, but should labour to understand it more fully (46).

    The limitations of that understanding are the focus of Robin Wiegman's *Object Lessons* (2012), which examines how academia has internalised an unexamined progress narrative and dependency on proliferating categorisations of identity. Tracing the histories of women's studies, queer theory, and white studies, among other discourses, Wiegman asks what has been learned thus far, and notes how categories are often figured, "fail", and are then reconfigured, as in the shift from women's to gender studies. Questioning the lived impact of these academic debates, Weigman's conclusion points to the need, as I discuss below, to recognise identity as processual.

17. Katherine Angel's tellingly named autobiographical text *Unmastered: A Book on Desire, Most Difficult to Tell* (2012) offers indicative statements such as: "I am afraid of repelling with my desire" and "[t]he desire to speak desire is a desire to burst through silence, to puncture" (116, 205). Recognising that she grew up with feminist resources unavailable to previous generations, Angel nevertheless grapples with how that same discourse "contained [her] desire" (186).

    Angel's exposure of her sexuality chimes with that of Naomi Wolf, whose historical and autobiographical *Promiscuities* (1998) acknowledges that her mother's generation "placed great stock in the value of female anatomical knowledge." As Wolf argues, "We were certainly grateful for the information; but we were also proof that sexual technology alone cannot solve a problem that is inherently social" (148). Ultimately, Wolf's tome affirms the ongoing relevance of the misogynist cliché by which "[w]omen's sexual past is still used against them to undermine their respectable present" (4).

    In her work on the state of contemporary female sexuality, Laura Kipnis cites the statistic that 58 per cent of women have yet to achieve

(artwork is available in Amy E. Elkins's "From the Gutter to the Gallery: Berenice Abbott Photographs Mina Loy's Assemblages" (2019).)

the orgasm that Loy's work venerates so highly (42). But Kipnis's tonally flippant *The Female Thing* (2007) oscillates between articulating the rationales behind the inaccessibility, for women, of intimate satiation whilst veering toward regressive victim blaming. A typically unhelpful Kipnis assessment that illustrates how little things have developed since Loy's time includes: "women just seem to end up defined by their bodies, or defining themselves by their bodies: a source of self-worth, a site of craziness, most likely both" (13).

18. In Loy's last book, *Lunar Baedeker and Time-Tables* (1958), she changed the title of her autobiographical poem "Anglo-Mongrels and the Rose" (1923–5) to "Anglo-Mystics and the Rose".
19. Loy's maternal grandfather began his working life as a carpenter, later ascending to the status of cabinetmaker; by contrast, her paternal grandfather descended from "the Lowys [who] had been wealthy members of the Jewish community in Budapest for more than a century before her birth" (*BM* 15, 17).
20. See chapter 9 of *Islands in the Air*, where Loy narrates how her mother, in a fit of rage, hurled her against a wall.
21. A fuller biographical account of Loy – one that includes her adult life, as well as offering an overview of her authorial and artistic trajectories – can be found in the Preface to *Nethered Regions*.
22. Loy's feminist incursions can be regrettably all too prophetic. Her critique of the passive supinity so regularly attributed to white middle-class female descendants of the Victorian age finds a still more oppressive extreme in the mid-twentieth-century Black Power movement, where it became a popular "quip" to assert "that the only place in the black movement for black women, is prone"; in 1970, Linda La Rue correctly attributed this thinking to "a white role ideal" (39). The full historic implications of this maxim are made stunningly clear in "Mama's Baby, Papa's Maybe: An American Grammar Book", where Hortense J. Spillers details the testimonial of Linda Brent, an enslaved African-American woman whose "vulnerable, prone body" was systematically raped in her sleeping quarters by her white male master and interrogated in turn by his suspicious wife (76–7).
23. I am indebted to Sascha Bru and the audience at the Modernism Research Seminar at the University of Leuven for pointing out these broader possibilities of my own work on Loy's esoteric Eros. Anaïs Nin and Clarice Lispector are ready candidates for more thematic, collective research on modernist feminist mysticism.

Part I

Chapter 1

Hearts Absented and Newborn: Loy's Esoteric Eros

In 1921, T. S. Eliot observes: "Those who object to the 'artificiality' of Milton or Dryden sometimes tell us to 'look into our hearts and write'."[1] Dissatisfied with this injunction, Eliot insists that examining the heart does not go "deep enough", as a good poet should be a "curious explore[r] of the soul" and the less revered human anatomy, "the cerebral cortex, the nervous system, and the digestive tracts" (290). In truth, readers seeking poetic interrogations of tissues and viscera are unlikely to turn to Eliot, the celebrated author of speakers contorted with anxiety about eating a peach or shrunk in horror at exposed downy hair on a woman's arm. Abject bodily innards are the modernist domain presided over by a James Joyce or a Mina Loy, not a Thomas Stearns Eliot. Yet Eliot's resistance to the sentimental, essential heart, that resonant poetic trope, symbolic yet vital, site of utmost pain and pleasure, is shared by Loy.

This elision is curious given how readily Loy focuses upon corporeality: the feet, legs, and genitals; the reproductive organs and digestive tracts discussed in the first volume of this *Anatomy*. Loy avidly read nineteenth-century poets consumed by extreme versions of the heart, among them Christina Rossetti, whose works Loy's father bought her alongside those of her more famous brother, and Walt Whitman, who lingered over the heart's inner workings and figurative, lovelorn bleeding (*BM* 40–1; Blair 229–31, 240). And the heart is crucial to Loy's fascination with immolation, as when she envisions an Aztec sacrifice wherein "feline priests ... gouged out beating human hearts to steam oracularly against the sky" (*EP* 25). Loy savours hearts torn asunder from the body, and this savouring is as prescient as she suggests: with like aggression on show, Loy considers love "a ferocious longing to unlock the centre of oneself with the centre of someone else" ("Colossus" 117). Notably, the vascular organ is only indirectly implied in this quotation; by Loy's terms, love may be as conceivably situated in the solar plexus.

The heart is renowned as the embodied centre of love, spirituality, emotions, and passions and, as such, appears synonymous with Loy's somatic creativity and politics. Superseding soul or mind in its anatomical specificity, the heart is "the most intimate part of an individual yet the most detached, in the sense that its actions cannot possibly be controlled" (Blair 2, 4). The dual function of the cardiac organ is consistent with Loy's satiric experiments with proximity and distance, an ideal cypher for her explorations of the self and relationality. Cultural history compounds these links: as Kirstie Blair affirms, the heart has been central to English literature since the medieval period, but Victorian poets were especially consumed with its activity – pulses, circulation, devotions, pathologies, alienations – to the extent that, from 1800 to 1860, "the culture of the heart often became a cult" reacting against the immanent socio-medical turn toward mind and nerves as bodily centres (4, 11).

This new anatomical focus reverberates in Eliot's twentieth-century diktat espousing the cerebral cortex, rather than the heart, as the correct poetic preoccupation. Figured as sun, king, and devoted husband to the body, the eighteenth-century heart was masculine, a gendering reversed in the Victorian era by its representation as a site of womanly, responsive feeling (Blair 5–6, 11). This feminisation infiltrated illustrations of doctors dissecting suggestively draped female corpses and, in one telling instance, holding a woman's heart aloft to "epitomis[e] the seat of her femininity and beauty" (Birke 116).[2] This gendered history subtends Loy's opposition to the cardiovascular organ. In its stead, Loy strategically develops a heart that is an ever-present absence, one inseparable from the psychological and an esoteric soul, or the predominant concerns of this volume. The next chapter uncovers how Loy grounds intellect and spirit in the dorsal corpus: the supine back, the rearward pineal eye. But we begin here with Loy's ethereal heartscape, which culminates in an Eros I define via feminist theorist Adriana Cavarero as "[s]exual and emotional inclination", a wilful turning away from rectitudes of logic, exoteric morality, and gendered constraint (3). In other words, this chapter listens for Loy's circuitous circulatory systems and attends to her oblique cardiac references, or what she provocatively calls "the percussion of Eros" (*CP* 17: 54).

"How should he know / he has a heart?", asks Loy of the father in "Anglo-Mongrels and the Rose" (1923–5), a question Loy readers might reasonably ask about most of her speakers (*LaLB* 113). Ever the satirical surgeon, Loy enacts coronary bypasses again and again, discussing the heart circuitously or at mocking remove. In her poems, passion is not heartfelt and immediate but ocular and anticipatory: eyes are as "full of love" as they are "of kohl", the cosmetic precursor of solicited attraction; when "we lif[t] / Our eye-lids on Love" we recognise it as a cosmos beyond immediate reach (*LoLB* 16, 56). Trembling marriageable women await amorous fulfilment from behind closed doors, where they "'Bore curtains with eyes'" and "'Plumb streets with hearts'" restless with unrequited desire, obediently awaiting a love god who will probe their bodies entire (*LoLB* 21). Unattributed dialogue, the latter line is an unfathomable fathoming. With it, Loy evades the clichéd excavations of unknown if desired hearts, instead equating streetwalking or prostitution with premarital courting, a trope common to the period, as I detailed in Chapter 3 of *Nethered Regions*. The opening lines of "At the Door of the House" (1917) up the ante of Loy's visual eroticism still further: "A thousand women's eyes / Riveted to the unrealisable". From the off, this intense, impossible scrutiny teaches us to mistrust the eagerly awaited appearance of "the Man of the Heart" in the Tarot reader's deck (*LoLB* 33).

With rare exception, Loy's love looks toward unattainable ideals or ruminates over the base aftermath of intimacy, the "erotic garbage", "caressive dusts", "pale trail[s]", and "weak edd[ies]" of "drivelling" sexualised humanity (*LoLB* 53, 121, 40, 59). Hence her painting *Untitled (Surreal Scene)* (c. 1935) shows a couple contained by an enormous ribcage, bent over as if in worship of a luminous heart held aloft by a sturdy artery; these lovers are entwined within outsized viscera that are as improbably located as the giant brain that lies to their immediate right. Loy's heart is thus intellectualised but also abjectified; her image tells us that, as lived condition, love is closer to the bowels that are, in this painting, the literal seat of feeling (Fig. 1.1). For Loy, we must "dissociate the idea of sex from the doctor" – sanitised scientific authority – and "associate the word love with douche bag" ("Biography of Songge Byrd"). In like base, circuitous spirit, Loy's "Modern Poetry" (1925) demands that the reader *listen* to contemporary verse, then locates its novelty in "the gait of [poets'] mentality" (*LoLB* 157). Eschewing the obvious, audible lyric heartbeat, Loy's novel rhythm is sourced in heady cerebrality and lowly feet.

In Loy's prose, the vascular organ can be deployed to mock the egomaniacal male, usually an avant-garde artist whose "'hardest'", diseased, or broken heart is initially resistant to affection before

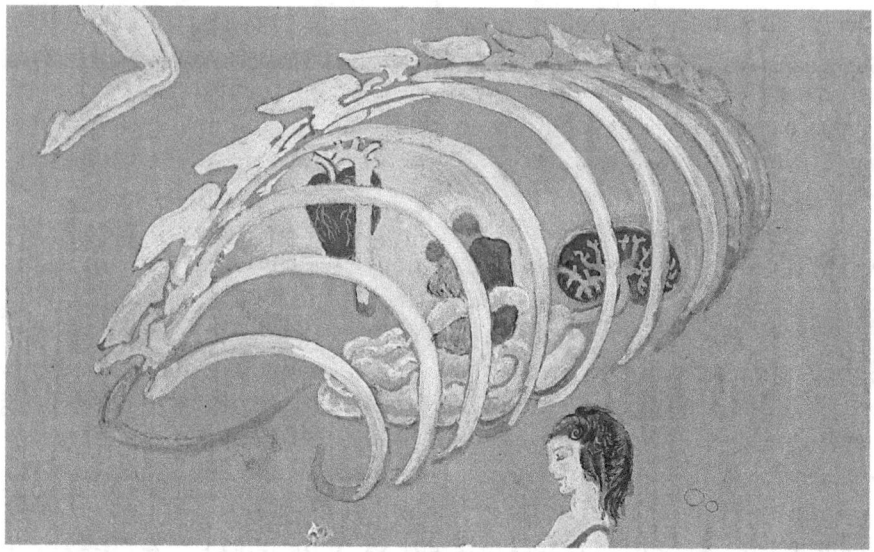

Fig. 1.1 Mina Loy, *Untitled (Surreal Scene)* (c. 1935), detail. Gouache with collage on panel, 20 3/4 × 16 3/4 inches (52.71 × 42.55 cm). Collection of Roger Conover.

submitting entirely to the same (*SE* 89, 97; 64, 106; *B* 2: 10). When male modernists use expressions of affection – "'dear heart!'" and "'Sweet heart!'" – Loy's narrative bemusement is palpable (*SE* 228, 203). For Loy, dysfunctional cardiac pumps are the real site of men's impotence, a truth most memorably deployed in "The Sacred Prostitute" (c. 1914–16), where a physical fight between Love and Futurism is facilitated by boxing gloves shaped into red flannel hearts. If the individual human heart is estimated to be the size of its owner's fist, these hearts are cartoonishly outsized, satirically disproportionate symbols of what is really lacking in heteronormative intimacy.[3] But even here, Loy's scepticism about cardiac strength can be discerned, as the strikes made by these gloves do not effect sufficient damage unless accompanied by "*a psychological blow*" (*SE* 208). To compel, hearts must work with mind and spirit, a truth emphasised by a moment of entrainment, or symbiotic rhythmic processes, shared between Love and Futurism: when Love comments upon hearing the couple's hearts beating, they are positioned "*for the purposes of communication with their temples pressed together*" (*SE* 212–13).

This same cerebral positioning defines the desultory pair of "Human Cylinders" (1917), who "[l]ean brow to brow   communicative / Over the abyss of the potential / Concordance of respiration". Excluding the circulatory system to which the heart belongs, this entrainment does not come to pass. Instead, reciprocal, coordinated intimacy is overpowered by "the frenzied reaching-out of intellect to intellect" (*LoLB* 40). The insufficiencies of the feeling, comprehending mind feed into Loy's lifelong critique of psychoanalysis, an incomplete science that, from her perspective, insufficiently acknowledges the spiritual, soulful, ecstatic, or feminine, and simply does not understand love. "Men are as yet so inexperienced that they are in all their most practiced pursuits—ignoramuses", writes Loy in the undated "Lady Asterisk.", going on to suggest that "great literature" is itself "the supreme confession of ignorance" where love is concerned. This is a confession Loy admires; studied unknowing is better than the pretence of total understanding. "[T]ake heart", admonishes Loy satirically, there is much yet to learn and create on love's behalf, and what is more, if we actually knew what love is, "[t]he sex-psychology of our era would become immediately meaningless" (*SE* 45). Take heart, recognise but mistrust the limitations of psychoanalytic terms: these coordinates will replicate themselves in this chapter, which focuses on Loy's esoteric approach to love, one that elevates matters of the heart to the spiritual, whilst incorporating an orgasmic, genital pleasure to the transcendent. Skirting the heart en route to all that the heart desires, Loy turns to love for its coherence, its capacity to overcome the anatomised and repressed self, one she sees too emphatically emphasised in phallic Freudian thought, especially where women are concerned. Or, as Loy puts it in an archived scrap: "Love is the extreme intelligence = / = the insight of one Being into another"; in turn, this insight creates a "structural inseparability" ("Notes on Metaphysics").

Loy blends preoccupations feminist and psychological with the psychical, keeping alive, as did many modernists, the Victorian fascination with the esoteric. "[U]ndermining scientific rationalism as a world view and rejecting the rationalist assumptions upon which it depended", *fin-de-siècle* occultism sought to "reconcile the secular and the spiritual", the self-aware with the divine, body with soul, all often – paradoxically – justified through scientific discourses, psychology among them (Owen, *Place* 13, 114). But where psychology replaced spiritual soul with irrational unconscious, the occult promoted "a renegotiation of self that sought an accommodation with a unifying and transcendental spirituality even as it underscored the self's multiplicity and contingency" (Owen, *Place* 116). Stressing subjective harmony, the occult paved the way toward self-realisation and a guilt-free rejection of outdated social morals, two goals with enormous appeal to Loy, who was a feminist opposed to the censoring of anatomy, sexuality, and women. The expansive malleability of the ancient occult particularly suited a Loy interested in heterodox religion, medicine, society, and aesthetic practice; a Loy consumed with the past – be it biographical, Victorian, or atavistic – who looked toward utopian futures; a Loy who privileged a spirituality grounded in the corporeal; a Loy whose ambivalence about psychoanalysis, itself indebted to occult ritual and knowledge, was never far afield from direct engagement in its methods. As Alex Owen asserts: "The crucial distinction ... between the secular sciences of mind and occultism (with psychical research often roughly bridging the two positions) is that an occult understanding of personal consciousness was always articulated in metaphysical terms" (*Place* 121). Forever in pursuit of a universal heritage, Loy considered herself as "an infinitarian", a being inextricable from the esoteric ("Street Sister" 41).

Encompassing a spectrum that runs from the materiality of theurgic or magical practice to the ecstatic divinity of mysticism, esotericism includes alchemy, arithmosophy, astrology, classical philosophy, Hermeticism, Kabbalah, New Age religions, occult practice (mesmerism, spiritualism, telepathy), Rosicrucianism, Swedenborgianism, and Theosophy. Often responsive to exoteric religions – Christianity, Islam, Buddhism, Judaism – the esoteric "discursive transfer" can draw on science, philosophy, philology, or the law (Stuckrad 84). Post-Enlightenment Western cultures developed an "antiesoteric bias" that either shoehorned esotericism into a presiding rationalism or defined it as oppositional: subversive, deviant, erroneous (Versluis 5). As opposition, the esoteric begins to exert an appeal on burgeoning avant-gardes keen to assert the viability of the irrational. Regularly drawing on pre-modern practices, thinking, and beliefs, esotericism is an irrefutable shaper of the culture of modernity: from a canonical literary perspective alone, its influence is discernible in the galvanism of Mary Shelley's *Frankenstein* (1817) or the mesmerism of Bram Stoker's *Dracula* (1897) (Faivre and Voss 53; Faivre 27). By extension, the esoteric has an under-examined purchase on high modernism: as Leon Surette compellingly asserts, for too long, scholars have disregarded the centrality of "the occult, mystical and secret history literature" to "the intellectual context in which literary modernism was born" (23).

This gap continues to beg redress in readings of modernist culture and politics alike. Underpinned by new archaeological discoveries, folkloric and anthropological treatises, as well as religious histories and movements, esotericism was discernibly adopted throughout the twentieth century by factions radical and reactionary, an influence spanning the anti-Christian, anti-positivistic mythologies of Marx and Nietzsche and the "pure" inner circle of Nazism respectively (Surette 93–4, 38). However diametrically opposed, these affinities were rooted in shared resistances toward orthodoxies of church and state, resistances that also defined avant-garde art movements. In 1906, the German sociologist Georg Simmel (1858–1915) observes: "politics, administration, justice, have lost their secrecy and inaccessibility in precisely the degree in which the individual has gained possibility of [a] more complete privacy" that dovetails with a gnosis by which "secrecy [becomes an] end-unto-itself" ("Secrecy" 469, 477). Secret or occluded knowledge "can be either euhemeristic (that is, allegorical and secular) or esoteric (that is, symbolic and sacred)" (Surette 22). By resisting legibility and revering the obscure, as well as directly engaging in occultism, modernist writers engaged in both forms. Members of vanguard factions, modernists embraced the content of esoteric gnosis and its methodologies, among them intensive writerly and interpretive practices that eschewed the obvious or status quo, as well as the fostering of select groups with whom to share this complex knowledge.

Esotericism is Loy's primary means of cohering the subject; in turn, it is by Eros that Loy unites self with world. Loy's esoteric Eros is the requisite counterpart to her satire; as a binary, satire and Eros cohere and structure Loy's oeuvre. Fundamental to her atavistic avant-gardism, the often libidinal life force that is Loy's Eros is, in Freudian terms, the complement to her satirical Thanatos, the drive to destruction on high alert to the limitations of mortality.[4] By extension, Loy's theoretical formalisation of an "esoteric Eros" occurs during World War II, is catalysed and driven by an all-too-real Thanatos, a counterbalancing terror of losses global and personal (*SE* 250). This theory is articulated in Loy's essay "History of Religion and Eros", an unfinished proselytising tract integral to this chapter, and in associated Loy writings, among them contemplative, expository works including "Tuning in on the Atom Bomb", "Mi & Lo", and "Censors Morals Sex." But as this *Anatomy of Mina Loy* contends, from her earliest writings, Loy uses satirical attack to generate intimacy, and her late recollections of familial intimacy reveal themselves as the ground by which she honed her skills in verbal sparring and invective. For, by Loy's own account, her satirical prowess was developed during childhood, is the artistic product of a "disheartened home" where "the only laughter ever heard [was] raised by herself" (*GI* 29: 144). Lacking the "motherly heart" Loy elsewhere attributes to a parental figure mocked and loathed, yet empathetically lingered over, Loy presents her own progenitor as a master of the ancient strategies from which satire is born: oracularity, judgement, malediction (*SE* 134).

Loy's mother prophesises for her firstborn daughter a miserable adulthood followed by a descent into hell; more than once, she inflicts curses upon her (*IA* 65: 66). And Loy recognises herself as sacrificial lamb to her mother's deific control and all-determining discourse. In a fragment of *Goy Israels* (1925–30+), Loy ruminates on the "Power" that "endows us with the endurance to suffer" and considers how justice "is prosecuted upon memory". Turning again to the cardiovascular organ as the site of immolation, she then asks:

> What is memory? Trot it along. There's Goy! Stuck in the past like someone just become aware that he's running into a lamppost.
> Look inside her! Her contents are a bunch of steaming nerves; quivering like the heart the Mexican priest jerked out of the breast of a living victim[.] (*GI* 28: 37)

Recollection is inseparable from the perpetually painful, clumsily shaming surprise of a past that prompts reminiscences of fierce injustice and images of violent sacrifice. Again, the heart in this passage metaphorically bypasses the literal organ: Loy's innards lurch, vent, and tremble "like" a vivisected heart of an indeterminately distant history, but circulate nevertheless. Yet what this anecdote implies is that heartlessness catalyses a pain that precludes the functional anatomy of the subject, as is affirmed in a later fragment – one uniquely sincere and direct – where Goy "empties [her] heart of its aching" by seeking out another heart as embittered and unfortunate. A peer is suggested, one who "band[ies] comparisons back and forth" by way of easing the perpetual "'bearing in silence'" required by their domestic circumstances, a companionship that seeks to heal "captive wounds" via "a drain of reciprocity … through which to interflow." Exceeding entrainment, these hearts share pestilence and oxygenation: the method is surgical and not without satire, as Loy redacts a passage comparing this pair to "helpless asses of misfortune apprais[ing] each others' loads" (*GI* 28: 59). Consistent with Loy's tactics, generative intimacy results from this combination of vulnerable heartache and narrative attack.

Loy often describes a need to bear in silence her mother's vocal cacophony. In turn, "The Voice" is a Loy phrase that becomes metonymic for the deeply frustrated, aspirant yet constrained Victorian mother. This experience prompts Loy's speculation about why domestic verbal abuse is perceived as humorous, as in the supposedly comic trope of the nagging wife, and, further, why women's emotional aggressions are not recognised as harmful (*IA* 68: 135; *SE* 34). Within these ponderings, we see Loy gathering the ingredients of the feminist satirical methods that will become the humorous counter to her more earnest theorisations on behalf of an anti-censorious, esoteric Eros. Notably, as genres and preoccupations, satire and mysticism politicise and proselytise. Sourced in injury, satire allows Loy to redirect and process injury. Because pain is confined to the individual, untransferable, it demands linguistic inventiveness, necessitates imaginative metaphor, provokes the very language that harm, be it affective or physical, so often strives to decimate or silence (Scarry 15). Stifled through her own development by "The Voice", Loy's esoteric ruminations on the neonate freshly arrived from the cosmos designate human entry into consciousness as coincident with the recognition of our own unique articulation, an "ecstatic throb in the cooing throat" that leads the way to a somatic "fanfare of self-expression" (*IA* 59: 4–5). What satire destroys, esoteric Eros rebuilds. An argument often assumed or implied about Loy is that she is a witty, experimental satirist early in her career, but abandons this mode as she reaches senescence, when her work becomes more realist, its transparently autobiographical thematics both more traditional and more occultist.[5] Against this lineage, I am arguing that esotericism and satire exist interdependently from the outset of Loy's writing, circling persistently if warily around the needs and desires of the heart. While Loy's ascriptions of aching hearts are few and far between, the steady beat of a sentience recognised most self-evidently in pain is always audible, be it scarcely submerged, mocked, or, as in the künstlerromans, the subject of so many of Loy's reminiscences. Focusing on the development of esotericism throughout Loy's oeuvre, the second volume of this anatomy, *Elevated Realms*, moves away from considerations of Loy's satirical modes toward tracing and substantiating their requisite counterpart, Loy's spiritualised quest for a liberating "heartsease" that is ecstatic, sexualised, but also familial and artistic, a love she calls Eros (*LoLB* 129).

The first section of this chapter establishes the undiscussed links between the esoteric and the modernist avant-garde, a lineage that begins with a rejection of Enlightenment rationalism before encompassing vanguard formation and methodologies. Tracing out associated historical, biographical, and epistemological trajectories in Loy's work, I show how, from the outset of her career, she models the modernist interdependence of mysticism and radical aesthetics.

The second section, "Loy the Adept: Esoteric Eros", drills further into the esoteric methodologies that underpin Loy's Eros. Recognising that the psychoanalytic and the occult operate symbiotically within Loy's thinking, this section turns to foundational overlaps and distinctions between Loy, Freudian psychoanalysis, and its mystical precursors and antecedents, among them Frederic W. H. Myers, Roberto Assagioli, Georges Bataille, and Surrealism. Where Freud anatomises the psyche in ways that rub salt into the deep wounds of Loy's perpetually split self, an occult-informed psychoanalysis harmonises spirit and soma, and, when wedded to a feminist polemic, feminine and masculine. This section concludes by contextualising Loy's feminist Eros, considering alternate, contemporaneous mystical approaches to love, intimacy, and gender in modernist literature and sexology. To further situate Loy's modernist coordinates, the chapter ends with "Ancient and Atomic Eros". Here I consider the classical, predominantly Platonic roots of Loy's Eros, juxtaposing her typically modernist reliance on distant sites of origin with her vanguard turn to a utopian, Eros-laden future paradoxically grounded by the ultimate Thanatos: the threat of nuclear destruction. Throughout Loy's oeuvre, access to and exposure of the internal pursuit of an elusive truth is a fierce, proximate grapple, alternately intimate, aesthetic, or intellectual, all terms that come to the fore in her esoteric Eros.

Loy the Initiate: Esotericism and Avant-Gardism

In Loy's "Lions' Jaws" (1920), F. T. Marinetti's avant-garde writings "crash upon" outdated "fashions in lechery" and "wheedle [their] inevitable way / to the 'excepted' woman's heart". Coaxed, cajoled, this anomalous female feels she aggresses against "Woman wholesale" in surrendering to Marinetti's charms; pursued and co-opted, she claims an ambivalent "Victory" (*LoLB* 47–8). This woman is of course Mina Loy, whose exceptionality within Futurist circles was a tenuous reprieve from its well-publicised scorn for women. But Loy refuses to be their sentimentalised or sacrificial heart, writing of her Futurist adventures with her tongue firmly lodged in her cheek. Along the way, she mocks the sincerity of her own feminist outrage against their constitutive misogyny, an outrage that does not overlook her willing investment in Futurist charisma and novelty, in its unabashed and now legendary public and artistic genius, or her consuming attraction to its leading figures. But as Loy gathers the experience and material that becomes the substance of her early

Futurist satires, pain has its part to play. In a letter to her close friend, American heiress and would-be mystic Mabel Dodge Luhan, Loy observes that "liv[ing] with the tempestuous F. T. Marinetti" made her feel "'uprooted and lost'".[6] In turn, Dodge counsels Loy that she need not feel bereft or confused because her "'roots are in the universe'" (Dodge Luhan 319). Celestial, the esoteric paradoxically grounds the burgeoning author, who, wounded, gathers up its resources to ready herself for satirical counterattack. So begins the intertwining of Loy's esotericism and satirical avant-gardism. Mysticism and comedy are similarly inextricable in Loy's epistolary claim, made during World War I, that she is writing a book – almost assuredly the scabrously funny *Brontolivido* (c. 1913–20) – that may be "no good" but which soothes because it gives her "that esoteric sensation of creating!" (Loy, "Series 1"). This same interconnectedness resurfaces in later life, when Loy evidently developed a habit of cutting out the comics from Sunday newspapers, "intend[ing] to arrange them in collage form . . . to demonstrate unfolding patterns in spiritual development" (*BM* 396).

Satire is everywhere present in Loy's first, incomplete, draft roman à clef, *Brontolivido*. But so too are manifestations of Loy's fascination with the esoteric, her drive to put down roots in the universe. From the outset of her writings, we see Loy equating esotericism with intimacy, with proximate associations, whilst developing an esoteric aesthetic that will be as central to her Eros as it is to her avant-gardism. The eponymous protagonist of *Brontolivido* is a fictionalised Marinetti said to have "catalogued [the] esoteric seductions" of Loy's protagonist-self, Jemima, for whom "his conversations fell like bombs among the solitude – induced static of her mind" (*B* 3: 9).[7] Loy's phrasing elevates desire and attraction to higher, unknown truths. Acknowledged, these passions have the capacity to violently disrupt and even short-circuit the individual intellect, bringing it closer to the "all-comprising static" Loy claims is readily available to "mystics" (*B* 2: 19).

This language of embattled esoteric intimacy resurfaces in Loy's *Esau Penfold* (c. 1910s–20s), where it begins to take on the terms of aesthetic theory. Struggling internally with thoughts of trumping the intimidating confidence of her new acquaintance "Geronimo", one of Loy's nominal variants for the Italian Futurist Giovanni Papini, Loy's female protagonist searches the recesses of her mind for facts that might throw him off his belligerent guard. Grasping anxiously at the prospect of an English cultural authority constantly paraded by her own mother, she recalls imperialistic high-water marks – 1066,

William the Conqueror[8] – but then resigns herself to Geronimo's superiority, a decision justified as follows:

> Besides, I liked his face, famous for being the ugliest in Italy. It projected an appealing sadness that picked out a pattern of beauty from the accident of flesh and bone, and this esoteric design advanced to consort with the misery hidden behind the outward harmony of my own features. (*EP* 23: 4)

More visual than literary artist at this point in her life, Loy creates a character who attends closely to what lies between and beneath Geronimo's facial lines, locating an expressive dichotomy within their militaristically "advanc[ing]" formations. Where she is inwardly miserable and outwardly beautiful, Geronimo's vexed interiority actively enhances his unsightliness, meaning an interdependent balance is struck between their countenances. This complementarity of spirit and soma, symbol and experience, mirrors the very esotericism ascribed to Geronimo's features. In response, Loy's character alternates between longing to confront Geronimo or bask in his appealing "occult impression" that makes her "sensibility fumbl[e]" (*EP* 23: 5).

A delineation of interpersonal esoteric connection, Loy's rendering makes a self-conscious portrait of Geronimo's physiognomy that acts as a model for Loy's theoretical equation of the esoteric and modernist artistry. In "The Metaphysical Pattern in Aesthetics" (1923), Loy argues that, historically, portraiture presents an arrangement "interposed between the artist's creation and the observer in the mode of a screen formed by the directing lines or map of the artist's genius." This screen is "the essential factor in a work of art" by which "[t]he old masters presented the esoteric plan of their individuality superimposed upon a 'subject'". Against this tradition, Loy argues, artists at the outset of the twentieth century "present the map of their individuality without the secondary reconstruction of the pictorial coherence of our customary vision" (*SE* 263). Juxtaposing realistic art with abstract, Loy conflates the representation of artistic individuality or novelty with an esoteric essence. By this conflation, the wilful opacity and inharmoniousness of modernist art – the Brâncuşis and Picassos upon which Loy so often comments – reflect subjective truths: modernists expose their unreconstructed, inconclusive esotericism, rather than hiding it beneath a finalised, exoteric congruity, or the surface legibility of traditional fine art.[9] Success for the modernist visual artist is gauged by how effectively their aesthetic coheres with their singular metaphysic, thereby embodying the appealing, resonant expression of their own "esoteric design" (*EP* 23: 4). Exposed, complex interiorities demand interpolation and interpretation, reminding us that the Greek *esoterikos* means "inward" or "within"; in turn, esotericists aspire to self-knowledge and realisation through the mystical.

Loy's early writings illustrate how esotericism can involve affiliation with the like-minded, be it an enlightened adept and a select group of initiates, or an intellectual or spiritual lineage passed on from one generation to the next (Asprem 10). Esotericism is also a methodology, a committed pursuit to the metaphysical, transcendent, or gnostic, to information or experience not immediately or readily available, be it philosophical truths, "cosmological mysteries", or inner comprehension of the spiritual and divine (Versluis 2). Often defined by "claims of higher knowledge and ways of accessing this knowledge", esoteric truths are understood to remain unutterable, requiring faith precisely because they are beyond articulation (Stuckrad 88). Promise overtakes achievement where gnostic methodologies are concerned (Asprem 434). By association and process, the esoteric positions itself outside of the status quo, prioritising the unorthodox in a manner that dovetails with Loy's avant-gardism. As "Metaphysical Pattern" details, Loy values her peers' incorporation and reinterpretation of the esoteric. And Loy's later, undated essay "The Logos in Art." similarly promotes artistic form – Cubist, modernist – that provides, at its most accomplished, a "divine 'view'" that an emblematic Christian "church" only rudely obstructs with its "ungainly edifice", its monumentalism, its cosmos-disrupting architecture. By this equation, experimental art accesses transcendence as exoteric representations cannot. Notably, even at her most esoteric, Loy's artistic forms remain embodied: they "spira[l]" classically and acrobatically "round the limbs"; they are "subjective conception[s]" leading to "subjective projection[s]"; they breathe upon logos itself, or divine universal reason (*SE* 260–1). Heterodox and vanguard by association, interiorly and corporeally attuned, Loy promotes an esoteric artistry.

Loy came of age in *fin-de-siècle* England, a period of "mystical revival" during which interests in the occult and alternative spiritualities permeated society: not only popular, esotericism was perceived as an analytic harbinger of a new, transformative age (Owen, *Place* 4, 8; Storm 96). A quick survey illustrates how readily Loy's biographical coordinates coincide with key aspects of that occult discourse. In 1882, the year Loy was born, London's Society for Psychical Research (SPR) was formed. The SPR mandate to study psychic and paranormal events directly influenced the emergence of psychoanalysis, a discipline arguably as immersed in an esoteric "inner gaze" as phenomenology, the philosophical movement that surfaced in the same period (Surette 85). Loy avidly read the work of the British SPR founder Frederic Myers, who coined the term "telepathy", and the French philosopher Henri Bergson, whose influential theories of time and embodiment are increasingly positioned within the phenomenological lineage.[10] Bergson became SPR president in 1913, and his promotion of intuition and *élan vital* made him incredibly popular within occult circles (Owen, *Place* 136–7). Formally founded in 1875, Theosophy became the most significant school of esoteric thought in England, and its influence is discernible upon Loy's first husband, Stephen Haweis, her close friend Mabel Dodge Luhan, and Loy herself, a subject to which I will return in Chapter 3. Furthermore, the formal development of Loy's esoteric Eros follows the publication of *Literature and Occult Tradition: Studies in Philosophical Poetry* (1930), Denis Saurat's demonstration of how esotericism is foundational to Western literature and modernisation, a book credited with setting in train the establishment of esotericism as an academic discipline in England and France.[11]

Loy converted to Christian Science in 1909, thirty years after it was established by US-born Mary Baker Eddy (1821–1910), and remained a loyal if distractible practitioner, prone to lapses and deviations. As Loy tellingly wrote: "there are so many kinds of C.S." (Undated letter, Loy to Julien and Joella Levy, Box 30, Folder 11, 1931). An outpost of the esoteric American New Thought movement influenced by Ralph Waldo Emerson and idealist, liberal beliefs in a heterodox transcendental spirituality "legitimat[ing] a mystical oneness with God", Christian Science centres on biblical interpretation, espousing spiritual individualism and a faith-based self-healing aimed at evolving toward freedom from suffering and adversity (Owen, *Place* 117; Versluis 149). To this promise, Loy was immensely drawn: while never shying away from the infliction of pain as a combative satirist, she turned to Science for its "unembellished non-contorted simplicity" that affirmed "the uneventful rhythm of life in the Absolute O.K.ness" (Letter dated 7 January 1928, Loy to Julien and Joella Levy, Box 30, Folder 8, 1928).[12] Given Loy's ambivalence toward Freud, it is noteworthy that Christian Science was perceived in her time as a popular alternative to psychoanalysis (Vetter, "Theories" 49). Loy applies the faith in a therapeutic manner, suggesting that it helps her overcome the trauma of her childhood, and with reference to the Science practice of regular spiritual "treatments", writes her daughter Joella: "I do nothing but treat myself against going gaga" (Undated letter, Loy to Julien and Joella Levy, Box 30, Folder 8, 1928). Loy's correspondence indicates that she kept her ear to the ground for word of good Science practitioners on whom she spent considerable sums for home visits; when living in Paris in the late 1920s and early 1930s, she appears to have occasionally attended a Science church and associated lectures and events with her daughter Fabienne.[13] But on occasion, Loy would abandon Science altogether, going to the doctor and "taking lots of physic", a choice justified by assertions that her esoteric proclivities chafe against extended exposure to any organised religion, and her right to explore "if an intellectual has not got the right to his own God" (Undated letter, Loy to Julien and Joella Levy, Box 30, Folder 13, 1933).

As will be underscored at the end of this chapter by an examination of the 1940s text "Tuning in on the Atom Bomb", even at her most devout, Loy practised and rejected Christian Science tenets at will. Loy used her religion instrumentally, turning to it more often in periods of illness and when she experienced needs for the creature comforts that fall outside of strict Science purview. Asserting her understanding of the difference between a "dangerous salvation" that was "not the 'provision of the Lord'" and Christian Science "demonstrations", or discernible manifestations of spirituality, Loy nevertheless systematically contravenes Baker Eddy's tenet that "'We demonstrate Life, Truth, and Love . . . . we do *not* demonstrate material things'" (Letter dated 15 December 1927, Loy to Julien and Joella Levy, Box 30, Folder 7, 1927; qtd. in Walker). Loy drew on Science when she hoped to secure a well-fitted set of false teeth or longed for the material success of the lamp shop she opened in Paris in 1923.[14] Rather cynically labelling her faith "C.S. Insurance", Loy repeatedly asserted: "In Christian Science you <u>can have</u> your cake and eat it too."[15]

Correspondence with Loy's extended family shows that they replicate her methods, so that Joella has specific angles of her face "treated" by a Christian Science practitioner in order to appear winsome in a photo shoot, and instructs her first husband, Julien Levy, to do his Science to bring about the success of his art gallery (Letter dated 21 April 1932, Joella to Julien Levy, Box 29, Folder 8, 1926–1980; Undated letter, Joella to Julien Levy, Box 29, Folder 9). Amidst encouraging Loy to "treat" her Paris flat with Science so that it can be sold, and calling in a Science practitioner to bring Joella's figure back from its post-partum state, even the often irreverent

Levy pauses to wonder about the legitimacy of their methods, an unusually moral stock-taking in a family correspondence that is frequently unabashedly grasping (Undated letters, Julien Levy to Mina Loy, Box 31, Folder 11, 1928–54). Loy complains about accruing incomplete Science practice that "pil[es] up like a national debt" that overwhelms and, when attended to, does not always demonstrably meet her personal needs ("Loy, Mina to Joella Bayer and Assorted Others"). And while Loy and Joella take it in turns to chivvy each other about their religious devotion, Loy rarely discusses Science as a means of enhancing her spiritual well-being.

Further complicating this picture is the truth that, to convert to her chosen sect, Loy had to turn a blind eye to some of its major teachings. Expressly countering the primacy of feeling corporeality in Loy's writings, Baker Eddy considered the ideal body a sensationless extension of a spiritual "Mind" not to be confused with "an entity within the cranium" (*Health* 92). Unlike Loy, Baker Eddy eschews "sentient material form[s]" and counsels bodily forgetfulness by way of overcoming the pain, heartbreak, loss, and injustice in which satirist Loy traffics (*Health* 280, 261).[16] Particularly telling is the fact that Loy remained openly fascinated by rituals associable with mesmerism, hypnotism, and spiritualism that Baker Eddy denounced as "false beliefs", no doubt as a defensive response to the widespread understanding that Christian Science was a pastiche of precisely these occult influences (*Health* 99; Versluis 149). Loy practised table-turning on at least one occasion, read her horoscope, pursued self-understanding through practitioners of numerology, longed to create a form of literature based on clairvoyant communication (*Insel* she considered an experiment in this regard), and actively sought out the truths of ancient philosophy.[17] In addition, Loy deployed Christian Science as a form of enchantment, what James Frazer in *The Golden Bough* (1890) considered sympathetic magic, or the belief

> that things act on each other at a distance through a secret sympathy, the impulse being transmitted from one to the other by means of what we may conceive as a kind of invisible ether, not unlike that which is postulated by modern science for a precisely similar purpose, namely, to explain how things can physically affect each other through a space which appears to be empty. (Frazer 12)

Loy expressly directs her Science practice at other people with a view to changing their behaviour, explaining this beneficence as follows: "in the old magic long before C.S. <u>you could only keep the power if you were constantly radiating it or handing it on</u>" (Letter dated

8 May 1935, Loy to Julien and Joella Levy, Box 31, Folder 2, 1935). While Loy aligns this power with Christian compassion and charity, its relationship to conjury is irrefutable, and is regularly acknowledged as such in her family's correspondence.[18]

Ironically, Baker Eddy learned about her own healing powers through a noted ex-mesmerist, the American clockmaker Phineas Parkhurst Quimby (1802–66), whose prowess is said to have inspired her pioneering religious journey, and who evidently coined the name "Christian Science" (Bloom 133).[19] Baker Eddy strove to foreground the inextricability of phenomena and reason, but the brand of mysticism she ostensibly rejects takes demonstrable precedence over sensory experience (*Health* 335, 80). Quite unlike Baker Eddy, Loy strives to maintain an interdependent balance between the spiritual and the corporeal. Because Loy values physicality and metaphysicality equally and fundamentally, Loy scholars have long been perplexed by the rationale behind her conversion to Christian Science, a subject addressed in the Preface to this volume.

Elevated Realms – An Anatomy of Mina Loy is grounded in the truth that Loy was a spiritualist magpie, sustainedly endorsing reincarnation, for instance, an evolutionary and ethical belief system propounded by Theosophy and rejected outright by the Christian Science to which Loy claimed allegiance. Come the late 1940s, Loy began following spiritual teacher Joel S. Goldsmith, a Jewish-born, long-time practitioner of Baker Eddy's teachings who left Science in 1945 because he felt its healing practice was no longer efficacious. Both Loy and daughter Joella were impressed by Goldsmith. Loy read his seminal text, *The Infinite Way* (1947), and paid him for consultations through the late 1940s and early 1950s, possibly beyond ("Loy, Mina to Joella and Julien Levy"). According to Joella, Goldsmith was a useful, appealing religious leader because he "streamlined the teachings of Science" (*BM* 414–15). Surprisingly, Joella proves only minorly concerned that her sister, Loy's youngest daughter Fabienne, expresses little interest in Christian Science, preferring instead the "French Catholic superstitions" to which she was exposed in her childhood in Paris, a time when she lived alone with Loy, whose religious influence might reasonably be presumed to dominate Fabienne's consciousness ("Bayer, Joella to Mina Loy and Fabienne Loy, 1917–1948"). But where Joella attended a Christian Science elementary school, Fabienne received some of her formal education through convents (*BM* 276, 372). Again and again, we are reminded that Loy's religiosity was nothing if not ecumenical: in the 1950s, she became fascinated by a left-wing Catholic collective in

New York, and subscribed to their magazine, *The Catholic Worker* (*BM* 423). In sum, Loy's faith in Christian Science appears conflicted, expediently deployed, and easily redirected.

From pursuing divine illumination to equating artistry with magic, Loy's contact with the full esoteric spectrum was lifelong. Negatively and positively, Loy was influenced by esoterically inspired members of the literati. A formative experience is telling: whilst studying art at the Parisian Académie Colarossi at the turn of the century, 20-year-old Loy was acquainted with a "British intellectual clique" highly cognisant of "the pillars of religion" even as "most of these brighter Oxonians & some of their fashionable female associates were dabbling in black magic." About this dabbling, Loy is excoriating: "Such students with their somewhat sinister conviction of being supermannish added to the then current pomposity of 'class' seemed to be ailing from a constipation of their humanity." Aspirant Nietzscheans, turgid humanists, the group was led by Samuel Liddell MacGregor Mathers, who Loy correctly identifies as Bergson's brother-in-law (*EP* 25). In 1887, Mathers co-founded the Hermetic Order of the Golden Dawn, an organisation that engaged in alchemy, astrology, magic, and spiritualism. Among its membership at this time were, famously, W. B. Yeats, and, infamously, Aleister Crowley, the English occultist who believed himself the messiah of a new cosmically magical age (Storm 153). Evidently, "[t]he most daring [of Loy's set]" sought out Crowley, "who roamed Montparnasse in search of recruits" (*BM* 78). Among the daring few was Loy's first husband. In Loy's *Esau Penfold*, Stephen Haweis relays a story in which Crowley begged leave from a late-night gathering due to a planned "'rendezvous'" at his home with "'that incredible beauty'" Mina Loy. Leaving the sexual tryst implicit, Crowley explicitly states his desire to sacrifice Loy to his eternal scopic pleasure: "'I shall take off her head ... and hang it from a ceiling-beam, over my bed, for ever'". Alarmed about the consequences to her reputation, only in retrospect does Loy realise that Crowley may have spoken "in fun" (*EP* 24). Her credulity is sustained by the magician's reputation. Crowley published tracts celebrating sacrificial rituals and transgressive intimacies that included his acolytes ingesting menstrual blood, and his much-discussed "magick" – an archaic spelling by which Crowley strove to distinguish his unique theurgy from mere trickery – was inseparable, for some, from what he proclaimed as his right to satisfy any sexual desire.[20] In his self-styled "autohagiography", Crowley makes passing references to Haweis, but offers no mention of Loy.[21]

In the aftermath of the Colarossi, Loy remained alert to black magical "ingenuity of Evil" (*LaLB* 300). When running her lamp-making business in Paris in the 1920s, she grew concerned that a "trusted forewoman was practicing a subtle form of black magic against her" (*BM* 366). And as late as 1950, she declaims against Surrealism as a movement "ethically hindered" because caught up in unethical deployments of the supernatural, praising the American Joseph Cornell (1903–72) as a visual artist capable of a "hocus pocus" that raises the Surrealist "sub-realism" to a white magical "incipience of sublime solidified" (*LaLB* 300–2). An archived sheet titled "White Magic" shows Loy describing this resurgent, transformative "Holy-magic" working in opposition to a contemporary, inevitably finite destructive trend ("Notes on Metaphysics").

Replete with racial overtones, Loy's theurgic hierarchy is contemporaneous with the then-burgeoning social science of anthropology, whereby black magic became a throwback widely attributed to the primitivised and marginalised: female "witches", Asian "exotics", and colonised cultures (During 6–7, 5, 10, 39). These stereotypes are evident in Theodor Adorno's assertion that "[t]he tendency to occultism is a symptom of regression in consciousness" (238). As an atavistic avant-gardist, Loy can embrace this supposed regressivity, positively equating magic and art in "Aphorisms on Futurism" (1914), where she likens the avant-garde mind to a conjuror finally freed from traditional constraints, or in the first clause of "Modern Poetry" (1925), which reads: "Poetry is prose bewitched" (*LoLB* 150, 157). Loy's associations of enchantment and creativity are consistent with nineteenth- and twentieth-century vanguardists who linked inspiration to a magic considered radical because it challenged the prevalence of post-Enlightenment reason. This "aesthetic dissent" began as early as post-1790 Romanticism, where writers lamented a lost connection with the universe and by extension, reappraised "old magic and mysticism", Neoplatonism and Hermeticism, among other doctrines (During 23). This aesthetic truth is consistent with the political truth that, come the nineteenth century, occultists were often reformers and activists, campaigning on behalf of women's rights, the working classes, and animal welfare, among other then-radical causes.[22] Malleable, the occult could be either atavistic or avant-garde.

Loy's fascination with and suspicion toward esoterically inclined vanguards takes its place in a long history that underscores the interdependence of her combative vanguardism and her mystical turn to love, or the binary defining her own aesthetic methods and associations. The word "esoteric" is first recorded in *Philosophies for Sale*, a satire by Lucian of Samosata (c. 125–80 CE) wherein Zeus auctions major philosophers at a slave market, a process comically exposing the material and utilitarian limitations of their metaphysics. When Aristotle is put on the block, he is promoted as exceptionally good value because he is "double": "one thing as seen from the outside and another thing inside" (329). Lucian's reference is to the doublespeak of ancient philosophy, which was often perceived as existing at odds – complexly, provocatively – with the noble lies by which people conducted their daily lives; as political philosopher Arthur Melzer argues, philosophy exacerbates the linguistic truth that "wherever there [exists] a threatening power differential, there will be coded messages of some kind" (136). Lucian's terms demonstrate how Aristotle offers an exoteric message to the casual reader, but with avid sleuthing, deeper esoteric truths are locatable in his writings. This internal mysteriousness breeds suspicion: just as Lucian scoffs at the supposedly elite, unattainable knowledge of Aristotle and his disciples, the Peripatetics, so too does Loy deride the Anglophone intelligentsia in Paris.

Loy mocks her migrant associates again in Florence, where she resided from 1907 to 1916. Led by Dodge Luhan, this second coterie is one Loy finds consumed by permissive talk that pretends at restriction: "Nature had been shunted up to a less ~~perceptible~~ absolute yet more esoteric ceremonial of taboo – / realities had been crushed out of cognisance" (*EP* 24). Lasciviously "natural", this talk eschews easy legibility: it is coarseness aiming at exclusivity, and Loy parodies, records, and thus perpetuates its clumsy incongruities, its mislaid truths. Loy's disdain exposes how avant-gardes aestheticise and politicise the paradox at the heart of esoteric rules of engagement: while heterodox ideas and truths are said to be incommunicable and inherently mysterious, their adherents believe that they require protection from profane influence, a protection that manifests as unique languages and rhetoric, and factions conversant with the same (Surette 93). Transparency can be democratising, but strategic concealment is not necessarily evil. As Simmel argues, secrecy is integral to all human relationships, and can be perceived as "one of the greatest accomplishments of humanity": trafficking in mysteriousness, secrecy can prompt a drive to know or understand, a comparativeness that can usefully generate reassessment of the self, circumstances, or the quotidian ("Secrecy" 462–6). That said, sanctified factionalism is eminently mockable, as Loy illustrates in *Brontolivido*, where Marinetti is the hyperbolic "prophet of a new religion" whilst Papini inhabits a mountaintop in an attempt to become God that fails absurdly (*B* 7: 6; 8: 30).

Leon Surette credits modernist avant-gardes with the first wholesale equation of their art with a "mystical vision" that remained unknowable to the uninitiated by design, identifying as early exemplars key Loy influencers: the French Symbolists, and the English Pre-Raphaelites, whose leader, Dante Gabriel Rossetti, wrote a last, unpublished book exploring Dante's relationship to heretical esoteric traditions said to have led to the French Revolution (Surette 81, 46). For Surette, modernists were unique in eschewing exoteric husks for the laying bare of esoteric kernels. Attuned to this association, Loy writes aesthetic treatises between the 1920s and the 1940s reverentially likening vanguard leaders to adepts: Picasso's audience is divided between discerning "disciples" and a myopic "uninitiated"; Gertrude Stein is "the enlightened" undeterred by "the unenlightened"; and William Carlos Williams's verse possesses "complete integrity of meditation" (*SE* 230–1, 233, 294). In 1921, Loy celebrates the restorative, alchemical "lyric elixir" offered by the American Romantic Edgar Allan Poe, a writer who engaged with the spectral and mesmeric; an authorial "[e]mpyrean" divinity is likewise lauded in her "Joyce's Ulysses" of 1923 (*LoLB* 76, 90). At times, vanguardism overtakes heterodoxy, so that Stein's writing becomes a compensation for the contemporary "bankruptcy of mysticism", whereby the ongoing and increasingly unmet human need for abstraction devolves upon experimental art and literature (*LaLB* 297). Loy's metaphoric esotericism pays homage to artists' transcendent tendencies. These honorifics extend to her fictions, where one vanguard leader is a figure for whom "*every gesture propounds vulgarity intensified to Divinity*" (*SE* 172). Another is capable of "mysterious ambulance in spatial mystery" and chastises his self-appointed mentor for failing to access "the emotions of the initiated", among whom he includes the Imagists (*SE* 172, 197). The process comes full circle with Loy's esoteric affinities: as I've noted, as late as her sixties, she finds succour in the teachings of dissident Christian Scientist Goldsmith, whose breakaway spiritual movement – effectively a subculture of a subculture – expressly refused to pander to the masses or advertise its teachings, instead purporting a quiet, conscious faith that likeminded practitioners would be drawn to him by "an invisible bond" of shared spirituality and understanding (27).

Today, the esoteric is often conflated with literary difficulty, or texts that make initiates of readers, demanding exegetical nous by way of accessing even the basic coordinates of an authorial vision.

With this specific meaning in view, a reviewer observes: "the hallmark of Loy's poetry is her esoteric and daring diction" (Ardam). Calling for an attentive, scholarly return to the esotericism of classical philosophy, Melzer champions the skills by which the ancients coded their unorthodox truths: wilful obscurity, ambiguity, and factual or grammatical error; oscillations between digressive dispersions and extraordinary terseness; the use of paradox, symbolism, allegory, irony, and satire (53–60). Drawn from Leo Strauss's influential "Persecution and the Art of Writing" (1941), the stylistic provocations Melzer lists are familiar terrain to any close reader of high modernist experiment in form and content, be it César Vallejo's *Trilce* (1922) or Virginia Woolf's *The Waves* (1931).[23] There are any number of reasons for the modernist turn to writing that drew so heavily on readerly reserves: aesthetic pleasure; accurate renderings of everyday resistances and internal chaos; evocation of subjective and ephemeral veracities; resistance to prescriptive, predictable literary realisms. Modernist difficulty is also a deliberate toying with constraint that bears comparison with Simmel's observation that esoteric and other secret societies generate strict rituals for the pleasure of precise observation and to create "a structure of formulas" by which to expand the society "into a comprehensive unity and totality" ("Secrecy" 480–1). But at its most pragmatic and incendiary, modernist difficulty dovetails with Melzer's philosophical esotericism, which withholds truths considered too dangerous for immediate or obvious release to the masses and their minders. Resisting censoriousness, embracing the uncertifiable and irrational, as well as difficulties of style and content, esotericism and high modernism share overlooked, fundamental coordinates.

Loy was always at home with the elusory: absolutism she considers a goal to be strategically avoided in art, if a convenient categorical catch-all for the mystic; deeming life a "great . . . mystery", Loy encourages her reader to "fare onward . . . even on impact with the '*unknown*'" (*SE* 228, 39, 247).[24] Claims to "understanding all things" Loy deems snobbish artifice (*SE* 146). But in a letter written in 1930, Loy attributed her own use of "obscure language" to aesthetic preference and, importantly, a need to "'get by the censor!'" (qtd. in *LoLB* 224). Esoteric in form and content, Loy suggests that she chooses the first consciously, the second, from political necessity. Both possibilities arise in Loy's "Apology of Genius" (1922), a poem in which she positions the avant-garde artist as proximate to the deific, if on high alert to legal restrictions on publicly circulated art. Written in the wake of the *Ulysses* obscenity trials and published just before copies of Loy's 1923 *Lunar Baedecker* (*sic*) were impounded in the USA, this poem considers Joyce's gifted peers stricken by their relationship with the occult and the divine: "[o]stracized ... with God" and "formed / by curious disciplines / beyond your laws", they are a collection of "mystic immortelles" awaiting "the censor's scythe" (*LoLB* 77–8). Loy reads literary indecency as alchemy, a "forg[ing of] the dusk of Chaos" into a "Beaut[y]" discernible to the clear-sighted and -minded (*LoLB* 78). Later archived fragments suggest that she equates these alchemical artists with the future-oriented example set by Christ himself, that "precursor of the ultimate" whose "magical sayings" are like boxes within boxes, outer containers housing his exoteric truths, the inner, knowledge "increasingly esoteric." For Loy, a modernist who values form as much as content, the "actual relics of [Jesus's] teachings" are best accessed through his "style" because "style is the man" and "in this case style is the divinity." Those possessed of "the more out-reaching intellect" are best placed to comprehend and value both the method and substance of Christ's highest and most resonant truths ("Notes on Religion" 14–15).

Fundamentally, Loy mistrusts the profane reader: "one has to ... avoid words with centuries of dirt & degradation clinging to them", she writes in her notes for her dialogue "Mi & Lo" (c. 1930s), adding, "You cannot expect your listener to bring an open mind – to your <u>clarifications</u>" (6: 166). This anxiety recurs in "Mi & Lo" proper, where Loy forthrightly identifies the need for a misleading authorial exotericism: "In an illogical society there is often the necessity for a temporary lie for the sake of ultimate truth" (*SE* 277). Yet "Mi & Lo" exemplifies what I consider Loy's expository esotericism, or her turn toward a greater openness about her own handling of the physical and spiritual mysteries of love; this dialogue is her attempt to bring into focus the meaning and direction of her high modernist "wanton dualit[ies]" and "infructuous impulses" (*LoLB* 53). Embedded in the manuscript of "Mi & Lo", "Censor Morals Sex." extends this turn: Loy insists that, due to contemporaneous "sex liberation", "censorship [has] defeated its own aims", precluding the need for esotericism. "There is no secret to be kept when 'all' are in the secret", she writes ambitiously, bemoaning yet perpetuating the persistence of censorship by using a long, redacting dash to avoid naming a potentially egregious portion of the human anatomy (*SE* 225–6).[25] And it is important to bear in mind that, even at her most overtly desirous for frankness fleshly or otherwise, Loy remains reliant upon a reader ready to tackle layered, enigmatic thinking, ellipsis, high register, and other taxing properties. These formal tactics evoke an ongoing concern about misapprehensions and misappropriations of Loy's own cherished truths.

While heterodoxy can generate clannishness protective or exclusive, Loy's expository esoteric turn unearths her ambivalence about this sequestering. This ambivalence is self-evident in her career-long oscillations between scepticism toward and worship of avant-garde esotericism, as well as in her willingness to stand in judgement of aspirations toward the divine or ideal. Where esoteric elitism is perceived as necessary and generative, it flies in the face of what Peter Bürger considers the great strength of early twentieth-century avant-garde movements: their bid to excise the divide between aesthetics – art as institution, or separate, lofty, theoretical sphere – and life.[26] Avant-garde praxis may well fuel Loy's late desire to articulate the esoteric machinations of her writing and age, to open a conversation about divine, climactic love in an alienating, moralising world. If accurate, this supposition significantly ups Surette's ante: not only does Loy, avant-gardist, denude her esotericism of the exoteric, she also self-reflexively discloses her esoteric process.

As initiate to Italian Futurist adepts, those self-sanctifying, elitist shock merchants who so brilliantly performed impermeable, radical aesthetics, Loy learned to reject censoriousness and hone her love of complex language and syntax. But Futurism is just one of many Loy initiations into vanguard circles, a history that encompasses art schools in London, Munich, Paris, and Berlin, Gertrude Stein and Natalie Barney's respective inner circles, the Arensberg coterie in the midst of New York Dada, and Surrealisms European and American. Having earned her faith in the camaraderie of these groups, as well as in the reader's willingness to decipher experimental aesthetics, late in life, Loy writes esoterically about a sublime Eros. Where Futurists dreamt of technological breakthroughs facilitating a parthenogenetic male reproductive capacity, Loy turns to esotericism for its promise of spiritual palingenesis, "literally 'backward birth' ... a death to the old life and a rebirth to a new, higher one" (Surette 15). "I am gradually coming to life again", Loy writes after a period of depression and artistic inactivity in Florence in 1914, "but don't feel the risorgimento will be complete – except in moments of optimism" (Letter dated February 1914, "Loy, Mina, 1913–1920, n.d.", Mabel Dodge Luhan Papers). Willed metamorphosis, palingenesis extends to occults aiming at cultural rebirth or "*risorgimento*" (Surette 50). Nostos, or the return home, is a secular version of the same. In her late künstlerromans, Loy undertakes both journeys, turning back toward the fraught past shared with her family of origin whilst advocating on behalf of an esoteric Eros that promises to transcend it. For, like Jove Ivon Corvon of her early, undated short story "Monde Triple-Extra", Loy is an avant-gardist from "disheartened stock" whose combative, prescient avant-gardism is matched by "a great longing" for a "newborn heart" (*SE* 57, 61).

Loy the Adept: Esoteric Eros

Loy's Esoteric Taxonomy

While scholars recognise the continued porousness of esoteric boundaries and methodologies, Antoine Faivre's esoteric taxonomy is widely referenced for its assistive utility, its capacity to provide clear checkpoints on often hazy cosmological journeys.[27] For Faivre, work can only be considered esoteric if it includes four intrinsic, often overlapping, characteristics or components. Esoteric category one is "the principle of universal interdependence" by which "[s]ymbolic and real correspondences are said to exist among all parts of the universe, both seen and unseen" (Faivre and Voss 60). On earth as it is in heaven, in the microscopic as in the macroscopic, the universe is a system of replications in need of and responsive to decipherment. For Loy, "the creation of a new being is the creation of a universe . . . in reduction, yet one as mysteriously complex and, could we conform to other dimensions, as vast as the one in which we are at large" (*CP* 19: 47). Similarly, Loy's esoteric essays exhibit a panentheistic belief in the inextricability of god and universe, so that "the first halves of the microcosmic forms in the human mind" are met by "the second halves in creative god-head" (*SE* 266). In Loy's writing, this symbiosis extends to the affective, to imposed pain: "All evil thought, all cruelty, the paralysed vitality of loneliness, the crushed vibrations of drudgery and the bewilderment induced by enigmatic injustices are broadcast through our universe and received by the collective human organism" (*SE* 292).

Emotion irrevocably links infinite to finite, as does human existence entire: descending "into the microscopic universe", individuals aim at "an intuitional ascent towards the cosmic". Or, by Loy's laconic equation: "Mediocosm = man" (*SE* 283). Where Christian Scientist leader Baker Eddy argues that "[a] sinning, earthly mortal is not the reality of Life nor the medium through which truth passes to earth", Loy's human being is precisely this: an intermediary uniting worlds material and spiritual, a conduit for cosmic truths (*Health* 72). For Loy, the human is living evidence of the esoteric belief that dualisms or "counter-powers" are "integral elements of cosmological processes" (Stuckrad 93). Loy's dualism dovetails with one of Faivre's relative categories, concordance, or "a consistent attempt to establish common denominators among two or more different traditions" (Faivre and Voss 62). As I've noted, Loy's movement between the esoteric practices of Christian Science and Theosophy are a topic addressed in *Elevated Realms*, which will also consider how Loy moves seamlessly between Christian and Buddhist referents in "Pazzarella" and *The Child and the Parent* (1932–6). Come "History of Religion and Eros", Loy's concordance is structural: this late essay is framed by the juxtaposition of Asian mystical practice against Anglo-Eurocentric rationality, science, and exoteric morality.

Faivre's second criterion pertains to the natural world, which esotericists perceive as animated, "alive in all its parts", and conjoined by "networks of sympathies and antipathies" (Faivre and Voss 60). For Loy, "[t]he source of all animation is the unique force of the universe" (*SE* 268). In Loy's poems, houses actively constrain, dolls and mannequins observe, streets are "[d]elirious", and the very moon is "[p]ocked with personification" (*LoLB* 81–2). Human and animal lives are equal: "[v]italized by cosmic initiation", a birthing woman of 1914 "leap[s] with nature" into parenthood, a process likened to egg-laying moths, nursing cats, and bluebottles feeding on a carcass (*LoLB* 6–7). Decades later, Loy writes of spotting "a minute roach" in her sink, and consciously refraining from killing it. To do so would be to "loose[n] upon the ether the vibrational shock that occurs on concussive ejection of life from a body", thereby "increas[ing] general anguish tapped by the human race" (*IA* 58: 4). Within this universal energy, magic – given pride of place within Faivre's second characteristic – plays with our expectations that all behaves predictably. Enchantment courses through Loy's writing from the malefic rituals in "Costa Magic" (1914) to the witchcraft, crystal balls, and fairy rings of her 1930s ballet "Crystal Pantomime". As Loy's later autobiographical writings articulate, her world is perpetually and potentially dynamic from childhood, when she recalls feeling at one with "the indestructible cosmos" to the point of making "advances in fairy air to communicative furniture" to "joi[n her] in a veritable dance of consciousness". Evidently, Loy occupied a divinely "increate" world, "possess[ing] the ability to animate ideas" and approximate "ceremonial magic" (*IA* 60: 11–12). This capacity to foster sympathetic networks – clairvoyance, theurgy – and "inhabi[t] rich worlds of [her] own creation" is the origin of Loy's adult artistry, early traits that were, evidently, commonly claimed by women of her generation who became active participants in esotericism and the occult (Owen, *Darkened* 207).

Loy's protracted redraftings of her early projective and perceptive animations bring us to Faivre's third category: the elevation of the imagination to "an 'organ of the soul' enabling access to different levels of reality" (Faivre and Voss 61). Loy's inventiveness is just such a catalyst: "travel[ling] farthest", her "creative man" obtains deepest consciousness, otherness, and "the outer universe" (6: 166; *SE* 272). Ultimately, for Loy, imagination is the most transcendent macrocosm, the veritable essence and driver of Platonic form: "The secret Universe of omniscient creative impetus comprises the power-house generating our obvious universe" (*SE* 237). In turn, God created the world "simply as raw material for the artist", who works the phenomenal and experiential into ideal "form", Loy's term for achieved, insightful aesthetic or philosophical metamorphosis ("Mi and Lo"). By so intensively delineating the evolution of her own creativity, Loy's autobiographical work aspires, in large part, to situate her as an artistic subject with a divine, mysterious imagination both innate and willed, thereby confirming her status as a genius with ready access to "that esoteric sensation of creating!" (Loy, "Series 1"). Recognising Christ as one of many "great mediates", Loy aspires to be Faivre's exemplary medium, using her creativity to negotiate the gap between the terrestrial and the spiritual, directing herself and her art toward gnosis (*SE* 271).

In combination, imagination and gnosis prompt the metamorphosis inherent to Faivre's fourth esoteric category, "transmutation", which includes an alchemical "modification of the subject in its very nature" and individual rebirth, or "the passage from one plane to another" (Faivre and Voss 61). Alchemy is allegorical for personal elevation: just as base metal becomes gold, so too might the individual ascend to the divine (Owen, *Place* 124). Transmutation usually escalates. Loy reveals her understanding of this process in "Auto-Facial-Construction" (1920), where she promotes herself as an adept of physiognomy prepared to teach others to "maste[r] their facial destiny"; the result of "initiation to this esoteric anatomical science" is "renascence for ... everybody who desires it" (*LaLB* 283–4). As the third chapter of this volume explores in depth, Loy's künstlerromans depict human birth as a transmutation of "the Infinite" itself, which involutes and self-contorts, remaining omniprevalent whilst "infinitesimally disappearing through a seedling point within itself to emerge as a human ~~soul~~ being". ~~Soul~~/being: Loy's infinitude is ever-proximate to the corporeal, and she protractedly labours to keep temporal eternities and corporeality aloft in her writings (*IA* 59: 2–3).[28] By extension, Loy directs her esoteric palingenesis to return to this originary sublimity, a nostos of the ineffable: her initiate strives toward a "presensate ecstasy" via the "Eros" that "is from the Creator broadcast to us" (*SE* 243, 248). By manipulation of will and breath, the mystic adept attains an illuminated ecstasy prevalent in Loy's work from *Brontolivido*, where it is "one of [Jemima's] happiest games" to "shu[t] her senses off habitude" and travel "unexplored universes", "transposable" life (2: 19). Roughly a decade later, in *Goy Israels* (c. 1925–30), Loy reaffirms her practice of meditative transcendence, describing it as a skill developed in childhood by which to generate "a retreat for recuperation" (28: 114). Consummated, satiated, Loy's Eros similarly transmutes into an "infinite sentience", an immortal mortality that she repeatedly characterises, as I discussed in the first chapter of *Nethered Regions*, as an innocence or virginity paradoxically rebirthed or returned to by knowledges carnal, intimate, or proximate (*SE* 250).

Loy's transmutative aim is mystical, prophetic, illuminating. Recognising "life in its dire disorder", Loy prioritises what she calls a "visionary Distance" enabling access to an "instantaneous eternity" (*IA* 58: 2; "Mi and Lo"). Loy admires Christ's ability, for instance, to "originate define & perpetuate the pattern of his 'vision'" to effect a global transmutation ("Mi and Lo"). Evident as early as her short story "Pazzarella" (c. 1914–16), Loy's esoteric Eros is her bid to occupy the role of visionary, to follow a path established by world-renowned spiritual teachers, Buddha among them. This vocation is typified by an individual who abandons youthful hedonism or domestic constraint, wanders rootless, then experiences a spiritual and physical nadir culminating in new knowledge, in reawakening and rebirth (Obeyesekere 24–9). Corresponding to this pattern, Loy's künstlerromans present the Victorian home of Loy's upbringing as prison, her mother as gaoler. Breaking free from those confines, Loy becomes a global traveller, inhabiting three continents and experiencing many trials by fire, including an unwanted pregnancy at the hands of her abusive first husband, the deaths of two of her four children, and a stint of near starvation when she was reunited with Arthur Cravan in Mexico in 1918. In "Mi & Lo" the trauma of this starvation is recalled as a means of interrogating the divide between body and soul and the efficacy of asceticism as a route to higher knowledge. Ultimately, Loy concludes, deprivation does not foster mystical illumination and its concomitant reconfiguring of temporality and spatiality.²⁹ Love, on the other hand, does: with pleasure, Loy notes that, when she was again in Cravan's long-awaited company, "distance got telescoped by locomotive power." Of their first days together, Loy writes: "Somehow we had tapped the source of enchantment, and it suffused the world. We must have anticipated the embrace of reunion as the consolatory Absolute which no perspective of Time could augment or reduce" ("Colossus" 117). This Eros meets each of Faivre's esoteric criteria: through it, macroscopic echoes microscopic, the universe is magically, imaginatively animated, and visionary reveries and passions fuel transmutative transcendence.

Cravan's love becomes Loy's benchmark and foundation, aim and ground of the transmissive proclivities that comprise Faivre's second, final relative criterion: "esoteric teaching can or must be passed from master to disciple following . . . a previously marked path" (Faivre and Voss 62). Teaching does not preclude individualism: in the modern Global North, the draw of the esoteric lies, in part, in its capacity to facilitate personal contact with the divine. In other words, the esoteric appealed to post-Reformation Europe precisely because it promised, as did Protestantism, "access[to] an 'inner church' through personal experience" (Stuckrad 92). Loy is in sync with this direct access to the deific, arguing: "It is not prohibitive to man, as the complete microcosm, to train his intelligence on his components and gain control of their potentialities . . . in order to transcend the restrictions of his overt senses" (*SE* 239). Loy's Christian Science promoted individual practice or "treatments", a methodology extended by Loy's subsequent adherence to Goldsmith's "Infinite Way", which precluded the need for teaching or books about God, instead propounding a spiritual wisdom contingent upon "*your own realisation*" (Goldsmith 12, 67). Individualist in practice, esotericism can be individual in formulation. Of the many examples of esotericists who generated their own systems, the English poet William Blake (1757–1827) is held up as an exemplar. Denis Saurat describes Blake as having "reconstructed an occult system for himself alone—which is indeed the acme of occultism and which will probably always prevent us from completely understanding him" (63).³⁰ Dubbed an "electric-age Blake", Loy similarly wrote unique, "[i]ntermittent . . . unfinishing" esoteric tracts set to retain aspects of the impenetrable forevermore (Kenner; *IA* 58: 3). For where "History of Religion and Eros" is a polished typescript, "Mi & Lo" is accompanied by notes indicating plans to further that dialogue; also central to this chapter are "Tuning in on the Atom Bomb" and "Universal Food Machine", both of which appear to have been intended as portions of a longer work. Like the autobiographical writings foundational to her sense of self, Loy's esotericism is never brought to a definitive conclusion, but she nevertheless expends considerable labour over four decades on künstlerromans and heterodox theories that speak to her aspirations and beliefs. "I think that first bit [of my novel] I have written 2000 times", Loy tells her son-in-law in 1932, comparing its progress and her thinking to "the drop of water torture on the scalp", a labour necessary, she feels, to achieve the aesthetic recognition and "pleasure that is often the result of a patient perusal of an individual expression" (Letter dated 28 November 1932, Loy to Julien and Joella Levy, Box 30, Folder 12, 1932).

Loy's uniqueness and incompleteness notwithstanding, these protracted writings indicate her desire to instruct; as she asserts about the writing of her mystical philosophical dialogue "Mi & Lo", she would like to write still more obscurely, but "[t]he trouble is ... I want the common housewife to understand what I say" (Letter dated 16 July 1930, Loy to Julien and Joella Levy, Box 30, Folder 8, 1930). With didactic tone and proselytising fervour, Loy is adept speaking to "the uninitiated" in "History of Religion and Eros" (*SE* 245). Writing of transcendence, Loy describes the obligation borne by the illuminati "to impart to others the formula for its inducement" (*SE* 243). By the end of this tract, she takes up that obligation, passing on "the ancient" understanding of "the electric incitement of Eros" mishandled and subverted by "[e]xoteric religion" (*SE* 247–8). Loy's re-estimation of sexual love in "History" extends, in her contemporaneous künstlerromans, to revaluations of familial and self-love, as well as to passions for beauty and art. These revaluations are as integral to Loy's palingenesis as they are to the reorientations at the heart of esotericism: its spiritual rebirths, its returns to the heterodox methodologies of classical philosophy, its "clarif[ications of] the complex ways in which people process – absorb, (re)interpret, (re)consruct, etc. – the idea of the past accessible to them".[31] Loy's revaluations can be overtly transmissive: in *Islands in the Air*, she announces herself "[a]ssured" of possessing "a precious knowledge to communicate to my fellows" (58: 5). Unspecified, this knowledge is withheld and gleaned esoterically: over a two-generation-long period, whenever Loy began to commit her thoughts to paper, "the least thing [she] caught a glimpse of . . . even a vestige astir in memory would dilate to a dimension of beauty defying rational analysis." For Loy, this mystical propensity is distraction, "magical quirk", an intoxicating mental "glitter" that facilitates a review of potentially "ugly" life (*IA* 58: 5). We observe this propensity in action as she gazes at her neighbours' windows, envisioning those alone as "illuminati" or, if married, "concording sublimely with the pulse of Eros' wings" (*IA* 58: 4–5). These revealing reveries set the stage for Loy's autobiographical transmissions whereby her past is measured against an Eros esoteric in its incommunicable perfectibility. Comparable to Zarathustra on the mountaintop or Christ in the desert, Loy is alienated city-dweller, "[n]o longer in touch with the world", yet readied to deliver the as-yet- "undistributed weight of [her] <u>communication</u>" (*IA* 58: 1, 5).

Esoteric Eros and Psychoanalysis

Loy equates the pursuit of love with occult practices such as Tarot reading as early as her 1917 poem "At the Door of the House" (*LoLB* 33–5). In her 1918 manifesto "International Psycho-Democracy", she issues a democratising call to uncover the secret power by which an esoteric, powerful social minority continually enacts a "hold" on the majority through "*strategical ideas*" that become "*social ideals*". Dissecting military might through an uncovering of the undisclosed machinations of power, Loy's express goal in this manifesto is "*To vindicate Humanity's claim to a Divine Destiny*", one that she believes should be exoterically accessible to all (*LaLB* 282). Combining Loy's preoccupations with the occult, the accessibility of mystical knowledge, and subjective satiation, the late, undated "History of Religion and Eros" remains Loy's most extensive, expository delineation of an esoteric Eros. "History" is also a culminating point of Loy's longstanding frustration at the limitations of Freud's otherwise impressive powers of sexual revelation initially discussed in Chapter 1 of the first volume of this *Anatomy*. Admirably, as Loy wrote in the 1920s, Freud established open discussion of sex; problematically, in so doing, he turned sex into a routine "duty", a universal habit lacking force or enchantment (*SE* 229). "History" is concerned with Freud's capacity to "illuminat[e] all but a blind spot, THE ELECTRIFICATION OF BLISS" or "that terrain" that has "become an infinitely extensible maze of introversion in search of Eros" (*SE* 251). In "History" we witness Loy striving to answer a question raised in "Censor Morals Sex.": "If as Freud infers— Religion and Sex are interchangeable—why not reintegrate both giving the people an impetus toward the equilibrium they require?" (*SE* 226). For Loy, religion is "psychic gymnastics", an "[e]xercise of the spirit" aspiring to "ENLIGHTENMENT ILLUMINATION ECSTASY" (*SE* 242).

Loy's ecstasy yields unhesitatingly to Adorno's critique of the occult relationship to the material: "The objects of their interest are supposed at once to transcend the possibility of experience, and be experienced" (243). Promoting amorousness as divine knowledge, Loy insists that it is the basis of an eminently human, affectively somatic fulfilment: in "Mi & Lo", for instance, unhappiness is deemed impossible for anyone who has achieved "the love [they] desire" (*SE* 274). Remaining attuned to the truth that Eros supersedes both the spirited ardour of Greek *thumos* and "fleshly desire", Loy nevertheless posits a metaphysical-yet-sensate orgasm as a foundational metaphor for the experiential apex of an Eros that includes and extends the sexual (Han 43–4; *SE* 251). As she puts it in *The Child and the Parent*: to "gauge the entire extent of our consciousness", we must do so via the "lightning intelligence" of sensation, seeking intensity, throbs and convulsions, "passions as inscrutable as the enduring eyes of the Boddhisatva", "mystic union[s]", and "occult relationship[s]" (*CP* 16: 56–7, 55). A passage in *Islands in the Air* clarifies the broad applicability of this orgasmic Eros:

> as there is an amorous orgasm which is the juncture of our sensibility with cosmic sentience, so there is a spiritual orgasm, the mystic's admittance to cosmic radiance, an intellectual one immingling with the intelligential ether, an aesthetic one on our impact with any of the myriad facets of cosmic beauty, so there is an orgasm of loving compassion, the lust of the humane. (*IA* 63: 41–2)

Love, religion, art, and intellection – in archived notes, Loy compares ideation to brain orgasm – offer satiations so great that they require a metaphor of the most overwhelming physical pleasure: sexual climax ("Mi and Lo"). This metaphor emerges in response to the visceral sensation that overtakes child Loy when she meets her adoring paternal grandmother for the first time; as recalled in adulthood, it is that relative's "loving compassion" that motivates Loy to pursue "the lust of the humane" (*IA* 63: 41–2). Later in the same künstlerroman, Loy recounts the aesthetic orgasm she experienced from a formative encounter with "cosmic beauty". Stumbling across a blooming lime tree festooned with an "interlaced shimmer of ivory into jade", "melodic fragrance", bees and delicately hung, spinning caterpillars, "filled with verdant juice", Loy's "aesthetic excitement" generates within her "body a faint electric nuclear response". This response catalyses an internalisation of "a projection of the vibrant lime" as Loy has the curious feeling of being penetrated by one of the larvae before her. Resolutely heteronormative, this incident affirms Loy's psychoanalytic leanings and resistances: offered as evidence of her youthful "precocious sexuality", Loy's focus on orgasm and its broad applicability as ideal psychosomatic repletion is an implicit critique of Freud's too-limited address of the same (*IA* 65: 75–6).

A like challenge arises in the mid-1930s künstlerroman *The Child and the Parent*, where Loy offers a lengthy reconsideration of heterosexual intercourse and its gendered ramifications, one careful to contextualise women's sexuality – as Freud does not – within the social and esoteric. Entering "the transformative state of love", Loy argues, woman "cannot wander in and out of the sphere of normal conditions as men do, or present, as it were, a surface to Love's contacts and associations, but that she is bound to absorb the phantasmagoric values to be found there, until they become integral to her make-up." In this instance, the phantasmagoric is not a prized gnostic knowledge, but the accumulated lived falsehoods by which gender inequities are culturally perpetuated. For Loy, the internalisation of these mythologies creates a dependence on woman's capacity to attract a male. As a direct consequence of this limited goal, woman becomes reliant on "the charge of the male electricity . . . to hold [her] egoless amalgam together" so that "when he withdraws his galvanic presence, [she] ceases to glow" (*CP* 18: 64). This process is self-eradicating and infantilising: "He returns to the world he has his business with, while she remains ethereally attached to his magnetic centre, as the child is materially attached to the umbilicus" (*CP* 18: 64). However so reduced, woman nevertheless remains cognisant of the fully desirous life, because she possesses "a sort of vaginal clairvoyance" by which "she can follow in [her mate's] emotions—(which his contact will whip almost to delirium)—" (*CP* 18: 65).

The potentially enticing powers of vaginal clairvoyance prove disappointingly limited: Loy's configuration gives male sexual prowess the upper hand, consigning women to a grasping tentacularity, or a parasitic relationship to the "vital sap . . . drawn from" their lovers. Borrowed lubricity notwithstanding, female nerves remain perpetually snapped, perpetually exhausted by "the ultimate fictitious value" by which they feel "entirely void" after the brief resuscitation of sex (*CP* 18: 65). Consequently, women are defined by an "inconclusiveness", a sentience or "mere being" that, at present, can only be brought into generative animation with the assistance or validation of male desire (*CP* 18: 66). Woman is reduced to partiality, her greatest success – only available to a "certain percentage of women" – limited to becoming a "concupiscence": the object of immense desire, a thing to covet carnally (*CP* 18: 67). When presenting this argument in *Child*, Loy revisits the terms of her "Feminist Manifesto" (1914) some three decades later, continuing to insist that, because society defines females via male need, women remain a mystery to themselves, and must look within "to find out what [they] <u>are</u>" (*LoLB* 154). In *Child*, Loy argues that the demands placed on women's appearance and flexibility have increased exponentially since her youth, concluding: "WOMAN – – the big Review – – still inconsummate" (*CP* 18: 69). Unsatiated in sex or self, woman remains malleable, unrealised.

These writings reconfirm Loy's understanding of herself as an esoteric adept with knowledge to give to select, willing initiates, a category that, in practical terms, may have ever only included Loy's eldest daughter. In her correspondence with Joella and Julien Levy when newlyweds, Loy pried into the details of their sex life, seeking assurance that Joella was realising intimate pleasure, and trying to prevent their "mak[ing] love ... along the old lines – you know, repentant male and sweetly suffering female." While next to no pragmatic advice emerges in this correspondence, it is implied that Loy imparts specific directions to her son-in-law in order to successfully bring her daughter to orgasm. For Loy, this achievement will "prove [her] theory to be correct", which in turn is permission "to write 'The' Anti-Freud." Reflecting the Victorian drive to evidence the occult, Loy considers her "enquiry" into the "neglected question" of women's intimacy both "scientific" and a corroboration of herself "as a prophetess!" (Letter dated 23 December 1927, Loy to Julien and Joella Levy, Box 30, Folder 7, 1927). While her microscopic attentiveness to her daughter's sex life unnerves, a truth exacerbated by her self-evident attraction to her son-in-law, Loy's invasive and triumphant letters assuredly confirm her desire to better Freud's presentation of women's sexuality.

Loy's emphasis upon the absented female libido in life and Freudian theory has proven prescient: she foresees second-wave feminist philosopher Luce Irigaray, who interrogates psychoanalytic gendered presumption, asking, for instance: why is woman's sexual evolution seen as intrinsically more difficult than man's? And: why must maternity supplant the erotic function in women? Fundamentally, Irigaray argues that "psychoanalysis ought to wonder whether it is even possible to pursue a limited discussion of female sexuality so long as the status of woman in the general economy of the West has never been established" (64–5; 67). Irigaray's critique is sourced in the second-generation psychoanalytic theories to which Freud gave circumspect credence, sources that have ideological and historical correlates in Loy. In "History", for instance, Loy notes that Freud cleared an escape route for sexual inhibition, a statement footnoted with a reference to Hungarian-born psychoanalyst Sandor Rado (1890–1972), who "reveals an unpredictable side-track toward insanity" (*SE* 252). Loy may refer to Rado's best-known publication, "The Problem of Melancholia" (1927), which argues that human beings are "most happy when living in an atmosphere permeated with libido" (49). Describing love as "perhaps the most powerful conception which we meet with in the highest strata of the mental life of mankind", Rado attributes our deepest melancholia to the loss of infantile love, a loss that is the basis for a fragmented selfhood that can propel untold aggression and mania (53). Based on the glorious experience of enduring love in infancy, the same essay posits what Rado termed the nursing infant's "alimentary orgasm" as a form of "narcissistic transport" that acts as a precursor to genital satisfaction ("Problem" 53–5). Rado's well-circulated reworking of the orgasmic is a viable prompt for Loy's articulation of orgasms amorous, spiritual, intellectual, and aesthetic. This supposition is strengthened by the fact that, as Loy was writing "History", her daughter Fabienne was working as a secretarial assistant and editor for Rado, who was then head of the New York Psychiatric Institute (*BM* 390). Furthermore, in a tract in Loy's archive dated at 1937, Loy mentions working on a translation for Sophia, her fictional name for Fabienne; Rado wrote in German, one of many languages in which Loy was fluent (Loy, "Promised Land").

Based on this Rado link alone, it is plausible that Loy was familiar with the work of Karen Horney (1885–1952), a German psychiatrist and psychoanalyst referenced by Rado and Freud; regrettably, her groundbreaking critique of psychoanalytic phallicism did little to budge their views that, due to anatomy, woman is forever consigned to lack.[32] Horney's oeuvre reminds us that Freud's theories were subjected to feminist critique from the time they were published. More precisely, Freud's immediate contemporaries recognised his failure to articulate a distinctive theory of female development, and his reinforcement of the supposed inevitability of women's physical pain and social exclusion, and Horney was a well-recognised figure amidst this dissent (Rubin 175, 185–6). Like Loy, Horney took express, protracted umbrage with Freud's diktat that anatomy is singular destiny and attended to the environmental factors that led to presumptions of women's genital and social inferiority.

Horney argued that Freud's masculinist theories overlook the very possibility of womb envy, or the entrenched fear of femininity traditionally exhibited by Western males ("Inhibited" 77; "Distrust" 112). What is more, Horney argued on behalf of woman's somatic superiorities, showing that pregnancy, for instance, is one area in which "woman has traditionally enjoyed a very clear advantage as regards bodily inspiration, [while] a man has had little choice but to turn to his soul" (Marshall 176).[33] Developing an archive of women's sexual pleasures, Horney insists, *contra* Freud, "that *from the very beginning the vagina plays its own proper sexual part*" in the life of those born with female genitalia ("Denial" 157). Horney also observes that Western society enforces the tacit rule that to be female is to be culpable in a way that inhibits women's expression of sexual desire ("Genesis" 53). In sum, Horney treats women's sexual inhibition as a socially constructed and enforced pathology – one eminently correctable – rather than the presumed, unexamined baseline of "civilised" society (Kelman 22).

This potential rehabilitation of female desire is the central theme of many of Loy's essays, her one known ballet, and her late künstlerromans, where she attributes sexual reluctance to the truths that women are not taught enough about intimacy or life, the failures of the male lover to accommodate or consider female pleasure, and the fear of pregnancy.[34] In turn, these critiques feed Loy's heterodox Eros. As Loy asserts: "Even the woman who is known as cold, but who would be more accurately described as smouldering, is capable of an esoteric kind of union with her man" (*CP* 18: 64). For Loy, information about female pleasure is gnosis, a higher knowledge withheld from all but an elect, satiated few (*CP* 18: 67). Implicitly affirming the ingredients of Loy's Eros, Horney presents women as most integrated in their approach to love and sexual intimacy, arguing: "the disassociation between 'spiritual' and sensual love ... is predominantly—indeed, almost specifically—a masculine characteristic" ("Monogamous" 95–6). Cohering feminised intimacy – the potentially transcendent and ecstatic – with the masculinised somatic is assuredly among Horney's proselytising goals, for whom not only women but men also must "be at home ... in the realm of eros" ("Distrust" 114). Furthermore, Horney recognises and deconstructs the expectation that women define themselves by romance; as Irigaray would later reassert, Horney recognises that "*'Love' has been [woman's] only recourse*, and for that reason she has elevated it to the rank of sole and absolute value" (Irigaray 51). Framed by quotation marks, this "'love'" is not Eros, which is distinct from the intimate clichés mocked throughout Loy's work, as in a 1921 poem where education is said to teach "How low men die / How women love—" (*LoLB* 75). Man's usefulness is comically juxtaposed with woman's affection throughout Loy's writings: "To man his work", she singsongs in a 1917 poem, adding: "To woman her love" (*LoLB* 38). And again, in the 1930s: "'Here is Love,' cries the great strong man, ''tis woman's whole existence'" (*CP* 15: 35). Rerouting Freud, both Horney and Loy aim at an intimacy that transcends the heteronormative traditions that stereotype or elide women's complex desire.

Seeking the harmonies of an esoteric Eros, Loy finds Freudian psychoanalysis insufficient to the truth of women's conditioning, or the actual cause of women's anatomical dissatisfaction. As importantly for Loy, the Freudian inner self is too vivisected. Freud's great contribution to twentieth-century Western thought is the parcelling of the psyche into "what is conscious and what is unconscious" (Freud, "Ego" 13). Divided against itself by design, the Freudian mind is a site of factionalism, aggressions, and competing drives. Some ideas ascend freely from the impassioned unconscious; those that don't are actively repressed by the reasonable ego, surfacing in dreams, fantasy, and psychoanalysis, or just staying put, doing invisible work on the individual. Freud's censorial focus is internal, working at the cross section of the superego or conscience and an id labouring to assert itself in a world become too civilised for its own hedonistic comfort. By contrast, Loy's relationship with authority is more outwardly directed toward societal mores and their gendered repercussions.[35] At its most extreme, Freud's "analytic dissection" of the contemporary relationship between the subject and society exposes a self at war with itself, "a displacement, a turning round upon [our] own ego" (Freud, "Ego" 23, 25, 34).

This displacement dogs Loy's childhood development: never assured of the response her behaviour might augur from her volatile parents, her "mind, which normally should work forwards, reverted; set out on that endless introvert journey in search of the motive attributed to it – imperceptible cause of harassing effect" (*IA* 65: 64). Rather than dissolve their marriage, Loy's parents grind themselves and their offspring into particulate, "triturat[ing] their lives in imposing their 'opinions'" (*GI* 28: 39). This fragmentation is the site of Loy's own existential crisis, and a version of the following lament runs through her writing, autobiographical and otherwise: "What becomes of individuality if it is only a confection of broken straws blown from the big hay-rick?" (*GI* 28: 106). Late in her life

Loy describes, prefiguring Beckett, the need to "go on [. . .] struggling through a sort of double life [with] half my conscious *esse* belabouring the other half with blows of inordinate apprehension" (*SE* 288). Creativity is her prime means of cohering this broken self: at art school, the adolescent Loy "anticipates a perpetual undulation of colour punctured by perfect form; [a place] where labour becomes creative leisure, and [her mother's] diatribes on 'taking pains' give way to a pleasurable weaving on the loom of sense, to patch the shredded fabric of her intellect" (*GI* 29: 132). The esoteric is another: describing the cycles of commotion in her childhood home, Loy writes: "morning for recuperation, the afternoon for the pulling of the self together – – – to face it anew. Magic – – – counter-magic" (*GI* 28: 128). An esoteric enchantment – magic, counter-magic – pivotally subtends Loy's subjectivity.

Rejecting Freud's anatomies of the psyche, self, and the female self in particular, Loy nevertheless follows psychoanalysis in coming to rely upon the cohering force of Eros. Psychoanalysis aims to restore the authority of the ego – alternately passive or masterful – over the unconscious, itself in perpetual thrall to a struggle between the libido, "sexual instincts", "self-preservative instinct", or Eros, and "the death instincts" (Freud, "Ego" 40, 56). Loy acknowledges this dichotomy, regularly pitting "LIFE" against "DEATH" in her poems; recognising the irresolutions of "ephemeral" couplings and "daily deaths"; characterising sexual desire as "the Will to Live" (*LoLB* 16, 64; *GI* 28: 123). Interdependent, these Freudian drives can fuse, defuse, or, in the case of Eros, be sublimated or redirected toward other goals and instincts ("Ego" 41, 46). To survive, the psychoanalytic ego affiliates itself with libido: "the clamour of life proceeds for the most part from Eros" ("Ego" 46). In this welter of self against selves, Eros "unite[s] and bind[s]", establishes unity ("Ego" 45). Freud repeatedly defends his Eros against charges of pansexuality, aligning it more closely with "the all-inclusive and all-preserving Eros of Plato's *Symposium*", a link he shares with Loy, as I address below ("Ego" 204, 218). But where, in "A Short Account of Psycho-Analysis" (1924), Freud seeks to demarcate his new field from "mystics" and "quacks", Loy believes that the esoteric is inseparable from a replete understanding of self and world; for Loy, psychoanalysis can only do its work when it foregrounds, rather than represses, the occult leanings from which it originated (191). In turn, Loy's portrait of Freud – drawn when she met him in Vienna in 1921 – is a tellingly spectral representation: emerging from pitch blackness, Freud's features are softened and ephemeralised, divorced from solid materiality; his gaze and brow are contracted in vengeful judgement, his mouth ajar as if for the obligatory apparitional wail (Fig. 1.2). In Loy's hands, Freud is unavoidably haunting, intrinsically occult. Deferential to the harmonising power the Freudian libido offered cultural constructions of the subject, Loy maintains that we remain in need of a feminist, esoteric spirituality in order to forge a replete whole of psyche and soma. Highly conversant with Freudian theory, Loy turns to Freudian antecedents and descendants in formulating her ideas about Eros and the self. In this regard, Freud might thus be seen as another of Loy's coronary bypasses, another evaded circulatory centre.

It was Frederic Myers (1843–1901), classicist scholar and a founder of the Society of Psychical Research, who first delineated the

Fig. 1.2 Mina Loy, *Portrait of Freud* (1921). Carolyn Burke Collection on Mina Loy and Lee Miller. Yale Collection of American Literature, Beinecke Rare Book and Manuscript Library. Permission granted by Roger Conover.

fragmented psyche, dividing it into "the empirical, the supraliminal Self" and the subliminal, "a more comprehensive consciousness, a profounder faculty" which we access in full after death (13). Myers's version of the unconscious, in other words, is linked to alternate planes of existence, a subject explored further in Chapter 3. As significantly, Myers perpetually seeks a mystical harmonisation of the fragmented self through Eros. Where, for Loy, Freud "infers" but fails to "reintegrate" the truth that "Religion and Sex are interchangeable", Myers presents them as continuous, representing different phases of an "all-pervading, mutual gravitation of souls" bound by love, "the energy of integration which makes a Cosmos of the Sum of Things" (*SE* 236; 61). These very topics are the ingredients of Loy's late "History of Religion and Eros". Around 1912, Loy attentively read Myers's influential *Human Personality and its Survival of Bodily Death* (1903). A history and a how-to-guide, Myers's is a compendium of paranormal experience – telepathy, visions, mystical ecstasies – written with the intention of hastening humanity's inevitable ascent to full integration with the cosmos. *Human Personality* went through three editions in its first year of publication, and was widely read by modernist literati, Loy's friend James Joyce among them; Freud framed his theory of the subconscious as an express counter to Myers, publishing his early findings in the *Proceedings of the Society for Psychical Research* in the same year that Loy first encountered Myers's work (Schneider 59; Cooper 21). Drawing on Loy's correspondence with Mabel Dodge Luhan, Sandeep Parmar points out that Loy eventually took issue with Myers's scientism, asserting that only through artistic practice could "the 'whole truth' of the creative self" be explored (89–90). These misgivings aside, Myers importantly, fundamentally reinforced Loy's belief that the self is generatively cohered and infinitely bound to the universe through an esoteric Eros.

As Loy read Myers, she was suffering from mental illness, and sought out the help of the Florentine psychiatrist Roberto Assagioli, whose writings she clearly found reassuring (*BM* 141–4, 146).[36] Assagioli (1888–1974) became famous for formulating psychosynthesis, an esoterically infused psychoanalytic method that he began theorising as he was treating Loy; Assagioli's mother was a Theosophist, and he was as interested in Blavatsky's cult as he was in Baker Eddy's Christian Science (*BM* 147). Psychosynthesis encourages the development of a controlled, centralised will rooted in interpersonal intuition, empathy, and beneficent love; what is more, it considers inspiration and "states of mystical consciousness" factual, pragmatically real (Assagioli 5–6). At every turn, psychosynthesis propagates self-harmony, exhibiting suspicion toward apportioning the psyche. By Assagioli's methods, the unconscious need not remain mysterious, as an integrated subjective centre can be identified from fragments of self-knowledge, "*a centre of pure consciousness*" that is aware of itself as a body, but more than a body; as in Theosophical doctrine, this essential, higher self is linked to genius and illumination, and aspires to be in tune with the cosmic order (55, 116–17, 27; Owen, *Place* 121–2). For Assagioli, the Freudian sublimation of Eros can become an alchemical transmutation, leading the libidinal energies toward transcendence in a manner consistent with Loy's esoteric Eros, if lacking Loy's feminist emphasis (49–53). Where psychoanalysis remains foundational to his methods, Assagioli believed that it places "exaggerated emphasis on the morbid manifestations and on the lower aspects of human nature" at the expense of the self-reflexive creativity that he cultivates in his patients. This creativity arises first from "careful introspection" – a term key to Loy's philosophical rumination on selfhood, "Mi & Lo" – and by cultivating the biographical and the visionary, narrative forms into which Loy leans eagerly in her later years, converging in her romans à clef (18, 35). Notably, the origins of Loy's romans à clef are precisely commensurate with her exposure to Assagioli's treatment. Myers and Assagioli are importantly anti-anatomising, integrating the divided self that runs like a gaping wound through Loy's work. Like Loy, they effect self-coherence through an enthused engagement with an esotericism that is in open conversation with the psychoanalytic. As evidence of Assagioli's undersung influence, it should be noted that Loy admired him sufficiently to include her portrait of him in an exhibition curated by Peggy Guggenheim in 1925; intensively discussed Loy mentors or associates Marinetti, Papini, and Stein were also so honoured (*BM* 339).[37]

Eros, Bataille, Surrealism

Loy's feminist resistance to Freudian Eros comes into greater relief when we consider her coordinates in relation to those of erstwhile mystic Georges Bataille, a figure similarly keen to rework and extremify the sexual teachings of psychoanalysis. Bataille is as preoccupied by Loy with "the heart of man", by which both mean "not the muscular organ, but the surge of feelings, the intimate reality that it symbolises" (*E* 184). Never neglecting her spiritual desires, Loy avidly pursues intimacies extreme, violent, unabashedly transgressive, intimacies that run counter to cultural expectations of docile, desexualised femininity. Her romantic reunion with Cravan in Mexico is brutalising, all-consuming, exposing; a mutual, catastrophic deluge that affirms Loy's foundational sentience – "being alive" – even as it "crashed the senses" ("Colossus" 117). For Bataille, "deep love" also prompts a desire "to be alive" solely for a passion that will necessarily remain only briefly requited, a passion that exposes the lover to the life and death of the "loved being", an experience that "has the flash of a cataract" (*IE* 121, 123).

Like Loy, Bataille defines love as the recognition of an equally unquenchable, agonising desire in another, one to which both parties only respond "in the transparence of an intimate comprehension" (*AS2* 113). "Passion fulfilled", writes Bataille, "provokes such violent agitation that the happiness involved . . . is so great as to be more like its opposite, suffering". Providing the requisite "anguish of desire", this satiation affirms individual continuity (*E* 19). Revelling in the truth that sexuality is unduly abjected, sullied, and denounced, Loy and Bataille maintain that the erotic "assent[s] to life up to the point of death", a sacrificial proximity by which it teeters – tellingly, generatively – upon the sacred (*E* 11). For both, the erotic is troubling, fascinating, a "supreme philosophical question" rivalled only by "mystical experience" (*E* 273).[38] In turn, both endeavour to liberate ecstasy from "confession" or castigation (*IE* 3). In "History", Loy argues that she draws upon the term "Eros" precisely by way of side-stepping the prudery so often ascribed to the word "sex" (*SE* 283). Similarly resistant to instrumentalising passion, Bataille nevertheless maintains that regulation enforces a transgression that feeds sexual excitement and importantly distinguishes hyperconscious human eroticism from unconscious animal rutting (*IE* 136). This excitement is aggressively gendered: Bataille asserts that men "cannot usually feel" capable of violating social laws and, consequently, long for a woman "to feel confused" in sex, to "accep[t] the taboo that makes a human being out of her" and a fully realised, if relentlessly predatory, male out of him (*E* 134, 39).

For Loy, social strictures on consensual intimacy are problematic precisely because they are founded on the abased feminine Bataille symptomatically reveres. Or, as she drily remarks in an essay against the modernist literary patriarchy, "man has never exhibited the least inclination towards a moral faculty" (*SE* 228). This "man" is neither capacious nor universal: drawn from "Conversion", Loy's 1920s essay critiquing the limitations of Freud's and D. H. Lawrence's phallocentrism, her quotation expressly excludes women, undermining the supposed inclusivity of "man" to good effect. But females do not escape Loy's rancour. In women, Loy satirises a buffoonish conformity to established "degrees of virtue" in order to evade "the thin-lipped spectre of dishonour", a conformity in which she knows herself complicit (*SE* 42, 142).[39] As the supposed transvaluator of values Friedrich Nietzsche all too typically asserts, "A woman who loves sacrifices her honour" (100). Given this pervasive authority of gendered norms, Loy considers taboo "mental congestion that obfuscates the directitude of [a] virility" that she significantly leaves unsexed, recognising its applicability to any consenting person's "right to realis[e]" their lust (*SE* 283). In Loy's day, to speak of virility in these inclusive, gender-neutral terms was nothing short of revolutionary.

"All profound life is heavy with the *impossible*", writes Bataille, equating ascetic religiosity and "flights of mysticism" with constraint whilst noting that "explor[ing] the farthest potentialities of being" may well involve "opt[ing] for the disorderliness and randomness of love" (*IE* 58; *E* 251). In Bataille's writings, love is "virtually the only emotion ... discusse[d] explicitly", and by love he means the body broken or wounded, forcibly in receipt of the intimate other (Cokal 84–5). Where both Bataille and Loy recognise the recuperative power of sex, Bataille's "love" is primarily somatic, only speculatively intellectual, and not transcendentally mystical (Cokal 86). To be fully transcendent, Bataille believes sexual ecstasy must shuck its necessary relation to horrors of abjection, yet he recognises that to desire another is to aspire to the universe, to a beyond (*E* 224; *AS2* 116). No less extreme, Loy is at greater ease with unkempt, aleatory love in all guises and contradictions. Furthermore, her esotericism feeds hope: for Loy, mystical ecstasy can reverse "our impossible" so that it "blossom[s] forth as *the* POSSIBLE", a belief foundational to the "infinite sentience" of her esoteric Eros (*SE* 243, 250).

Haunted by Catholicism, triumphantly phallocentric, Bataille is Loy's immediate peer – both expressly interlink sexuality and spirituality through the 1930s to the 1950s – and resonantly symptomatic of the religionist thinking Loy's esoteric Eros strives to redirect. Throughout her late writings, Loy maintains that access to a divine "source of presensate ecstasy", or the fount of earthly Eros, was first discovered by ancient Asian seers who became protective about their capacity to attain communion with the universal "abstract potency" (*SE* 243, 249). But despite their precautions, Loy insists that misinterpretation did take place: as Eastern ascetic discourses proliferated, eager followers confused the "mortification of the flesh" with "an *automatic transmutation of virility*" (*SE* 247). Incapable of attaining transcendence, maladapted but eager disciples came to perceive the unyielding body as faulty and incompetent, and thus anti-sexual exoteric religions – Christianity among them – grew out of a combined desire for a secrecy that became repression, and an anxious mystic impotence, an acquired or inherited inability to perform one's way to illumination.[40] To reinterpret a stanza of Loy's "Joyce's Ulysses" (1923): "The Spirit" became "impaled upon the phallus" or, in this instance, a masculinist anticipation of a body primed for easily achieved ecstasy (*LoLB* 88). By contrast, the true adept is a "genius [who] would never have snubbed the Creator with a derogation of 'The Flesh'" precisely because that flesh is microcosm to the macrocosmic Creator from whence it sprang, and therefore cannot be inherently bad (*SE* 248).

The troubling consequences of misunderstanding "the amatory passion" range from religious celibacy, which Loy deplores, to a greater social tolerance for violence than is extended to the pleasures, consolations, and comforts of Eros (*SE* 283–4).[41] Citing the medieval propensity to torture the sexually non-normative as a deliberate extreme, Loy condemns the punishment historically "inflicted on sentient human beings" who sought only the harmless succour of love and intimacy (*SE* 250). That this castigation is inseparable from patriarchal mores is reasserted in Loy's archived notes, where she suggests that communists might expose how the "sex mystery" was propagated by capitalists keen to limit sex to reproduction by way of maintaining a larger population to exploit ("Biography of Songge Byrd"). Patriarchal limitations on sensuality recur in Loy's "Faun Fare" (1948), where she illustrates how, from ancient Athens to contemporary Manhattan, intimacy has been overruled by the belief that Eros is and belongs to the male; by contrast, Loy proselytises to "Votaries of Venuseros" or initiates to a "bisexual norm" comprised of goddess and god, Aphrodite and Cupid (*LoLB* 128). A privileged man, Bataille treats sexual prohibition as enticing constraint; a constrained female, Loy writes excoriatingly against the damage wrought by self-frustrating exoteric prudery.

Commensurate with Bataille, a phallocentric modernist sexual mysticism is never in short supply. One need venture no further than D. H. Lawrence's *The Plumed Serpent* (1926), where, against the backdrop of a contemporary Mexico restored to potency by a paternalistic, brutal, reductive paganism, protagonist Kate Leslie contemplates "how wonderful sex can be, when men keep it powerful and sacred, and it fills the world" (453). But it is Bataille's associates and occasional enemies the Surrealists who sail most closely to the landscape of Loy's Eros. Loy and Breton were neighbours in 1930s Paris, and the introduction to Maurice Nadeau's influential *The History of Surrealism* (1945) claims Loy for this vanguard movement, citing both her and her husband Arthur Cravan among its early progenitors, even as critics have repeatedly noted that Loy's own relationship with Surrealism, which she relabelled "sub-realism", was defined by ambivalence (Shattuck 30). As Paris agent for the Julien Levy Gallery in the late 1920s and 1930s, Loy became an under-acknowledged expert in Surrealist fine art, but was never wholly convinced, writing Levy in 1931: "I wish there were some really big genius in surrealism – of all the schools I have 'met' in the last 30 years it seems the one, that <u>could</u> be wholly satisfactory" (Undated letter, Loy to Julien and Joella Levy, Box 30, Folder 11, 1931).[42] Loy's hesitation notwithstanding, the preoccupations shared by Loy and Breton make for an extensive list that includes the esoteric and the occult (mysticism, mesmerism, spiritualism, telepathy, clairvoyance, magic, accursedness, hallucinatory and trance states); radicalism and avant-gardism; sexuality (desire, transgression, anti-censoriousness); the feminine (figured as irrationality, hysteria, madness, and in Breton's case, as a site of lust); orientalism and primitivism (in both cases, all too often reductive and appropriative); the past (childhood, atavism); the aleatory ("being alive is a queer coincidence" [*CP* 20: 15]); heightened consciousness (genius, humour, satire); somnolence (passivity, the subconscious, dreamscapes – see, for instance, the oneiric conclusion of chapter 7 of Loy's *Islands in the Air* or her attempt at analysing her own dreams in "Notes on Metaphysics"); and, most significantly, Eros.

Historically speaking, both Loy and Breton become more preoccupied by love as the Second World War is on the horizon, and their configurations of Eros significantly overlap. Fascinated by Freud's theorisation of Eros as driver of the pleasure principle, as well as a unifier of the individual ego and the phenomenal, Breton insisted in a 1941 interview "that 'we must all learn to read with and look through the eyes of Eros'" (qtd. in Mahon 15). Like Loy, Breton saw things to reinterpret in Freud. For instance, the Surrealists strategically deviated from the ultimate psychoanalytic goal, as they did not aspire to a mental or emotional well-being that might restore subjective "normality" (Ades 192). Both Loy and Breton presented Eros as gnomic, pursuable, but never contained or fully known, "not susceptible to any proof, other than the experience itself which is ... construed as an act of faith" (Ades 188). Akin to the Society for Psychical Research before it, Surrealist research sought to combine the scientific with the marvellous. But where the SPR pursued the irrational to prove its inherent logic, Surrealists sought to locate and abide in the "arational" (Nadeau 86–9; Caws, "Translator's" xiv). Meant to nurture the individual mind, this arationality was, as Surrealist Raymond Queneau put it, "'a mysticism of a new kind'"; for some, it involved a turn to Eastern philosophies and religion, thereby cementing a Victorian lineage via Schopenhauer, Emerson, and Blavatsky, all of whom looked to similar sources (qtd. in Nadeau 114–16). In accord with the orientalism of Loy's "History", and its avowal of a transcendent Eros, in *Mad Love* (1937), Breton asserts that "unique love comes from a mystic attitude", adding that it relies upon interrelated dichotomies key to heterodox thinking, among them mysteriousness and exposure, magic and chance (7, 19).

Loy and Breton could be too absolute about Eros, using it as salve to all that ails the contemporary subject. At its best, Loy's love is totalising in the sense that it includes every human participant equally. Breton's is differently totalising: he pursues "*certain* love, such that it can only be proof against everything"; he insists that "absolute love" is "the only principle for physical and moral selection which can guarantee that human witness, human passage shall not have taken place in vain" (Breton, "Nadja" 185–6; *Mad* 117). Loy's love can take on this Bretonian idealisation, as is evident in the diction of "History of Religion and Eros" where she speaks of the adept's ability to access the complete, indestructible absolute – soul or beyond – a process she hopes to achieve through love (*SE* 241). But it is absolutism that exposes the cracks that divide Loy's Eros from Breton's, cracks well illustrated by Suzanne Cordonnier (previously Muzard), one of Breton's lovers, who states: "Love is a trap for lovers in quest of the absolute." Here Cordonnier is perfectly aligned with Loy's resistance to romantic cliché, her infamous insistence that "Women must destroy in themselves, the desire to be loved" (*LoLB* 155). As for Loy, Cordonnier's "absolute" is the infuriatingly ineradicable feminine ideal. As she avers: "I have often been much flattered, much moved by homages paid to me by Breton in public, but never won over in private by habits that broke the spell" (190). A compensatory chivalry, a performed, ephemeral reverence for the sacrificial virgin or self-immolating mother matched by a totalising derision for the whore: these are the absolutes Loy and Cordonnier recognise as infiltrators of an otherwise ideal Surrealist Eros. Instrumentalised sexism, this gendered traditionalism troubles critical appraisals of how the Surrealists deployed Eros philosophically, politically, and artistically as a revolutionary counter to *passéiste* values and morals, among them flagging spirituality and artistry; fascism; the post-World War II reclamation of "normality"; and the censorious French regime during the Algerian War of Independence (Mahon 72, 83, 109, 143).[43]

As for Loy and Bataille, the key distinction between Loy and Breton is feminism. Surrealist Eros is, all too often, a permission to venerate misogynist harm: "seducing" the reluctant virgin; stalking an "alluring" woman in the street; participating in male exhibitionism; presenting the idealised female body as eternal, static, natural; insisting upon the "uncanniness" or grotesquery of the maternal body.[44] As Susan Rubin Suleiman reminds us: Woman as the Surrealist cypher for love often has little to do with the lived reality of womankind (13). Breton admitted as much in a candid transcript of a 1928 roundtable on sexuality dominated by male surrealists, where he baldly stated: "Having to consider the question of a woman's sexual temperament would in itself make me unable to continue to love her" (Pierre 47).[45] Breton's foregone consideration is at the heart of Loy's esoteric Eros, which we might read – consistent with Sarah Hayden's canny interpretations of *Insel* – as wilful antipode to the unwitting impotence of the Surrealist revolution.[46] In its overemphasis on the female form as signifier for Eros, Surrealism, at its best, anatomises and spectacularises the fear and aggression that drive paternalistic Thanatos (see Foster, *Compulsive* 10–11). At its worst, it reinforces the same. Bataille proves surprisingly canny in this gendered instance, if insufficiently self-reflexive, naming Surrealists "mystic-mongrels" – a term commensurate with Loy's 1958 retitling of her epic satire "Anglo-Mongrels and the Rose" as "The Anglo-Mystics of the Rose" – who "safeguard the most vulgar virility while at the same time opposing sloppiness and bourgeois oppression with technical trickery" ("Castrated" 28).[47] These attitudes recur as late as the catalogue for the 1959 *Exposition InteRnatiOnale du Surréalisme*, where Breton described Eros as "'a privileged place, a theatre of initiations and prohibitions, where the deepest processes of life play themselves out'" (qtd. in Mahon 152). Of the raced and gendered privilege his work exuded he evidently remained unaware. Many critics have continued in this tellingly unwitting spirit, so that Nadeau, chief Surrealist historiographer, argues: "The surrealists, who more than anyone else have magnified love (and woman), sought to transcend the psychological realm in which it had immemorially been confined and to pin it, too, on the dissecting table" (158). For the contemporary feminist reader, there is sardonic comedy in Nadeau's second use of "it", which becomes an ungrammatical, anatomisable female substitute. By this multivalent pronoun, Surrealist Eros dissects a superficialised femininity, remaining fearful of or blind to the coherent intimacy Loy pursues, an Eros that demands recognition of female virility and male emotional vulnerability alike.

Throughout her oeuvre, Loy avows an Eros-based esotericism unambivalently informed by feminism. With reference to "Songs to Joannes", Steve Pinkerton lauds Loy's ability to create "an alternative and already-profane poetic space" as counter to and reappropriation of "the abiding ideological significance of the sacrosanct" (13). Consciously, strategically embroiled in the very religiosity she derides, Loy subverts it from within, making room for women's divinity and transcendent ecstasy, thereby avoiding what Pinkerton aptly delineates as "satire's stubborn if unintended capacity for consecrating the subject it means to skewer" (94). But Loy's religiosity is not a uniform category, as she consistently distinguishes between the paternalism of the exoteric and the liberating potentialities of the esoteric: the "dull-dong bell", for instance, of a Catholicism that "toll[s] a drudgery / of exoteric / redemption"; a supposedly charitable Christianity that attains to esoteric ecstasies by aligning itself and its members with the mind-altering succour of alcoholism (*LoLB* 140–1). We repeatedly witness Loy seeking out a non-dualistic, feminist esotericism, one celebrating an interconnected, holistic world view whilst prioritising experientiality, intuition, and transformation over logic, reason, and the status quo.

Feminist gnosis, writes Karen Voss, accounts for and celebrates the somatic and the spiritual alike, treating bodies as neither fundamentally nor ideologically differentiated by genitals or gendering (18).[48] Just so does Loy's recovery of pleasurable sentience uphold the body as a crucial conduit to the spiritual and the intellectual whilst extolling sensual pleasure regardless of sex, striving to expose and rewrite contemporaneous literary fictions of "an interminable procession—of ladies 'possessed' in floods of delight" (*SE* 256). In her "Feminist Manifesto", Loy argues that sex is expression with tremendous power to harmonise and equate: "The only point at which the interests of the sexes merge—is the sexual embrace" (*LoLB* 154). From the start of her authorial career, Loy's gendered equilibrium is overt challenge to the autonomous, upright "I" of a patriarchal Western philosophy that has so resolutely resisted inclination, a postural metaphor for passions, desires, and instincts that turn selves outward: "Eros pulls the subject out of itself, toward the other" (Han 3). Of these longings, the greatest cause for consternation has long been "eros" or "[s]exual and emotional inclination toward a person"; artistic inclination runs a close second (Cavarero 3). Drawing her terminology from this classical lineage, infusing her impassioned theories of intimacy with psychoanalytical, mystical, and ideological thinking, Loy's feminist esoteric Eros makes virtues of precisely these desires.

Modernist Mystical Feminisms

Loy's feminist Eros can be situated within a broader category of esotericism that "draw[s] upon sexuality as a primary basis for mystic-magical power", one traceable through Hindu validations of sexuality, or the Swedenborgian celebration of non-monogamous conjugality (Versluis 139; Owen, *Place* 99). The pervasiveness of this tendency within modernist discourse is indicated by *The Varieties of Religious Experience* (1902), where the American philosopher and psychologist William James (1842–1910) feels compelled to critique the contemporary "fashion" of "criticising the religious emotions by showing a connection between them and the sexual life", a link he considers as preposterous as reducing spirituality to digestive satiety or respiratory "inspiration" (10, 12). Keen to uncouple spirituality from physiology or the psychosomatic, James nevertheless enthusiastically conveys the "deliciousness" of mystical visions, those "highest states of ecstasy" that prompt swoons, elude language, and provoke "organic sensibilities" in ways exceeding "anything known in ordinary consciousness" (412). James's referents include Teresa of Ávila, the sixteenth-century Spanish nun who famously recorded her bouts of rapturous mysticism. Attending to a like history, Denis Saurat's influential *Literature and Occult Tradition* (1930) asserts that sexuality has long been esoterically celebrated as an animating, generative principle affirming universal correspondences. For Saurat, Kabbalah attributes world origins to a divine sexual union between a paternalistic god and his own feminine power; in turn, mortals engaging in sex are at their most deific, "in full co-partnership" with their god, whose continued flourishing is contingent upon their satiation (95–111). While the Jewish mystical traditions that might link us to Loy's Judaic heritage are not expressly lingered over in her writings, in her archive, she notably reformulates this precise Kabbalistic premise, writing: "Orgasm = the microcosmic projection of the paroxysm of creation" ("Notes on Religion" 16). And a version of this hermaphroditic deity informs Christian Science, a religion widely understood to attract women of Jewish descent, among them Gertrude Stein and Mina Loy (Appel 115–17; *BM* 131).

In "Songs to Joannes" (1917), Loy's version of an originary esoteric intimacy expands and contorts heteronormative coupling: "Where two or three are welded together / They shall become god". The orgasmic depersonalisation of this "Me you – you – me" leads to the peaceful, restorative soteriology of "the terrific Nirvana" (*LoLB* 58). In her guide to Christian Science, Baker Eddy offers a more conventional, chaste variation on this nonetheless revolutionary theme, denoting God as "Father-Mother" (*Health* 331). A Cartesian dualist who monistically champions abstinence and condemns our "world of sin and sensuality", Baker Eddy is an unlikely sexual mystic (*Health* 57, 82). But significant claims have been made about Baker Eddy's proto-feminist "support for a transgressive, authoritative, public female subjectivity", claims sustained by today's pro-feminist Science adherents (Simon 379).[49] In its early years, the majority of Christian Scientists were women, and in 1907, when Mark Twain devoted an entire book to critiquing and satirising the faith, he figured its devotees as unattractive harpies who strong-armed puling husbands into joining its male minority (Macdonald 104). As ever, satire exposes threat: a powerful, pioneeringly female religious leader, Baker Eddy was reviled in the press by physicians and clerics who dubbed her a middle-aged hysteric or domineering shrew (McDonald 95, 98). But as Katie Simon argues, Baker Eddy considered gender an intellectual concept that had no place in a debased, insignificant material world, and thereby predated Judith Butler in positing sexual identity "as culturally constructed and available for resignification" (381).[50]

Furthermore, by propagating a feminised deity, Baker Eddy anticipates Irigaray's assertion that "'as long as woman lacks a divine made in her image she cannot establish her subjectivity or achieve a goal of her own'" (qtd. in Simon 382). Irigaray does not speak symbolically; without an idealised self-projection, she firmly believes that women will remain "claustrophobically confined to the role of the Other" (Shreiber 477; Simon 382). Othering Baker Eddy knew first-hand: she lived a life of chronic pain, penury, and loss before founding a church composed of people who usually came to her with bodies unmoored or unwell. Baker Eddy, in other words, represents the very coordinates Maeera Shreiber ascribes to Loy as a poet and mystic, who, "in taking the broken or ageing female body as the site of illumination, offers a powerful reconfiguration of the well-known association between women and lack, as well as making an importantly unsentimental claim for feminism and religion or spiritualism as complementary rather than adversarial discourses" (471). Coupled with her unending drive to a restorative (if ultimately unachievable) wholeness that likewise defines so much of Loy's oeuvre, this is the Baker Eddy who might logically appeal to the feminist Loy. But in truth, it is impossible to discern how closely Loy adhered to Baker Eddy's writings: as late as November 1933, or nearly a quarter century after converting to Science, Loy writes her daughter and son-in-law to say that she plans to follow some advice to read all of the Science founder's writings, a comprehensive process in which she had evidently not yet engaged (Loy to Julien and Joella Levy, Box 30, Folder 13). That said, Loy was in regular contact with Science practitioners – predominantly women – who might be presumed to have imparted foundational tenets to her during her regular one-to-one "treatments".

Integrally, Loy and Baker Eddy articulate a symbiosis between the guiding, powerful human Mind and "the divine Principle, Love" that "encompass[es] all true being" (*Health* 355, 496). We hear like thinking in an archived Loy fragment: "love is recognition of the individual's collective identity in God" ("Notes on Metaphysics"). In her writings, Loy concurs with Baker Eddy's premise that love promises healing, harmony, spiritualisation, and transcendence, "support[ing] the struggling heart until it ceases to sigh over the world and begins to unfold its wings for heaven" (*Health* 96, 57). Making these claims, Baker Eddy may be influenced by Emerson's espousal of an impassioned, transcendent Over-Soul, also dubbed Love or Eros, which he considered "the essential cosmic force, the glue that holds the universe and humanity together" (Gougeon 5, 7). But Baker Eddy is also a Christian attuned to the New Testament maxim that "God is Love" (1 John 4.8). And as will be discussed further in Chapter 3, many nineteenth-century heterodoxies emphasised a purely good deity incapable of wrath or evil, a truth as evident in Christian Science as it is in Theosophy, a faith that posited God's essence as "Joy and Light and Love" (Besant 28). This emphasis recurs in the work of Loy's post-1940s religious guide Joel S. Goldsmith, who admonishes his followers to "come out from the old Judaic ideas and beliefs of a God of punishment and reward" and recognise, in a reciprocation of Loy's definition of love, that "Christ is the love of God in you" (84, 110). Loy can be seen wrestling with, and attempting to abandon, like Jewish traditions in her correspondence.[51]

But unlike these faiths, in her own expository esotericism, Loy, well-schooled in the New Testament from childhood, actively resists the Christian diminishment of the relationship between the individual and the flesh as inextricable from "sin, lust, and death" (*BM* 30; Rivera 1). Attending a Christian Science tea party in Paris in 1930, Loy comes away disgusted at the truth that "people in [Science] are still 'shying at lust'". This "shying" is a red rag to Loy's sex-positive bullishness, and she struggles to keep her rage under control, writing: "I appreciate chastity – but not on the assumption that it is the right side of a 'wrong'". Loy considers "[t]he intelligentsia" – among them, presumably, her avant-garde associates – "<u>too</u> dirty", but Science practitioners she condemns as "too <u>dirtily</u> <u>clean</u>", too prone to "wash themselves in the putrescence of the ~~conquered~~ subjugated vices –" (Undated letter, Loy to Julien and Joella Levy, Box 30, Folder 10, 1930). Cognisant that "the immateriality of God was the linchpin of the Western masculine symbolic", Loy persistently satirises the Christian feminisation and derogation of the flesh in her literature (Rivera 6). Witness her scabrous assertion that "the fleshly bond between mother and daughter does sometimes deposit disgust in the daughter's subconscious"; her knowing presentation of a misogynist who refers to his lover as "a lump of female flesh"; or, in another story, a gay man who "reached a higher plane having eschewed the devil in woman's flesh" (*SE* 14, 70, 103).

In turn, Loy's esotericism takes express issue with "religion's war against the flesh", observing that, like our desire, our skin is a gift of the Creator, "an instrument" facilitating Eros that should be treated with respect (*SE* 248, 250). Here again Loy may assert her Jewish roots, as Christian doctrine prided itself in spiritually surpassing "Jewish law [that] insisted on the importance of the flesh", most notably in the mark of kinship and procreation that is circumcision (Rivera 35). But while Loy's Eros is an undeniable challenge to "the prudish and moralising Christianity that coloured her middle-class Victorian childhood", it is also a corrective to all censorious orthodoxies (Steinke 500, 494).[52] For the anti-somaticism Loy identifies extends well beyond nineteenth-century England: as Enrique Dussel argues, cultures Hindu, Persian, Greco-Roman, Buddhist, and Taoist have judged corporeality as unethical, as beneath the divine soul, a valuation perpetuating negative, conflicted thinking about sexuality, even as it justifies the domination of the enslaved, the poor, and women, or those traditionally defined by the body and/or its needs (13–14). While Loy pursues a divine transcendence that arguably positions her within this conservative, binary-driven lineage, she is feminist in insisting that the sexualised body incontrovertibly facilitates our journey toward comprehending a mystical beyond.

There exist notable *fin-de-siècle*, sex-positive precursors to the feminist orientation of Loy's esoteric Eros. Here we might turn to the self-described "tawny student of Esoterics", African-American Rosicrucian Paschal Beverly Randolph (1825–75), whose *Eulis! The History of Love* (1874) advocates on behalf of a mystical, sublime approach to sex (47). Ever mysterious, Randolph's soul is most loving when sustained by a satiated, respected body, and as a direct result, he demands greater equality between the sexes, discussing, with remarkable introductory frankness, the need for men to better acquaint themselves with women's vulvas in order to generate the vital "lymph" key to happy heteronormative domesticity (7). Randolph begins as he means to go on: while not shying away from gendered essentialism or distinctly biased phrases such as "wedded harlot", he encourages husbands to consider how their failures might contribute to their wives' adultery; he speaks with sympathy and outrage about backstreet abortions; he satisfyingly denounces the ubiquity of misogynistic male discourse and men who treat women as "an appendage" rather than "partner or equal" (14, 21, 20, 80). Marriage Randolph venerates as "the most potent and tremendous energy and agency in the entire material and hyperphysical universe", a cosmos watched over by a deity both male and female that we access by "learn[ing] to Love" (31–2, 194). Loy echoes many of Randolph's precepts and preoccupations, as when she argues that marriage is a foundational, "occult relationship" that "stimulates" the often tragically unmet "latent tactile impulses of a satin-lined Venusberg" (*CP* 17: 55).

Many of Randolph's ideas recur in the work of a thinker with whom Loy assuredly came into contact: the openly gay British utopian socialist Edward Carpenter (1844–1929). Like Loy, Carpenter admired and associated with Havelock Ellis and Emma Goldman, and was influenced by Frederic Myers; Carpenter's "cosmic consciousness" permeates the writing of Loy's friend Mabel Dodge Luhan and Loy's 1914 "Aphorisms on Futurism" (Dalrymple-Henderson, "Mysticism" 33). In *Love's Coming-of-Age* (1896/1906), Carpenter connects love and "cosmic energies and entities", describing "the passion of sex" as the "divine made actual and realisable" (3, 159). His sexual mysticism insists on the interdependence of terrestrial and celestial, establishing concordances between Eastern mysticism and European Christianity, and imparting on behalf of improved sexual understanding (147, 16–17). Carpenter berates his contemporaries for denigrating sex by foregrounding its pleasure over the "deepest soul-union" it enables (15).

Echoing Randolph, Carpenter's male is overwhelmingly impassioned, his female inherently, troublingly passive, if refined. This essentialism notwithstanding, Carpenter deplores the expectation that woman "sacrifice [her] personal interests and expansions in the ever-narrowing round of domestic duty" (38). Born of "universal soul", Carpenter's "perfect love" transforms human into god (21). Crucially, Carpenter's Eros is built on discernibly feminist foundations. In her "Feminist Manifesto", Loy tells her reader that men and women "are at the mercy of the advantage that each can take of the others [sic] sexual dependence", a dependence, as mentioned above, only set aside in "the sexual embrace" (*LoLB* 154). With less animus, Carpenter argues: "in order to be love at all, love must be ... free from any sentiment of dependency or inequality" (85). Atypically open and urgent about the long-overdue prioritisation of women's satiety, Randolph's and Carpenter's sexual mysticisms actively counter the self-effacing puritanism affirmed by emergent feminist discourse at the end of the nineteenth century, a moral legacy with which contemporary feminism continues to contend. Unusually forward-thinking, both men emblematise how Western *fin-de-siècle* occultism was preoccupied with contemporaneous renegotiations of gender and sexuality progressively, regressively, and so centrally that these debates significantly fractured or disrupted the operation of some occult organisations, among them the Theosophical Society and the Hermetic Order of the Golden Dawn (Owen, *Place* 111–12).

To enable fair access to sexualised transcendence, Randolph and Carpenter articulate plans to release women from entrenched quotidian inequities, evincing a pragmatism rarely seen in Loy's writings. Claiming that the "bread and butter" of feminism "bores [her] rather", Loy instead focused on the psychosexual and spiritual transformation of womankind; as she wrote when the First World War heightened her sense of gender disparity: "What I feel now are feminine politics, but in a cosmic way that may not fit in anywhere" (Undated letter, "Loy, Mina, 1913–1920, n.d.", Mabel Dodge Luhan Papers; Loy, "Series 1."). In lieu of hard strategy, Loy feelingly articulates women's oppression, and theorises a countering universalised if feminist esoteric Eros. Loy shares this mystical solution with her modernist associate the American writer H. D. (1886–1961), an individual with whom Loy came into contact both personally and as an author.[53] H. D.'s *Notes on Thought and Vision* (1919) goes without direct reference to lived gendered disparities yet propagates two centres of human consciousness: brain vision, or intellect, and "womb or love-vision", the stuff of dreams, but also the quotidian

(20–1). For Loy and H. D., sympathetic thought, shared goals, and the excitations of attraction prompt over-brain and womb-brain to think and perceive; for H. D., only love reveals the gnomic, "the mysteries of vision" (22; see *Anatomy* volume 1, chapter 4). Drawing on Christian, Chinese, and ancient Greek sources, H. D. sketches out a sexual mysticism that prioritises a healthy, beloved body as "a means of approach to ecstasy", a vision most focused, regenerative, and deific when rational brain and loving womb work symbiotically (46, 23). Incorporating female sensuality into their validation of women's capacities to think, create, and envision, Loy and H. D. anticipate more broadly applied post-war reclamations of the erotic.

The German-American philosopher and theorist Herbert Marcuse (1898–1979) initiated a return to Eros that shaped 1960s countercultures. Like Bataille, Marcuse draws on Marxist and Freudian tenets in his writings; his famous *Eros and Civilisation* (1955) actively refigured the basic precepts of psychoanalysis. Where Freud defined culture as "[t]he methodical sacrifice of libido . . . to socially useful activities and expressions", Marcuse asserted that, as the fear of scarcity need no longer drive existence, humanity should now prioritise the polymorphic erotogenic zones of the body and the pleasures they engender (23, 47). In so doing, our species might resist a sexuality unnecessarily reduced to "genital supremacy", one expressly designed to leave the rest of the body free for an often-alienated labour (23, 47, 163). Prioritising eroticism over toil, Marcuse maintains that, by realising our individual desires, we will circumvent the increasingly amplified destructive instincts of contemporary Western civilisation entire (50). Marcuse shares coordinates with Loy: both resist censoriousness, or "outlawing . . . expressions of Eros"; both recognise that sacrifices individual and social, rather than pleasure, remain at the heart of contemporary too-functional society; both posit Eros as a "striving for Eternity" that generatively critiques the resignations and limitations of existing conditions; both turn to Plato as a model for the "celebration of sexual origin", and in Plato's wake, both celebrate Eros as intrinsic to aesthetics (Marcuse 54, 89, 186, 169, 143). Furthermore, Marcuse's celebration of libido as a prime guiding force recalls the vitalist principles that beguile Loy; his is a return to a universal, timeless energy both animating and synchronising.

But Marcuse is far less alert to the gendered ramifications of Eros than Loy: in complete accord with the Oedipal complex, Marcuse posits Womankind as "the supreme pleasure" and is openly hostile to the intimacy that drives Loy's feminist Eros; by Marcuse's figuration, men in particular become trapped by the singular loyalty love presupposes (73, 62).[54] For Marcuse, Freudian drives irretrievably define humanity, and culture is their product; to suggest, as does Loy, that society is patriarchal is to redirect attention from the foundational Freudian psyche that Marcuse considers universal, biological, and sacrosanct. In Marcuse's psychoanalytic reading, neuroses emerge from an amorphous civilisational repression, not from the historicised particularities of identity. In sum, essentialism and the sexual double standard taint Marcuse's thinking. What is more, while his call to establish a "libidinal rationality" that effectively eliminates the Freudian reality principle suggests a turn to a transcendent desirousness, Marcuse's Eros is a utopian vision adamantly materialist, resolutely anti-spiritualist (162–3). Given the above, the writer and activist Audre Lorde (1934–92), who came of age just as Marcuse's theories came into being, is a clearer descendent of Loy and her feminist peers. Recognising Greek Eros as a multiplicitous, foundational love that exceeds sexuality, Lorde writes extensively of how its etymological descendent, the erotic, can affirm the female self "in the face of a racist, patriarchal, and anti-erotic society" (55, 59). In a redirection of Marcuse that mirrors his expansive and utopian terms, Lorde's eroticism is "an assertion of the lifeforce of women; of that creative energy empowered, the knowledge and use of which we are now reclaiming in our language, our history, our dancing, our loving, our work, our lives" (56). A site of replenishment and provocation, Lorde's erotic is a cohering, nurturing drive inseparable from the political and intellectual, but also, importantly, the spiritual (56).

However discernibly trailblazing, Loy's and H. D.'s modernist feminist mysticisms were not taken seriously by their male peers. If her romans à clef are taken at face value, Loy was dubbed a "'busy little mystic'" by Futurist leader Marinetti (B 8: 6). Purportedly, H. D. was considered Ezra Pound's "'Dryad' or tree-sprite initiating him into the mysteries of the vital cosmos" (Gelpi 8). As William James tells us, the mystic temperament has long been aligned with psychopathology, acute moral sensitivity, and a sentimentality at odds with "your robust Philistine type of nervous system, forever offering its biceps to be felt, thumping its breast, and thanking Heaven that it hasn't a single morbid fibre in its composition" (16, 25). In delineating a gender-equitable gnomic transcendence, Loy and H. D. challenge their respective vanguard Philistines, whose dismissals by diminution speak to the threat posed by their feminist visions. These visions were expressly informed by that "great Athenian group" that included Socrates, and by Sappho, who, as

H. D. acknowledged, brought emotional wisdom, genius, and bitterness to her own highly physical "clamours" for Eros (21, 65). Loy shares this admiration, imagining Sappho "stroking my neck with [her] silver fingers", "her face ... a cross between The Madonna and the full moon". Reworking the New Testament story by which archetypal fallen woman Mary Magdalene washes the feet of Jesus Christ with her tears, notes in Loy's archive show her envisioning "smear[ing Sappho's] feet with my brains".[55] For Loy, such an act would be an "homage to Sappho, the immune, serene" a reverential ritual she imagines as compensation for panicked instincts that she wishes to keep concealed, hidden ("Biography of Songge Byrd"). Replacing romantic lachrymae with the fatty tissues of her anatomised, pulverised mind, Loy's is a deeply abject vision of a self-sacrificing intellectualism that elevates Sappho to the status of a deity so powerful that Loy herself is overawed just imagining her presence. This tribute – both feminist and masochist, intimate and violent – speaks to the depth of Loy's allegiances to the ancients. With a view to situating Loy's esoteric Eros more fully within like modernist paradigms, the next section of this chapter turns to both its classical origins and futuristic aspirations.

Ancient and Atomic Eros

> *Sex!* This word, at last, overflows with so many misassociations. To clarify its future significance, sex must be renamed. Meanwhile, for "sex", let us substitute *Eros*. Somehow the sound of the Greek cupid survives unsullied. (*SE* 247)

Aiming toward revolution, Loy reaches to the past, drawing the term "Eros" from ancient Greek culture by way of avoiding her contemporaries' conflicted presentation of sexuality as "beatitude and secret filth" (*SE* 247). Loy shares this propensity with Myers, for whom Platonic love is "earthly passion" that is "the initiation and introduction into cosmic sanctity and joy", as well as "Eternal Goodness and Beauty" (61). She shares it also with Freud's *Civilisation and its Discontents* (1930), where "Eros" signals sexual and life-preserving instincts threatened by Eurocentric civilisation, its proprieties, technologies, and anxieties that centrally include the fear of losing love itself (125, 132). Concern about civilising harm is, at times, uncomfortably present in Loy as racist primitivism, as when a late poem focuses on the "ancestral smoulder" evident in an African-American performer whose "posturing" of "an overwrought Eros" too palpably fascinates (*LaLB* 216).[56] But it is the classical lineage that most consistently preoccupies Loy: her earliest published use of "Eros" occurs in "Lunar Baedeker" (1923), a poetic travel guide to a carnivalesque moon that is virginal concubine, an "[o]dious oasis" morbid and lively with excess. From oxymoronic and cultural surfeit – the poem alludes to Zoroastrian, Asian, Egyptian, Turkish, Christian, Roman, and Greek mythologies and practices – "Eros" arises "obsolete" yet flying, as if toward the introductory morning star, the "silver Lucifer" also known as Venus (*LoLB* 81–2). A consummation of Greco-Roman love deities may well be under way.

In later writings on culture and Eros, Loy reserves her greatest negativity for sexuality sourced in the Judeo-Christian exoteric religious tradition: "The serpent in Eden is symbol of extreme imposture – – – / The substitution of 'sex-morality' for humane morality" (*SE* 250). Off the winding back of a base, beguiling snake, biblical teaching insists upon our "originary inclination to evil" (Cavarero 4). By Loy's characterisation, this evil is sexualised so that prudishness and censoriousness take compensatory precedence over benevolence or agape. Rejecting this history, Loy turns to ancient philosophers, only to find every one of her best "metaphysical ... epigrams ... posited with an absolutely appalling lack of vim – – Which proves – that the sage who sits on his tail and meditates will mechanistically come to the same conclusions – whether 'it' be an old man in the year 3000 BC or a lady of 'certain' age in 1930 a.d." (Letter dated 16 July 1930, Loy to Julien and Joella Levy, Box 30, Folder 8, 1930). Equating her own wisdom with that of classical thinkers, Loy's spirited readiness to stylistically best ancient philosophy is a thin veneer over her indebtedness to its ideas. Most self-evidently, we might suppose that her turn to a classical past is wholly reliant on the supposition of "the typical Greek tendency to glorify ... the intrinsic value of sexual love" (D. Levy 285). But while carnality is assuredly integral to Loy's thinking, she aligns her esoteric Eros with the ancients primarily because she shares their perception of love as an ineffable if definitive truth, triangulating its knowledge with desires for beauty and goodness facilitated by aesthetic inclinations. In these regards, Loy's Eros echoes Plato's *Symposium* (c. 385–370 BCE), which presents philosophy as "the translation of eros into logos" (Han 52–3). For Loy as for Plato, "the creation of beauty", be it through intellection or creativity, "is always an act of love" (*G32* 27). As importantly, Loy's love is atomic: the basic unit of materiality and inclination that she understood as inseparable from its potential for nuclear destruction. Hence, when she was asked what she most happily anticipated in a 1929 questionnaire by *The Little Review*, Loy answered: "The release of atomic energy" (*LaLB* 305).

The story of a dinner party held by the poet Agathon, the *Symposium* is propelled by each guest offering a panegyric on love. Socrates brings the formal proceedings to a close with a discussion of love imparted to him by the seer Diotima. Beginning with love of an individual body before moving outward to all beautiful beings, Diotima's Eros hierarchy ultimately extends to love of soul, morality, and bodies of knowledge before culminating in "the vast ocean of beauty" that brings forth wisdom eternal (*Symposium* 92–4). Ascending from sensuality to the metaphysical, Diotima privileges a divine love powerfully discernible in Western philosophy, literature, and religion. But just as Socrates finishes relaying Diotima's teachings, Plato's narrative takes an abrupt turn that challenges this orderly hierarchy. Socrates's lover Alcibiades arrives drunk, late, and dishevelled. Rather than offer an encomium on love, Alcibiades launches into a disquisition of Socrates and their unconsummated relationship. In the intimate portrait that follows, Socrates approximates the divine: Alcibiades reveres him as war hero, ascetic, and superlative scholar. Believing himself the most astute about Socrates's inner beauty, Alcibiades openly yearns for their greater physical intimacy. As Plato reports, speech unmoors audience: "When Alcibiades had finished, the freedom with which he had spoken raised a general laugh, because he seemed still to be *amorously inclined* toward Socrates" (emphasis added; 111). Dismissible as comic, Alcibiades's passion affirms how love relies on a virtuous spirituality that is importantly (un)balanced, thrown off kilter, by physical intimacies. Where Diotima's Eros hierarchy fails to mention pleasure, Alcibiades's protracted lament confirms a message implicit within Plato's *Symposium*, namely that "the ordering of eros to absolute beauty does not in principle exclude generous and desire-laden companionship [but] intensifies it" (Santas 74; Schindler 219). Exoterically promoting spiritual love, Plato's narrative irony equalises loves metaphysical *and* physical.[57]

Homer's contemporary, the Greek poet Hesiod, considered Eros "the most handsome among the immortal gods, dissolver of flesh, who overcomes the reason and purpose in the breasts of all gods and all men" (ll. 120–3; 6). Tasked with coordinating the universal elements, Eros became symbiotic with life-giving harmony.

Eros is later demoted to the god of human love, but also passion and feeling, and "even in th[is] diminutive form the cohesive and progenerative element[s are] conspicuous" (Gougeon 7). According to Socrates's interpretation of Diotima, Eros is the offspring of Penia, or poverty, and Poros, variously translated as plenitude, contrivance, or the "'way'", the leader, friend, or lover who guides us through "uncharted terrain" (Han 52). A spirit comprised of lack and fulfilment, uncertainty and wisdom, Eros is neither discernibly mortal nor immortal, but interposes between humanity and the gods in pursuit of the beautiful and the good. Eros, then, appears an ideal candidate to lead us from the exoteric toward the esoteric. These are the self-same roles ascribed to the philosopher of antiquity, who never attains sought truth just as Eros, to survive, maintains a middle ground between enticing, frustrating desire and pleasurable satiation (Secomb 21). As a result, the *Symposium* is widely interpreted as Plato's recognition that the desires for Eros and truth are symbiotic, akin, even as his *Phaedrus* (c. 375–365 BCE) reaffirms how Eros and truth represent longings to which we are beholden unto madness.[58]

In the *Symposium*, Socrates is both a knowledge-seeking philosopher and, as subject of Alcibiades's encomium, a stand-in for Eros itself, a figure who, as Alcibiades discerns, is perfectly capable of the controlled detachment and proximate playfulness love requires (Scott and Welton 13; *Symposium* 103). Plato's conflation of Eros and truth is radical and potentially inconsistent: it undermines the rectilinearity presumed integral to the philosophical tradition that he elsewhere famously allegorises. In Plato's *Republic* (c. 375 BCE), Socrates has us envision a cave of shackled, hunched individuals from whom the philosopher alone breaks free to stand up, step outside, and turn his face toward illuminating light. Guided by a desire to liberate, the philosopher's altruistic return to the cave leads to his violent death at the hands of those who fear and resist his insights. As Cavarero attests, this allegory idealises upright rationality, privileging authority and individual autonomy over care and otherness (46–8). It also idealises the exoteric.

By stark contrast, the *Symposium* concludes by affirming a carnality worthy of Sappho, a direct influence on both Plato and Loy. Plato references Sappho with palpable admiration and respect throughout his writings, the *Symposium* inclusive. Loy's appreciation for Sappho was similarly long-standing: well before she envisioned anointing Sappho's feet with her own brains, Loy boasted in a 1916 letter that her "Songs to Joannes" were "the Best since Sappho" ("Series 1."). It has been convincingly demonstrated that, in this poem sequence, Loy borrowed directly from Sappho's remaining fragments, and allusion is always homage (Blau Duplessis 58–9). In Sappho's writing, Eros is profoundly physical, a force that "sh[akes her] heart like a wind falling on oaks on a mountain", a "limb-loosening . . . bitter-sweet, irresistible creature", a "pain-giver" (93, 147, 175). Articulating a similarly unabashed amorous inclination, Alcibiades extends a warning rebuff to the otherwise unimpeachable, divine Socrates about the importance of intimate needs. But in fact, desirability is integral to the Eros hierarchy Socrates reiterates via Diotima, which, after all, aspires to transcendence through the beauty that motivates not only knowledge, but also art.

As Eros, aesthetic inspiration presupposes the capacity to be "moved by an external power, something that resides outside [the self] but is nonetheless irresistible and generates talent" (Cavarero 92). This creativity can be physical, as in biological reproduction, or spiritual, a "creative desire of the soul" begetting wise and virtuous progeny through poetry, craft, or law (Plato, *Symposium* 90–1). Posited as more enduring, spiritual reproduction is preserved by passing on one's wisdom or skill to an interlocutor, student, or receptive public. Via Plato's notably female seer Diotima, this metaphor situates "'philosophy [with]in the realm of love, nurturance, and procreation'"; through it, "'new ideas are the natural product of a well-chosen union between . . . virtuous human beings'" (Wendy Brown qtd. in Secomb 16). Avant-gardist to her core, Loy's creativity may not operate in strict accordance with Platonic virtue, but it does follow his Eros in striving toward a truth born of abstraction and carnality. Loy's artistic genius regenerates the divine in its complex entirety, an "image of God" conjoining deific "voice" but also "offal"; a forging of the crudely unknown and chaotic with an eye always upon "that imperious jewellery of the Universe / — the Beautiful—" (*LoLB* 88, 78). For Loy, the "gravid day" that "spawns" within and as a consequence of *Ulysses* enables Joyce to transcend the "Empyrean emporium" of Babel itself, taking up the role of "rejector—recreator", a figure whose illuminations are inextricable from the unsayable, the machinations of a necessarily circumspect "sub rosa" (*LoLB* 89–90).[59] Failed, this dualistic, comingling impetus is acknowledged in poem 24 of "Songs to Joannes", where Loy's speaker's "procreative truth" is drained by insufficiently significant "lusts and lucidities / And prayerful lies" (*LoLB* 62). Lacking expansivity, desire and illumination invert divination, generate dishonest supplications and petitions that speak to the yearned-for ideal against which they fall short.

Unique among philosophers for foregrounding "love as an absolute vital power", Plato remains resonant, according to Simmel, precisely because he locates the origin of love in the expansive cosmos, a "metaphysicalizing" that surpasses the strictures of post-Renaissance individualism ("Eros" 236, 242). Love exceeds us to such an extent, Simmel contends, that even "the Beyond" can be perceived as "an inadequate designation" of its presence ("Eros" 244). In sum, Simmel accords with Plato's implicit argument in the *Symposium* that "sexual love opens the doors of the total personality widest", likening this ego exposure to how the artist, through art, offers us her or "his entire nature" ("Sociology" 457). Loy is similarly preoccupied by Eros as gnostic and aesthetic truth. Like Plato, Loy draws upon intimacies central to esotericism, which as rhetorical strategy or mystical belief requires connectivity, lingering, proximity, and the immediacies of intuition. Strauss claims that the esoteric texts of classical philosophy occlude disruptive truths beneath an accessible, edifying message, and should be understood as "'written speeches caused by love'" ("Persecution" 504). Critics have sought an attribution for Strauss's quotation in vain, but it has been interpreted as a validation of the transmissive proclivities considered fundamental to esoteric discourse. By this reading, the esotericist's innate desires to communicate, teach, and liberate despite the risks these processes can involve are motivated less by secrecy and elitism than by a philanthropic desire for love (Dinan 252–3). Indebted to Strauss, Arthur Melzer similarly describes the student of esotericism as a lover reading a letter from the beloved, seeking out indicators of ardour, Freudian slips that give the lie to unspoken sentiments, and repeat, fervent analyses of repetitions, symbols, omissions, dangerous thinking, and internal contradictions (290–322). This metaphor is discernible in the work of esoteric scholar Karen Voss, who asserts that, when we want to know something, we aspire to fall in love with it, become one with it, allow it to transform us (17).

Following these Platonic and gnostic legacies, Loy generates an exoteric esotericism about Eros, a pedagogical bid to prise open a love that must always remain, to some degree, ineffable, manifesting itself beyond language. If classical philosophy is an impossible "quest for universal knowledge, for knowledge of the whole", Eros has been interpreted as "the truth of that whole" (Strauss, *Political* 11, 227; Berg 108). Celebrating its somatic and intellectual mystery, Loy nevertheless believes we can know more about Eros than we do: we can right the historical wrongs of Western socio-sexual morality by authenticating lust as a "sane *impulse*"; furthermore, we might reconsider why the "amatory passion" is so vilified when it might be better perceived as "the only passion that can do no harm to anybody" (*SE* 283–4). And of course, for Loy, a fulsome pursuit of Eros demands recognition of women's desire, a sincere welcoming of authentic, uninhibited female pleasure. Against a longstanding exoteric overlooking and mistreatment of the body, Loy values both body and soul via a feminist Eros that is drawn from antiquity, that is equal parts longing and aspiration, as well as satiations emotional, physical, intellectual, and divine.

Importantly, Loy's theorisation of an esoteric Eros is also part of a failed attempt to reanimate and shore up the fragments of her own ruins. "Ghosts of manuscripts written at odd whiles", these expository writings are both a "book [Loy] had felt impelled to write" and the substance of her own "inhibition", her own fear of no longer "preserv[ing] her incognito" (*IA* 58: 3). Remaining tied to bodily inclinations, Loy's late, self-reflexive esoteric prose exhibits an anti-anatomising impulse, an "eclosion" or emergence from concealment that coheres her long-standing references to the female body as "[w]racked", split, or partial (*LoLB* 67). Thus, Loy rallies herself at the outset of *Islands in the Air*: "To gather up, to put together, to elucidate!" Then questions: "To what end? Perhaps the relief of a not uncommon anxiety to produce proof of having, oneself, existence?" (*IA* 58: 6). Plato's procreative legacy is on Loy's mind, one achievable by reconsiderations of Eros writ large through her life, through recapitulations of loves familial or sexual. But why turn to complex, messy, insatiable love and desire to cohere the self? Observing how, through twentieth-century psychoanalytic and philosophical thought, the "autocratic, integrated and cohesive ego" was regularly dissected and fragmented, Cavarero counsels: "Instead of breaking its vertical axis into multiple pieces, one could try bending it, giving it a different posture", inclining it away from its erect stance, either inward, toward itself, or outward, toward otherness (11, 32). Through art and love, Loy approximates new postures in the manner Cavarero describes, working toward a flexibility within her own subjective mental and emotional frameworks, structures that she often describes as battered to obliteration or repressed to ossification.

That Loy maintains any healthy relationship to her inclinations is remarkable given that pain in her Victorian family of origin is primarily affective. By humiliation, child-Loy was denounced, manipulated, abused. Where her mother continually requires "self-abasement", her father "put[s] her shame out of countenance" with "his exhortations to glory". While both parents are united in their class aspirations, Loy is torn between maternal, Protestant censoriousness and paternal, Jewish incitements to intellection and ambition and, as a direct consequence, develops a "cloven ego" (*GI* 28: 64). Family conflicts intensify as Loy enters sexual awareness. Mistakenly informed by a peer that giving birth is always a near-death experience for women, Loy becomes ill "in horror of [human] origin", eventually locating the courage to ask her mother for a reassurance that becomes another excuse to humiliate. Calling her "leper" and outcast, her mother tells her to isolate herself and "'guard [her] disgusting secret carefully'" (*IA* 65: 77–8). Loy historicises the fear prompting the sadism, noting, for instance, that her father cleaves to the traditional Jewish view that women are constitutively impure and must be kept under a watchful eye (*GI* 28: 47). Against the insistence of twentieth-century moralists that the world is no longer as it was, Loy asserts: "At the close of Victoria's reign [sex] formed an incessant obsession of the respectable." So all-encompassing was this forbidden subject that it disrupted concentration and led to rabid censoriousness (*IA* 67: 114). This is the divisive status quo that Loy's esoteric Eros strives to ameliorate, her oeuvre repeatedly positing an introspective being who rejects the alienating, entrenched sexual shame of occidental puritanism for self-reflexive inclinations that unite her more seamlessly with art, cerebrality, and otherness. In the early "Aphorisms on Futurism" (1914), Loy demands that "retrograde superstitions" be abandoned, pledging to "shout ... obscenities" at the blushing propagator of such backward thinking; her contemporaneous "Feminist Manifesto" insists that "social regeneration" will dovetail with the elimination of women's sexual shame (*LoLB* 152, 156). Come "International Psycho-Democracy" (1918), the suppression "of Man's fundamental desires" leads to "Cosmic Neurosis", and this pattern recurs in late works including "Mi & Lo" and "The History of Religion and Eros", both of which extol the virtues of heightened consciousness whilst conclusively affirming lust and bliss (*LaLB* 279).

"[E]xtreme enigma" in Loy's "Bewilderness", Arthur Cravan is proof that love coheres and another catalyst of Loy's "desire for continuity and meaning" (*LoLB* 130; Parmar 103). Noting that the eminently performative Cravan appeared to her in many guises in their first encounters, Loy observes that it was only "through intimacy" that these separate identities "coalesced into a single man" ("Colossus" 108). Disappeared, Cravan occupies the rubbled centre of Loy's ruins: once "Adonis" to her Venus, he has become "the bloom of beloving / decoyed / to decay" (*LoLB* 130). By Loy's telling, she and Cravan were the originary human described by Aristophanes in the *Symposium*: two conjoined bodies severed by a Zeus so envious of their power that they were condemned to seek proximity to their other half forevermore (*Symposium* 59–62). A recollection of Cravan emerges, for instance, in Loy's description of love as a twinship marked by a continual reach for communication with the inviolate core of the other (*CP* 20: 14–15). Or, as she puts it in an interpretation of the Gospel of Saint Mark: "'Whom god hath joined together let no man put asunder,' undeniably confirms the derivation of Eros from the divine abstraction, delimiting the self in the peace of participation, of being no longer contactless in a mysterious universe" (Mark 10.9; *SE* 249). The embodied couple – serene, touching, grounded by otherness – affirms the spirituality of love. Ideally, this embodied couple is married, as another reference to Mark confirms. According to Loy: "'They twain shall be one flesh,' described the sense of a tangible bond, a vibrational co-identity of perfectly married people, as if the Eros union bequeathed to them a continuous reciprocal radiation" (Mark 10.8; *SE* 248). In this regard, Loy chimes with Baker Eddy's insistence that, in marriage, "[u]nion of the masculine and feminine qualities constitutes completeness" (*Health* 57).

This affinity is troublingly straight, rectilinearly consistent with exoteric religious and state law. But Loy can and does transcend these heteronormativities, positing Love, for instance, as "hermaphroditic" (*SE* 197). And in the late, unpublished poem "There is No Love Alone", Loy delineates an alchemical Eros in which unquantified, ungendered prone "bodies" ecstatically attune themselves to the cosmos, forming a lyric "duet" that is the only clear coupling (*LaLB* 233). Yet Loy cleaves to marriage, a truth perhaps attributable to a retrospective reimagining of a husband lost too soon and too tragically, whose love was constitutively incomplete and mysterious as all love is, but was also experientially unavailable for the last forty-seven of Loy's eighty-three years. After their wedding, Loy and Cravan were buoyant with the "exaltation" and "canonization" of their love, their eyes haloed with "happiness"; thus sanctified, they were grounded by the architectural foundation they had laid, "perceiv[ing] in [their] united joy a divine cementation" (*EP* 25). Late in life, this solidity eludes Loy. "Everything's been funny in my life", Loy stated aged 82, "But it wasn't funny losing him, we got on wonderfully" (Loy, "Mina Loy: Interview" 241). Burke argues that Loy's attraction to Cravan was subtended by her understanding that he shared her belief in a higher power and, as significantly, her understanding that artists and geniuses "could intuit the divine" (*BM* 244). As Loy puts it in 1949, Cravan was an "ill-relinquished" ideal, an "acme of communion // who made euphonious / our esoteric universe" (*LoLB* 129). Always Loy's Eros, Cravan becomes her cosmos, the desire transporting her to divinely harmonious truths, representations, logos. In his wake, she is "dumb / in answer / to [his] dead language of amor", extinguished by his explosively unexplained departure: "inhumed in chasms, / craters torn by atomic emotion / among chaos" (*LoLB* 131).

To conclude this chapter, I will attend to the reverberations of Loy's lovelorn "atomic emotion", or, more precisely, the atomics that run molecularly and explosively through her oeuvre, from the "radio-active onrush" of birth, to the corporeal "atomic volume or cellular structure" that renews itself throughout our lives, to Loy's youthful epiphany that the material world is neither solid nor immune to miraculous transpositions by the human will (*IA* 60: 12; *GI* 28: 37).[60] Consistent with the scientific preoccupations of popular culture and literature, and with Loy's own interest in physics, one that overlapped with a Christian Science veneration of the same as offering access to a dematerialised world akin "to the world of pure Mind", atomics are the mechanism by which Loy rallies classical Eros into a futuristic "Eros-Bliss" that affirms the longevity of her esoteric vision (Armstrong 211; *SE* 249).[61] Against the blatantly reductive claim in "Mi & Lo" that "the amatory passion" is "[t]he sole passion that is not destruction", the presiding preoccupation of Loy's "History of Religion and Eros" is the relationship between intimacy and detonation, be it ecstatic or fulminatory (*SE* 283). The metaphor of explosivity is grounded in historical event: Loy is either prompted by the prospect of atomic warfare or writes in the aftermath of the mass destruction of Hiroshima and Nagasaki on 6 and 9 August 1945 respectively. Although these archived documents, unpublished in Loy's lifetime, remain undated, Loy alludes to the writing of "History" at the outset of "Tuning in on the Atom Bomb". "Tuning" announces itself as undertaken during a break from another piece of writing about "the danger induced by extracting force from Power"; "History" begins with a veneration of power as "creative dynamism" both conscious and constructive, and a condemnation of force as derivative, unthinking, and dangerous (*SE* 286; 238–9). Furthermore, "History" critiques the occidental direction of its accumulated force into bombing, and this intertextual allusion clarifies Loy's otherwise opaque reference to nuclear warfare in the title of "Tuning"

(*SE* 238). In other words, it is the threat of human extinction that appears to motivate Loy's most extended formulation of an expository esoteric Eros.

Observing that "modern science successfully harnesses intangible phenomena", Loy transposes the consequences of the splitting of the atom – first achieved in a University of Cambridge laboratory in 1932 – to mystic contemplation. By "identifying the microcosmic with the macrocosmic in the energy of the atom", writes Loy, mystics access the "eternal moment" (*SE* 246). Himself an "ego-laboratory" and "complete microcosm", the mystic "train[s] his intelligence on his components", ultimately transcending the phenomenal realm by mobilising the force latent in his own individual atoms whilst allowing a universal ether to "interpenetrat[e] his atomic structure" (*SE* 239, 241). As did Victorian occultists, Loy draws on modern science to ratify esoteric practice: based on the then-recent uncovering of atom anatomy – only discovered in 1913 – Loy reminds her reader that these minute particles are solar systems in miniature, the universal in the finite (Fountain Eames 32). By extension, a mystic "suffusion by the infinite" is replicated in the electric release of Eros. Affirming the desiring body, this release is "a flash of attainment to an infinite sentience, resulting in perfect relaxation", an eruption into divinity, followed by the attainment of Nirvana (*SE* 250). But in the context of Loy's meditations upon the atom bomb, this blaze is equally legible as a repurposing of the weaponised heat flash of nuclear fission, one Loy expressly articulates as an "invers[e]" explosivity that is corrective and prophecy (*SE* 249). In the past, Loy argues, there existed an esoteric Eros that was misinterpreted by the masses. This misinterpretation "exploded in the human mind, leaving a debris of sadism to infiltrate religious institutions", prompting "the bursting (again, explosive) excitement induced by the filth-bliss confusion of the sin centuries" (*SE* 251, 249). As a counter to these occidental fulminations, Loy anticipates an esoteric "Eros of the future [that] subordinates mere flesh to vibrational co-ordination promoting release of the intrinsic electrification inducing Eros-Bliss"; in Loy's day, atoms were commonly said to vibrate (*SE* 249; Morrisson, *Alchemy* 91). Still volatile, this "intrinsic electrification" is Loy's new and improved esoteric Eros, one sufficiently self-controlled to avert risking further "'explosion'" on the frontier between the celestial and terrestrial, or the threshold between "secret" and "overt" where Eros resides, "metaphysically intact, yet available to sensate experience" (*SE* 251).

In "History", Loy's esoteric Eros is catalysed by and transmuted from weapons of mass destruction. Recall that Loy's ideal couple experiences "a continuous reciprocal radiation that distance does not disrupt", one that may well fuel the "atomic emotion" Loy ascribes to her recollection of Cravan's love (*SE* 248; *LoLB* 131). Technological change has long fed occult practice: after Morse Code was invented in 1837, testimonials appeared affirming encounters with "rapping spirits"; with the advent of photography, blurred images proffered "proof" of ghosts (Thurschwell 23). At the turn of the twentieth century, advances in communicative technology "create[d] a new metaphorics for imagining intimate relations"; the telegraph and telephone, for instance, added legitimacy to telepathic discourse (Thurschwell 36, 8). And as Mark Morrisson has shown, from the turn of the twentieth century to the outset of World War II, occultism – alchemy in particular – and atomic science dovetailed in their shared fascinations "about the nature of matter and energy", meaning that the esoteric was increasingly "explained in terms of radiation" (*Alchemy* 5, 10, 12). Combining the idealised communication of telepathy with the atomic, Loy envisions an eternally reciprocal couple that emits heat, light, electromagnetic or brain waves, and possibly subatomic particles that overcome the communicative complexities of time and space. But where we might intuit Loy likening a mystic's vision to "a radio-television broadcast in three dimensions", her affirmation of love as sourced in a totalising, destructive illumination is an alchemy of near-unimaginable dimensions, one whereby Thanatos is reborn as Eros (*SE* 245).

Loy's paradoxical formulation can be substantiated through Cavarero, for whom the atom is the primary unit of inclination: its willingness to turn toward otherness is the origin of all phenomena, inanimate and animate. "In the history of philosophical cosmogonies," Cavarero asserts, "the world itself comes into being when atoms—which otherwise fall through a vacuum with inexorable, rectilinear motion—touch, thus subjecting their movement to a tiny swerve" (94). Loy's Eros is a like aggregating veer, a reconstitution of the component self, a willed, necessary exploitation of the energy housed within each molecule of our being. Gazing upon the desirable Joannes in *Brontolivido*, Loy's female protagonist finds herself overwhelmed by "his terrific Impersonality" which reveals itself "as God first revealed himself to the seeker after truth, as the plasmic atom – – –" (*B* 8: 27). In Joannes, this fictionalised Loy pursues an ultimately unattainable Eros as a philosopher seeks knowledge, the believer epiphany, the scientist or mystic access to the primary transporting vehicles of life itself.

Destructive and productive, bomb or base unit, riven or inclining, the atom and its physics generatively complexify Loy's Eros throughout her oeuvre.[62] Writing *Brontolivido* during World War I, Loy claims that, in compiling a taxonomy of her "esoteric seductions", Marinetti's "conversations fell like bombs among the solitude – induced static of her mind" (*B* 3: 9). Alone, inward, within, Loy-as-character embodies the etymological interiority of word "esoteric" as she attains the static she ascribes to mystical transcendence. Her mysteriousness prompts Marinetti's intimate dialogic battery, his onslaught from above that either facilitates Loy's Nirvana-like state or is an inveigling from which she defensively retreats. Either way, there are premonitions in this ambiguous, scrawled manuscript anecdote of Loy's later "flash of attainment to an infinite sentience"; within it lie the components of an explosively esoteric Eros underscored by Marinetti's witness of the first aerial bombing in history, as well as his abiding passions for epic warfare and the molecular materiality that warfare brings into fragmented focus (*SE* 250).[63]

During this same period, Loy associated with Christian Socialist activist George D. Herron (1862–1925), who advocated on behalf of universal embrace of a divine love, common to us all, by way of making our world "the kingdom of heaven" rather than "ground to powder"; for Herron, "[t]he wreck and welter" of the First World War, "the possible dissolution of our civilization, is nothing other than the world's collision with love" (*BM* 146–7; Herron 20–1).[64] As late as 1961, we witness Loy revisiting like coordinates in one of her last publications, "Time-Bomb", a poem that echoes "Apology of Genius" (1922) in celebrating avant-garde artistry as an esoteric pursuit capable of "translat[ing] eros into logos" (Han 52–3). In "Time-Bomb", the present moment continually detonates, rupturing past and future, as an outlaw populace stands guard over the resultant "unknown   dawn / strewn   with   prophecy". Where past esoteric Eros explodes leaving "a debris of sadism", this time-bomb generates "ruins" that are the substance of an ideal future (*SE* 251). Echoing the shunned genius mystics of "Apology", the "valorous   disreputables" who stand advance guard over this future are "sentinels" navigating a perpetually instantaneous explosivity that perpetually makes it new, makes it totalisingly unfamiliar. Like Loy's esoteric Eros, these "fugitive[s]" mediate metaphysical and physical, seeking transcendence over a haunting, all-too-mortal reality, or the staying "goggle   of   death" (*LoLB* 123). "History" foregrounds the esoteric Eros of sexualised love, "Time-Bomb" attends to aesthetic passion. Again and again, Loy shows us how the heterodoxies of the esoteric and the avant-garde work in tandem. Drawing on themes of combustibility and inclination, both of these texts delineate how momentous fissures or divides – between temporalities, self and other, renegade artists and society – potentially reveal and regenerate the cohering truths of the divine.

Potentially, but not always, as atomic, esoteric Eros is also a site of anguish and an anxiety that can return us to infantile "panics" (*SE* 287). In *Insel*, Mrs Jones witnesses "an inconceivable reversion of a standard transmutation" in the eponymous protagonist, who modifies his formerly sadistic propensities into "the indiscriminate love of a saviour" (126). Esoterically, transmutation is totalising alchemical change or rebirth to an alternate, usually higher, existential plane. Insel's ascent Jones labels anomalous perversion, an offering from an undiscerning adept. Thus framed, Insel's reversal cannot yield an ideal love, and in what follows, Mrs Jones finds herself "the agent of his—my—dematerialization", experiencing a cataclysmic dissolution in which "[t]he life force blast[ed] me apart instead of holding me together" (*I* 127). In "Songs to Joannes" the bond forged by "[m]e you – you – me" leads to "terrific Nirvana"; in *Insel*, an encroaching, proprietorial passion reduces the protagonist "he—she" to a distinctly "atomic despair", generating a consciousness "pulveriz[ed]" to particulate, "shattered . . . to splinters" (*LoLB* 58; *I* 127, 131). The decimation is total: recognising Insel in her features, finding her very physical being bisected by temporary paralysis, Jones feels she has been punished for "dabbling in the profane mysteries", and ends their relationship (*I* 131).

The apocalyptically premonitory events of "Tuning in on the Atom Bomb" similarly produce "a shattering terror of the limited incarcerated within the illimitable" within Loy's psyche, one likened to an "explosion blast" (*SE* 286). Writing "History", Loy becomes acutely aware of a "perilous secret" drawn from "ancient time" that she cannot access, yet experiences as a cerebral detonation; Loy thus becomes a medium for a mystical knowledge that behaves like contemporary nuclear fission, an experience she – expository esoteric – is keen to transmit (*SE* 286). In what follows, Loy details a vision that reworks Virgil's story of Aeneas, whose quest to find a new homeland after the Trojan War results in a journey to the underworld to visit his dead father, a passage enabled by the golden bough he locates and offers to Proserpina, winter queen to Pluto, king of the afterlife. Sitting in her New York garden, Loy sees a "branch, bronzed by some unnatural blast" that overwhelms her as she "faced a glaucous continuity of evacuated space, a universe constructed of intangibles ... reflecting nothing". The branch is "soulless", the disappointment "global" (*SE* 287). Where Aeneas's visit to Hades gains him access to the shade of his father and assurances that his offspring will found the Roman Empire, Loy's "Tuning in on the Atom Bomb" is imperialism in reverse, a world saturated and then obliterated, or book 6 of the *Aeneid* for the nuclear age. "[C]onfronted with the prestidigitation of an unreasonable universe", Loy encounters not sleight of hand, but the prospective atomic razing of earth (*SE* 287). Loy affirms as much in "History" where she chastises the occidental misuse of warring "BLIND FORCE" by which "man, mistaking destruction for dominion, furthers the ultimate menace to his perfectability" (*SE* 239). Occidentals deal in a force that bombards, unmooring intellection from clear intention (*SE* 238). In the process, atomic explosivity derails the most ideal human potentiality and experience, transcendent Eros.

An urgent, contemporary rereading of a classical text, "Tuning" illustrates how the gluttonous occidental misuse of force can devour its own, as Loy yields to an anxiety she casts as a "force in fear of itself" (*SE* 287). But this very explosivity – cultural, personal – affirms Loy's pursuit of esoteric over Judeo-Christian truths. Like any active Christian Scientist, Loy regularly read biblical passages alongside the writings of Mary Baker Eddy, and before her "unaccountable transformation" or vision she expresses an unfulfilled intention to read the Bible (*SE* 288). In its wake, she turns to the Bible for a comfort that only fosters rebellion. Loy locates St Paul's maxim to the Corinthians: "for the letter killeth, but the spirit giveth life", a phrase that pits humanity as the mortal, "fleshly" substance of God's word, or "the epistle of Christ . . . written with the spirit of the living God" (2 Cor. 3.6 and 3.3). By Paul's metaphor, humanity embodies God's logos. Loy interprets Paul's spirit as "all conscious Power", his letter as a "derivative unconscious force", phrases that recur near-verbatim in "History". But in "Tuning", Loy takes express issue with Paul's diminution of humanity, remarking: "at once it was as if the very roots of the supreme knowledge were being torn up" in a "ruthless tornado" by which God sees fit to "correc[t] his creature, purely for *being* as created." Having made humanity in his likeness, God unjustly holds mortal beings "endlessly responsible" for failing to reject, even supersede, the form he created (*SE* 289). Deific replications, humanity surely does not deserve "the celebration of doom" Loy now perceives in the exoteric New Testament (*SE* 288).

This crisis of faith cements Loy's "black-out vision—phantasmagoria of the exoteric religious debacle" (*SE* 288–9). Within it, she resists Christian rectitude and accepts – anxiously, neurotically – that mystical understanding "shattered scripture" (*SE* 289). Neither comfortable nor hopeful, the experience catalyses Loy's reminiscence of a childhood defined by "ill-mated parents" and "the consequent catastrophes of maturity" (*SE* 287). Loy's vision, in short, effects a rebirth, a palingenesis whereby memories "rearose" from the "dreamy hollows" of her mind (*SE* 287). "Rearose" situates this experience in an insistent past tense. Arising again, these repetitions and returns are the substance of Loy's late autobiographical writings exploring filial and artistic inclinations, complements to the esoteric Eros of "Tuning" and "History" (*SE* 287). As early as 1918, Loy articulates how human life is too often a "wear[ing] out" of "imperfectly functioning" organisms whose "social condition [is] safeguarded and preserved by the blowing up of other millions of human organisms", a scenario she likens to "the nightmare of a criminal lunatic" (*LaLB* 279). Suspect technological advance propels Loy away from the exoteric toward the esoteric, toward palingenesis, cultural rebirth, or the *risorgimento* by which she envisions overcoming the past – hers, the world's – through the heterodox, transcendent love articulated in the companion text of "Tuning in on the Atom Bomb": "The History of Religion and Eros".

In Loy's family of origin, fear and destruction too regularly supplanted affection and intimacy. From her wracked beginnings, Loy becomes a poet who fearlessly examines pains emotional and physical, from the suffering that exceeds bodily confines in birth, unifying opposed sensations in "lascivious revelation", to the "agony" of old age and mourning that "ends in an equal grave / with ecstasy" (*LoLB* 6, 130). Where Loy's Eros soars its way towards the orgasmic, her Thanatos crawls on bloodied knees toward the same. Like love, pain is gnostic, exceeding communication, yet it is also a grounding unifier of soma and spirit. These shared coordinates are inextricable: thus, in *The Child and the Parent* (c. 1932–6), as in "History of Religion and Eros", Loy chastises ascetic and ecclesiast alike for prioritising pain and misrepresenting Eros as all-too-pervasive self-indulgence, given that even sexual pleasure brings untold suffering, be it through childbirth, abortion, or sexually transmitted disease (*CP* 16: 52). We have much to learn about our bodies, insists Loy, calling, as does Myers before her, for "[a] transcendental observer who could look into this unexplored territory" (*CP* 15: 54). "It is, of course, a mystery how a single cell can hold together", writes Myers, noting that the mystery intensifies when "cells cohere in a conjoint and independent life". To better understand the smallest units of the physical body, Myers argues that we ought to spend more time examining "that unseen or spiritual plane" wherein lies "the origin of life" (21).

In a passage from *The Child and the Parent,* Loy takes on the role of Myers's transcendent observer. In it, Loy argues that although we perceive ourselves as "islands in the air", we are in fact comprised of "the rush of infinitesimal races" running along "the fronds of our forestal nerves", and asks us to envision how "our being is sustained through the shaping of the indiscernible destinies of invisible collaborators". Holding this vision aloft, Loy pays especial homage to "the boom of the sensitive dynamo, the heart, to which the currents of our life are confluent, receiving and expelling their pouring velocities". Sensitised, dynamic, Loy's heartbeat in this specific, unusual instance is explosively present. For Loy, our innards become evident in two ways: firstly, when we become "a butchered horror" as a consequence of harm, or, secondly, "in such rare moments of inverted consciousness as occur when we are coming out of a swoon". In these rare moments, and these moments alone, Loy attests, "can we listen to the existence of our own heart" (*CP* 15: 54). Forever mocking sentimental platitudes – hearts contented with material well-being, pure women with hands on hearts – Loy remains alert to cardiac organs extreme, exposed, and essential, extending its circulatory powers to the riven sentient body (*SE* 163, 220). As she writes in notes for "Mi & Lo": "Suffering is but peevishness in all but the great of heart" ("Mi and Lo"). Loy's esoteric Eros aims to overcome divides, a truth literalised in her late story "Agony of the Partition", where the narrator, resident of an urban boarding house, leans upon the thin wall separating herself from another tenant: "[f]limsy to vibrancy", this wall exudes the corporeal rhythms of that individual, rhythms that ultimately overtake the speaker's breath and circulation. "I was made heavy with responsibility", Loy's narrator imparts, "and soon, under those feeble winds I could feel a stranger's heart beat on my compassion" (*SE* 6). This synaesthesia is as much anxious torture as reassuring connection. Through it, the beating heart becomes a signifier of the unknown and unknowable, the immediacy of the material organ gone spiritual, gnostic, "suprapersonal" (Simmel, "Eros" 241).

Swooning, sexing, obliterated by lust or pain, Loy's is an extreme and porous body, vulnerable to combat, open to ecstasy, in constant pursuit of transcendence. As such, it is unsurprising that Loy developed a feminist satiric practice whereby attack on what repulses or discourages is not, as per tradition, in aid of concretising distance between author and enemy, but proximity. Loy's esoteric Eros, in other words, aspires toward an unattainable plane of intimate reprieve, consolation, and bliss that is earnest, constitutive counterbalance to her lifelong sardonic drive. This duality fuels the explosive capacity of Loy's Eros and its determination to draw an ecstatic victory from a then-novel and still-nauseating capacity for unprecedented destruction, a love realised by exceeding the bounds and breakage of the individual atom, a love that replicates its aggregative inclination. Loy transmutes the function of the atom bomb just as she aims to cohere the decimated parts of her self and her past. In the process, she envisions a world where Eros might be as explosively influential as global war. Hers is a sex-positive, intimate utopia where the amatory passion overcomes what she delineates in "Human Cylinders" (1917) as "the lucid rush-together of automatons" hopelessly hoping to "form one opulent well-being" (*LoLB* 40).

In *Civilisation and its Discontents* (1930), Freud's consideration of humanity's driving anxiety about the prospect of losing love is rooted in his growing concern about the extremisms of European fascism and Russian communism (113, 143). Like Freud, Loy observes a symbiosis in anxieties about Eros and global aggression. Unlike Stein, Loy turns to esotericism as a means of redirecting and mitigating mounting apocalyptic tendencies. In her "Reflection on the Atom Bomb" (1946), Stein demands not withheld information, but transparency, not "secret weapon[s]" and "death rays", but attuned, lively mortality (161). By contrast, Loy leverages the atomic open secret into an intimacy that generatively compels, withholds, and detonates. Stein's promotion of the transparent and self-evident is commensurate with the sham anti-exegetical premise of her writing, the stylistic truth – one often proclaimed by Stein herself – that her diction is generally simplistic and repetitive, even as her baffling syntax demands the closest and most forceful interpretive methodologies. But Loy too takes part in a feint and jab: overtly challenging the rationality of occidental thinking, she repurposes scientific "[r]adiation ... 'fourth dimension,' and relativity" to foreground "the epistemic room [they create] for soul, or spirit, or even an astral realm". In the process, Loy exhibits "a scepticism about scientific materialism" that foments alternate epistemologies and esotericisms (Surette 286). From her first writings, Loy hones these skills, redirecting the presumed passivities and supinities of occult practice toward a feminist visionariness and transcendent dorsality. It is to these early writings that the next chapter will turn.

Notes

1. The source for "look into thy heart, and write" is Philip Sidney's *Astrophil and Stella*, a text composed in the 1580s (Hodgson 114).
2. The image in question is a portrait by D. Simonet completed in 1890; it remains untitled in Birke.
3. As caricatures of sentimental romance, the flannel hearts of "Sacred Prostitute" may find their origin in Loy's post-1910 Florence drawings *Heart Shop* – an image of love for sale – and *Ces Coeurs*, which evidently depicted "young ladies . . . emptying captured hearts from a wheelbarrow" (*BM* 129, 138). Now lost, these images were produced alongside drawings entitled *Ladies at Tea* and *Ladies Fishing* (*BM* 129). As the rigid formalities of Victorian teatime and its attendant ladies are often subjects of Loy's satire, it is plausible that Loy's quaint subject matter evinced barbed intent.
4. The death drive that complements Freudian Eros does not bear its Greek name, Thanatos, in Freud's work, but the term is widely used by critics discussing these ideas in his writings.
5. As a ready example of this interpretive line, we might turn to the table of contents of *The Lost Lunar Baedeker*, where Roger Conover begins with a section entitled "Satires: 1914–1923", thereby separating this genre and mode from, for instance, Loy's "Later Poems: 1930–1950" and from Loy's epic satire "Anglo-Mongrels and the Rose: 1923–1925". Conover's thematic chronology has proven pervasive. Sandeep Parmar's *Reading Mina Loy's Autobiographies: The Myth of the Modern Woman* (2013) argues that Loy's romans à clef exhibit the importance of Victorian origins and influence in an oeuvre too reductively considered consistently vanguard. Setting aside the occult and psychoanalytic leanings of Loy's earliest writings, Christina Walter also maintains that "the lodestar of the mature work" is Loy's "conclusion that opaque psychophysiological forces bear on subjectivity" that she aims to bring "as far as may be, into the reader's line of sight" (147).
6. Dodge's mystical leanings ran the gamut from the hire of a Vedanta swami, whose teaching sessions Loy briefly attended, to her late-life appropriations of indigenous culture and spiritualism on her estate in Taos, New Mexico (*BM* 132–3; 296). When Loy lived in Florence, Dodge dabbled in Theosophy and Christian Science; the latter she soon abandoned because she felt it prompted no personal change (*BM* 121).

She replaced Christian Science with cultivated upsurges of strong, serene feeling that she labelled Nature (Dodge Luhan 311, 319).

7. The punctuation in this quotation is uncertain: it could read "among the solitude-induced static of her mind" (*B* 3: 9). The variation is minor but significant: in the instance I quote in the main body of the text, the Martinet induces the static; in the above instance, solitude is its cause. The solitude, however, remains constant.
8. Why does Loy's mind turn to the date of the Norman conquest of England? An answer lies in *Goy Israels*, where Loy describes herself as a child hungry for knowledge who is constrained by her mother's imperialistic mien and agenda, which infects the familial environs in which Loy grows up, but also means that, when she learns history, she "never gets farther than William the Conqueror 1066" (*GI* 28: 61). "[F]arther" is typed "father" and the central "r" is added by hand above. The Freudian implications of this typo are self-evident, given that Loy repeatedly defines her migrant, Jewish father by his passive acquiescence to his wife's Englishness.

    The reference to William the Conqueror in *Brontolivido* lends authority to Loy's repeat claims in her künstlerromans that her Victorian mother's voice permeated her consciousness throughout her life, as it is to that voice that her mind turns in this anxious exchange, in adulthood, with a future lover.
9. Loy's argument in "The Metaphysical Pattern in Aesthetics" is reinforced by Leon Surette's thesis that, in *The Cantos* (1915–62), Loy's associate and modernist peer Ezra Pound created an "esoteric compendium of 'modern thought'" or the laying bare of an obdurately unprocessed, if aspirationally elite form of knowledge culminating in a creative vision (Surette 36). Surette's theory will be further acknowledged later in this chapter.
10. For more on this association, see Michael R. Kelly's *Bergson and Phenomenology* (2010).
11. With *Historia Critica Philosophiae* (1743), the German historian Johann Jakob Brucker was the first to undertake a systematic history of esoteric bodies of knowledge. But it was not until the mid-twentieth century that the history and study of esotericism became an academically recognised discipline. Influenced by Denis Saurat, Frances Yates's seminal *Giordano Bruno and the Hermetic Tradition* (1964), which argues that modern science emerged from esoteric practice, is considered pivotal to this transition (Stuckrad 80). Yates worked at the Warburg Institute, which is devoted to the esoteric; founded in 1944, it remains associated with the University of London. Further formal recognition is evinced by the creation of a chair in the history of esotericism in the religious studies department of the Sorbonne in 1965 (Faivre and Voss 59).
12. This quotation emerges in a letter where Loy encourages her daughter Joella to use Science as her prime medical support when giving birth

to her first child, as doing so will ensure a painless labour. Where Joella prosaically argues that "all treasures spring of themselves from love and pain", Loy vociferously counters: "NO from love and pleasure". Chiding Joella for turning to Western medicine during her pregnancy, Loy celebrates her sister Fabienne as a better demonstrator of Christian Science principles because "she can overcome severe pain – instantaneously" (Letter dated 7 January 1928, Loy to Julien and Joella Levy, Box 30, Folder 8, 1928).

In indecipherably dated or undated letters in the same archived folder, Loy again holds up Fabienne as an exemplary Christian Scientist because she is getting braver about going to the dentist, whilst another letter insists that Science can hold all pain at bay, "even toothache". These are just some of the countless examples in Loy correspondence affirming her belief that Science provides the skills and stoicism to transcend fear and physical suffering.

13. References to Christian Science proliferate throughout a great deal of Loy's correspondence with Joella and Julien Levy, but are particularly abundant through 1927–32, when Loy is living in Paris, the newly married Levys are establishing their livelihoods and starting a family in New York, and Fabienne is transitioning from childhood to adolescence (see Loy to Julien and Joella Levy, Box 30, Folders 7–12 (1927–32). On 28 April 1935, Fabienne reports to her sister and brother-in-law that Loy has begun attending a new Christian Science church in Paris (Fabienne Lloyd to Julien and Joella Levy, Box 30, Folder 6, 1929–74).

14. According to Burke, Loy asked daughter Joella to "treat" her lamp shop by way of dealing with her anxieties about her indebtedness to Peggy Guggenheim (*BM* 359). In the late 1920s, Loy would again ask Joella and her husband Julien, also a Christian Science convert, to "treat" her situation as she struggled to manage her shop and debts (*BM* 369).

15. The equation of Science with insurance arises in an undated letter from Loy to Julien and Joella Levy, Box 30, Folder 10, 1930. Loy asserts the "eating your cake" cliché in undated letters in two folders of correspondence to Julien and Joella Levy (Box 30, Folder 10, 1930; Box 30, Folder 8, 1928).

16. As Tim Armstrong observes, this rejection of the body in Christian Science in fact extends to all material forms, which "Spirit" is meant to transcend (209). Offering an extended account of the international popularity of Christian Science, particularly after the First World War, David Ayers similarly notes that "Eddy's emphasis on the subordination of matter to mind, and, consequently, on the unreality of matter, seems as if it ought to have major implications for Mina Loy's beliefs and aesthetics" (223). Acknowledging that many esoteric systems were available to adult Loy, Ayers suggests "we should conclude that Christian Science theology, and not merely its healing practice, was

accepted by Loy" but also collates reservations about the same that emerge in Loy's *Insel* (224). As discussed in the Preface to this volume, Armstrong resonantly argues that the Christian Science doctrine was a mixed and malleable one, in that it rejected the body, yet used it as its primary gauge of spiritual well-being, meaning its ethereally, transcendent soul continually and necessarily returned to the material self in a way that corroborates Loy's own somatic emphasis ("Loy" 210).

17. In a letter dated 9 December 1934, Fabienne rapturously describes visiting friends in Paris with Loy and practising spiritualist table-turning and rapping until two in the morning (Fabienne Lloyd to Julien and Joella Levy, Box 30, Folder 6, 1929–74). On 4 February 1936, Loy speaks of reading her horoscope and having it correspond with the outcome of a session of numerology (Loy to Julien and Joella Levy, Box 31, Folder 5, undated). Elsewhere, Loy writes about seeing a "fashionable numerologist" on a visit to London (Undated letter, Loy to Julien and Joella Levy, Box 30, Folder 13, 1933).

    Loy's "vision of an entirely different kind of literature . . . most *clairvoyante*" arises in an undated letter in a folder that frequently refers, as she does in relation to this quotation, to wanting to write a fictionalised biography of Richard Oelze, the protagonist of *Insel* (Loy to Juliena and Joella Levy, Box 31, Folder 5, undated). Loy writes about consulting an encyclopaedia of ancient philosophy in 1930, noting that the truths contained by the "sage[s]" therein are not unlike those she seeks out in her own time (Undated letter, Loy to Julien and Joella Levy, Box 30, Folder 8, 1928).

18. "You must always be absolutely truthful for the magic to work", writes Loy to Julien Levy in relation to directing his Science practice at his clients; similarly, Julien commends his wife Joella for sending a letter "full of good magic and Science" (Letter dated 23 December 1927, Loy to Julien and Joella Levy, Box 30, Folder 13, 1933; Letter dated 13 June, Julien Levy to Joella Levy, Box 29, Folder 7, 1928).

    In Loy's family, Science "magic" extends to hexing or cursing, as when Loy's daughter Fabienne states in 1954 that she doesn't want "to put a thought on" Loy when she realises that her mother is so ill she will need to go not to a Science practitioner but to a much-dreaded hospital (Fabienne Lloyd to Julien and Joella Levy, Box 30, Folder 6, 1929–74). As Loy writes in a letter possibly dated 19 January 1933, no one should "ever deny or lose the principle of C.S." without anticipating certain disaster to ensue (Loy to Julien and Joella Levy, Box 30, Folder 10, 1930).

19. According to Harold Bloom, Baker Eddy's resistance to mesmerism manifested itself as a concern that some of her current adherents or past disciples were deploying "Malicious Animal Magnetism" or directed ill will against her; as Bloom attests, the ferocity of her disavowal of this occult practice speaks to its proximity to her own creed and process (136, 144).

20. See Storm 166, 173; Versluis 138; and Owen, *Place* 218.
21. Burke's relaying of the Crowley anecdote is considerably more discreet than her source text, Loy's *Esau Penfold*. Burke reduces Crowley's plan to a bit of "gossi[p] about his desire to know Mina" (*BM* 78, 83). She also sets aside Loy's struggle to reassure Haweis that she has never met Crowley, about whom she knows only that he wears a bejewelled turban (*EP* 24). While Haweis uses Crowley's claim to implicitly question Loy's fidelity, he is himself in an extra-marital relationship at this time, and it is he, not Loy, who actively courts Crowley, details not presented in Burke.

    Haweis's archived memoir indicates that he planned, in 1903 or 1904, a Parisian exhibition of his photographs of Rodin's sculptures alongside Crowley's sonnets on the same (*BM* 92). If Crowley's "autohagiography" is to be believed, this plan did not come to fruition. Crowley describes Haweis as, firstly, a visitant of Mathers, who became Crowley's enemy after the latter was ejected from the Golden Dawn; secondly, son to the famous H. R. Haweis, author of *Music and Morals* (1871); and, thirdly, an artist who "achieved a certain delicate eminence" (335). Haweis evidently undertook a portrait of Crowley intended to grace the latter's *Collected Works* (341). The two were in close enough contact that Crowley could mock the hypocrisy of Haweis's mistress, who expressed horror at a "premature" kiss in Crowley's *Alice: An Adultery* (1905) manuscript – as the title suggests, a collection about an affair – even as she was intimate with the married Haweis (50–1).
22. See Thurschwell 19; Owen, *Darkened* 121; and Winter 131, 147.
23. Melzer's argument and tactics are lifted near directly from Strauss; for the latter, see Strauss, "Persecution", pages 496–9 in particular. For Melzer, the would-be esoteric reader will take pleasure in the laborious task of acclimatising themselves to complex thinking in a bid to work toward an unacknowledged truth (223).

    Melzer's directives to that reader are inseparable from the task of literary close reading, and include exceptionally slow, careful, and intimate connection with texts; avid sleuthing for keys and clues; setting aside ready presumptions about suspect characters or speakers – villains or buffoons for instance – who may represent authorial truths; and the pursuit of conspicuous omissions and anomalous textual structures (290–322).
24. While critics often cite Loy's claim that "[t]he aim of the artist is to miss the Absolute", less quoted is the latter half of this statement, which reads: "whereas the mystic impulse is to embrace a 'ready-made' in the way of absolutes" (*SE* 228). Potentially pejorative about the mystical, Loy arguably ascribes a canniness to this esoteric line of inquiry whilst elevating it to a lauded modernist art form, however performative or conveniently deployed. Within art, Loy also celebrates its capacity to convey "the unpresentable in presentation that causes it to exceed

replica" or strict mimesis (*SE* 261). Like esotericism, art brings us closer to the impossible, the unreachable.

25. This elision is discussed in greater detail at the outset of Chapter 3 of *Nethered Regions*.

26. I refer here to the central argument of Peter Bürger's influential *Theory of the Avant-Garde* (1974), namely, that the avant-garde strives to obliterate the divide between art and praxis. While Bürger's argument pertains more legibly to Dada than the Futurism that goes undiscussed in his text, his work endorses vanguard political radicalism. By stark contrast, Arthur Melzer recognises that esoteric methodology can be offensive to a democratic and relativist world view, but nevertheless celebrates the "frankly elitist" rhetorical style and inner circles it necessitates (220). Directing our attention to the privileges inherent in complexity, protracted intellection, and select fraternities or coteries, Melzer insists that the philosopher separate himself from society and conceal ideas that may be interpreted as objectionable (91).

27. Concerns regarding Faivre's model include the limitations of its historical parameters: it is seen as too rooted in the European Renaissance, and too tied to heterodoxies diametric to Christianity, when many forms of esotericism emerged in conversation with Judaic or Muslim traditions (Asprem 26; Stuckrad 83). Furthermore, esoteric scholars take issue with Faivre's labelling of esotericism as "a specific form of thought"; Hanegraaff, for instance, argues that esotericism would be better categorised as an "idea complex" or "a cluster of related ideas recognizable over time by virtue of family resemblance" (117).

28. Returning to her own formulation of infant transmutation in *Islands in the Air*, Loy declares: "This is no mysticism", instead contending that she offers a distinct, accurate recollection of "a precocious flash." But as part of this esoteric suppression, she tellingly labels the same experience a "preliminary illumination" that gives pause regarding the continuity between "transient body" and "'spiritual' continuum'", a question she provocatively leaves open (*IA* 58: 7).

29. Soul is the seat of happiness, body the site of suffering, Loy attests. But this relationship is interdependent: soul is audience to the body's suffering, and the pleasure of the soul filters through the body. Soul does not *need* illumination because it *is* illumination, and its conceptions can appear more intense – erroneously so – than bodily experience. To read about starvation, Loy argues, is to feel angst at the injustice of that experience, but nevertheless to recognise "the simple poignancy of conception of starving". To starve, on the other hand, is not to transcend the self, but to be mired in the phenomenal: constant thoughts of death, past meals, fixations on shops full of food, and the overwhelming feeling of being "an awful fool" (*SE* 275).

30. Another example of an individualist esotericist is the eighteenth-century Freemason Johann George Schrepfer, who created his own set

of "para-Masonic rituals" that brought him into conflict with his fraternal organisation and society more generally (Hammer and Stuckrad xiv–xv).
31. See Surette 50; Melzer 364; and Hanegraaff 117.
32. Freud and Rado reference Horney's essay "On the Genesis of the Castration Complex in Women", first delivered as a lecture at the Seventh International Psycho-Analytical Congress in Berlin in September 1922. Freud does so in "Some Psychical Consequences of the Anatomical Distinction between the Sexes" (1925), where he describes Horney's essay as "valuable and comprehensive" yet persists in presenting the biologically sexed female as emotionally damaged and inferior due to her phallic lack (258). Similarly, Rado's "Fear of Castration in Women" (1933) insists on the extraordinary pleasure of the phallus that goes, in Rado's opinion, under-recognised by Horney. In turn, Rado believes penile superiority reinforces female "anatomic depression" that can result in flight from men (read: lesbianism), frigidity, aggression, or masochism ("Fear" 87, 93). In addition, Roberto Assagioli, whose close links to Loy I will soon discuss, refers repeatedly to Horney in *Psychosynthesis*, using her work to justify ways of learning and dissenting from Freud's model, but also as a set of ideas with which his writings are in generative conversation and disagreement (13, 26, 52, 167).
33. In his article "The Ecstasy of Mina Loy", Alan Marshall briefly relates this specific Horney argument to Loy's ecstatic presentation of birth in "Parturition" (1914).
34. See for instance, from *Stories and Essays of Mina Loy*: "My Catholick Confidante", "Havelock Ellis", and "Lady Asterisk."; Loy's ballet "Crystal Pantomime" also fits this mould. Examples of this contextualising recur in Loy's künstlerromans; see *Goy Israels* (27: 33–5) and the conclusion of *The Child and the Parent*, where chapters 7 to 11 are devoted almost exclusively to a disquisition on constraints imposed upon women, particularly their sexual ignorance and subsequent frustration. The titles alone indicate the direction Loy takes: "Ladies in an Aviary", "The Hewn Tree" (a critique of the Tree of Knowledge in the Old Testament Garden of Eden), "The Dissatisfied Bride", "A Certain Percentage of Women – –", and "The Outraged Womb" (*CP* 15–19).
35. Freudian guilt is in low supply in Loy's autobiographical writings, where she remains suspiciously if consistently innocent of all charges held against her from the inception of her childhood consciousness to her own turn at parenting. Loy's resistance to examining her conscience may contribute to the truth that even the inherent inwardness of her esoteric proclivities is, through Eros, turned outward, toward otherness and an infinite cosmos.
36. In correspondence, Loy observes that "[s]ome of the younger insurgents raided my nice good Assagioli – the other night – and recited excerpts

from his writings" (Letter dated February 1914, "Loy, Mina, 1913–1920, n.d.", Mabel Dodge Luhan Papers). The insurgents are likely Futurists who appear to have used Assagioli's work as the basis of a spontaneous performance piece. This 1914 quotation confirms Loy's familiarity with Assagioli's written treatises; in a letter from the same archive file dated 28 March 1913, Loy also mentions socialising with him.

37. After drafting this chapter, I discovered Tamara Beauchamp's impressive dissertation, *Enemies of the Unconscious: Modernist Resistances to Psychoanalysis* (2014). In Beauchamp's chapter on Loy, she too follows Burke's cue regarding Loy's association with Assagioli, drawing out excellent arguments about how the psychosynthetic method is discernible in Loy's 1918 "International Psycho-Democracy" manifesto (262). Arguing as I have here that Loy turns to second-generation psychoanalytic theorists by way of resisting some Freudian precepts, Beauchamp points out, for instance, how Loy's manifesto exhibits an anti-war stance consistent with Assagioli's own, whilst emphasising the need to move toward the highest, most replete version of the self (260, 263). As both volumes of this *Anatomy* illustrate, this self-cultivation of the artistic, genius subject recurs throughout Loy's writing, and is consistent with Assagioli, Bergson, and Myers. See also Chapter 1 of *Nethered Regions* on Loy and evolution.

38. While Bataille's interest in mysticism is widely recognised, at the outset of *Inner Experience* (1943) he tells us that we will find "states of ecstasy, of rapture, at last of mediated emotion" in his rendering of consciousness that we will be inclined to equate with the esoteric. Working against this association, he argues that he pursues "experience laid bare, free of ties, even of an origin" (*IE* 3). Writing in the same period, Loy similarly shuns the label "mystic" in relation to her own esoteric writings, claiming, like Bataille, that she exposes not divine but experiential truths.

    Bataille's contemporaries and critics appear unconvinced by his distinctions. Sartre labelled Bataille a "new mystic" (Biles 64). Susan Rubin Suleiman argues that, in Bataille, "the self-preserving husbandry of everyday life becomes subordinated to the excessive, quasi-mystical state we associate with religious ecstasy and generally with the realm of the sacred" (75). Alexander C. Irwin believes Bataille evinces a raw, convulsive, and immediate mysticism (108). A last example: among the types of "disruptive nonknowledge" that Bataille advocates, Elisabeth Arnould lists "mystic, erotic, poetic" (86).

39. Loy equates the status quo with an unfulfilling, outdated "Moral Order" in many works (*SE* 57). In "Piero and Eliza.", the female protagonist originates from a "middle-class morality" that sees her pursue an unsatisfying relationship with a closeted husband (*SE* 99). "In Maine: Green's Colony" is Loy's fictionalised anthropological study of an upwardly mobile American community infected by a

wayward, perverse puritanism. Finally, "Lady Asterisk." mournfully spoofs the constrictions on women's sexuality that pervade even the self-aggrandisingly liberated upper classes.

Loy's daughter Joella articulated some of the contradictions in her upbringing that expose the depths of Loy's own allegiance to "the thin-lipped spectre of dishonour" (*SE* 142). Of her own writing, Loy would only allow Joella to read "Anglo-Mongrels and the Rose", pronouncing the rest unsuitable for "*'jeunes filles'*". And while Loy was evidently open in private conversations with her daughters, she strictly forbade them from indicating that they knew anything about sex in public or social settings. Loy also insisted that Joella be a virgin at marriage, and effectively chose a husband for her based on his good social and financial standing (Bayer, "Interview, Burke and Bayer").

40. Loy refers obliquely to this same theory in the eighth chapter of *The Child and the Parent*. Describing the human body as a site of "vital instability" that wavers continually between pleasure and pain, she argues that only pain elicits sympathy in our fellow humans, and that society has become "almost prohibitive to pleasure". As modernity developed into this "raptureless regime", Loy writes, the Christian faith "appointed us to doff the flesh and invest ourselves of the spirit." Meanwhile, "The ecclesiast ostracised the flesh, the laity were persuaded they indulged the flesh, while Eros distributed his misleading literature" (*CP* 16: 52). The "misleading literature" in question is the doctrine of the ancient Eastern seers referenced in "History" that Loy's esoteric Eros strives to correct. Further ruminations on the exoteric mishandling of sex, and containment of "sin" via marriage, recur in Loy's "Notes on Metaphysics".
41. Consistent with her rejection of asceticism in "Mi & Lo", a footnote to "History of Religion and Eros" disparages "[t]he esoteric 'career' of chastity" as "aimless". The exception proving this rule is Catholicism's celibate "'Vocation'" (*SE* 248). Loy's tone and punctuation convey the same suspicion toward the priesthood as a nineteenth-century anthropologist might direct toward the survival of pagan rituals (Storm 99). This claim is confirmed by Loy's earlier resistance to chastity in "The Black Virginity" (1918). In this poem, priests are infantilised yet intimidate, and the speaker feels innately, immediately sexually shamed in their proudly chaste company even as she aligns said priests with old predatory men (*LoLB* 42–3).
42. "[A]s sub-realism", Loy maintains that Surrealism needs an artist as revolutionary as Joseph Cornell to draw upon, and then surpass, its themes and approaches (*LaLB* 301). Loy reiterates this need for Surrealism to transcend itself in *Insel*, where she defines her eponymous protagonist as "'too surrealistic for the surrealists'" (*I* 104). As an art agent, Loy had repeated contact with Breton, whose work she solicited for Levy's gallery. Breton no doubt cultivated and valued,

his relationship with Loy, not least because of his desire to publish Cravan's manuscripts, for which he needed Loy's permission. As Sarah Hayden articulates, the Surrealists claimed Cravan as their forefather, a cultural link Loy resisted (130).

43. According to Alyce Mahon, this theoretical strain was evident from the 1938 Surrealist exhibition to the 1959 *Exposition InteRnatiOnale du Surrealisme* (both in Paris) and beyond, motivating Herbert Marcuse's influential, countercultural *Eros and Civilisation* (1955), as well as Bataille's *The Tears of Eros* (1961).

    The Surrealist influence on Marcuse is discernible in his presentation of psychotherapy as "a course in resignation" to the "precarious condition" that is "[n]ormality". Or, as Marcuse summarises: "psychoanalytic therapy aims at curing the individual so that he can continue to function as part of a sick civilisation without surrendering to it altogether" (195).

    The Tears of Eros is an art-historical text framed by the theoretical terms of Bataille's lengthier, denser *Erotism* (1957), which certainly reflects Surrealist fascinations with Freud's sex and death drives, with the (often degraded) feminine as a site of desire, and in its heteronormativity and homophobia.

44. I refer here to Paul Eluard's "The Queen of Diamonds" (1926), a tale of the appeal of predating upon numerous virgins with the refrain or justification "Loving love" (171–2). "Hands Off Love" (1927) is a much-anthologised Surrealist tract that defends Chaplin's right to disown his children and have affairs because his 16-year-old wife "tricked" him into marrying her; at its end, Chaplin is valorised for heeding always the call to love, the "proof" of which is a willingness to pursue strange women in cities (author unidentified 153). In this spirit, we might also consider this sentence from Breton's *Mad Love*: "This young woman who had just entered was about to reappear in the street, where I was waiting for her without being seen"; Breton takes pleasure and feels hope as he instigates fear in the woman who "flee[s] before [him], ceaselessly intercepted by the darkness of moving hedges" (43). A last example: Salvador Dali's "The Surrealist Conception of 'Sexual Freedom'" (1930) details how a man is expelled from a train due to exposing himself to a woman. Dali considers the man's act among "the purest and most disinterested" whilst envisioning, with evident relish, how "the girl" was "plunged . . . into a tremendous and delicious confusion" (qtd. in Nadeau 305).

    According to Mahon, in preparing for their 1938 exhibition, the Surrealists refused the mannequins delivered to them, choosing a different model which they felt better embodied the "'Eternal Feminine'", namely, a model of beauty ironically commensurate with a twentieth-century feminine ideal: "svelte bodies, fashionable hairstyles, long eyelashes and slim breasts" (44). As Mahon writes, "the Surrealists primarily explored Eros in terms of the female body and uncanny spatial play which exploited the association between the mother/womb and a fear of castration/death" (18). Mahon is singularly celebratory of this equation of marginalisation and the irrational. Of the 180 images her book contains of Surrealist renditions of "love", none include naked white men.

45. This roundtable was one of twelve held between 1927 to 1932. In another, Breton enthuses over love as "the one thing alone in life which is not denied and forbidden to us" (Pierre 77). Shortly thereafter, the limitations of this "us" become painfully self-evident: without irony, Breton dismisses outright as a potential recipient of his love any woman who "embod[ies] all the mental qualities" he values, genius included, should she possess a "single [displeasing] physical detail" (Pierre 81).

46. In this critical spirit, Hayden argues convincingly that Insel's madness critiques the Surrealist exploitation of (an always feminised) lunacy; that Insel embodies Surrealist "goals, aspirations, and personalities" taken to an ambivalent extreme; that Jones's understated laughter at Insel's worst misogynies should be read as a satiric, rueful critique of Surrealist presentations of femininity; that Insel-as-Surrealism is ironically and tellingly weakened by his sexual interactions; and, lastly, that Loy's novel entire illustrates the failure of the Surrealist revolutionising ethos (134, 139, 148, 156, 158).

47. As I discuss in the Preface to *Nethered Regions*, Loy changes this title in the second and final book she publishes in her lifetime, *Lunar Baedeker and Time-Tables* (1958).

48. Drawing heavily on the historical work of Deirdre Green, Voss contemplates the reverberations between Renaissance mystical consciousness and feminist consciousness-raising, as well as the esoteric primacy of individualism that is echoed by, for instance, "the personal is political" maxim of second-wave feminism (8–9).

49. Christian Science practitioners continue to proudly assert their sect's female founder, refusal of a male-only god, and ongoing challenge to the paternalism that continues to define many exoteric religions, noting, for instance, that a "pure, spiritual ideal" is one that male and female Christian Scientists alike are taught to emulate (Moore; see also Snow).

50. In *Science and Health*, Baker Eddy asserts: "Gender is mental, not material" (508). Whilst noting that this statement opens up the possibility that gender can be discarded, Simon is careful to consider that it might also reinforce extant binaries by suggesting that gender, as currently understood and practised, belongs to the spiritual realm, and thus should be respected rather than disrupted (Simon 393).

51. As one example of this spiritual and cultural conflict, Loy writes that her "Jewish blood always keeps me longing for relations – the trouble

is I don't belong to my relations" (Undated letter, Loy to Julien and Joella Levy, Box 30, Folder 11, 1931). At issue is a paternalistic family structure, one conceivably associable with a patriarchal deity.

52. Steinke offers a detailed reading of how Loy grapples with the inherent contradictions of Victorian evangelism, pointing out, for instance, that the narration of "Anglo-Mongrels and the Rose" exposes how "anthropomorphizing God whilst simultaneously turning away from the realities of the human body creates a paradox difficult to reconcile" (500). As a consequence, Loy's protagonist, the girl-child Ova, searches for "more substance in divine representations", a substance the writer Loy often sources in the religious imagery Steinke explores in her writing (500, 506).

53. H. D., or Hilda Doolittle, was a close friend of Loy's associate Marianne Moore, and correspondence exists indicating that H. D. asked Moore to convey her impressions of Loy (*BM* 292). H. D. was also in a long relationship with Bryher, who married Robert McAlmon, whose connections with Loy are extensive. McAlmon published Loy's *Lunar Baedecker* in 1923 and fictionalised her in *Post-Adolescence* (1923). In turn, Loy celebrates his humour and writing in "All the laughs in one short story by McAlmon" (*SE* 219–20). In 1925, McAlmon's *Contact Collection* included both Loy and H. D., and in that same year, Loy praises H. D.'s abilities in her essay "Modern Poetry". Vetter writes cogently on the relationship between Loy's and H. D.'s respective religio-scientific discourses, noting, for instance, their shared emphases on electric currents and electromagnetism (*Religio-Scientific* 60–1).

54. Marcuse persistently presents love in negative terms. Sex he perceives as subsumed to love, with its "enduring and responsible relations" and "the historical result of a long and cruel process of domestication" (163). This process has resulted in the "monogamic family" that Marcuse defames with real passion, noting it puts obligations on men in that it "restrict[s their] monopoly of pleasure" (72). For Marcuse, love has been used to dignify a sexuality that ultimately needed no such defence (163).

As Linda Martín Alcoff avers, Marcuse's theory of Eros is a "utopia . . . open to the critique that although he holds out the possibility of positive forms of intersubjective relations, his portrayal of these relations mirrored the 'free love' ideology of the 1960s, which were hardly based on mutual recognition and accountability to others and in fact generally resulted in the denial of full sexual subjectivity to women" (65). Given that *Eros and Civilisation* was published in 1955, Alcoff's "mirrored" should be a more pioneering term: foregrounded, perhaps, or established.

55. That Loy was aware of this biblical symbolism is apparent from an incident Burke recounts about her year in Mexico with Cravan, 1917–18. At one juncture in their troubled and impoverished travels, Loy elected to bathe Cravan's feet, sorely blistered by badly fitting

boots; by Loy's account, through this act, she became "'the Magdalene in ecstatics'" (*BM* 256). See also Chapter 3 of *Nethered Regions* on feet and prostitution, or streetwalking, in Loy.
56. In "Negro Dancer" (c. 1930–50), Loy strives but ultimately fails to foreground the theatricality at stake. That African Americans have exceptional access to "[t]he cosmic spasm" of love is a claim that first appears in Loy's "The Widow's Jazz" (1927), where African-American music and dancing "mimes . . . the encroaching Eros / in adolescence", prompting Loy's recollection of her own transport with Cravan (*LaLB* 216; *LoLB* 95–7). Again, homage portends primitivist or appropriative positions, as, through the poem, Loy renders African-American dialect and envisions herself as a victim of the Hindu practice of sati. See also Chapter 1 of *Nethered Regions* on Loy's relationship to primitivism.
57. This argument is drawn, in part, from Plass 45.
58. See Secomb 10; Berg x, 103; Scott and Welton 25; and Stannard 124; on *Phaedrus* see Rowe xxi.
59. This linking of base and ideal recurs in Loy's paean to Wyndham Lewis, where that modernist artist and writer is posited as an artist-god whose "geometric Chimeras" and "Nirvanic snows" are "austere", his figures "celibate", yet never far afield from the generative "radiance / of suns and moons" or the abjection of "silent entrails" (*LoLB* 91–2).
60. In *Islands in the Air*, Loy recalls an art-school tutor explaining to the students that the world is not solid, because comprised of atoms. She writes:

> It flashed through my mind that this was the explanation of how the man in the Bible got/bolted out of a dungeon. I could feel there was some 'control' in the brain with which he, knowing how to use it, could pass atoms through the spaces between the atoms in a wall of stone. (*IA* 67: 104)

61. As Rachel Fountain Eames argues: at the turn of the twentieth century, "contemporary ideas about subatomic particles were linked with emergent technological phenomena, electricity, X-rays and radio-waves, and radium, that quickly captured the public imagination" (32). Mark Morrisson extends this assertion to popular fiction, noting that "[w]ithin a decade of its discovery, radium had invaded almost every subgenre of fiction—including science fiction, occult, adventure, western, detective, and romance fiction" (*Alchemy* 28).
62. In her article "'Snared in an Atomic Mesh': Transcendent Physics and the Futurist Body in the Work of Mina Loy", Rachel Fountain Eames focuses on the science of Loy's preoccupation with physics and the atom, brilliantly tracking Loy's play with the materiality of bodies through "Songs to Joannes" and her early poetic satires on the Futurists, where physics becomes a metaphor for human relationships so that, for instance, Marinetti is often posited as nucleus to Futurist electrons or disciples (33–8).

Prioritising different sources, I am coming to different conclusions than those delineated in Fountain Eames's article, which I discovered when redrafting this chapter. For Eames, Loy's utopian view of atomic dispersal is intertwined with "modern sexuality and female experience"; on these fronts, we agree (47). But, for Eames, Loy's atomic aspirations end with the detonation of Little Boy and Fat Man in 1945. As this chapter asserts, I situate Loy's anxiety about totalising, molecular decimation as early as her 1930s novel *Insel*, and argue that atomic destruction counter-intuitively becomes a central driver of Loy's cohering esoteric Eros, or the very subject at the centre of "History and Religion of Eros".

63. Around the time that Loy embarked upon *Brontolivido*, Marinetti was a war correspondent who witnessed one of the first instances of aerial bombing during the Balkan Wars: the 1913 Siege of Adrianople. He also published a manifesto insisting that artists distance themselves from the "obsessive 'I'" by incorporating "the whiz of atoms" and "the infinite life of molecules into poetry", merging both "with the spectacle and drama of the infinitely huge, for it is this fusion that represents the total synthesis of life itself" ("Destruction" 126). The sounds of war – gunfire, bombing, sword clashes – are among Marinetti's most esteemed means of expressing a "love for matter" and "its vibrations" ("Geometrical" 140).

64. The publication of Herron's *The Menace of Peace* (1917) is precisely contemporary with the writing of Loy's *Brontolivido*. The titular threat refers to Herron's concern that people are willing to accept a peaceful end to World War I at any cost, without delivering appropriate retribution to the German perpetrators Herron unmitigatedly blames. Herron also believes that true love is not afraid to judge or conquer; he presciently argues that humanity is at risk of Germany adopting a "pseudo-socialism" that, if left unchecked, will see that nation rule the globe in another two decades (10–11, 73).

An influential Christian Socialist who replaced Nietzsche's will to power with a "will to love", Herron turned to the Stoics, Christ, Buddha, and the mysticism of the *Theological Germanica*, precedents for an ideal love he considered "the eternal and inviolable constitution of our being" (*BM* 146–7; Herron 16–17, 20). Like Loy, Herron professed a belief that humanity's "mission in the universe" was "cosmic intimacy" and asserted that true love is not afraid to judge or conquer (9).

Part II

Introduction

Backs, Nerves, Eyes: From Proneness to Visionary Transcendence

Across the top of a sheet in her archive, Mina Loy writes Sunday 21 January 1917, the word "Geronimo.", and number one.[1] Having situated her page, she begins:

> I would try to rearrange a human situation that through my own undoing had changed vis à vis to turning of the back. Try to create a loophole whereby Geronimo could return, with honour, to the point of departure.
> Nights I meditated on this acme of dilemma a woman could find herself in. Finally I managed a concoction of skits on his litterateur's attitude, my current obsession with the sex war, hung on a string of whimsical suggestions for him to set events in such callous reverse, he could turn the (Time)-tables on Brontolivido. Remarks on crude virility which men so overestimate suffusing me with blushes as I wrote – were necessary, as I knew, in rebuttal of the flabbergasts' opinion of him.
> In all, a parody attempting to make this unconscious man conscious of an opportunity – – – – to forgive me! (*B* 6: 13–14)

Reconnoitring, rebounds, reversals, rebuttals, repetitions: this passage turns in upon itself, involutes, its author contorted by false remorse and genuine shame. No longer on face-to-face terms with lover one, Loy contrives a scenario to ensure that he feels he has bested lover two and his acolytes. Reassurances of Geronimo's virility, she hopes, will remedy the dissenting rectilinearity he now shows her, his back metonymic for a departure her complex tactics strive to undo, however contrary to her modesty or feminism. To face Loy, Geronimo must save face by "turn[ing] the (Time)-tables" on Brontolivido: steal advantage, invert the unbalanced equation of their relationship, become more *au courant* than the globally famous leader of the Futurists, reduced by Loy to "flabbergasts" or flaccid merchants of shoddy shock, lumbering prophets of a progression that moves backward, through recoil, as much as it gains ground. Next to this passage, Loy carefully pens the word count, "(139)"; beneath it, she observes: "Note re poets remarks on above – – – / Truth remains the one unrevealable scandal" (*B* 6: 14). If there is a truth gone amok here, it seems to be Loy's own uncertain desire, which is alternately shunned or subsumed by the men she puzzles over. The "concoction of skits" to which she refers is almost assuredly her short story "Pazzarella". Products of the tail end of Loy's decade in Florence, these narratives were written before and through 1917. They distil Loy's intimacies, from 1913 onward, with Italian Futurists F. T. Marinetti (Brontolivido) and Giovanni Papini (Geronimo).[2]

Roughly two decades later, Loy articulates a return to a distinctly different point of departure, namely, the inception of consciousness, or the moment at which the child-self becomes "an actor on [its] own stage". Whilst still a "microcosm", writes Loy, the neonate is:

> A seedling of all evolution [that might contain] not only the reflorescence of the past, but also a germination of the ultimate blossom of consciousness, and that, in the cyclic manner of secret things whose end is in the beginning, it starts its unfoldment in a flashing synopsis of the eventual illumination of man: as if will were the urge upon us of Evolution, to arrive, through a patient voyage of elucidation, at the point of departure. Only this time by the light of our own reason. (*CP* 13: 31)

Not illumination, but reillumination; not a single bloom, but a reproductive cycle; not a distant destination, but an informed, autonomous return to a known, viable moment of egress. This second passage is drawn from Loy's *The Child and the Parent* (c. 1932–6), a roman à clef that combines esoteric meditation and feminist polemic with the story of Loy's artistic origins.

Both Loy quotations perform an inward turn with a view to a harmonious ideal: in the first, romantic love; in the second, a heightened self-awareness, a self-consciousness intimacy of the self and its cyclical relationship through the phenomenal world back to the transcendence from which it originated. Passage one traces out the over-arching narrative of Loy's first dialogic strand of autobiographical writings. This creative line runs from 1914, when she begins writing seriously, until the completion of *Insel*, a text drafted between 1933 and 1936: again and again, Loy posits a female protagonist enamoured by, if sparring with, a male artist figure to whom she consciously prostrates herself, patiently awaiting his "insatiate leave-takings & deferred returns" (*B* 8: 4). From this wilfully prone position upon sacrificial altars, Loy's women ultimately become exasperated by their objectification and exclusion at the hands of their adored male triumphalist. From beholden supinity, these women endeavour to resurrect themselves; many succeed.

This mistress narrative, so to speak, runs alongside another that emerges most coherently in Loy's "Anglo-Mongrels and the Rose" (1923–5). In this second autobiographical preoccupation, a variant of the künstlerroman, Loy considers the vexed relationship between her Victorian family of origin – one defined by a vengeful mother, a vacillating father, and their resolute middle-class aspirations – and the development of her artistic will and consciousness. Throughout, Loy "retrospeculates", a term I borrow and bend from the neologism "introspeculates" Loy coins with reference to an expansive reflexivity by which "the mind unbuilds itself for a divine re-edification" (*SE* 281). Retrospeculating, Loy shows how she forged her legacy, moving from prone infant to adulthood, overcoming those who turned their backs on her, near-autodidactically willing her own transcendence through her cultivated passions for beauty and revelation. By retrospeculation, Loy details her embrace of an aesthetic Eros. This autobiographical process is fuelled by Loy's entrenched understanding that the forward-facing, masculinist avant-gardes with whom she associated drew upon posteriority, or what lay immediately behind them, to generate their celebrated "originality".

Loy recognised, in other words, how twentieth-century vanguards had not surpassed the nineteenth-century discourses they claimed to shun, among them occultism, decadence, misogyny. By delineating her past so fulsomely, Loy uncovers the gendered difference of her own ascent to vanguard practice whilst exposing the deceit repressed in unthinking adherence to Ezra Pound's "make it new" or T. S. Eliot's poetics of impersonality. Instead, Loy consciously embraced the esoteric palingenesis or "*risorgimento*" discussed in the previous chapter, a process feeding her own self-aware, ongoing "psychic rebirth" (Surette 50; Parmar 46). Loy defined herself by her combative familial origins: in her romans à clef, she articulates how her past led her to satire, vanguardism, feminism, and a mysticism by which she theorises an Eros that makes symbioses of gendered difference, body and soul, being and cosmos, third and alternate dimensions. In the process, Loy affirms the female vanguardist's rearguard status, one that in artistic circles earns the epithets laggardly, contemptuous, or kitsch. Working her arrière-garde designation to full advantage, Loy shows how women's intellection and creativity are more than lost causes futilely defended.[3] Behind the scenes, relegated to the back foot, Loy orchestrates a cutting-edge feminist vision. As David Wills asserts: "If the dorsal names the unseen, that is not the same as the invisible" (12). Loy understands that what lies behind can determine the future, arrière metamorphosing into avant.

Loy's romans à clef exhibit a dialectics of reversal emergent as early as *Brontolivido*. Versos of this manuscript contain drafts of the "Songs to Joannes" (1917) poem sequence confirming Loy's belief that attraction is fuelled by repulsion, or near-insurmountable separation and opposition: "Let meeting be the turning / To the antipodean" (*LoLB* 65; *B* 4: 5). Technically speaking, the turn is never effected in "Songs". Instead, sexed humans clash, recognise differentiation, dissatisfaction, and their own insufficiencies: love is insatiable madness, love is divinely oppositional. These humans "[b]e[g] dorsal vertebrae" – a bit of spine to prop up the self, a bit of spine to incline toward others (*LoLB* 65–6). These backs extend the inclinatory Eros of the previous chapter, underscoring how digressions from "forward linearity mak[e] reference to what is behind", evoke "a decelerating [rearward] pull" (Wills 5). For Loy's esoteric Eros is a propensity resolutely crooked, reaching back and toward, a contortion unmasking the self-perpetuating illusion of a sexual ethics that begets the unethical.

Recognising that individuals tend to enjoy uncircumscribed practice of their own "'amoral' sophistication", Loy remains alert to the "somersault[s] of morality" perpetrated by male modernist iconoclasts, Picasso among them (*SE* 225, 377). Female modernists who similarly attempt to escape "vertical caste" with "somersault descent" into the bohemian underworld do not fare quite so well: rather than transcending their own esoteric heights, they fall for men they consider "di-vi-ne", who resemble Buddha (*LoLB* 98–9). Attacking, but also paying homage, Loy satirises avant-garde men who do not conform to what Adriana Cavarero describes as the philosophical preoccupation with the upright man, "literally a subject who conforms to a vertical axis, which in turn functions as a principle and norm for its ethical posture" (6).[4] An ambitious female avant-gardist, Loy aims at a like revolutionary propensity, a similar liberation, but remains aware that, when idealised, women are maternal incliners, leaning protectively toward the vulnerable child; when vilified, women are unstable, the subject most readily unmoored by love, itself an "attack against the self's balance" (Cavarero 6). Conventionally, Western thought champions the autonomous rectitude of the upright 'I' whilst resisting inclination, itself a postural metaphor for passions, desires, and instincts that turn the self outward, toward otherness.[5] Given this intellectual and affective history, Cavarero regards Eros as the greatest challenge to rectitude, with artistic passion following close on its heels (3). Loy's feminist esoteric Eros is founded upon this very challenge, and her passions – loving, sexual, familial, platonic, aesthetic – lean and reach, welcome a constitutive imbalance, an asymmetry making demands upon the insular, autonomous self (Han 16).[6]

Positioning is a feminist issue. As Iris Marion Young has shown, by an imposed "female comportment", women and girls are discouraged from using a full range of mobility, instead evincing a "permanent posture of [self-]disapproval" ("Throwing" 144; "Women" 180). Posture preoccupies the feminist Loy, who presents women lying constrainedly in the pockets of their male beloveds, within which they find themselves "compromising / Between the perpendicular and horizontal" (*LoLB* 44). A satirist as embattled as she is experimental, Loy is consumed by the turned back, the prime anatomical figure of dissent (Wills 212). Her early artworks include images of male figures swooning, their backs curved into the arms of inclining women; in *Consider Your Grandmother's Stays* (1916) Loy depicts a woman bursting out of her furbelow onto the page, defying her restricted torso with unanatomical bulges and cartoonish torsions. In the 1940s, Loy invented a "corselet": called "Armour for the Body", it facilitated spinal alignment during sleep and throughout senescence (Loy, "Inventions"). In "Anglo-Mongrels and the Rose" (1923–5), Loy demonstrates her awareness that the back was a site of vulnerability from an early age, attending to the forlorn tippet worn by a working-class girl on the street: "at the back / her plait / hump[ing] itself over it" (*LaLB* 159). Stooped posture and prescient gaze anticipate the dowager's hump Loy's corselet seeks to avoid. Looking on, Loy is admonished by her governess to walk straight to avoid the inevitable fate of the "'horrid ragamuffin'" (*LaLB* 160). Loy internalises these injunctions, presenting the infant Arthur Cravan to the "Anglo-Mongrels" reader as a boy of good appetite and superlative posture: "devouring his pap / it is as if a pillar of iron / erects him / in place of a spine" (*LaLB* 150).

Cravan's admirable mightiness is extendable to the *fin-de-siècle* images of Loy's family included in Burke's biography, a group that includes the busked, adamantly erect maternal figure at the heart of so much of Loy's discourse, and another photograph of Loy at 3 or 4 years old, sitting atop a sofa back, her spine ramrod straight against the wall behind her. These images set the stage for Loy's fascination with the unyielding structure of domesticity, and her own retroversion to that very scene. But all such returns to a point of origin are doomed to failure: "[b]ack, in all its singularity, begins in repetition", and as a result, its logic "is always doubled up" (Royle 151). Of backward proliferations, Loy is all too aware: reflecting on how she was "jammed between the pair of opposites" that were her parents, she notes that within this vice-like, obliterative grip she "acquired an accidental 'infinity complex' and 'manifoldisation'" (*B* 7: 21). Composite, constrained and strained, Loy's background transcends unification and directs her toward the cosmos, forming the ground of the incomplete developmental maps that combine nostos with the gnostic by way of directing Loy's artistic beginnings and her feminist avant-garde legacy.

Reliant on backs metaphorical, postural, theoretical, and anatomical, Part II of this book is divided into two interconnected chapters, "'The Supine Event'" and "The Blind Back". The first of these two chapters focuses on Loy's story "Pazzarella", attending also to its companion text, the draft roman à clef *Brontolivido*. Positioning the Futurists as more arrière- than avant-garde, Loy satirises their rectilinearity and unexamined positivism. To do so, she posits a female protagonist who strategically leads her vanguard associates by passively reclining. Subsections of this chapter address the various forms of indolent repose with which Pazzarella is associated, beginning with the feminised experience of mental illness regularly associated with derangements of brain, nerves, and spine. In "Decadent Languor, Somnolence, and Male Violence", Pazzarella's languidness, her tendency to proneness, is presented as an aesthetic and ideological posture against which the Futurists railed and aggressed. Using "Pazzarella" as a limit case for her own theory of satire whereby ferocity engenders intimacy, Loy exposes male aggression as the pre-eminent Futurist nightmare: a *passéiste* convention. Building on Loy's understanding that Futurism and her own idealised love are reliant upon magical thinking, "Enchantment, Supinity, and the Hypnotic Gaze" exposes the theurgical roots of Loy's esoteric Eros. Recognising the latent occultism of her Futurist peers, Loy satirises them as irrational enchanters, porous mediums, embodiments of the Decadent sphinx, and finally, as the punchline of her own narrative joke, her "vindication of female psychology" (*SE* 97). Throughout, Loy moves from the willed passivities of hypnosis, mesmerism, and spiritualism, or the eighteenth- and nineteenth-century occult practices marrying body, mind, and cosmos, toward the psychoanalytic therapies that came to dominate the twentieth. Concluding this discussion, "Telepathy, Voices, and Visions" demonstrates how Pazzarella's complaisance enables her to hone her skills at reading the unsaid and unknown, generating a feminist vision that draws its strength from deploying esotericism and psychoanalysis in combination. For Loy, visions are subliminal manifestations that effect discernible change on the exoteric, paternalistic rectitude she critiques. As Loy argues in "Mi & Lo": supinity is expansive, mystical opposition to the presumptions of power and authority embedded in the perpendicularities of the hyperrational.

Loy's rearguard critique of hyperrationality continues into the second chapter of this section, "The Blind Back", which attends to a Loy anatomical figuration as paradoxical as it is foundational. Briefly referenced by Loy critics thus far, the blind back is overdue for extensive analysis and replete contextualisation. Loy's blind back is anatomical truth – we cannot see what lies behind us – and, in Loy's hands, a mystical portal by which we access distant pasts or transcendent, Eros-laden futures. As constraint, the blind back is crucial to the development of the gendered self in Loy's künstlerromans, as it has particular resonance for the domesticated female; as theoretical construct, the blind back bears relation to the retrocognitions of thinkers integral to Loy's sense of herself as a genius, among them Bergson and Myers; as a site of the visionary it is akin to the pineal eye propounded by Theosophy and Bataille, but also the utopian fourth dimension much celebrated in Loy's era. Via the blind back, Loy seeks to cohere the splintered, artistic being that is the subject of her equally fragmented late prose. Like Loy's strategically passive supinity, the blind back is another of Loy's deceptive anatomical figurations: ostensibly disabling or disabled, it proves ecstatic and liberating. It is ironic, if consistent with Loy's abjecting processes, that she elevates an unseeing posteriority alongside her instatement of her artistic legacy, her unique perception. Elevates, rather than erects: even at the level of the spine, Loy maintains greater adherence to the deviant curve than the straight line.

Notes

1. Loy does not include the year. The twenty-first of January was a Sunday in 1912 and 1917. As Burke suggests that Loy met Marinetti in or around 1913, and the text for *Brontolivido* includes rough drafts of

"Songs to Joannes" as published in 1917, I am assuming that Loy is writing in the latter year.
2. The pages that follow the quoted passage contain a brief biography, in French, of the Italian Futurist Giovanni Papini, and reference his evidently disconcerting psychology (*B* 6: 16–17). Loy's most protracted interactions with the Futurists occurred in Florence from 1913 to 1917; as is indicated by his thinly disguised presence in her draft *Esau Penfold*, Loy first met Papini, albeit at a distance, between 1907 and 1910 (*BM* 114). *Brontolivido* also includes prose, themes, and dialogue reworked for Loy's contemporaneous story "The Sacred Prostitute", discussed in greater detail in Chapter 3 of *Nethered Regions*.
3. Charles Altieri, who describes the arrière-garde as the dividing line between avant-garde and all else, notes that these divisions "facilitate a far too easy contempt for what one has projected as in the rear (or in arrears)" (633). In Natalie Adamson and Toby Norris's sophisticated depiction of the arrière-garde, they argue that this term "cannot be simply and reductively identified with what some critics would call rearguard or kitsch, implying a deliberately retrograde and reactionary stance" (18–19). For Adamson and Norris, "arrière-garde bears within it a telling ideological inflection . . . referring to the defence of a cause that one already knows to be lost" (19).
4. The parents of Jove Ivon Corvon give up on a "Moral Order", thereby generating a famously vanguard son; Ian Gore of "The Three Wishes" spurns "[t]he abstract authority of a moral concept" with similarly creative results, as does arch-creator The Loony, or he of "abortive morals" in "The Pamperers" (*SE* 114, 165). And while, in Loy's "The Sacred Prostitute" and "Pazzarella", male vanguardists behave deplorably with little consequence, her mockery is surely tinged with a desire for the same impunity, the same recognition.
5. Cavarero's theory of inclination works against the rectilinearity of a broad swathe of the Western philosophical tradition that includes Plato, Kant, and Levinas. Hannah Arendt's *The Human Condition* (1958) and "Some Questions of Moral Philosophy" (1965) are prime sources for two of Cavarero's key themes: inclination and natality.
6. Cavarero's arguments lend additional meaning to Loy's wry claim, discussed in the previous chapter, that "man has never exhibited the least inclination towards a moral faculty" (*SE* 228). By Loy's inverse reasoning, to be moral is not to be statically erect, but to wilfully lean away from the self's centre of gravity. As she writes in "Mi & Lo": "Morality is not a behaviour but a discovery", a journey toward a point of arrival, a "clarity" that requires not only a conservative "domination" and "utilisation" of the senses, but also a respectful "perfect understanding" of the same (*SE* 271, 277). Ultimately, Loy's virtue inclines toward others to sustain the self: "Morality is to give all you have and still possess all" (*SE* 271).

Chapter 2

"The Supine Event"

Scissions are lines metaphorical and experiential that Loy challenges. Testing the bounded bonds shared by attack and affection is Loy's artistic *raison d'être*, and she effects this test, in part, by chipping at ossified ideological and intellectual binaries: male/female, rational/irrational, science/mysticism. Most obviously, body/mind: in March 1914, Loy writes her first husband: "I am not intellectual enough to become a futurist – But I am intelligent enough to have given up everything else" ("Loy, Mina to Stephen Haweis"). Intellection is one kind of cleverness; intelligence is body, world, soul, spirit. Loy's mission is as deconstructive as it is esoteric: championing "counter-powers" as the "integral elements of cosmological processes", the occult often "blur[s] the usual distinctions between real/unreal, inner/outer, and subjective/objective" whilst performing its own illusions as absolute truth (Stuckrad 93; Owen, *Place* 129). Loy's journey toward a visionary esoteric Eros is discernible within her earliest Futurist fictions, among them her short story "Pazzarella" (c. 1914–17) and its unfinished companion text, the draft roman-à-clef *Brontolivido*. While Nietzsche's espousal of a transcendent Overman, sovereign to his own truth, greatly appealed to turn-of-the-century occultists such as Loy's Parisian peers, the Futurists drew on Nietzsche's strategic contrariness, combative action, buffoonery, and crucially, his will to revolutionise systemic cultural value: it is a Futurist refrain that "the will to renewal is all" (Owen, *Place* 133; Marinetti, "In This Futurist Year" 232). Foundational to contemporary avant-gardism, Futurists upheld a regenerative drive that included overt disdain for the past, with its imprecisions, nostalgias, disorders, traditions, and "mildew"; following in Nietzsche's footsteps, Futurists promulgated "a healthy forgetfulness" (Marinetti, "Geometrical" 135). Emblematising their aggressive passion for modernity, their internationally published call to arms, "The Foundation and Manifesto of Futurism" (1909), "*celebrate[d]* the very inhumanity of the new machine age" (Nicholls 83). Recognising the tremendous hold that art exerts over the public, the Futurists set out to "purge it of sentimentalism" and tired romance, "creating instead an art that glorifies individual strength and freedom, the victories of science, and man's increasing dominion over the dark forces of nature" (Marinetti, "Necessity" 70). Futurist ideologies validate the upright, powerful, fact- and forward-driven subject, impose order over the fecund, messy, uncontainable physical world, and reject "the tyranny of love", or the affective, intimate totalisation integral to Loy's thinking (Marinetti, "Battles of Trieste" 161).

In Loy's writings about the Futurists, the violence is vanguard, but also up close and personal, transgressive and transformative. Loy's lived experience is readily discerned within her protagonists' coordinates, as is her uncertainty about herself and her participation in the hyperbolically masculinist Futurism. Critics often cite Loy's brilliantly ambivalent riposte to the eponymous Futurist leader in *Brontolivido*: "'Now you ... are everything I despise in Man, raised to the Nth power – Yet I respect you – because I recognise in you an enemy worth understanding[']" (*B* 5: 3). Loy actively interrogates the Futurists' interior motives, hoping that even they "must know that each of us carries a potential universe of pain within ourselves" (*B* 8: 27). Yet, despite bravados brooding or exuberant, the Futurists wear surprisingly limp external armour, their very physique "seeming to convey – it was for her to mould" (*B* 5: 20). Rather than active agents rushing toward triumphal points of arrival, Loy finds the Futurists caught "in activated suspension; taut between projection and *re*projection" (*B* 2: 18). Adjectivally, Loy undermines Futurist novelty, derogating their "'*reactionary*'" misogyny, their enthusiasms for "*reb*[irth] in the satisfaction of buckling to the fresh attack", their "*reiterative re*surrection" (emphases added, *B* 2: 51, 5). Consistent with her affective and somatic emphases, Loy takes issue with their performances of emotional "*recovery*" and an ease oxymoronically located in "nostrils flaring *re*pose" (*B* 51, 5). For Loy, the Futurists merit a prefix that *re*turns, undoes, or negates; their very creativity she likens to "the *re*crudescence of the experimenter", an ambivalent, recurrent state of affairs (*B* 9: 12). Where Marinetti considered himself the leader of a movement "affirm[ing] the continuous perfection and endless progress of humankind ... as absolute principles", for Loy, Futurism moves hindward, lumbering through recoil, trafficking in points already reached ("War" 53).[1]

Driving Loy's satire of Futurism is a critique of the defining "fable of modernity", or the presupposition that society is constantly propelled away from a fixed, outdated past toward an aspirational now always just beyond reach (Storm 7–8). Working against this pervasive mythology, Loy underscores the Futurist allegiances to rectilinearity, from their ideological absolutism to "the inviolate perpendicular of [their] trouser creases" (*B* 5: 16). Yielding and circuitous Eros, or "[s]exual and emotional inclination toward a person", is one means by which Loy effects her critique, as is foregrounded in poems that disavow possessive love or lust, espousing "propensity" above all, or observe faces "sloping toward perception" (Cavarero 3; *LoLB* 3, 111). Another is the resolutely supine feminised body, an idealised, derided, and narratively critical trope that runs through Loy's oeuvre, evident from the "sleeping-beauties" scorned by Don Juan in Loy's early play "The Sacred Prostitute" to her undated draft poem "Passivia", which features Pazzarella's doppelgänger, a figure prepared to "spread herself out on the highway / of adolescence / prostrate to the presence / of the male principle of the universe" (*SE* 189; Loy, "Passivia"). Similarly, in *The Child and the Parent* Loy defines the "fallen woman" as subject to enforced non-sentience, "prone in the coma of the evoked" (15: 41). Consistent with this patriarchal positioning of the female, the narratively maligned John Straher of "In Maine: Green's Colony" expresses a desire that his love interest, Lucy, become bed-ridden so that he might nurse her back to health (*SE* 49).

In the later, undated story "The Agony of the Partition", Cassandra is rejected by a lover, becoming a dorsally defined, passively wracked female "lying upon her incomparably betrayed bed of a bride" (*SE* 12). In the contemporaneous *Insel*, Loy has protagonist Mrs Jones fill a painting overall with every scrap of her writings and stitch up the garment's openings before tossing the entirety into "a superfluous room", thereby turning the products of her intellect into a prostrate version of herself, all with a view to keeping her creativity away from the invasive gaze of housesitting Insel (*I* 23). Come "Letters of the Unliving" (1949), Loy begins to romanticise female prostration, expressing a senescent yearning "to drift in lenient coma / an older Ophelia / on Lethe", a trope repeated in another late poem, where Loy details the feminised moon's capacity to "suffuse the self", an experience "[c]oercive as coma, frail as bloom" (*LoLB* 132, 146). Further evidence of welcome lethargy arises in the undated "Maiden Song", wherein resides a songstress who can "anaesthetize all sense / save listening" and who "close[s] the eyes" on blissful "arias of languor" (*LaLB* 237). Loy's deployment of enforced and willed female lethargy is lifelong.[2]

Loy's early satires establish her fascinations regarding inclinations and supinities. These works focus on "remingling[s]": witting, intimate repetitious encounters between a female protagonist (alternately named Jemima, Sophia, or Pazzarella), who is in dialogue with variants of Marinetti – Brontolivido, the Martinet, Mafarka – and Papini, rendered as Johannes or Geronimo (*B* 8: 25). Ruminating upon these unsatisfying exchanges, Jemima speculates: "something had gone wrong with the modern man, as far as construing him was concerned; *he had turned on his propensities* – with a challenge – & into whatever corner he pushed woman at the blade point of his self consciousness[,] *pricking her if she lay still* – slashing at every stir – he never forgot she was there" (emphasis added, *B* 8: 24). Über-modern representative of masculinity, the Futurist attacks women who symbolise passion and disposition, affects that crimp his resolute, all-consuming onward and upward. But resistance contorts, effecting twists that exert still more pressure on the cherished illusion of autonomous uprightness. Ever more frustrated, the Futurist skewers and incises the prone, expectant female precisely because she dominates a male consciousness newly tasked with "keeping a watch on himself" (*B* 8: 24). Violence is a time-worn response to the repugnance femininity elicits within patriarchal cultures. Loy updates this misogynistic truth for the twentieth century, observing how women's increasing demands for respect and recognition merely whet modern man's "paradoxical ingenuity" and augment his valorised combativeness (*B* 8: 24–5). All too often, revolution is return.

By Loy's reckoning, woman can never be supine enough for contemporary assaultive man. Free of overt historical detail, Loy's satirical argument nevertheless echoes the suffragettes' passively resistant refusals to participate in censuses or pay tax to governments that did not recognise them as fully enfranchised citizens, tactics developed in tandem with Mohandas Gandhi's "*satyagraha* or spiritual resistance to unjust laws", first deployed in South Africa in response to the Asiatic Registration Bill of 1906 (Liddington and Crawford 111). Epitomising wilful inaction, "Pazzarella" nods to these well-publicised, international nonviolent protests; its ethos certainly underscores Loy's thinly disguised claim to be "secret service buffoon to the Woman's Cause" in her dealings with the Futurists (*LoLB* 49). That said, Loy's protagonist is less activist than transcendental supernaturalist. Countering the Futurist faith in science, technology, violence, action, noise, and all – yes, all – things erect,

Pazzarella engages in occult practices that navigate the complex terrain between sacrificial self-renunciation and potent wilfulness, traversing eighteenth-century mesmerism and nineteenth-century spiritualism along the way. Pazzarella asserts and reasserts the primacy of what Loy later labels "the supine event", itself an expansive, mystical counter to "the perpendicular event" of alert, progressive rectitude (*SE* 270). Where the Futurists longed to raze and purge the "outmoded", Pazzarella is a passive, contagious throwback to mores and movements the Futurists despised, reserving special rancour for the Decadence Pazzarella so self-evidently embraces (Marinetti, "War" 54).

Paradoxically, Pazzarella leads by literal, anatomical repose, and by a surprisingly progressive arrière-gardism. Her strategic atavism exposes Futurist posturings: Pazzarella's tendency toward nervous collapse proves enchanting and empowering; mediumistically prone, she stealthily occupies the swooned-over ground of a telepathic narrative, effecting a supernatural triumph that goes unrecognised by her obdurately self-absorbed Futurist paramours. By Loy's reading, Futurist leaders ascend mountains in futile pursuit of deification; they refute truth and love, which Loy equates, considering nothing "'more itself than Love is'"; against Futurist pessimism, Loy seeks out an "esoteric reason" that will shore up her position (*B* 8: 30). In 1903, Frederic W. H. Myers pronounced love "the simplest and most universal expression of that mutual gravitation or kinship of spirits which is the foundation of the telepathic law" (277–8). Affirming the telepathic impulse for which Myers remains best known, Pazzarella is Loy's counterargument to early masculinist avant-gardes: she delineates Loy's inclination toward an esoteric Eros, one that privileges women's capacity to voice the visionary.

Spinal Irritations and Nerviness: Feminised Lunacy

"La pazza" means madwoman. To this gendered noun, Loy adds the Italian pronoun "ella", or "she", as if to compound the abject femininity at stake. There is no small echo here of "Cinder" – another base term, referring to combustive residue – "ella", the fairy tale in which female servitude is rewarded by privileged heteronormative intimacy. Consistent with this paternalism, Pazzarella's love interest Geronimo claims he bestowed her name upon her in the opening pages of a story that appears exclusively told from his point of view (*SE* 65). Historically, madness has been feminised, seen as inextricable from the irrational overpowering of the mind by the morally suspect, all-too-natural body. Sanity, by contrast, is reasonable, measuredly discursive, intellectual: masculine. For the past three centuries, women in the Global North have far outnumbered men in receiving mental health treatment, a statistic complementing pervasive literary representations of female lunacy from Shakespeare's Ophelia to Charlotte Brontë's Bertha Mason to Breton's Nadja (Showalter 52, 250). In eighteenth-century England, nervous disorders became emblematic of the aristocratic, pampered English constitution, problems believed compounded for women due to their constrained mobility, ineducation, and enervating, sensitising reproductive systems (Logan 18, 32, 24). These views encroached upon and shaped the nineteenth-century England of Loy's birth. Improbably deemed both too rebellious and too easily commanded, women's nerves were believed susceptible to hysteria and neurasthenia, illnesses that came into prominence in the 1870s. Nearly indistinguishable from hysterics, neurasthenics were believed to be more passive, more "cooperative, ladylike, and well-bred" (Showalter 134). Also known as "spinal irritation", neurasthenia is described by nineteenth-century sexologist Havelock Ellis as "a weakness of . . . both brain and spinal cord" revealed "by a tendency to over-action and irritability of the nervous system, morbid sensibility, and mental anxiety" (Showalter 136; Ellis, *Man* 379).

Ellis's anatomical emphases respond to contemporaneous developments in the study of female insanity. During the nineteenth century, understanding of the vertebral column was transformed "from a large bundle of connecting wires for the brain into a congress of distinct nerve centres, called ganglia, with semiautomous control over their distinct regions of the body" (Logan 166). From about 1840, the spine and ganglia were newly interpreted as receptors of reflex sensation, impression, and bodily or organic mechanism, while sophisticated cognition was attributed to the cerebrum alone: ideas, emotions, intellection, and pivotally, the will emphasised by Nietzsche and Futurism (Winter 287–90). Predictably, medical studies "confirmed" that the ratio of spinal cord to conscious brain was greater in females than males throughout their lives; physiology, psychiatry, evolutionary theory, and social commentary subsequently reinforced how women's intemperate reproductive systems arrested their nerval development (Ellis, *Man* 140; Oppenheim, *"Shattered"* 185). In an era where the will was the epicentre of mental health, autonomy, and intelligence, women were said to lack adequate, appropriate backbone (Oppenheim, *"Shattered"* 44, 182). Victorian women were diagnosed with "'hysterical affections of the spine'" and prescribed resorts where they spent their days in Bath chairs, the elongated precursor of the contemporary wheelchair designed with an insistence upon full-length repose (Owen, *Darkened* 78). Women's madness was contagion, threat, and unethical justification for male violation: in an 1886 study of abused women, one British surgeon attributed husbands' propensity to violence to a specific degree of spinal curvature shared by their victimised wives; women "predispos[ed] to insanity" were thus blamed for "driv[ing] men mad" (Showalter 107). As Loy was coming of age, women were appraised as unduly, threateningly, in thrall to their reflexes, led more by spine than brain.

In the hands of Euro-American women, feminised supinity became cause and effect, curse and salve, illness and inadequate cure. In 1852, Florence Nightingale likened the daily life of the Victorian lady to "lying on one's back, with one's hands tied and having liquid poured down one's throat" without hope of an alleviating, terminating suffocation (34). The indolence imposed upon said lady made her insomniac, a form of mental illness circularly requiring still more repose during the day, while at night, she became a living "corpse, which lies motionless in its narrow bed" as her spirit roamed "at large among the stars" (Nightingale 43, 51). Enforced passivity was a gateway to active rebellion, a celestially directed ambition. In the notorious New Woman story collection *Keynotes and Discords* (1893), George Egerton's narration was said to "'personify our modern nervousness'" and "women's 'psychic atavism'". As Roger Luckhurst details, Egerton's proto-feminist tales "signalled refinement and sympathy beyond the brutishness of masculine nerves", a strategy similarly deployed by "Decadent men who refused muscular masculinity by embracing *la névrose*" (220–1). Egerton's female protagonists "stretc[h] motionless" when seated or lie alone upon the hills, "quive[r] nervous[ly]", and laugh hysterically, yet also aspire frankly to masculinity, losing themselves, for instance, in visions of commanding crowds of men (10, 13–15, 20). Alert, intuitive, highly sensitised, and intelligent, by their embodied positioning, these women refuse "the long crucifixion" of Victorian heteronormativity and foresee Judith Butler's famous claim that gender binaries remain in place by "posturing as the foundational illusions of identity" (Egerton 159; Butler, *Gender* 46). Wilfully resistant and femininely receptive, these figures significantly predate Loy's Pazzarella.

Atavistic neurosis, then, propels the feminine *fin-de-siècle* outsider forward, and this is a tradition Loy knew intellectually and personally: in late 1912, a few years before she wrote "Pazzarella",

Loy was diagnosed as neurasthenic. As was consistent with treatment for spinal irritation, at her most ill, Loy was confined to a bed in a darkened room and discouraged from reading or conversing. Through her months-long convalescence, she witnessed the departure of her first husband to Oceania, wrote to her friend Mabel Dodge Luhan about the likelihood of a superconscious counter to Freud's subconscious, read Myers's *Human Personality and its Survival of Bodily Death* (1903), and enlisted the expertise of the influential exponent of psychosynthesis Roberto Assagioli (*BM* 141–6). Responsive to her own experience, Loy wrote about women perceiving themselves or perceived to be on the verge of mental and emotional breakdown, female speakers obsessed with their sexual primacy, an ardour inextricable from anxieties about the ever-present threat of "insane asylums", women keen to evade "the psycho-pathic wards" of the lauded male's "abandoned harem" (*LoLB* 27, 46). These speakers include the woman of "The Effectual Marriage" (1917), who plays at domestic bliss with a self-proclaimed male genius blind to her needs, a woman whose story remains partial, constrained by gendered expectation and the easy assumption that she is unreliable, dismissable because prone to madness (*LoLB* 36–9). From her own state of nervous collapse, Loy began to plot foundational intellectual and esoteric coordinates, as well as a journey to New York to cement her artistic autonomy. That Loy's well-being returns with her abusive husband's departure does not seem coincidental: as Elaine Showalter argues, "[i]n case after case [of female invalidism], immobility, sensitivity, loss of appetite, and depression seem to be forms of sexual withdrawal, the body protecting itself against further invasion" (140). Feminised spinal impulses may be involuntary, but they are not without cognition.

Insanity has long been perceived as bestially abject, a "somatic dysfunction [by which] the mind regress[es] into autonomic, reflex action" (Luckhurst 96). But since Plato, insanity has also been celebrated as conduit to the sublime, to divinely inspired prophecies, to poetic visions bestowed by the Muses, and to the totalising derangements of love (*Phaedrus* 23–5). This binary is superbly captured in Giacomo Balla's *La pazza* (1905) (Fig. 2.1). Balla's painting is one of a portrait series of the disenfranchised entitled *The Living*; in combination, Balla's title and content echo Loy's associations between a too-minimally acknowledged human sentience and disenfranchisement.[3] *La pazza* is static precursor to Balla's *Girl Running on a Balcony* (1912), a neo-Impressionist work produced in the same year as his much-touted Futurist celebration of motion and fourth

Fig. 2.1 Giacomo Balla, *La pazza* (1905). National Gallery of Modern and Contemporary Art of Rome. By kind concession of the Ministry of Cultural Heritage, Activities, and Tourism. ©ADAGP, Paris and DACS, London 2016.

dimensionality, *Dynamism of a Dog on a Leash*. As Christine Poggi argues, *La pazza* reveals Balla's defiance toward nineteenth-century discourses on hysteria, and his familiarity with the now-contentious photographs authorised by Jean-Martin Charcot (50). A professor of anatomical pathology, Charcot ran clinics at Paris's Salpêtrière that drew large crowds – Freud among them in 1885 and 1886 – eager to see hysterics perform whilst hypnotised (Showalter 147–55). The associated photographs capture women prone in padded rooms, clothes falling from their bodies, convulsed in ecstasies legibly sexual or religious.

By wilful contrast, Balla portrays his neighbour Matilde Gabini on the threshold of the balcony of a bourgeois home, standing erect if off-kilter, fully if raggedly clad. At Gabini's back, the sun shines over an undulating yellow crop distantly bordered by the luminous greens and blues of woodland and a determined, if suggestively thin, celestial beyond. Before her lies a darkened interior, and her own shadow is ominously framed by the inward-opening door. As Poggi argues, the juxtaposition of darkness and light compellingly suggests the interpenetration of reason and lunacy; Gabini is ambiguously placed between the two, meaning the viewer is enveloped by, and implicated in, the shadow of her madness (60). The shoes awkwardly clutched in the crook of Gabini's right arm signal a protective endurance and lowliness, perhaps a desire for grounding. Religious symbols and gestures martyrise Gabini: her upraised finger, laid next to her mouth, evokes the silenced mind of the mentally unwell and hagiographic or oracular proselytising; her ruddy hair is unkempt aura; her heaven-gazing eyes draw on a standard iconography of suffering; the pronounced blue-grey drips of paint on her forehead invite comparison to the blood induced by Christ's crown of thorns. The contortion of Gabini's spine is particularly noteworthy, as it heaves toward her left clavicle in a cruel, uncontrollable parody of the figural contrapposto celebrated in canonical, classical works of art, Michelangelo's *David* (1501–4) among them. Against presumptions about lunatic performance so prevalent in biased medical diagnoses of "capricious" womankind, these art historical details speak truth to the pain – mental, physical, social, communicative – endured by those experiencing mental illness.[4]

Unlike John Everett Millais's beautifully prone, agape *Ophelia* (1852) or Tony Robert-Fleury's prurient *Pinel à la Salpêtrière* (1876), Gabini is neither objectified nor made complicit in her demise. Instead, Balla discerns frank pathos in his subject's expression, one that appears attuned to the beyond. We assume that it is this Balla that Marjorie Perloff labels "a humanitarian socialist", a figure less discernible in the Balla who writes manifestos professing a "love of danger, speed and assault" with a concomitant "loathing of peace and immobility", or who, come the 1930s, designs Futurfascist tennis and golf wear (36; Balla 203). In 1909, *La pazza* was exhibited in Rome and at the Paris Salon d'Automne of which Loy was a member, although she did not submit or attend that year (Poggi 41; *BM* 114). But Loy would assuredly have known of Balla, not least because, alongside Marinetti, he created well-publicised scandals with his fiercely nationalistic, anti-neutral Futurist sartorial designs and manifestos of 1913 and 1914, perceived by many Italians as war-mongering provocations (*BM* 175). A clothes designer herself, Loy may have had Balla on her mind in 1942 when she created a Victory dress emblazoned with a large "V" as the United States entered the Second World War (*BM* 175, 395). But as early as *La pazza*, allegiances are discernible between Balla and Loy. For, like Balla's painting, Loy's "Pazzarella" foregrounds the intimacies, squalid and sublime, of female lunacy, and delivers a sustained assault against the postures and postulations imposed upon the mentally unstable woman. Importantly for both painting and story, spinal irritation is a conduit to the visionary, and, in a manner that foreshadows Loy's late theories on the blind back, a portal to alternate planes.

Decadent Languor, Somnolence, and Male Violence

Supine of manner, supine of posture, Loy's Pazzarella incarnates the will-lessness ascribed to the Victorian female. Vapid, passive, her "fragile body" exudes "a vague evaporative quality" and her facial "lines of suffering" go "undefined"; awash in "cerebral confusion", in her, "the vital rhythm [is] disjointed" (*SE* 74, 65–7, 96). "[D]isquieting", "tremulous", Pazzarella shuns debates about free will, too certain that "confirmation of [her] choice[s] is beyond her power" (*SE* 67, 75, 68). When not resolutely retiring, Pazzarella is given to emotional volatility: a fit of screaming, an all-encompassing sob (*SE* 74, 93–4). When her apathy works in his favour, Geronimo is pleased; when it challenges his inclinations, Pazzarella evinces "[t]he contrariness of women!" (*SE* 70–1; 94). Yet Pazzarella is masochistically obedient to patriarchal command: when one lover tells her not to have a baby with the other, she refrains; when war breaks out, she promptly dons a nurse's uniform and "fix[es] her cheated eyes on chimerical Duty" (*SE* 77). Inactivity and ennui exhaust Pazzarella, who exemplifies Florence Nightingale's testimonials to the effect that middle-class women raised in the nineteenth century can spend days at a time idly prone, processing the minutiae of their confined, male-dominated lives (*SE* 87). Surveying Pazzarella's domicile, even unempathetic Geronimo "shudder[s]" at "the blank expanses of Time shut into those charming rooms" (*SE* 68). As in Balla's *La pazza*, constraint warps the female body, so that "taut nerves distor[t Pazzarella's] face in a rigid resignation" and she walks "with an angularity that must have irked her limbs." Bemused by this lived rigor mortis, Geronimo diagnoses Pazzarella's neediness as self-generated pathology, a "suicidal mania" that he maintains is cause, rather than effect, of his neglect (*SE* 81–2). Against these insurmountable odds, Pazzarella vainly hopes that "there is some elemental truth concealed in woman's love that men do not suspect, but which will some day make amends for our monotony" (*SE* 85).

Pazzarella progresses decadently, towards degeneration. Originating in nineteenth-century France, Decadence was enamoured with art above all, but also demise, deformity, failure, paradox, excessive style and consumption, non-heteronormative sexualities, negative affects, and crucially, the marvellous, supernatural, oneiric, and irrational. In turn, occultism throve in the cultural milieu Decadence established (Owen, *Place* 9). From page 1 of Loy's story, Pazzarella is adorned in decadent detail: "seated before the tarnished gilding of a dilapidated clavichord, she let her idle fingers under their crepuscular jewels crawl over the keys, evoking tired melodies" (*SE* 65). Like the protagonist of Joris-Karl Huysmans's *Against Nature* (1884), Pazzarella flourishes against circadian rhythms: "There was something about her of a plant that has matured in a cellar as though she had had to draw her alimentary light from an enduring twilight" (*SE* 66). Affirming the decadent paradox whereby the artifice at the core of modernity is presented as organic wellspring, Pazzarella encounters Nature at night, discoursing with her on paved city streets (*SE* 74). Paul Verlaine's "Langueur" (1884) remains a pre-eminent Decadent anthem, a paean to this wonderfully multivalent state of consuming distress, lamentation, and desire coupled with a totalising lassitude. Consistent with the terms of Verlaine's sonnet, Pazzarella exudes languorous torpor, an enervation frustrated, voluptuous, and unorthodox – "evok[ing] the couplings of butterflies and reptiles" – with the power to "congea[l] [Geronimo's] veins in a glacial passion" (*SE* 70–1). Come their fourth visit, she is splendidly, mournfully bed-ridden:

> Pazzarella looked a trifle faded, laid out on a sofa lapped in her silken gown and propped with cushions, occupying herself as usual with her tea things which were set on a low table. This body gradually desiccating for want of caresses, this potential mother empty of fruit, must necessarily continue throughout her steady undoing to distribute her circles of amber and sugar gewgaws. A woman resigned, who, while her life was ebbing from her, seemed ceaselessly to be pouring it out from a silver pot for casual callers with hands that were livid with calm. (*SE* 79)

Pazzarella's seething hands are the only ripple in this otherwise pristine decadent pool, a *mise-en-scène* appropriately replete with weary lounging, ornament, preserved inutility, and a gratifying reproductive incapacity.[5] Pazzarella hosts lying upon her well-supported, feeble back. Next to her, Geronimo observes how autumn – decadent season *par excellence*, lavish precedent to winter demise – "impinged on every nerve in her sensitive body" (*SE* 80).

To claim Pazzarella as a decadent character is, to some degree, to travel a well-travelled path in Loy criticism. As Marissa Januzzi writes: "Modernism, in Loy's hands, is decadence with a studied difference" (415). Jessica Burstein quotes and counters Januzzi in this regard, arguing that "there is an aesthetic of continuity in Loy's workings". For Burstein, Loy drew on the artistic preoccupations of the previous century in her visual work, deploying those just-passed fashions as a means of resisting "the avant-garde account of the new" (155). To acknowledge and rework these arguments: the continuity Burstein identifies resists outright replication via Loy's use, in her early work, of *fin-de-siècle* aesthetics as satiric tools by which she takes issue with the Futurist fear of passivity and effeminacy, whilst acknowledging that Decadence is a major – if not *the* major – site of modernist innovation. In short, Pazzarella's all-encompassing lethargy runs counter to Loy's oft-cited epistolary claim that Marinetti's Futurism was, for her, a personal awakening, one echoed in her 1915 poem "Three Moments in Paris" (Kouidis, *Mina Loy* 8; *BM* 178). Underdiscussed is the subversive appeal of slumber in this poem, which opens upon "brother pugilist[s]" roaring all-too-manfully over the head of a drowsing, eternalised woman who wants her reflexes to hold sway, to be "animal woman" free of the insistent tussle of masculine "cerebral gymnastics" (*LoLB* 15). This provocative pairing of lethargy and aggression is thematically central to many of Loy's writings on the Futurists; by this binary, Loy intertwines the monomania of Futurist combat with the decadent enervation that was, by default, a major catalyst of Futurist energy.[6] Accordingly, while the feminised disregard for intellection is satirised in "Three Moments", the desire to return to somnolent, domestic peace is sincere. For, as discussed above, Loy maintains a yearning for blissful "arias of languor" into senescence (*LaLB* 237). Loy recognises Decadence as the generative ground from which modernism sprang.

Loy's acute understanding of Decadent mores is visible as early as her 1906 image *L'Amour dorloté par les belles dames*, or *Love Pampered by Beautiful Ladies*, in which a slender, naked male collapses supine into a circle of five impeccably dressed, beneficent Victorian women, one of whom catches him just before his assuredly elegant back hits the ground. By this artwork alone Loy demonstrates her knowledge that Decadents archly performed effeminate demise from the reliable vantage of a male privilege lacking only in heteronormative virility.[7] In turn, Futurism was pre-eminent among early twentieth-century avant-gardes that conflated femininity with a vociferously rejected Decadence (Nicholls 76).

Unquestionably misogynistic and homophobic, the Futurists signalled their loathing of Decadence by the pejorative use of "languor" and a thoroughgoing resistance to somnolence, a pattern to which Loy falls prey on one occasion.[8] With Futurism, Marinetti promises, "[t]here'll be no more [of] the languid actions of the prostitute as she moves her hands over the body of her worn-out client" ("Dynamic" 194). In Marinetti's "New Ethical Religion of Speed", city streets are "rivers of languid fire" passively awaiting heroically fast vehicles, while "Sunday crowds" exhibit "[i]mmoral languor" (254). Like Papini, Marinetti was one of many modernists who despised "the effeminacy of crowds" considered too suggestive and irrational ("Dynamic" 194).[9] In his anti-Decadent autobiographical work, *The Failure* (1913), Papini's greatest fear is a permanent affliction of "languorous indifference, on a dead level, in fog of grey, even, monotonous memories, with no lightning flashes of desire, no thunderbolts of action" (320). For Papini, to want "dull, bestial slumber" is to be "drowned in Nothingness", while to be bed-ridden is to experience "indescribable humiliation", "impotent rage", and "spasmodic purposeless strain" (282–3). Similarly equating rest with weakness, Marinetti propagates "a healthy insomnia", and begins his first Futurist manifesto as follows: "My friends and I had stayed up all night" ("Battles of Trieste" 164; "Foundation" 11). In *Mafarka the Futurist: An African Novel* (1910), Marinetti's eponymous protagonist designs his ideal son to be so strong of will that his muscles automatically strengthen at the first signs of exhaustion, thereby evading "'the sombre sickness of deep sleep!'" (187).

Mafarka's mother is Languorama, a moniker akin to Pazzarella in coupling a feminised exhaustibility with the third-person present "ama" of "amare", the Italian verb for "love". Marinetti appears as Mafarka in "Pazzarella", a story satirising the Futurist belief that men are "sleepless hero[es]", while passive women languish, complicit in their fated mental derangement (*Mafarka* 187).

Lacking staying power, Pazzarella is a believer: in hope, in God, in men, and most especially, in love: "'One must believe—love *IS*'" (*SE* 69). Confronted with her faith, Geronimo professes his allegiance to "reason" and his capacity to "entrenc[h him]self in his own lucidity" (*SE* 66). But violence undoes Geronimo's rationality. Linguistically, Geronimo's aggression is endemic: he shatters Pazzarella's silence with harm, considers her "prey", and envisions sucking life from her body, castrating her, or lacerating her with wounds (*SE* 67, 72, 75, 79, 76, 81). In response, Pazzarella implacably enjoys Geronimo's variousness and the pleasures of touching him; once, for her attentive pains, she is slapped across the face (*SE* 85, 92, 76). The viability of Pazzarella's consistently affectionate hapticity as return for Geronimo's mockery and enmity strains the reader's credulity to the breaking point. With "Pazzarella", Loy explores the limits of proximity as satiric method.

Geronimo's one-sided brutality sets this story apart from the contemporaneous *Brontolivido* and "The Sacred Prostitute", texts where sparring takes place between a male and female couple, but in which the female more readily holds her own against male assault. Despite the self-evident violence of "Pazzarella", the narrative gaze on the couple's interactions is so microscopic that the unethical intimacy at stake blurs all-too-feasibly into heteronormative expectations of gendered Western society. The intimacy between Pazzarella and Geronimo begins with rape, a startling truth made strategically mundane, everyday, discountable. In other words, Loy presents this assault realistically: as in most incidents of sexual violence, it takes place in domestic privacy, victimising a woman who has previously been in willing contact with the assailant. In "Pazzarella", Geronimo's rape is preceded by questions inert and inane:

> ... after apparently listening to all I had to say, [Pazzarella] suddenly exclaimed, "'But whatever *is* philosophy, and why do your eyes strike off such icy green sparks?'"
> Ah, then there was no withholding myself, and I did throw myself upon her. In a seductive delirium of destruction I determined to put an end to her. When I regained my calm, I found I had only possessed her.

> 'I am so fond of you,' she sighed.
> 'The worse for you.'
> 'My affection—'
> 'But are you mad?'
> 'I am a woman.' (67)

In *Discourses on Satire and Epic Poetry*, Dryden tells us that the poet John Donne mistakenly "perple[xes] the minds of the fair sex with nice speculations of philosophy, when he should engage their hearts and entertain them with the softnesses of love" (14). Incapable of gentle love, Geronimo, like Dryden, appears threatened by the philosophical ambitions of "the fair sex". But his assault does not decimate as planned. In return for his criminal act, Pazzarella tours Geronimo through "the pitiable emptiness" of her flat, a ritual he likens to the "Pascal Benediction" – a priest's blessing in honour of the sacrificed Christ – or "an exorcism", but most likely a "consecrat[ion]" of her abode "to a man who had just raped her" (*SE* 68). Equating her vacuity with that of her lodgings, Geronimo misses the import of Pazzarella's mournful gesture, her attempt to sacrifice herself still further to his cruel, exacting godliness. As is *La pazza*, Loy's madwoman is a martyr: violated, she offers Geronimo biscuits, calls him the perfect lover, and validates male "'possession'" of woman as "'the coronation of masculinity'" (*SE* 70). Loy directs our credulousness toward a woman who fully succumbs to misogynist rape mythologies: a woman who not only "asks for" assault but savours the bond it generates between herself and an aggressor whilst the violent event is subsumed by "the gewgaws" – the paltry trifles, playthings – of her marginalised and ever-diminishing lived experience (*SE* 79).

The permission given masculinity is total, the substance of Loy's fiction far from novel. These tired misogynistic mythologies underpin the fictions of some of Loy's clearest, closest lines of influence in this period of her life, among them Italian Decadent Gabriele D'Annunzio.[10] The first story of D'Annunzio's *The Book of the Virgins* (1884) focuses on a fragile, newly sexually aware young woman named Giuliana who is given to solitary, near-hysterical fits of laughter imbued with a sensualised languor.[11] The precise terms ascribed to her onanistic, lethargic pleasure are disturbingly repeated in Giuliana's recollection of a brutal rape she experiences at the hands of a man entrusted with shuttling letters between herself and a prospective lover:

> But at that moment, she thought, she had not resisted, not called out, not made any attempt to oppose him; she had succumbed, powerless,

not being able to make out anything any more, feeling nothing but a great joy mingled with pain flowing through her body, feeling nothing but the violence of repressed nature rebelling throughout her being. Then the reflection of that feeling disturbed her flesh anew with an infinite, languorous tenderness; and in her muddled consciousness she ceased to have any ideas of her own. (35)

Giuliana's sensibilities are deranged, her will weak. In her story, as in "Pazzarella", abuse is figured as satiation deserving a narrative berating. Pregnant due to the assault, Giuliana "found herself in a nightmare brought about by her sin", but the rapist garners no narrative reprisal (37). Giuliana procures an illegal abortion, then collapses in a pool of her own blood, "struck by a paroxysm of convulsions" grotesquely echoing her past laughter (49). As does Pazzarella's, Giuliana's trajectory degenerates: this concluding scene depicts Giuliana as hysterical madwoman, punished for her tentative, solitary forays into *jouissance*, susceptible to spasm, supinity, and self-decimation. If D'Annunzio critiques Catholic strictures by demoralising his young protagonist so absolutely, legible sympathy is absent from the story entire.

"We must fight against Gabriele D'Annunzio at all costs", Marinetti writes, anxiously aware of his own debt to his predecessor's "Nietzschean cult of action and energy", and thereby seeking fault in D'Annunzio's decadent nostalgia, romantic sentimentalism, "fatalistic ideal[isation] of Woman-Beauty", and hyperbolically transgressive eroticism (Nicholls 83; Marinetti "Renounce" 45). But for Loy, Marinetti's "florescent gallantry" gave the "sensation of irruption into a D'Annunzio novel" (*B* 2: 9). Certainly, Marinetti's own portrayals of gendered violence eschew novelty. For Pazzarella's validation of rape as affirmation of masculine sovereignty is surely an allusion to the infamous Futurist celebration of sexual assault as a laudable outcome of welcome war. In the "Futurist Manifesto of Lust" (1913), Valentine Saint-Point condones mass rape as "the conquerors' due", normalising it in "natural" masculine desire and regenerative need, tendencies she extends to "[t]he modern . . . hero in any field" and male artists in particular (71). A book-long homage to male violence, Marinetti's *Mafarka* begins in the aftermath of a battle. The spoils of war include 4,000 "negresses" confined to a foetid pit where they are systematically raped and killed by hundreds of soldiers. Looking on, Mafarka berates the rapists only because they have been promised these women's bodies in return for treason against him (27). This complicit condemnation follows the collapse of Marinetti's fast-paced narrative bombast into a slow, pleasured lingering over the women's sexual anatomy and supinity. Pages are devoted to "pitiful eyes contorted with pain, dread and lust", prolonged attention paid to a beautiful victim who begs for more violence from an assailant mislabelled "lover" (25). Marinetti makes victims willing participants in his apocalyptically racist, misogynistic fantasy, a charge readily extended to D'Annunzio's attribution of "infinite, languorous tenderness" to Giuliana's recollection of rape.

With "Pazzarella", Loy responds to a surfeit of Italian misogyny that culminates in the most direct influence upon her earliest satires on male violence: Papini's "The Massacre of Women" (1914), a satirical manifesto published in his journal *Lacerba* on April Fool's Day. As Matthew Hofer comprehensively demonstrates, "The Massacre of Women" was Papini's revenge for his 1914 schism from Loy, after which she embarked upon a two-month relationship with Marinetti. A reworking of Swift's "A Modest Proposal" (1729) that anticipates Valerie Solanas's *Scum Manifesto* (1967) and its infamous call to male gendercide, Papini's manifesto tests the truth of the Futurist's much-touted scorn for women by advocating global gynocide, an annihilation of both women and "the eternal feminine" ("Massacre" 255). Acknowledging that his proposition will distress men aged 15 to 55, Papini insists that women are generally useless, too sexually and amorously irresistible in a world where love means only pain. Therefore, men should take evolutionary precedence, and heteronormative sex should cease. "Literature has . . . construct[ed] a whole fairy-tale backdrop around a primitive physical need, one that is quite simple and pleasurable but should not have become the central post of life's merry-go-round", writes Papini ("Massacre" 253). Hofer reads "Literature" as a "thinly allegorised Loy" (236). In response, Loy writes the satirical anti-fairy-tale that is "Pazzarella", the sharpest and most precisely aimed tine of her many-pronged rebuttal to Papini's misogynist article; above the title of one "Pazzarella" manuscript, Loy writes: "Parody of Gio's Work" (*SE* 333). There is much to mock: Papini's *The Failure* describes women as parasites, vampires, and thieves; alongside "Massacre", this work no doubt contributes to the ire of Loy's "The Sacred Prostitute" as well as her "Feminist Manifesto" (159).[12] The publication of Papini's article is directly referenced in *Brontolivido*, where Loy has Marinetti publicly refute Papini via his own unwitting displays of misogyny, including a lampoon of his fellow Futurist as so sexually inexperienced – feminine, infantile – that he cannot be held accountable for his "*reductio ad absurdum* of the sex-question" (*B* 7: 7–8).

On the entrenched extent of male violence, Loy and the Futurists agree. But Loy desacralises Futurist aggression, exposing virile masculinity as Marinetti and Papini's worst nightmare: a *passéiste* convention, one Loy signals too loudly with the indigenous appellation she appropriates for Papini: Geronimo.[13] Given this ubiquitous truth, "Pazzarella" argues that women's affections towards men can only be sourced in unproven faith, or, more precisely, by inhabiting an irrational state of enchantment where disbelief is willingly, necessarily suspended. The irrational is key: to Geronimo's outraged questioning of her sanguine, post-rape proclamations of fondness, Pazzarella summarily equates lived femininity with a lunatic acceptance of male violence: "'I am a woman'" (*SE* 67). If all women teeter vertiginously on the edge of madness, women in love must be still more fatuous madwomen, *le pazze straordinarie*. By extension, Loy demonstrates that both love and the vanguard "Flabbergast" movement are reliant upon magical thinking, or "the belief that thoughts and desires can directly transfer themselves to, and transform, the material world, other people, the future" (Thurschwell 6). Shot through with decadent languor and somnolence, Loy's magical thinking incorporates an exposing, mesmeric intimacy, a backward-looking spiritualist anticipation, and a symbiotic telepathic exchange demanding suspended wilfulness and hypnotising gazes. Irrational and loving at its very core, Loy's magical thinking undoes Futurist rectitude whilst it normalises – makes integral, foundational – a madness too often, too narrowly, ascribed to women alone. Here, again, the esoteric dovetails with the vanguard, culminating in an articulation of Loy's esoteric Eros sourced, in this instance, in eighteenth- and nineteenth-century occult practice.

Enchantment, Supinity, and the Hypnotic Gaze: Mesmerism and Spiritualism

From antiquity, magic has challenged the rectitude of Western empiricism, philosophy, and Christianity. In turn, occult practice has been linked to mental imbalance and concomitant dorsal and nerval sensitivities: mesmerism was perceived as a stimulus to brain and spinal cord, telepathy a consequence of highly attuned ganglia. Posture and imposture were key to these processes: the mesmerist usually stood over a recumbent-cum-prone patient; psychic porousness – wilfully malleable, often unconscious – sparked admiring wonder and moral concern.[14] Well into the 1930s, Marinetti outwardly championed an intellectual rectitude that encompassed a universal and "enthusiastic glorification of scientific discoveries and machines" ("Futurist Year" 232).[15] Yet Marinetti was a descendent of French Symbolism, a movement that privileged interiority, intuition, and the inexpressible, and his earliest writings include Rosicrucian and kabbalist tendencies, an esotericism to which he returned in 1920, after breaking with Mussolini and becoming leader of Milan's Occultism Circle (D'Ambrosio 296, 303). While heterodoxy is discernible in Futurist writings until the 1930s, Marinetti was careful to cordon off his own occult interests as purely pragmatic, scientific (D'Ambrosio 314, 322). Nevertheless, as Matteo D'Ambrosio amply demonstrates, there are strong links between Futurism and the occult, many of which resonate with Loy's concerns, including the transmutation of occultist language to shore up Futurist "vitalism"; the strong presence of esoteric adherents in the Florentine Futurist chapter with which Loy was closely associated; and Marinetti's discernibly heterodox fascination, post-1920, with discovering new senses, an interest with clear overlaps between Theosophy and Loy's determination to conflate the spiritual and the corporeal, both discussed further in the next chapter (D'Ambrosio 297, 298, 303). While Futurist occultism is often noted, rarely "thoroughly examined", it is clear that early twentieth-century Italy, in contemporaneous league with its European neighbours, "permitted the esoteric", and that the Futurists – both sceptically and curiously – read occult literature and engaged in séances, as well as being influenced by Eastern religious traditions and parapsychology (Celant 36–7).

Feigning fidelity to Futurist self-promotion as "earnest experimenter[s]", Loy's Futurist satires expose and hyperbolise their links to past, popular esoteric methods (B 6: 7). In so doing, Loy plays on the truth that the schism between enchantment and knowledge has never been absolute: before the nineteenth century, science was known as natural or plain magic, nature and the subject were said to be animated, and occultism extended itself into human anatomy via magnetic and electrical flows perceived as constitutive of the nerves, connecting body and will, or galvanising consciousness (During 49, 21). From the late eighteenth century, practices such as mesmerism and, later, spiritualism, sought to externalise this enchanted soma, to make it visible to audiences eager for proof of symbiosis between the occult and the rational. That Loy directly associates these discourses with Futurism is consistent with her non-exoteric and vanguard inclinations alike: as Simon During attests, after the Enlightenment, only small esoteric communities – selective, ideologically aligned groups – took seriously the conveyance of love, attraction, sympathies, and antipathies through an enchanted universe (283). But where Loy locates self-transcendence in an esoteric Eros, for Marinetti of the 1910s, the period when Loy was closest to him, the "psyche" is most ideally "transported" by the fruits of scientific discovery: "a day's train journey", global media, or an opera singer's recorded voice ("Destruction of Syntax" 120–1). Loy's writings uncover the mysteriousness behind Marinetti's propaganda on behalf of the mechanical. In the process, Loy drew upon a public conflation of sorcerer and Futurist, as is clarified by an article published in 1920 by Marinetti devotee Eva Amendola (later Kühn), a writer who went by the pen name "Magamal", or the name Marinetti gives the tragic brother of the eponymous hero of his novel *Mafarka* (D'Ambrosio 305–8). In "Futurist Occultism", Amendola insists that the Futurist man is a transformational, "*electric, extended being*", a genius whose health-giving powers are born of his symbiosis with technology, rather than the occult, as anyone other than the most base *passéiste* can clearly ascertain (321–2). The vehemence of Amendola's protest speaks to the prevalence of the very associations she seeks to discourage, associations central to Loy's artistry and her satirical methods.

Enchantment facilitates Loy's deconstruction of binaries, be they female and male or irrational and rational: "most of what gets classified as contemporary esotericism or occultism came into being as an attempt to repair the rupture between religion and science" (Storm 15). Loy's satire assaults opposites only to clarify their proximity, their interdependence. And her confidence in the esoteric is consistent with the frequently made charge that, in these domains, women have been predominant adepts, mediums, and leaders (Ellis, *Man* 388). In modern, patriarchal Europe, woman's supposed porousness, her capacity to receive divine ecstasy and inspiration, made her both enchantable and prophetic, a subject suspect and ideal. Mediumistic Pazzarella is thus accurately presented as vacillating between passive stupor and assertive control over her own soul, begging the alarmed Geronimo at one juncture to test her briefly confident self with his usual insults. In response, he charges her with manipulation, a facility by which "'women can so easily penetrate the souls of others'" (*SE* 71–2). Flavoured with a dash of misogynist cliché, malleable languor becomes threatening clairvoyance. But Geronimo's presumption rests on historical precedent. As Havelock Ellis writes: "The phenomena of mesmerism, animal magnetism, etc., now usually grouped under the head of hypnotism, have always been specially identified with women" (*Man* 355).[16] Hypnosis was equated with occult quackery, and prominent *fin-de-siècle* physicians considered "any entranced condition ... a pathological abnormality" (Oppenheim, *"Shattered"* 301). Feminine, weak, passive, somnolent, diseased: to be hypnotic is to be diametrically opposed to predominating Futurist values.

These gendered stereotypes strengthen Loy's assault on the Futurist-cum-enchanter, a lampoon that comes to fruition in "Pazzarella" but begins with *Brontolivido*. In what follows, I offer a very close reading of phrases in both texts that are charged with occultism, showing how Loy portrays Marinetti and Papini as ambitious if misguided mesmerisers, hypnotists who wield charisma, authority, and a forceful gaze with a view to controlling, rather than healing or understanding, their followers, be they fans or lovers. Both fail: Marinetti because celebrity and virility matter more to him than any truth gnomic, aesthetic, or ideological; Papini because, by sacrificing his lover to his needs, he figuratively devours her wholesale, thereby finding that he has involuntarily incorporated and become the malleable, passive feminine he so despises. In close reading and contextualising the relationship between vanguard proselytising and occult practice in Loy's early works, I seek to overturn and nuance the assumption that *Insel* is Loy's first and predominantly "negative depiction" of these realms; throughout Loy's oeuvre, a well-deployed, conscientious esotericism is the very ground of meaningful avant-garde practice (Armstrong 214).

Within the incomplete text that is *Brontolivido*, Loy plays upon an occult dichotomy by which mysticism is perceived as a self-surrender that potentially unites – passionately, lovingly – human will and cosmos, whilst magic aggressively, scientifically pursues the authoritative forging of will with intellect. Where the mystical is the methodology at work in Loy's feminist, esoteric Eros, magical mastery "shored up the masculinist personae of late-Victorian men who sought spiritual enlightenment", and only appealed to women hungry for a power gendered male (Owen, *Place* 88–9). Pazzarella's precursor, "'busy little mystic'" Jemima, embodies the combined weakness and wilfulness attributed to the occult-oriented female (*B* 8: 6). Where Pazzarella believes heterogeneously, ecumenically, and against the odds, Jemima actively reaches for an object for her faith. "All I want in the world is to Believe in something", says Jemima to Brontolivido, adding: "The thing I want – escapes me – it's probably I'm willing to concede – an attenuated reflex of the facts you fisc – just as likely again – it transcends them" (*B* 5: 2, 4).

Brontolivido promulgates facts as a state manages its expenditure. Describing herself as a reflex respondent to his authority, Jemima also implies that her inclinations outpace Brontolivido's own. And when Brontolivido assures Jemima that she need have faith in nothing but him, her reply again confirms and derails woman's presumed susceptibility: "Woman is omniplastic – she can mould herself to the vision of any man stronger than herself – She is merely potential prior to her impact with man – it would be for her an economy of time could she invoke the oracle" (*B* 5: 2). Woman is omniarch, ruler of her own malleability, an assertion giving traction to her latent prowess, staying power to her prophetic access. By turns submissive and powerful, Jemima repeatedly accedes to, then transgressively supersedes, male expectation.

Aligned with priest, god, prophet, or mystic, Loy's Brontolivido is a plausible candidate for Jemima's efficient oracle. But however spiritualised, his vision remains notably terrestrial, even abjectly grasping: a "martyr to reputation", Brontolivido is Jemima's "Apostle of the Common-place", parading "gesticulant imperatives" from which "the worn-out air receded" (*B* 4: 4, 6). For Jemima, he is slightly more convincing as magician than priest: "'I <u>conjure</u> you'", Brontolivido tells her pliant self, ironically calling upon atavistic magic even as he directs her to always look futuristically forward, never back, for fear of being left behind (*B* 4: 4, 7). "[I]n his hands" Jemima "felt like the conjuror's hat – from which he produced with his instinctive perspicacity – all kinds of attractions, which she had mislaid in her introspection" (*B* 8: 4). Omniplastic woman again precedes the visionary male: the magically animated prop foresees the conjuror's powers of enchantment, object overtaking subject. Jemima's enchantment proves contagious: in the final archived file of *Brontolivido*, its titular protagonist admits that, when he met Jemima, his thinking about women was simplistic, but insists that he now longs to change through "magical strategic – of determined re-self assurance" (*B* 9: 4–6). Primitive, irrational magic possesses declarative power, reconstituting or *re*-selfing even those resolutely attached to forward momentum. But this magic requires skill, possibly genius, and faith: "in his secondary phases – uninspired" Brontolivido "was just an ignoble plagiarist – of this magical self in him" (*B* 9: 20). Tasking Brontolivido the Futurist with irrational magical aspirations, Loy shames him a second time by characterising him as a failed enchanter.

That Loy perceives Brontolivido as unwittingly defined by the pull of past practices is written into his names as well as his methods.

A collage of Italian terms for dinosaur, moaner, and stormy enragement, "Brontolivido" casts Marinetti as an outdated grumbler; by Loy's alternate moniker, "The Martinet", he is a traditional, merciless disciplinarian.[17] These backward associations are reinforced by avowals of his allure, the "appallingly ~~perfect~~ dynamic" "misogynistic magnetism" by which rooms "vibrat[e] with his emanations", a synaesthesis undoing Brontolivido's performance of "Bombastic superman" holding himself aloft from the herd (*B* 8: 2). For, underneath his armour of Nietzschean will, Brontolivido recognises "his cosmic significance as the exponent of the '~~Life~~ Magnetic Force – & wanted to translate it transiently for the comprehension of anyone he had to get in touch with" (*B* 9: 18). Brontolivido's intimacy with his audiences – personal or public – is one-sidedly mesmeric, a "magical gift" that is an unquestionable draw to Woman, who Jemima posits as "a magnet of both positive and negative poles" (*B* 8: 4; 2: 53).

Mesmerism springs from the same eighteenth-century soil as galvanism: both scientific theories sought to reanimate somnolent beings or dormant aspects of the human mind through "a continuous current [or] unifying force of biological life" labelled "electromagnetism" (Faivre 27). An esoteric adept, originator Franz Mesmer (1734–1815) claimed that animate beings and the cosmos were connected by a universal fluid. Surfacing as illness, particularly "disorders of the nerves", imbalances in this ideally reciprocal relationship could be restored through mesmerisation, a practice Mesmer considered "'the application of nature's own agent of harmony, animal magnetism'" (Crabtree 18–19). In "Incident" (c. 1930s), Loy combines galvanism and mesmerism, describing "Life" as a "magnet to a sort of universal electricity" (*SE* 39); come "History of Religion and Eros", she continues defining "Life as a Deific Electricity … conveying to us our animation, our intelligence, our intuition" (*SE* 240). Loy's electricity aspires toward proximity with the celestial; similarly central, Marinetti's electricity serves godlike humanity. Marinetti aims for a future in which electric currents meet all basic needs, thereby freeing humanity to embrace "the fullness and stolid resistance of their wills" ("Electric War" 221–2). Placing equal value on his "intellectual influence" and "the power of [his] animal magnetism", Marinetti's use of the latter phrase is not Mesmer's ("Against Marriage" 310). Instead, it refers to an exclusively male sexual charisma over which Marinetti exercises a control notably absent from the ladyfolk with whom he comes into regular, amorous contact, women deemed "hysterical" by Brontolivido and Jemima alike (*B* 5: 9–10).[18] Against an electromagnetism fuelling masculine desire and individualism, Loy insists upon Marinetti as a mesmeriser beholden to a universal, symbiotic intimacy with the cosmos.

The mesmeric heyday began nearly a century before Loy wrote *Brontolivido*. Concurrent with the steady professionalisation of medicine and science, mesmerism was popularised in mainland Europe and England in the 1830s, and proliferated into the decades that followed, becoming a much-debated practice undertaken in theatres, lecture halls, treatment centres devoted to its workings, and private residences (Winter 6, 41, 131, 112, 155–6). Sessions involved a mesmeriser leading their subject into a suspension of their will for up to an hour at a time. Upon entering this waking somnambulism, the subject became unguarded about exposing what would be called the subconscious self: open to directives; capable of channelling alternate personalities or the sensory experiences of the mesmerist; insensible to pain, but also, for those actively seeking healing, responsive to magnetic cure (Winter 31, 68, 77, 88). Mesmerism involved contact, either directly in the skull-reading known as "phreno-mesmerism", or indirectly: via a significant object sent through the post; the gaze shared by mesmerist, patient, and audience; or the "curative passes" of the mesmerist's hands held suggestively just above the patient's body (Owen, *Darkened* 124, 109). Mesmerised, women were believed particularly vulnerable to sexual assault, yet were also charged with seduction, play-acting, and worryingly powerful oracular qualities; mesmerising, women were presumed predatory (Winter 93, 101). Never scientifically proven, mesmerism was a crucial antecedent to spiritualism and psychoanalysis due to its advocacy of healing trance, its call to expose the inner life of the mind, and its pursuit of what exceeds conscious understanding (Owen, *Darkened* 109–10). As late as the 1880s, the Society for Psychical Research housed an active Committee on Mesmerism alert to the possibility "that mesmeric rapport 'may be represented as only a special extension of [. . .] 'telepathic' sympathy between two organisms'" (qtd. in Luckhurst 103, 72).

As in *Brontolivido*, and in accord with contemporaneous gender politics, the organisms in question were most often a male mesmeriser and a female patient. Women were believed especially susceptible to "'hypnotic' phenomena" due to their "more primitive nervous centres" and their exceptionally responsive, all-consuming bodies (Ellis, *Man* 400). Loy reaffirms this hierarchical dynamic in "Pazzarella", where Geronimo asserts himself as a manipulator of Pazzarella's vitality and will, "spread[ing] about us a receptive somnolence closed in upon her breath" (*SE* 81). As were many mesmerists, Geronimo can be exhausted after a session grappling with the magnetic pull of his patient, describing departures from Pazzarella as a much-needed opportunity to "breathe in freedom again" (*SE* 70). Recognising "definite points of contact between myself and this disquieting person", Geronimo understands that his supremacy over Pazzarella relies on proximity: on one occasion, he feels "desperate, fearing that at a few yards' distance [he] lost some of [his] power over her" (*SE* 66–7, 94). By the story's end, Geronimo's prowess seems assured: Pazzarella "quiet[ed] under [his] touch, sank into a state of coma, leaving [him] at liberty to investigate" (*SE* 95). "[K]eeping company" with her totalising unconsciousness, Geronimo contemplates her scientifically, holding her spirit "like an object in [his] hands" and locating himself within its "vortex of mist" (*SE* 95).

From this sublime vantage, Geronimo, like Brontolivido before him, promotes himself from mesmerist to ancient god or oracle capable of creating womankind, of providing Pazzarella's defining "axis ... to revolve on" (*B* 5: 18). But as in mesmeric practice, Geronimo's mastery is continually challenged by his patient's unpredictable truths, experiences, and behaviours: ultimately, good mesmerisers must be receptive mediums. We witness this reciprocity in Geronimo's promise to provide Pazzarella with a transcendent ecstasy, a promise in which Loy plays upon established social fears about the sexual vulnerability of the hypnotised. Proper Futurist, proper Nietzschean, Geronimo tells Pazzarella that after he "'animat[es]'" her with a lusty, prophetic gaze that reveals "'[her] salvation'", he will promptly forget their "celestial innocence of mutual possession", while for her, this memory will prove all-consuming (*SE* 84–5). Striving to contain his permeability, Geronimo's analogy unwittingly cedes experiential control to Pazzarella, who, now hypnotist, retains sole recollective autonomy over their shared history. Similar inversions of masculinised mesmeriser and feminised recipient recur throughout "Pazzarella", emerging most legibly in demarcations of the couple's shared gaze.

Mesmeric sessions usually began with an extended visual exchange between practitioner and patient, and Loy foregrounds a like ocularity in *Brontolivido* and "Pazzarella". While Brontolivido is an excellent public mesmeriser, an intimate, symbiotic gaze is not his forte; instead, the misdirected or misinterpreted visual exchange is a continual site of contention between him and Jemima.[19] This very contentiousness sets the stage for the mesmeric visuality of "Pazzarella": it is in *Brontolivido* that Loy's female protagonist first finds herself drawn to Johannes/Papini/Geronimo precisely because of his penetrable gaze, a prospect catalysing her withdrawal from the blindsiding Brontolivido. Of her first contact with Johannes near a Florentine olive grove, Jemima recalls: "He had descended the hill as if his eyes still stared from its summit at something recessive . . . . It was in some way . . . as if she had passed her own self" (*B* 3: 17). Johannes's visual trajectory encompasses great heights and the regressive, occluded, or yielding; in it, Jemima sees a like perspective, a like vision. Initially, "Pazzarella" is less mutualising. Instead, Geronimo and Pazzarella wrestle, in gendered ways, for visual recognition from the other: Pazzarella's eyes seek out clairvoyance and the unknown, which Geronimo derides as an impenetrable bewilderment, preferring her eyes submerged, darkened, or lifeless (*SE* 66, 69).[20]

In turn, Geronimo's affection reinvigorates Pazzarella's gaze. Observing without recognising pattern, Geronimo tells us that the mere "sentimental inflection" of his voice elicits "[t]he drama of a whole life . . . in [Pazzarella's] eyes" from birth to death to "purification"; offering her a photograph of himself as a child – a rare Futurist nod to pastness – he observes her "receptive eyes" (*SE* 72, 80). Against Geronimo's visual gauges of her pleasure, Pazzarella is desperate to puncture Geronimo's oracular mastery, labouring too long, too futilely, to have him see her perspective. Determined to have Geronimo follow her visual lead, Pazzarella places an open book beneath her eyes in order that her bibliophile paramour might offer her a proxy "'look of adoration'" (*SE* 90). To her plea, in their eighth and final encounter, that they embark upon making "'the supreme discovery together'", a journey that will begin with Geronimo having a "'[l]ook in [her] eyes'" and "feel[ing] the beat of [her] heart", Geronimo comments only that her heart "*was* irregular" whilst averting Pazzarella's scrutiny (*SE* 90). Geronimo's most sympathetic gaze is reserved for "the primitive monkey" printed on Pazzarella's bedspread, or he who looks at Geronimo in a "brotherly fashion" affirming Geronimo's regressively survivalist tendencies, his inability to access open, frank human intimacy (*SE* 93).

As unwitting medium, Geronimo is propelled into oracular acquiescence. Against Pazzarella's charges of his short-sightedness, Geronimo keeps his eyes "fixed on her hypnotically", intoning: "I can extend the scope of your sensibility until it comprises a universe, and this universe being myself, can disappear from one moment to another" (*SE* 83–4, 87). Insisting on his mastery over Pazzarella, Geronimo fails to notice that a desirable equilibrium is achieved in their shared gaze, which mesmerically supersedes the need for coherent speech, as in their fourth visit, when he proves able to "sustain a tacit expectancy of immanent collaboration between us—expression of eyes and inflection of voice stressing the *entente* of accomplices", an *entente* that repeats itself in their fifth confrontation, a wordless pause in the street where he and Pazzarella "sto[p] for a while to observe each other reciprocally" (*SE* 80–1). Blind to her beneficent visual supplications, deaf to her pleas for recognition, in visit four Geronimo is climactically confronted with Pazzarella's powers as she lies on her "inarticulate deathbed". Restlessly looking in the mirror, he finds his gaze unrecognisable, his eyes those "of a stranger":

> Wondering what had happened to them, I peered into their brightness for some time. At first I could make out nothing, but gradually I became aware of a putrefying mass, a turbid residuum lying at the bottom of their wells. Luminous sepulchres of vanquished emotions, of petrified humanity, such had been my eyes. But now, beneath their inflexible logic, the effrontery of their wile, lay the decaying remains of an embryonic spirit, an almost imperceptible reflection of Pazzarella's dying. Had this wretched creature contaminated my very soul, insinuated her tenacious interrogation to the very stronghold of my wisdom? (*SE* 91)

"It was in some way [...] as if she had passed her own self", Jemima asserts after taking stock of Johannes's gaze in *Brontolivido*; in "Pazzarella", Geronimo's visual return to self is derailed by a macabre, even decadent, epiphany of his spurned lover. The muddiness at the base of Geronimo's eye-wells recalls what he sees when he claims to hold Pazzarella's spirit "like an object in [his] hands": "a flux of nebulous matter" (*SE* 95–6). Averting Pazzarella's gaze has not shored up his ruinous mesmeric powers: instead, Geronimo has become Pazzarella's medium, a spiritualist channelling the essence of her haunting soul as her body is on the brink of expiration. Through an oracular mutuality by which Geronimo feels violated, Loy implicitly, expertly questions the male scopic regime and its systematic objectification of women.

Each encounter in "Pazzarella" gauges the degree to which the eponymous protagonist succumbs to a protracted living death at the hands of a patriarchal society in which she cannot locate ease or purpose, voice or vision. Channelling the story of an increasingly spectral woman, the narrator becomes *de facto* spiritualist by necessity, a role particularly fitting in Geronimo's case, given that spiritualism descended from and is explained by "a mesmeric framework of quantifiable fluids and forces" (Owen, *Darkened* 20, 25). Attaining European popularity in the latter half of the nineteenth century, spiritualism involved entering trance to access the otherworldly: visions, the voices of the deceased, and, if sufficiently powerful, spirit materialisation (Owen, *Darkened* 39, 5, 42). Extending the feminised roles of healer or Angel in the House, spiritualists were most often women prepared to undertake the self-renunciation requisite to channelling other beings: "A medium gave herself, sacrificed her 'self', to another" (Owen, *Darkened* 112, 7, 10, 233). Like sacrifice, mediumship was performative ritual: séances, often held within the home, were ceremonies over which women most often presided, directing the proceedings and assertively centralising themselves within the scopic economy (Owen, *Darkened* 227).

In "Pazzarella", Geronimo takes up spiritualist characteristics: he describes lovemaking as a parental, soothing "rocking" (*SE* 81); by the story's end, we will understand that he is the immolated punchline of its extended joke. More crucially, Geronimo likens Pazzarella's embodied somnolence to etherealities hagiographic or diabolical: she is saint, virgin mother, and "female Buddha", but also accursed serpentine temptress and outcast scapegoat, nightmarish incubus and vampire (*SE* 95, 78).[21] Be she good or bad spirit, Pazzarella haunts Geronimo, a truth adding import to the decadent "fading colours and clouded mirrors" of her "boudoir", a room distinctly echoing Baudelaire's better-known "dusty boudoir" of "pale pastels" and "withered roses" (*SE* 65; *Flowers* 147). Both Baudelaire and Loy channel speakers who, eternalised by passive indolence, approximate infinite death in finite life; "Nothing is longer than the limping days", writes Baudelaire in "Spleen (II)", attributing to ennui a "dulling lassitude" that "[t]akes on the size of immortality" (*Flowers* 147). A ghostly throwback to a prior era, decadent Pazzarella attains a degenerating climax that forces her narrator to evolve in accord with nineteenth-century occult history, moving through mesmerism to spiritualism. As it reaches its conclusion, "Pazzarella" is increasingly akin to a séance for the not-yet-dead rather aptly presided over by an anticipatory Futurist said to venerate "system[s] of postponement" (*SE* 75).

Both protagonists desire Pazzarella's imminent demise: from their first meeting, Geronimo longs to "silence her, for once and for all", and in typically placatory turn, Pazzarella is at pains to reassure him that her death is imminent (*SE* 66, 81). But Pazzarella's eagerly awaited deathbed scene lacks finality: instead, it awkwardly, protractedly conjoins vomited soul and agonised splutter, faltered step and coma, before culminating in avian resurrection. Pazzarella neither dies nor recovers. For Baudelaire, convalescence is a state of genius weak and strong, innocent and knowing, feminised and masculine: "a return towards childhood" by which the sick individual is dazzled anew by the world whilst retaining an adult's "sound nerves", analytic strength, and "will" ("Painter" 7–8). The narrative of "Pazzarella" moves toward just such a revelatory conclusion, one marked by a distinctly Loy-like feminist turn.

For, whilst looking backward to a paternalistic decadent lineage, "Pazzarella" also attends to Loy's early understanding that extreme passivity – extending to incapacitation – is highly desirable in Victorian children and women. "Every child of that era was aware of what it meant 'to go into a decline' for they could not learn too early of the consequence of wet feet or sitting in a draught", Loy recalls, adding: "In a literature of smug fatalism, the 'nicest' children cross flickering finger on a hollow torso draped in calico; and even longer girls lie out at full length on the first disappointment in love" (*IA* 65: 67–8). Reverence is extended to children ascetically emaciated by illness or malnourishment who seek God's blessing, enacting the sign of the cross over prone bodies with weak fingers; infantilised, grown women likewise prostrate themselves to romance. Envying "recumbent", "waning" women "about to fly to heaven", Loy and her sister set off in "quest of tuberculosis", dousing themselves in water that they believe is "brimming with consumption", courting Thanatos as "a practical joke on [their] elders" (*IA* 65: 68). The "joke" is active resistance: if Victorians believe, following Poe, that the death of a beautiful woman is purest poetry, Loy takes this premise to logical extremes. This childhood satire of Victorian aggressions – rigidity, censoriousness, misogyny – is self-prophesising. With it, Loy retroactively anticipates Pazzarella's languorous breathlessness, and Geronimo's pleased recollection of her "lain at [his] flank, weak for the want of 'life'" (*SE* 96).

Feminist passivity dovetails effectively with Loy's esotericism, her lifelong fascination with meditation, her affirmations of a subliminality accessed via genius or sleep, and, as I will soon discuss, the visionary. Harshly punished for a childhood accident, Loy enters into a meditative state to transcend the "subjugation of the body" imposed upon her, a skill compounded by her latent command of "concentration"; in *Brontolivido*, Loy describes "[o]ne of her happiest games" as "shutting her senses off habitude – & getting into unexplored universes" (*CP* 12: 23; *B* 2: 18). With these skills and cosmic aspirations in view, Loy's late, unpublished esoteric writings advocate on behalf of "the supine event". Countering "the perpendicular event", proneness allows the universal life force to circulate more freely through the body. In the process, we renounce "our cooperation with active time" and can access "fourth-dimensional consciousness" (*SE* 270). Loy writes of a drive to a transcendent meditation in the same period that she encounters Christian Science renegade Goldsmith, whose teachings, emblematised by *The Infinite Way* (1947), were grounded in meditation as a means of reaching self-understanding and God. Goldsmith's method is passive and authoritative: observing that the only thing in the world over which we have agency is our own consciousness, he expressly conflates esoteric meditation and Christian prayer, assuring his followers that by ruminating over God's unknowable existence regularly throughout the day, their "finite sense" will disappear, and in its stead will emerge a "vision without boundaries" (119). The first stage in his methodology? To sit still, "spine straight". From this quiescent position, one can learn how to access an infinite "Truth" (35). "Supine event[s]", then, can progress into the beyond, exceeding ready comprehension or expectation (*SE* 270). Consequently, although she is consigned to recumbence by the resolutely perpendicular Geronimo at the end of Loy's narrative, Pazzarella should not be underestimated.

Pazzarella's illness gestures to Baudelaire's era-defining precepts, then parodies Oscar Wilde's edict that women are sphinxes without secrets: it is Pazzarella's narrative refrain to assert that women are in possession of a "secret truth" that she appears ready to impart, à la Baudelaire, from her sickbed (*SE* 91).[22] This secret, as discussed in the third chapter of *Nethered Regions*, is that female sexual pleasure is unduly gnomic knowledge, meaning it is known only to an elite inner circle of "the satisfied" (*CP* 18: 67). But Pazzarella gains no opportunity to proselytise on behalf of women's orgasmic delights: she is stopped by Geronimo's forceful push back into the mattress, silenced as he blithely asserts that the solution to woman's riddle resides within him (*SE* 96). In so claiming, Geronimo approximates the sphinx, one of an array of feminised monstrous figures – chimeras and sirens among them – who appear in Decadent scenes of convalescence, their half-human, half-animal status echoing the liminalities of individuals neither dying nor healthy (*SE* 96).[23]

This liminality actively deconstructs: as Barbara Spackman asserts, in Decadent literature the feminine is exempted from portrayals of male convalescence, only to be reincorporated in a later "secular conversion", thereby facilitating the celebrated androgyny of genius (ix). Thus Nietzsche, who affirmed and denied his Decadent allegiances, evades fixed thinking by taking up the shifting terrain of convalescence via metaphors of generative "illnesses" such as pregnancy and birth (Spackman 93).[24] So too do supposedly anti-Decadent Futurists envision parthenogenesis as the apex of their ferociously masculinist vision. In "Pazzarella", Geronimo curtails Pazzarella's insight into women's truth, yet incarnates the very femaleness he represses and oppresses.[25] Poised to embark on a revelatory disquisition upon the womankind dubbed "omniplastic" in *Brontolivido*, Geronimo negates its totalising prowess. By his framing, woman is merely "raw material ... so plastic in its untouched condition, that it offered untold possibilities of formation" (*SE* 96–7). Androgenised genius, mesmerist-cum-spiritualist-cum-visionary, Geronimo is now discernibly impassioned, his rectitude palpably on the incline. But Geronimo's enthusiasm remains as aposiopetic as Pazzarella's truth: he is cut off mid enunciative flow by parallel dashed lines running horizontally across the page that enclose the terse, metanarrative assertion: "Manuscript long ago lost" (*SE* 97). Loy's assault on Giovanni Papini's Futurist misogyny – both published and personal – is not quite complete.[26]

Telepathy, Voices, and Visions

Like Lily Briscoe of Woolf's *To the Lighthouse* (1927), Geronimo has "had [a] vision" recognised in full by its recipient and a narrator alone (281).[27] Loy expressly constructs "Pazzarella" to avoid this gnomic fate. Through her pursuit of the curative powers of Roberto Assagioli's psychosynthesis, examined in the previous chapter, Loy was learning how to cultivate visions by way of generating a self-realised future as "Pazzarella" was being written (*BM* 147). For Assagioli, harmonious, generative periods of "renewed inflow of superconscious energies" in the life of any individual should be continuously kept "present before the inner eye" as a visionary goal (53). A like goal emerges at the end of Loy's story. To Geronimo's firm but false "The End." is appended a "Note sent with M. S. S." written by a newly intrusive female narrator who insists upon having the final say. This epistolary postscript indicates that "Pazzarella" is not solely Geronimo's creation, but rather an "opus" long threatened as a "vindication of feminine psychology" (*SE* 97). Marinetti and his Futurist friends stay up all night writing their first manifesto; so too does Loy's letter-writer claim to have written her treatise from dusk until dawn, adopting Futurist aggressive polemics and somnolent refusals alike (Marinetti, "Foundation" 11). Neither addressee nor sender is identified: the salutation is "Sympathetic Enemy", the incomplete valediction merely "Your affectionate" (*SE* 97). Pazzarella to Geronimo? Loy to Papini? Perhaps. But in their glaring absence, the names universalise: the letter could be written to any or every man by any or every woman.

As importantly, conclusionary note and parodic story begin with ferocity and conclude with open-ended intimacy, replicating Loy's satiric methodology in fine. Porous, mediumistic, yet in strategically commandeered control, this epistolary narrator asserts her telepathic access to Geronimo's thoughts whilst recovering disparaged, shunned womankind as innate psychologist *par excellence*: "Whether it is that truth is more powerful than determination, or fantasy less fantastic than truth, or that woman, being incapable of thinking, reads the thoughts of others. However that may be, this is how it turned out" (*SE* 97). Is this Frederic Myers's definition of love as "exalted" if "unspecified telepathy"? (277). An incomplete sentence points to an unstated narrative truth, one that overturns a taxonomy of discernibly masculinist fictions regarding limitations or drive, illusory or ingenious appearances, and women's malleable cognition. "Pazzarella" now requires rereading through a multiplied narrative gaze. What is more, through the sharp focus of its conclusionary lens, the reader is informed that "Pazzarella" relays a complete authorial vision: conscious, expectant, and palpably feminist. Artists have always perceived themselves as prophetic, attests Leon Surette, noting how that tendency is shared with the esotericist, the only difference being that the latter is still more assured of their judgement and vision (281). Self-avowedly, Loy's narrator is both.

Mysticism has been defined as "'the negation of the veracity of communicative language, and the belief in a non-communicative truth lying in a symbolical fashion deep within revealed divine language'" (Joseph Dan qtd. in Hanegraaff 124). Within these mystic pursuits, "'visions and voices [are] forms of symbolic expression, ways in which the subconscious activity of the spiritual self reach the surface-mind'" (qtd. in Surette 82). This passage from Evelyn Underhill's *Mysticism: A Study in the Nature and Development of Man's Spiritual Consciousness* (1911) was marked in the copy owned by T. S. Eliot (Surette 82). Externally imposed upon the willing, perceptive individual, visions begin life as trans-verbal communications. Once experienced, the vision requires interpretation and articulation, moves from affective, internalised epiphany to artistic or linguistic representation. In short, a successful visionary possesses the foresight, creativity, and command that Geronimo continually overrides in Pazzarella, most notably through his subsumption of her voice. "'Listen—'", Pazzarella implores Geronimo as she descends into lifelessness; in resistant response, he hears her "word cr[eeping] round the room like a dumb crowd" (*SE* 90). For Geronimo, the passage from Pazzarella's cognition to enunciation is a prone, volitionless journey by weak stealth, a base navigation of the "eternal non-impartation" of her miring in the "incommunicable" (*SE* 90).

Pazzarella's inarticulacy can be linked to neurosis: feminised hysterics were regularly diagnosed with somatic and verbal incoherence that undermined their authority, yet also gave narrative shape and sound to their occluded experience (Logan 3).[28] For these reasons, hysteria has been interpreted as a "female language ... oppose[d] to rigid structures of discourse and thought" and an "ineffectual response to the frustrations of women's lives" – enforced "powerlessness and silence" in particular (Showalter 160–1). The conclusion of "Pazzarella" arguably conforms to both points of view: a cohering female voice garrulously surfaces after Geronimo's definitive announcement of an end point, even as Pazzarella succumbs to a well-known symptom of vocal hysteria, the making of animal sounds (Ellis, *Man* 412). As Geronimo tells us: Pazzarella's "exhausted voice transform[s] for the future to the trill of a bird", a metamorphosis confirming Pazzarella's underdiscussed trauma by aligning her with Philomela of Greek myth, a rape survivor who may well be among the first Western "hysterics" (*SE* 97). By this same allusion, Geronimo is condemned as the rapist we know he is, and feminised again: "woman speaks as the bird sings, she alone is capable of teaching the language", writes Symbolist, Decadent author Rémy de Gourmont, and with this quotation in view, it is notable that Geronimo finds himself incomparably attuned to Pazzarella's "twittering" ("Women" 120; *SE* 97).[29] Pliant, confused, Pazzarella's trilling body speaks its objectification, a truth adding import to her barbed retort to Geronimo's accusation that her passivity is odious: "'It is to this your intellect condemns me'" (*SE* 83). As Geronimo's vision, Pazzarella is accursed to acquiescence.

Yet this very complaisance primes Pazzarella's visionary and telepathic capacities. Suspiciously unbiddable, visions require a "passive cerebration" at odds with "the idealization of the active thinking ego or 'I'" (Obeyeskere 9). Throughout modernity, like receptive mental passivities have been recovered by thinkers of the Global North, from the "mystical consciousness" discussed by American psychologist William James to the perception of God via "'the eye of the passive intellect'" espoused by the sixteenth-century Spanish mystic St John of the Cross (Obeyeskere 7; qtd. in James 41). Contemporaneous clues suggest that it may well be a "too preciously bound" tome from this "Saint John" that Pazzarella reads on her deathbed, as the precise terminology of his *Precautions* recurs in Loy's companion text, "The Sacred Prostitute" (*SE* 90).[30] But it is Sigmund Freud, arguably the most famous theorist of the malleable human mind, who appears in the climax of Loy's fictional duel between intuitive occultism and willed, logical cognition. After all, "Pazzarella" enacts a revenge upon the "feminine psychology" adumbrated by Freud himself, an allusion clarified earlier in the story when Geronimo recounts the Oedipal triangle, a theory confirming, to Geronimo's immense satisfaction, that by finding the father in the arms of the lover the "woman takes root, flowers, and finally disappears" (*SE* 97, 80). Focused upon the erasure of its titular protagonist, "Pazzarella" is propelled by the misogynistic implications of Freudian theory; via a feminised occult prowess, the conclusionary *volte* reveals that women do not disappear quite as easily as Geronimo imagines.

Loy chooses her weapons well, wielding them to reconfirm her abiding belief that the self can only be fully understood when the esoteric and the psychoanalytic operate equally and in tandem, their methodological allegiances and divergences clearly on show. As Suzanne Hobson cogently argues, the Loy who wrote the essay "Conversion" (c. 1920s–30s) posits psychoanalysis as a cult that is too often too proximate to an exoteric religion, one steeped in a paternalistic traditionalism that threatens both female freedom and creative licence (248–52). If Hobson is correct, Loy's assault not only resists the enormous leap of faith Freudian thinking requires, but also actively challenges the esoteric origins of psychoanalysis, origins Freud both acknowledged and resisted. Given that he uncovers his understanding of the unconscious through careful observation of hypnotic methods, Freud could not fail to credit a "reciprocal sympathy" between psychoanalysis and occult practices centred on mediumship and clairvoyance ("Psycho-Analysis and Telepathy" 178–9). Yet Freud maintained that his emergent science might clarify, and thereby master or supersede, occult mysteries, telepathic communication among them ("Some Additional" 138).[31] In striving to make legible the irrational and obscure – be it the unconscious or the unspoken – psychoanalysis and telepathy both require a willed suspension of disbelief, a turn away from the transparency of reason. Recognising that "woman, being incapable of thinking" is deemed as illogical as the unconscious, Loy extols her ability to "rea[d] the thoughts of others" (*SE* 97). Visionary outlaw, Loy's conclusionary narrator best embodies a combined esotericism and psychoanalytic nous, a symbiotic methodology that remains central to Loy's lifelong, ambivalent critique of psychology, one consistently resistant to purely empirical readings of the mind, as is discussed in the first volume of this *Anatomy*.[32] Combating both the hyper-rational Futurists and the "incorrigible mechanists and materialists" that are psychoanalysts – the phrase is Freud's ostensibly self-deprecating veneration of a scientism Loy more damningly considers a deceptively "mechanised mysticism" – Loy's narrator insists that Geronimo's exacting, controlling narrative be read through an ungovernable, feminine, and cosmically transcendent point of view ("Psycho-Analysis and Telepathy" 179; *SE* 228).

From a historical vantage, Loy's expository pronouncement of "Pazzarella" as telepathy completes the journey of her story from eighteenth-century mesmerism into the century of its composition. In 1920, Loy acknowledges her attraction to clairvoyance as an occult preoccupation, and conflates this extrasensory perceptivity with the telepathic, writing, "I find . . . clairvoyance can be a power, in some cases, which can be entirely & continuously relied on – to be compared to calling up for information by telephone" (Letter dated 1920, "Loy, Mina, 1913–1920, n.d.", Mabel Dodge Luhan Papers). Decades later, Loy avows in "History of Religion and Eros" that humanity has always had exceptionally sensitive exemplars whose scientifically explicable "quirks of perception [are] comparable to telepathy, television . . . etc." (*SE* 239).[33] Telepathic communication emerged as an area of study courtesy of the Society for Psychical Research (SPR), founded in England in 1882. Buoyed by increasingly discussed transmission theories of electro-magnetism and contagious disease, the SPR investigated mesmerism, hypnosis, spectrality, and spiritualist mediumship, leading to the hypothesis that communicative sympathies might well exist between living organisms, and that telepathy might prove "'an all-important method or instrument for testing the mind in its hidden parts'" (Luckhurst 78, 88, 72, 73). Founder of the SPR Frederic Myers, established in the previous chapter as a major influence on Loy's understanding of psyches coherent and genius, not only introduced Freud to England, but also coined the term "telepathy" (Thurschwell 19).

"[D]irect and supersensory communication of mind with mind" Myers considered "the first law . . . of the spiritual or *metetherial* world" (8). Like mesmerism and spiritualism, telepathy is trans-verbal, capacious exchange: for Myers, it is not only "a quasi-mechanical transference of ideas and images from one to another brain", but encompasses love and the clairvoyant visions of genius upon which the seer or sensitive hones a "narro[w] and exact[ing] gaze" (277). Deployed in the service of evolution, telepathy was seen as a superstitious, unsubstantiated throwback hardwired into human nerves (Thurschwell 26). Against this premise, Myers argued that telepathy was a power capable of propelling human development forward, a power in which women, so often tagged with cognitive and volitional degeneracy, were "*progenera[te]*" or categorically advanced (Thurschwell 27; Luckhurst 214). A *de facto* claim to telepathic progeneracy is the substance of the conclusionary missive of "Pazzarella", and it performs powerful narrative work: if Geronimo's narration is channelled, the story becomes a vindication of our eponymous protagonist's martyrdom. Armed with this knowledge, telepathic progeneracy prompts the prospect of a vanguard sisterhood that counters both Geronimo's Futurist "brother[s] in arms" and a psychoanalysis that does not acknowledge, as Geronimo himself recognises, females as individuals, or the possibility of "relationship among women" (*SE* 70, 80). Drawing on a long-established occult lineage, this progeneracy envisions a triumphal feminist mysticism, one commensurate with Loy's view that "the seer" is "composed of racial – primeval cosmic memory or awareness" and "also the memory of the future" (Letter dated Easter Eve, Loy to Julien and Joella Levy, Box 30, Folder 13, 1933).

In Loy's hands, progeneracy is mysticism that prompts observable, physical change. "I have often had an impression," writes Freud, "in the course of experiments in my private circle, that strongly emotional coloured recollections can be successfully transferred without too much difficulty" ("Some Additional" 138). The placidity of Freud's observation is nowhere in "Pazzarella", where charged encounters provide ample fodder for telepathic exchanges leading to novel, intuitive understanding. "Had this wretched creature contaminated my very soul, insinuated her tenacious interrogation to the very stronghold of my wisdom?", asks Geronimo, awash in suspicion (*SE* 91). The answer is yes, the evidence postural and postulating. For Pazzarella's decadent languor ultimately infects and redirects Geronimo's somatic rectitude. Their tête-à-têtes initially take place standing, with much ado made of Pazzarella's inclining toward Geronimo, letting "her face f[a]ll onto [Geronimo's] waistcoat, for instance (*SE* 68). But by their third exchange, it is Geronimo who "s[i]nk[s] into an armchair" upon which Pazzarella perches (*SE* 70). In subsequent encounters, Pazzarella's tendency to "fall back" will be matched by a Geronimo increasingly "seated" or at repose, be it "beside her" or "settled down comfortably" nearby (*SE* 89, 94, 93, 96). Come their fourth encounter, Pazzarella lies upon her sofa as Geronimo puts his "head in her lap . . . incubat[ing] that rapacious womb in a promising warmth" (*SE* 80). Despite his pejorative language, their bodies enact a level and levelling playing field, a consenting interaction of "male" reason and "female" fecundity that catalyses their most generative conversation about their relationship, gender, and sexuality.

From this shared, prone vantage, Geronimo describes sex as a "'mutual possession'" in which "'inequalities [are] razed'", thereby channelling Loy's personal correspondence, as evinced by her "Feminist Manifesto" (1914), sent in a letter and unpublished in Loy's lifetime, where Loy makes precisely the same argument (*SE* 84–5; *LoLB* 154). At an alternate narrative juncture, Geronimo calls Pazzarella the "'odalisque of an able surgeon!!'" (*SE* 73). Geronimo's insult unwittingly parodies Pazzarella, who in a letter described her lover Mafarka/Marinetti as an "able surgeon" (*SE* 70). "Odalisque" originally referred to a woman in a Turkish harem who served the concubines; the odalisque's low status rose if she was considered attractive enough to capture the attention of the Sultan. In more recent contexts, "odalisque" refers to any enslaved prostitute or, still more generally, a sexually attractive woman. In art history, odalisques are portrayed with provocative consistency: from François Boucher's *L'Odalisque* (1749) to Jules Joseph Lefebvre's *Odalisque* (1874), these women are naked, sprawled, idealised, eroticised: the male epitome of female recline. But in this instance of sofa-bound, conjoined receptivity, Geronimo is odalisque to Loy's surgical satire: unknowingly parroting his author's manifesto, Geronimo is anonymised, feminised, his mental submissiveness an echo of his physical proneness. Loy's decision to have Geronimo espouse a key tenet of her feminist manifesto is a curious one. It might be read as a means of legitimising her own view, or as a satire comprehensible only to herself and American art patron Mabel Dodge Luhan, who was the sole recipient of the document in question. Given that "Pazzarella" also went unpublished, both texts might be read as drafts feeding into Loy's more assured view of the ecstatic dissolution of hierarchy in the sexual embrace writ large in "Songs to Joannes". Still further, this quotation creates a *mise-en-abyme*, given that, as was discussed above, "Pazzarella" is a direct response to Papini's own published manifesto, "The Massacre of Women".

Geronimo recognises his internal change, and this moment of anagnorisis further validates Loy's claim for intimacy as sex-war salve: to Pazzarella, Geronimo proclaims: "'See, I, in my turn, am passive. Profit by it!'" (*SE* 86). But Pazzarella knows that she cannot capitalise on Geronimo's affections as readily as he does upon hers, and thus restlessly rejects her love for Geronimo with the definitive: "'I *object*'", a polyvalent resistance that articulates the objectification it stands against (*SE* 86). Similarly, Geronimo has earlier suggested that Pazzarella is "'[i]n love with love'" in a way that he suspects may exempt his individuality; this ultimately groundless fear propels his relentless drive for still more masculine autonomy (*SE* 69). Pazzarella longs to be seen and partake in an idealised love; Geronimo wants an insatiable recognition; each falls increasingly supine upon their respective sword. The sex war is far from over, but a demonstrably embodied progeneracy wins this battle. In the end, Geronimo has the last word, yet Pazzarella maintains her postural authority.

Making a cameo appearance in Loy's *Insel*, Geronimo appears to have changed little, telling Mrs Jones that she is "'no psychologist'", and taunting: "'You just walk into a man's brain, seat yourself comfortably in an armchair to take a look around—afterwards, you write down all you have found there'" (*I* 147). Conscious at last of the internal joke of his narrated relationship with Pazzarella, Geronimo labours to undermine Pazzarella's supine authority, her esoteric and psychological prowess. Like any belated riposte that replicates the terms set by an interlocutor, this denunciation is as much homage as insult. By it, Geronimo continues his implicit acknowledgement of the "'postural model of the body'" begun in "Pazzarella", or the non-linguistic communication that demonstrates how the body relates to the world at large, and other individuals in fine. Where females are instructed to constrain themselves, subsequently hesitating where assertion or bravado is needed, or failing to make good use of the lateral space the vertical body allows, Pazzarella's is a body that, even when prone, strives to overcome "a conceptual mapping" of corporeality that systematically diminishes women's "value, relevance, and imaginable possibilities" (Alcoff 108).

"Pazzarella" is a tale of an intimacy that struggles to flourish amidst hard-wired combativeness. Its occult leanings challenge Futurist rectitude, but also validate inclination, receptivity, the unknown and uncontainable, and the prospect of a feminist transformation of Eros itself. In the decades following "Pazzarella", Loy continues to be guided by Myers's belief that, under telepathic law, individual lives, love, and religion are bound by "one all-pervading mutual gravitation of souls" – this is the very foundation of her esoteric Eros (61).[34] Loy also aspires to Myers's clairvoyant consciousness, drafting and editing transformative woman-centred visions in her prose, visions that extended to her novel *Insel*, which aimed at becoming "an entirely different kind of literature . . . most *clairvoyante*" (Undated letter, Loy to Julien and Joella Levy, Box 31, Folder 5, undated). In "Incident" (1919), Loy briefly dislocates her spine from her cranium whilst crossing a city square; this moment of arrested circulation and forced repose gives her access to a metaphysical realm first terrifying, then sublimely peaceful as Loy patiently awaits an "intuited revelation" ultimately staved off by a reanimating "universal electricity" (*SE* 37, 39). The anecdote takes place during a conversation between Loy and Emily Greene Balch, Nobel Peace Prize winner for her work with the Women's International League for Peace. Is it about feminism that Loy and Balch "argu[e] humorously" whilst crossing a city square? (*SE* 36).

"Incident" is referenced in *Insel*, where Loy triangulates a decimating transmutation effected by the eponymous, mystical protagonist to a brief mental imprisonment in the mind of a beatific girl who died after an operation meant to cure a disability, an experience not unlike the disembodied "sensation of utter helplessness when dislocating [her] cervical vertebra" (*I* 130). Empathy between women portends visionary transport again in Loy's undated anecdote "Street Sister", which opens upon a narrative "I" described as

> that uncircumscribed entity, an infinitarian, traditionless, almost conditionless, I have been privileged, but so seldom, to slip over the psychological frontier of that unvisited region where those others withhold the confidences of their deprivation, and see the light that lingers in the shadow of mankind. (41)

This narrator will find a "half-deflated heap" on the pavement, a "deranged" street woman unwittingly receptive to the gazes of passers-by to whom Loy offers money and care. Defeated together by local shopkeepers who refuse to help or serve the pair, the experience of "absolute equality" transforms the bedraggled, half-frozen woman with a "totally unoccupied gaze" to "a perfectly normal human being, with light in her friendly eyes" ("Street" 42). This transmutation is literalised by the enchanting effects of Loy's infinitarian clairvoyance, her ability to see into a beyond that exceeds the obvious, given, or assumed.

Recollected, "Incident" and "Street Sister" stretch and compress time, invert spatial confines, and find resolution in a heightened awareness of a sublime realm validated by quotidian female companionship.[35] To lesser degrees, these coordinates recur in visions fictional and experiential throughout Loy's oeuvre, perhaps most tellingly in "Hush Money" (c. 1917–22), where Loy ascribes to her male protagonist, Daniel Bundy, a "delicate feminine intuition of poets" enabling "vision[s] of those signs and portents that men so often miss" (*SE* 33).[36] Daniel is visiting a father needled to chronic illness by his overbearing wife, Daniel's mother; possessing both a domineering mother and a tendency to reverie, Daniel is a typical medium (Owen, *Darkened* 207). In poets like Daniel, Loy's narration confirms, "nature seems to attempt to substitute the mother they should have had 'outside' them with a mother inside" (*SE* 33). The vision is generative, feminine, protective, sympathetic, and compensatory: these are founding principles of Loy's genius and the substance of the künstlerromans to which we will soon turn. Combining idealised, maternalised inclinations and transcendent perspectives, "Hush Money" affirms that Loy's telepathic, visionary progeneracy works toward an Eros as informed by feminism as it is by the esoteric.

Easily dismissed as lunatic, for Loy, visions affirm the intuitive, fantastical "knowledge that tends to be suppressed when hyperrationality holds sway over our lives" (Obeyeskere 4). And in a further satisfying counter to publicised Futurist mores, visions are "altered states of consciousness" that validate somnolent states idealised – rapture, reverie, trance – and reviled: thoughtlessness, mechanical action, habit, madness, and trance.[37] Telepathy, too, requires a mental receptivity that plays brilliantly to Futurist anxieties about imperceptible or undiscerned female autonomy whilst underscoring Loy's satiric methodology. As its very coinage indicates, telepathy is as foundationally paradoxical and corporeal as Loy's satire: "an oxymoronic distant (*tele-*)" is made inseparable from "intimacy or touch (*pathos*)" (Luckhurst 1). Both Loy and the Futurists flout outdated sexual morality, but Loy's challenge is rooted in the generation of a more egalitarian intimacy that is not an express Futurist goal. Yet, in its own way, Loy's satire is as anticipatory as Futurist aesthetics; the labour of ruminating and writing is sustained by the desire for change.

Loy's strategies of counter and allegiance are not wholly singular: consider Italian Futurist Enif Robert's "A Tranquil Thought" (1917), a contemplation that concludes by arguing that "women, smiling in a fecund silence, are continually sharpening their minds to contend with myopic males and—who knows?—perhaps even with . . . their monopoly of intelligence" (243). There is more than a glimmer of Pazzarella's decadent languor in Robert's sphinx-like image, and Loy assuredly works in tandem with what Lucia Re describes as a young, female Futurist generation that succeeded in enacting "a subtle war of position, not an openly confrontational war of manoeuvre" against their own vanguard (122). Among this group was Maria Ginanni (1891–1953), the editor of *L'Italia futurista* (a journal established as counter to Papini's male-only periodical, *Lacerba*), who confronted the Futurists with her literary form, content, and focus. Ginanni focused on the banal and minute, rather than the speedy and violent (Re 117). Like Loy, Ginanni deployed the implicit power of the feminine and occult, writing in 1917 of how the "fingers of my soul would like to take hold of your impalpable strings and intertwine them with the most delicate gentleness and the sharpest lucidity of my genius"; describing destiny itself as "sustained by the crumbling tremor of our hypnotically enslaved hands!"; and celebrating, as does Loy's "Lunar Baedeker" (1923), an "immense night" that expressly validates neither logic nor technology, but a distinctly Symbolist "nucleus of intuition" (Ginanni 466–7). United by their experimental aesthetics, these feminist writers shared a willingness to use past vanguard and heterodox movements as evidence of the backwardness, traditionalism, or indebtedness of the bellicosely forward-thinking Futurists.[38]

Loy's uniqueness lies in her deployment of occult practice as a satiric weapon by way of moving toward a greater interpersonal intimacy and cosmic harmony. Hence she celebrates passive if strategic proneness; hence her depiction of a utopian level playing field between the sexes is as postural and embodied as it is epiphanic. Like the visionary, telepathy, too, looks forward whilst circling back toward a self-affirming present. Derrida describes telepathy as "the prophecy returning to itself from the future of its own to-come", a phrasing chiming with the origins of satire as prescient judgement, even as it echoes the dorsal returns of Loy's narrative dialectics (4). Underscoring the telepathic circling structuring "Pazzarella", the language of turn and turn about runs beyond and through its narrative: Pazzarella's head is turned; Geronimo overturns everything, love included; Pazzarella begs Geronimo to turn to him, to come over to her side, a prospect he finds unsavoury given her willingness to turn her back on him (*SE* 73, 72, 89, 90, 88–9). These postures reinforce the embodiment of Loy's dialectics of reversal, of backs that are physically and narratively structural. In "Pazzarella", a female psychologist channels Geronimo's aggression, disregard, and misogyny toward the eponymous female victim so that it redounds upon her perpetrator, the Papini who purports that, should men like him continue living with womankind, they "cannot help but love her – and loving her we cannot help but serve her – and in serving her we are cowards, we are betrayers of our true destiny" ("Massacre" 256). The pain of attraction, the unbearable lived truth of his subsequent loss and suffering, are glaringly over-exposed in Papini's masochistic "satire". His is an unwitting paean to the very love he hopes to excise from the world.

In the 1920s, Papini's Futurist comrade and enemy Marinetti would yield entirely to proselytising about the essential nature of loves platonic and amorous. Marinetti's surfeit of affect appears most notably in his poems to his wife, the Futurist Benedetta Cappa, written between 1920 and 1938. "Poems to Beny" include homages to "the perfumed ecstasy" of his beloved's skin, occasionally awkwardly juxtaposed against Marinetti's brutish virility: "Dear presence in the gushing of blood-desire" (136). Notably, in these poems, Marinetti actively celebrates languor, particularly when it collapses the divide between himself and his wife: "Distance distance I no longer see her I see her better / for she sleeps next to me in her bed like a drowsy / sea on a summer night" (137). Marinetti's authorial interest in love arises alongside an esoteric return thinly veiled by a scientism that does not prevent Marinetti being publicly, widely recognised as an occultist (D'Ambrosio 301–2, 312). Looking over her shoulder at the decimated past she shares with Papini in "Pazzarella", Loy's concurrent "The Sacred Prostitute" oracularly anticipates Marinetti's embrace of sentimentality, intimacy, and the irrational. Like any good psychologist, Loy recognises the Freudian truth that fear bespeaks desire.

"Pazzarella" moves chronologically if implicitly through the occult fascinations of the eighteenth, nineteenth, and twentieth centuries toward a feminist visionariness and psychologisation of a misogynist male co-protagonist. The esotericism of this story, and before it *Brontolivido*, is relatively subtle, hinging on gestures, gazes, and potent phrases, a discourse subtending the verbal sparring about vanguard aesthetics, gender, and heteronormative commitment that is Loy's overt focus. Nevertheless, the esoteric presence in these earliest

Loy writings incontrovertibly demonstrates her deep awareness of the long history of European occult practice and its ties to psychoanalysis, coordinates discernible from the outset of her authorial career.

Come the 1930s, Loy centralises these occultist leanings in the final instalment of her dialogic romans à clef, *Insel*. Able to see through, penetrate, and exit the material world at will, Insel is phantom to his co-protagonist Jones, who is, like Pazzarella, another Loy avatar. Insel is an "innate mediu[m]" replete with "magnetic field" and continually emitting "healing *Strahlen*" (rays or beams), with whom Jones shares a telepathic intimacy, an "accidental clairvoyance" (*I* 27, 111, 115, 47). Throughout this novel, Jones is both psychologist and spiritualist, her every visit with Insel as much therapy as séance, as ideally astute about both discourses as the narrator of "Pazzarella".[39] Atavistic, primitive, but also a transcendent if unrecognised Buddha or Christ figure, Insel is esotericism embodied, "submit[ing] to an unknown law enforcing itself through him" and "doing sentry duty before his own secrecy" (*I* 119, 124). "I definitely penetrated (into) his mediumistic world," boasts Jones, but in truth, she and Insel interpenetrate incessantly, taking it in turns to become flotsam in the gyre of the other's involution (*I* 47). Gesturing to Loy's ever-present decadence, *Insel* regresses rather than progresses, and Loy signals this degeneracy when Jones acknowledges that, with Insel, the "'entente' in the visionary lethargy of that primeval chaos we were able to share was fundamental and secure", so that the couple "drowse[s] in an impotence of arrested development", children too familiar with the rules of their own heterodox games (*I* 114, 122). *Insel* sputters toward an internal narrative failure that echoes how, for Loy, it is an unsuccessful attempt at her new "*clairvoyante*" literary genre (Undated letter, Loy to Julien and Joella Levy, Box 31, Folder 5, undated).

As time intervenes and Jones's pursuit of Insel's gnosticism yields little truth, lethargy is overtaken by reality. "[T]he work [Insel] no longer seemed able to do waxed so sublime in his visions" and those of Jones, but visions, Jones realises, they will remain (*I* 122). Decidedly demoted to lesser being – "[o]ur relative positions entirely reversed" – Insel becomes the "vindictive psychiatrist" that was Pazzarella-cum-Jones (*I* 142). In turn, Jones recognises that their relationship has been pure madness: outside of their shared hallucinatory zone, "the earlier iridescent Insel" appears "a figment of [Jones's] insanity", a vision born of lunacy that will never yield the intimacy or aesthetic catalysts Loy's narratives tend to seek (*I* 146). With *Insel*, in other words, Loy takes the narrative arc of "Pazzarella" full circle, back to the state of average well-being that precedes the mental illness of *La pazza*. Proving yet again that revolution is return, with the completion of this orbit, Loy abandons her vanguard protagonist couplings for a re-examination of the self, a reconsideration of her own singular origins. Drawing on the anatomical dorsality crucial to nostos, the contrapposto of a self-reflexive subject, Loy's late romans à clef, her künstlerromans, theorise a transcendently perceptive dorsality, the corollary to her early preoccupations with the spinal irritations of madness, empirical perceptivity, and positivist propulsions. From the somnolent, sublime supine event, Loy turns toward a blind back that is portal to a fourth-dimensional cosmos.

Notes

1. Lines redacted from the *Brontolivido* manuscript expose the insecurity behind Jemima's otherwise bravura performance of the salty dame, and indicate that Loy was unwilling to apply this prefix to her stand-in: "understanding nothing of herself – [she] was as usual ~~heavy~~ leaden within – ~~her self reproach~~ her bewildered disapproval" (*B* 3: 22). Loy's rewrite redirects both the censure and the return implicit in "self *reproach*" away from Jemima and toward the Futurists.
2. It is not only women who are prostrated in Loy: notably passive or marginalised men share this experience. In "Hot Cross Bum" (1950), Loy describes the rest of a homeless male New Yorker as follows: "prone / lies the body of the flop / where'er he drop" (*LoLB* 143). In "Anglo-Mongrels and the Rose", Jewish Exodus is a too-passive, sleepy figure; so too in Loy's story "Hush Money" (c. 1917–22) is the father, Mr Bundy, at the mother's protracted and vicious mercy, "l[ying] like a log in his bed" (*SE* 30). As does Bundy, Loy's Insel accesses a nocturnal transcendence, even as narrators liken both male figures to a fallen-in or extinct volcano when somnolent (*SE* 31; *I* 81, 83, 93–4). Triggered by lying flat on the back, this combined access to sublimity and primordial abjectness is echoed in Loy's formulation of the blind back, to which I will return in the next chapter.
3. For more on this Loy association, see "'Being Alive': Sentience" in Chapter 1 of *Nethered Regions*.
4. Elaine Showalter observes how, alongside the physician Josef Breuer, Freud developed a more respectful attitude toward the female hysteric that challenged views – Charcot's among them – that her words were less relevant than her physical symptoms. In short, Showalter credits Freud with recognising that many Victorian hysterics were bright, strong-willed individuals whose symptoms were predominantly tied to

social circumstances, rather than female biology. This awareness did not always play itself out in practice, as is illustrated by Freud's disregard for Dora's family circumstances in his diagnosis of her hysteria (Showalter 158–9).

Showalter's discussion of hysteria has since been critiqued by Elizabeth A. Wilson, one of many scholars encouraging a greater feminist attentiveness to the biological, material body. For Wilson, Showalter does not attend sufficiently to the bodily symptomologies of nineteenth-century hysterics, their lived experience of pain, discomfort, and disorienting physical conversions. *Contra* Showalter, Wilson maintains that Freud's psychoanalysis is importantly founded in both bodily symptom and the experiential (6).

5. It is a trope of Decadent fiction, often remarked, that male protagonists tend to be the final, sole descendent of a grand, aristocratic lineage (see, for instance, Weir 94). This claim holds for Jean des Esseintes in *Against Nature* (1884) and Andrea Sperelli of D'Annunzio's *Pleasure* (1889). With this lush description of empty-wombed Pazzarella, Loy adds a female protagonist to this lineage.

6. Loy once described Papini as possessing a "'languorous yet, at the same time, blustering voice'" (qtd. in *BM* 162). In "Sketch of a Man on a Platform" (1915), Loy mocks Marinetti's absolutism and machismo by aligning him with "the airy-fairy of the ballet", a beast "snuffl[ing] the trail of the female", and a predominantly unproductive celebrity. His genius, Loy writes, is limited to "the activity of pushing / THINGS / In the opposite direction / To that which they are lethargically willing to go" (*LoLB* 19–20). Thundered, "THINGS" implies rancour and contestation, an agential bellowing counter to women's objectification. To be "lethargically willing" is to be unwilling, nearly inanimate, and Loy affirms this ambivalent state whilst accusing the Futurist leader of disrespecting its legitimate vagaries. Pushing in opposed directions is also crucial to the machinations of "Pazzarella", which culminates in the eponymous protagonist begging Geronimo to "come over *on [her] side*" (*SE* 90).

7. In her writing on Decadence, Rita Felski argues that the dandified male becomes a gauge of modernity, his status grounded in a "displa[y of the] traits the dominant ideologies of his day identified with women: passivity, languidness, vanity, hypersensitivity, a love of fashion and ornamentation" (1095). Submissive and susceptible, this male nevertheless maintains an authority unavailable to women:

> The feminised male deconstructs conventional oppositions between the 'modern' bourgeois man and the 'natural' domestic woman; he is male, yet disassociated from masculine rationality, utility, and progress; feminine, yet profoundly unnatural. Whether hailed as subversive or condemned as pathological, his femininity signals an unsettling of automatized perceptions of gender, whereas feminine qualities in a

woman merely confirm her incapacity to escape her natural condition. (1099)

8. Loy's "Piero and Eliza." centres on a marriage of convenience that allows "decadent" Piero, newly returned from Paris, to spend time with "lethargic" cafe-haunters in Florence, contemplate his decor, and mock or patronise his spinsterish wife, who remains unaware that she married a gay man (*SE* 99, 98). Presented as homophobic stereotype, Piero's unlikeability is attributed to his sexuality; notably, this story is one of the few instances in which Loy uses the term "decadent".
9. As will be noted below, Geronimo reduces Pazzarella's speaking voice to that of the "dumb crowd" ("Dynamic" 194; *SE* 90). For widespread modernist perceptions of the crowd, see Bellamy 73–4.
10. Loy lampooned D'Annunzio's national celebrity in "Lion's Jaws", a poem she published in *The Little Review* in 1920, and in her essay "Library of the Sphinx." she is sensitised to his absurd romanticism and entrenched misogyny. "Library" mocks how, in D'Annunzio's novel *The Flame of Life* (1900), "the lovers stagger about in a mist—in a state of *débile* hysteria" (*SE* 246). Loy goes on to consider D'Annunzio a "type of man in literature" who beatifies women only to condescend to them (*SE* 256). This very "type" is taken to violent extremes in "Pazzarella".
11. In D'Annunzio's "The Virgins", three fits of masturbatory laughter are ascribed to Giuliana. The first occurs when she is alone at home, recovering from a life-threatening illness. Putting her feet on the floor for the first time in months, Giuliana "laughed, laughed because laughing imbued her with a pleasant languor, a subtle pleasure, quivering throughout her being" (11). On another solitary occasion, Giuliana finds a vegetable cupule at the back of a drawer that is full of seed, which she delightedly blows over herself, laughing; a drowsy lethargy follows this sexually fertile scene (17). In the last such instance, Giuliana undresses and looks at her naked self in front of the mirror, again experiencing "a mad burst of hilarity" that "shook her whole body" (30).
12. Hofer's brilliant article makes the link between Papini's "The Massacre of Women" and Loy's "Feminist Manifesto", and illustrates how Loy repurposes Papini's too-sentimental satire in her poem "The Effectual Marriage" whilst remaining in conversation with his literary technique come "Songs to Joannes". Hofer makes no mention of "Pazzarella", *Brontolivido*, or "The Sacred Prostitute".
13. Geronimo was a well-known indigenous American hero in the modernist period whose biography was published in 1905. For several decades in the latter half of the nineteenth century, Geronimo took part in the North American Frontier Wars (also known as the Indian Wars) that began in the seventeenth century. An Apache, Geronimo aimed to secure his tribal lands in Mexico and Texas. "Apache" was a term used

by Loy's peers as a synonym for an admirable rogue (see, for instance, Carl Van Vechten's *Sacred and Profane Memories* [1932]).

On the one hand, Loy uses Geronimo's name as a racist compliment to Papini's virility: indigenous men surface in Loy's writing on a few occasions as over-simplified cyphers for the sort of desirable "primitives" who really know how to satisfy women. Hence the rejected harem of Loy's story "Monde Triple-Extra" finds refuge in convents or in eloping with Apaches, and the Victorian, polite Tea Table Man of "The Sacred Prostitute" claims to hide an aborigine within (*SE* 59, 191–2). On the other hand, Loy's Apache is also violent against women, given to cuffing his beloved or dragging her by the hair (*SE* 256), behaviours initially ascribed to the Futurism character in Loy's "The Sacred Prostitute", meaning Marinetti may preceded Papini as the first Futurist "Apache" (*SE* 198).

The historical Geronimo's given name was Goyahkla, widely interpreted as "One who yawns". Suggesting lassitude to a Western ear, this name counters Geronimo's fierce legacy, even as it is a fixed component of the popular lore that sprang up around this outlaw-cum-hero, one with which Loy may have been familiar (Debo 13). If accurate, this derivation may further co-opt Papini into the supinity and somnolence Loy ascribes to Pazzarella.

For more on Loy's treatment of indigeneity, see also "'Primeval Recognitions': Primitivism" in Chapter 1 of *Nethered Regions*.
14. In addition to being a perceived cerebral stimulus, mesmerism was often used by invalids eager to upright themselves (Winter 67, 216). Consistent with nineteenth-century neurology and occult histories, telepathy was perceived as an access to the inner workings of the mind facilitated by the nerves: in 1897, Society for Psychical Research members postulated that "'[a] sensitive may be one who possesses the telepathic transmitting or receiving ganglion in an advanced state of development'" (qtd. in Luckhurst 89).
15. Marinetti repeatedly equates "the lightning development of science" with either the machine or "the marvellous conquest of speed" ("Necessity" 64; see also "Open Letter" 105; "Artistic Movement" 278). From 1910 to at least the early 1930s, Marinetti counsels people to "cultivate and glorify the triumph of science and its everyday heroism", calling special attention to groups such as *passéiste* Spaniards and aspirant Futurist cooks, who should equip their kitchens "with scientific instruments" such as ozonisers, ultraviolet lamps, and dialysers ("Futurist Proclamation to the Spaniards" 101; "Manifesto of Futurist Cuisine" 398–9).

For Marinetti, writers should embrace "the ideal of a great and strong scientific literature [and] extol the most recent discoveries", as should thespians, be they Futurist, followers of the Tactilism branch of Futurism, or those interested in generating a *Gesamtkunstwerk* for

the stage (on Marinetti's scientific directives to writers, see "Battles of Trieste" 160–1; "Proletariat" 308; "Address" 335; for his scientific directives to thespians, see "Manifesto of Futurist Playwrights" 182; "Abstract Antipsychological" 390; "Total Theatre" 405).
16. As Thurschwell notes, "The Saltpêtrière [Hospital] maintained that only the already hysterical (primarily female patients) were hypnotizable, and that hypnosis was a phenomenon of illness"; their *fin-de-siècle* French associates, the Nancy School of psychotherapy, propounded a more gender-neutral hypnotic efficacy (41). Ellis acknowledges these debates in his text, and subscribes to elements of both, arguing that, while everyone is hypnotisable, the vast majority of hypnotherapy is conducted on women. Unusually for his time, Ellis believes that a degree of sanity is required for hypnosis to succeed: "for it is notoriously difficult to hypnotise the insane even with the exercise of very considerable skill and patience" (*Man* 356).
17. The Italian for brontosaurus is "brontosauro"; "brontolare" is mutter, grumble, complain, or groan; "brontolone" is grouchy or grumpy; "brontolio" is moaning or whingeing. "Livido" refers to livid, black and blue (as in a bruise), angry, and enraged; a "cielo livido" is a stormy or dark sky. At one point, Loy toys with "Brontolurido" (*B* 3: 12), thus replacing rage with the disgusting, foul, filthy, or sleazy.
18. This animal magnetism is overwhelmingly on display in Marinetti's *Mafarka the Futurist* (1910), which foregrounds its eponymous protagonist's virility at every turn. The marriage of animal magnetism with intellectual and creative generation recurs in Marinetti's discussions of the foundational Futurist "words-in-freedom" aesthetic, or the elision of syntax, paring down of punctuation, and use of noises, experimental typography, and prose forms in poetry, all of which Marinetti considers "the lyrical, transfiguring extension of our animal magnetism" ("Geometrical" 139).
19. Jemima often gazes upward or sidelong only to see a lover who "[b]rush[es her] with a sweep of his eyelasing" (*B* 5: 7). With rare exception, Marinetti's look oscillates between sentimental wooing and brutal cuts; in turn, he continually chastises Jemima's gaze as too chaste, too romantic (see, for instance, *B* 6: 10).
20. The terms used to describe Pazzarella's eyes include "extinguished", "dull", dark-lidded, "bloodshot ... in a purple pit", or blind (*SE* 74, 81, 87, 94, 93). Preferring her gaze bludgeoned, Geronimo is genuinely alarmed when, after she has had sex with another man, Pazzarella's "eyes no longer sought for anything" (*SE* 71).
21. By Geronimo's own admission, the persistence of Pazzarella's one-sided affection elevates her to sainthood: her commitment to him may be a "contemptible beatitude", but heteronormativity nevertheless elevates her to "a virginity of spirit" and keeps her from pointless martyrisation to other men (*SE* 67, 71–2). Recognising Pazzarella's desire to parent

both him and their potential offspring, Geronimo couches motherhood as a holy series of "saintly consecrated gestures" (*SE* 80). And although Geronimo mocks her sodden, weeping form on the stone stairs of her flat as *Pazzarella de le Scale di Pietra*, his pun nevertheless extends to Pazzarella Michelangelo's paean to a sacralised motherhood, *La Pietà* (*SE* 94). Against these more transcendent religious characterisations, Pazzarella is also a cursed figure: the tempting serpent of Genesis wound round Geronimo's midriff, or a cleansing Jewish outcast, "'the scapegoat to carry the load of [Geronimo's] spleen'" (*SE* 82, 76). More demoniacally, Geronimo compares Pazzarella to "an incubus of desire" and a vampire; he suggests that she cohabitates and communes with spirits in need of exorcising (*SE* 78, 81, 68).

22. Wilde's short story "The Sphinx without a Secret: An Etching" was first published in 1887.
23. As Spackman observes:

    > Androgyny as a spiritual principle is haunted by the monstrosity of the hermaphrodite; the metonymic chain produced by that hermaphrodite ... is made up of a series of monsters, the majority of which are considered female. Harpies, sphinxes, and sirens are part woman, part animal; the chimera, part lion, part goat, part dragon, is considered a she-monster. References to these monsters appear precisely in the scene of convalescence in which the male protagonist is feminised; they seem to mirror his own condition. Part woman, part animal, they are the demonic versions of the convalescent as part woman part man. If the 'altro spirito' the convalescent experiences is androgynous, then the 'altro corpo' might be imagined ... as the body of a woman with the head of a man. (77)

    In the penultimate scene of "Pazzarella", Loy depicts this "altro corpo". "'You are only an intellect'", Pazzarella has told Geronimo; he is a half man, and as he appropriates sphinx-hood, he is just that: a male brain attended by Pazarella's leaden, prone female body (*SE* 84).
24. To elaborate: in *The Genealogy of Morals* (1887), Nietzsche compares emergent thought to the pains of parturition; in *The Gay Science* (1882), he asserts that "'spiritual pregnancy produce[s] the character of the contemplative type, which is closely related to the feminine character: it consists of male mothers'" (qtd. in Spackman 93).
25. Loy may borrow this trope from Marinetti: as Cinzia Sartini Blum argues in relation to *Mafarka the Futurist*, the penalty for the expulsion of the female in Marinetti's novel is the return of the repressed; like Geronimo, Mafarka is haunted by a female lover and by a sorrowful mother (77–8).
26. Far more bombastic than "Pazzarella", Papini's *The Failure* (1913) is, nevertheless, a like promise of triumphant resurrection disguised as a self-castigating martyrdom. The linkages are specific as well as structural. For instance, in chapter 21, "And Not a Word of Love?", Papini

offers a litany of misogynist insult before taunting the reader to despise him outright, just as Pazzarella begs Geronimo to insult her (159).

27. *To the Lighthouse* closes upon Lily labouring toward a singular, unshared vision that drains her in the same way that spiritualists often described themselves, post-séance, as exhausted: "It would be hung up in the attics, she thought; it would be destroyed. But what did that matter? she asked herself . . . . It was done; it was finished. Yes, she thought, laying down her brush in extreme fatigue, I have had my vision" (281).

    Without referencing Lily's epiphany, Julie Kane provides a good overview of Woolf's combined loathing toward and co-opting of nineteenth-century esoteric preoccupations. Likening Woolf's moments of being to mystical experiences, pointing to her repeat use of terms such as "aura" in her fiction and aesthetic theory, as well as her references to out-of-body travel, the immortal soul, and distinctly telepathic communication, Kane maintains that there is a discernible mystical turn in Woolf's later writings, an argument often made about Loy (see, for instance, Armstrong 205).

28. For Freud, the illegible symptomologies of the mentally imbalanced "can be traced back to incompletely suppressed psychical material, which, although pushed away by consciousness, has nevertheless been robbed of all capacity for expressing itself" (emphasis removed, *Psychopathology* 279). However forward-facing the individual, the body stammers its past difficulties as best as it can, a truth Freud universalises in his affirmation that "we are all a little neurotic" (*Psychopathology* 278).

29. Philomela endures rape and mutilation at the hands of her brother-in-law, King Tereus of Thrace. Having taken her revenge with her sister's aid, Philomela begs the gods to save her from the return of his wrath and is turned into a bird. There is a like fraternal assaultive link in "Pazzarella", when Geronimo describes Mafarka/Marinetti – the other Futurist who is intimate with Pazzarella – as a "brother in arms" near-indistinguishable from himself (*SE* 70).

30. "The Sacred Prostitute" culminates in the appearance of a character named "Reality" who Loy's stage directions describe as "a composite person called World-Flesh-and-Devil" (*SE* 214). While many Christian theologians have written on this symbolic triumvirate of temptation, the *Precautions* of Saint John of the Cross (1542–91) expressly directs itself this grouping. Moreover, *Precautions* was written for cloistered nuns in Beas who copied and circulated the text; appositely, Loy's "The Sacred Prostitute" is similarly situated within a female community, namely, the brothel that is the play's setting.

31. For Freud, the distinction between mysticism and psychoanalysis – both transgressive, unconventional discourses – is empirical: occultists put faith before proof, while analysts possess a scientific mindset,

pursuing and submitting to natural laws that further their understanding of "the unconscious element of mental life" ("Psycho-Analysis and Telepathy" 178–9). But there is slippage in Freud's resistance to equating occultism with psychoanalysis, as when he argues that thoughts might be transferred between individuals in "the moment at which an idea emerges from the unconscious", or the very moment his analytic practice pursues ("Some Additional" 138).

32. See the "'Cosmic Force': Vitalism" section of Chapter 1 of *Nethered Regions*.
33. The ellipsis in this quotation is Loy's.
34. Myers perceived consciousness along a spectrum that "could extend 'down' towards the autonomic physiological functions . . . but also 'up' to the sublime possibilities of clairvoyance and telepathy" (Luckhurst 109). In "History of Religion and Eros", Loy's desire to "cooperat[e] with the electric inspiration of Deity" similarly leads to access to Myers's metetheriality or, in Loy's terms, a "*gravity upward*" (*SE* 244).
35. On visionary distortions of time and space, see Obeyesekere 34 and 36. "Incident" is exemplary in this regard: in briefly accessing "eternal existence", Loy finds her "liberated self, the body-contour and the intervening space telescoped into one another" (*SE* 37–8).
36. Satirising and thereby furthering this supposition, Loy's "Monde Triple-Extra" presents vanguardist Jove Ivon Corvon, whose "vision" transforms an otherwise unremarkable charwoman into his feminine ideal (*SE* 60). Furthermore, the "black-out vision" of Loy's "Tuning in on the Atom Bomb" is grounded and aggravated by a workaday conversation with her daughter (*SE* 60, 288).
37. Post-Enlightenment Europe is the notable exception in an otherwise global respect for trance, rapture, and vision; for Gananath Obeyesekere, the phrase "altered states of consciousness" is inherently pejorative, as it erroneously implies that humans are and ought to be in full mental command at every waking moment (20). The lack of control inherent to the vision is long understood: conditions can be arranged – meditation, séance – to welcome a vision into being, but, like its reception, its arrival is never guaranteed.
38. Noting that critics have attended too closely to Loy's relationships with Papini and Marinetti, Laura Scuriatti has uncovered further links between Loy and the wider Florentine cultural context, including its female Futurists. Discussing Ginanni and her husband Arnaldo Ginna as possible models for the Gina and Miovanni of Loy's "The Effectual Marriage", Scuriatti also considers ties between Loy's presentation of maternity and that of Milanese poet Ada Negri (1870–1945), showing how both Negri and Loy work against Futurism by positing female reproductivity as a form of genius (54–9).
39. Here I benefit and differ from Andrew Gaedtke, who wonderfully reads the dual protagonists of *Insel* as engaged in a form of lay

psychoanalysis defined by fluid patient/doctor roles (156–7). My arguments also resist Tamara Beauchamp's reading of *Insel* as a joke about the coterminous nature of telepathy and psychoanalysis; instead, I am suggesting that Loy understands the complex esoteric history that leads to psychoanalysis, and perceives theories of the mind without mysticism as incomplete (278–80).

Chapter 3

The Blind Back

Blindsiding Dorsality

The quotidian truth that human beings cannot see what lies behind them is a decades-long site of contemplation for Mina Loy, who defines human vertebrates as "three[-]dimensional organism[s]" cognisant of and defined by a "BLIND BACK" (*SE* 279, 407). Anglo-Europeans figure the past as rearguard, as the known that accumulates behind us as we catapult ourselves each day into the unknown. By this temporal figuration, autobiography disturbs Loy because it creates "a freak continuity" through which "the Past lay before [her]" (*IA* 58: 3). "Being alive from the inside", writes Loy, "feels like having an open window where others see our solid face", even as "[w]e stare across the ocean of phenomena while it washes away the façade of our torso and flows into our blind back" (*CP* 20: 7). A permeable contour, the dorsal defines Loy's sentient being, is the limit point of the self and interaction. Telepathy Loy likens to friendly backslapping; clairvoyance sees through the individual, effecting a volte-face when it reaches the spine (*I* 24, 72). The back structures our body, our past structures our being.

As if incomplete, blighted, or ill-adapted to an as-yet-sunless primordial world, Loy's back is unseeing correlate to a material reality she considers unperceived, linking our obdurate, intrinsic myopia to an atavism as substantive as it is, potentially, threatening and overbearing. As a site of overbearing rectitude, the back is an anatomical and metaphorical spine through Loy's writings on her Victorian upbringing, the locus of limits imposed on rigidly busked women blind to the often painful effects – on themselves, on others – of their stunted experience and aspirations, or the very affective and gendered consequences Loy excavates in her satires and romans à clef.

Through her mythology of the blind back, Loy rewrites her familial ancestry, replacing genetic heritage with a story of origin by which Loy emerges from the universal ether, an ideal cosmos to which she can transcendently, triumphantly return.

Tautology fully on show, Loy's back is profoundly backward. But paradoxically, from her earliest writings, Loy theorises coordinates by which the human back is a portal to a beyond. In this regard, the blind back marks the start of human life, is the threshold by which we navigate a higher realm as our bodies remain tethered to the third dimension. The blind back offers access to an alternate plane imbued with visionary potential, is the launching ground for a transcendent artistry confirming universal interdependence, the anatomical ground of planes divine and inspired, planes that artists like Loy can access at will. Uniting Loy's arrière-garde and mystical proclivities, the blind back reasserts Loy's coupling of the vanguard with the esoteric; at its most illuminating, this unsighted dorsality manifests Loy's aesthetic and visionary Eros.

While a few Loy scholars have acknowledged the presence of the blind back in her late work, this chapter offers a sustained, contextualised exploration of its development throughout Loy's oeuvre, whilst interrogating the multiple resonances of this foundational, pervasive focus. Loy's blind back contains multitudes: memory, regressions, utopias, creativity, genius, subliminality, introspection, metaphysics. It is fulcrum on the scale of universal mass weighing the "incalculable tonnage" of the infinite, the "source of all animation" that pushes our mortal lives up against the pressure of phenomenal reality (SE 268). Linking ocularity, nerves, feeling, insight, and soul, the blind back is a phenomenally replete motif of Loy's presiding atavistic vanguardism, the feminist politics that guide her aesthetics, and her relationship to contemporaneous heterodox, philosophical, and scientific discourses, among them Theosophy, Cartesian duality, pineality, and fourth dimensionality. In sum, the vicissitudes, contradictions, and potentialities of the blind back represent the anatomical zenith of Loy's lifelong drive to cohere fragmentary being: by a mystic dorsality, Loy connects anatomy to the universe entire.

Drawing on Loy's domestic architectural metaphors for the blind back, the first part of this chapter, "Origins: Home and Legacy", considers how Loy equates house with body and, come her late romans à clef, the spine with ascending structures. Confronted by the strictures of her early homes, Loy vows to establish an expansive artistic legacy. "Atavisms: Retral Drag" attends to Loy's concern that the blind back presents an ever-present lapsarian risk by which weak-willed individuals – her protagonist Insel among them – become too bound by the past that cumulates behind us. Against this antecedence, "Geniuses: Retrocognition" juxtaposes Loy's blind back with Bergson's evolution and Myers's subliminality, both implicitly past-oriented theories that foreground the creative genius by which Loy defines herself. "Decimations: Bowed Backs" examines the vulnerability of the unduly laboured and ossified feminised back that Loy commandeers into a site of intimate risk and ecstatic self-dissolution.

This relation between blind dorsality and esoteric Eros subtends the second half of this chapter, which foregrounds Loy's oscillations between the primordial and the futuristic in her rendering of the blind back. In "Backing and Forthing: Pineal Eye, Fourth Dimension", Loy's dorsality is juxtaposed with Descartes's and Blavatsky's moral readings of the pineal gland, or rearward, mystical third eye. Providing the first sustained reading of Loy's relationship to Theosophical evolution, involution, and reincarnation, sections on pineality and rupture demonstrate how Loy's rearward vision is set alight by the very sexuality that Blavatsky and her ascetic followers condemn. In its wilful excesses, Loy's dorsal orb bears remarkable resemblance to the volcanic parietal organ Bataille celebrates in "The Pineal Eye" (c. 1930s). An assault on Western rectilinearity is Loy's and Bataille's shared concern, and this polemic informs the conclusion of this chapter, "Utopia: Loy's Artistic Fourth Dimension", where the blind back is explored as a portal to the malleable modernist presentation of alternate dimensions. For Loy, the third dimension is a site of pain, the fourth, of a pleasure best accessed and represented by the artist. In her künstlerromans, Loy posits an artistry that relies upon and supersedes mysticism, alchemically transmuting suffering into legacy whilst exhibiting an awareness that her faith in the unknown and unknowable may be the only structural, lasting axis of her own irrevocably fragmented being.

Origins: Home and Legacy

For Loy, the human back is a threshold, behind which lies infinity. She believes this positioning becomes evident in infancy, when the human neonate arrives on the planet possessed of an "unbroken child-consciousness" that remains at one with "cosmic continuity" while its physical being "stands inquiring on our threshold", attempting to understand and integrate with the three-dimensional world (*CP* 11: 14–15). Significantly, Loy's narrative allows her to replace her biological connection to her family of origin with a creation story in which the universe is parent to all human beings, even as chance informs that individual's placement within a specific locale; to what Loy labels "the jugglery of birth" I will return (*IA* 59: 2). As the infant peers inquisitively into this foreign, phenomenal world, its back remains a conduit to eternity, a doorway that Loy alternately figures as a portal to expansivity, or a seal upon our material constriction. Reworking the cliché by which the eyes are conduit to the soul, Loy suggests that through these organs we can see the weighty, ominous palpability of our individual connections to the beyond.

As early as *Brontolivido* (c. 1913–20), Loy has her female protagonist seek the reassurance that her male love interest is connected to an infinite rearward gravitas: "She looked into his eyes – trying to see whether they were empty – or whether they had shut off something behind" (*B* 8: 27). Unspecified, this valved current is the "something infinite" that another Loy character accesses best upon awakening, porously liquefying as he ascends reality through skilfully manipulated blind behindedness: "To his soul there was no limitation once he had shut his eyes" (*SE* 139). Mediumistic, this figure involutes, inclining toward himself, prising open the backstop upon which he lies in order to surpass reality and access an ocularly guarded infinity that emerges throughout Loy's oeuvre. In a 1914 poem, the "ambiente" seeking eyes of a café clientele "[t]rai[l]" their evolutionary, bestial past "behind them"; roughly four decades later, Loy recalls the defensively expressionless eyes of a London streetworker whose fortressed gaze nevertheless exposes the infernal pressure of "her own brain battering on the back of [her eyes]" (*LoLB* 16; *IA* 69: 142). Through heightened self-consciousness, the Loy individual can overcome the "reality" that "is the seal of the creator on nothingness" (*SE* 279). This seal appears as early as 1918, when Loy proclaims: "'Self' is the covered entrance to Infinity", an expression that becomes a decades-long refrain; as late as 1950, for instance, a Loy poem pays homage to decimated New Yorkers "turning a dorsal retaliation / on closed entrance" (*LaLB* 281; *LoLB* 136).

Portal to endlessness, Loy's blind back is constructed as an express counter to "REALISM'S BLIND FORCE" (*SE* 239). "Choked" though we are by "the tatters of tradition", for Loy, we can access infinitude spatiotemporally and somatically. Throughout her writings, eternity manifests as a pressure of "incalculable tonnage" bearing down upon the embodied being, a metaphor that first arises in Loy's description of the oppressive "Night" as she walks with trepidation through the Mexican jungle in 1917 (*LoLB* 71;

SE 141–2). "[A] shaft of rushing 'force', with an impact-potential of incalculable tonnage descended from above" runs along Loy's vertebrae in the "Incident" of 1919, an experience that she returns to in "Visitation of Insel" (c. late 1930s), where this "incalculable voltage conducted by the spinal column" is theorised as "the force that drives us" (*SE* 37; *I* 160). Looming, this power can "crush th[e] body to infinitesimal fractions of atoms"; running down the spine as lightning rod, it likewise possesses the potential to reanimate, to clear "blocked up channels", offering voluminous relief (*SE* 38; *CP* 20: 1). Encountered, the force draws us out of ourselves, proliferating our subjectivity *ad nauseam*, "giv[ing] us the impression of being the witness of our own experience, of witnessing that witness and of witnessing that witnessing, until there is no end to the multiplication of the witnessed witness within us" (*CP* 20: 1). Intractable, the blind back brings this existential tongue-twister to a close, shutting the door firmly on introspeculation run amok. For if humans remain "a covered entrance to infinity", this containment directs and orders: "Being alive is a 'walling in' by our blind back[,] a convenient housing of our biological perfections, for otherwise who can tell but that we might be looking out of front and back windows at once[?]" (*CP* 20: manuscript scrap 1). Delineator of our third dimensionality, gateway to the "[n]onentity of force, of pressure, more pressure", the blind back is threshold to the "limbo ever present" to humanity, is site of ascension and circumscription alike (*SE* 287).

Valve, seal, shutter, wall, door, threshold: Loy's diction presents the blind back as domestic architecture. As such, the blind back is a defining feature, both as anatomy and edifice, of recalled childhood experiences that establish the foundations for the later theory and thematic. From her earliest writings, Loy aligns home and self, presenting the room as "an enlargement of the body", and "windows and doors" as "versions of the senses" or, as Loy puts it, spaces through which "scattered mental currents" can "be set to words" (Scarry 38; *IA* 58: 5). At its most ideal, the home constricts protectively to release "the human being's most expansive potential" (Scarry 40). By claustrophobic contrast, Loy recalls her family dwelling as narrow to suffocation, one among many "sheltered homes of the nineties" where "daughters were bullied to maturity" and "subject to prohibitions unmodified since babyhood" (*IA* 67: 91). The ripple effect of Loy's own leaden *fin-de-siècle* upbringing can be observed in her lifelong bids to uncouple the domicile from the individual. In "Aphorisms on Futurism" (1914), Loy insists that we must "FORGET" that we inhabit homes in order to "live in [ourselves]";

for Loy, "the smallest people" – those, presumably, with the most limited world view – "live in the greatest houses", remaining bound by outer shell rather than expansive phenomenal pith (*LoLB* 149). Resistance to the residence-self recurs in Loy's play "The Pamperers" (1920), where the protagonist is Houseless Loony, a name equating homelessness with a madness his followers interpret as genius. "Turn everything upside down and inside out . . . and you'll get on",[1] the Loony is counselled, a phrasing that recurs in "Piero and Eliza." (c. 1920s), where Loy's unhappily married occultist Eliza observes that the very "planes of the walls [of her home] seemed to turn inside out to withhold the fulfilment of life from her" (*SE* 181, 100).[2] Houses may live and breathe like the subject – Loy's family home in St John's Wood, London is "a discreet lady, with its turret decollate" – but Loy's stronger characters resist becoming overdetermined by the husks we inhabit (*IA* 63: 33).

The exception to this rule is the person preoccupied by portals or thresholds that bear resemblance to the blind back in being traps *and* sites of liberation. A subset of Loy's early poems – "Virgins Plus Curtains Minus Dots" (1915), "The Effectual Marriage" (1917), and "At the Door of the House" (1917) – focuses on women keen to pass through a literal or figurative doorway toward heteronormative loves suspiciously idealised, their highly problematic, patriarchally romantic promise satirically on show. By extension, in Loy's later work, entryways are metaphoric for penetrated vaginas, so that the feminist creation mythology emergent in *The Child and the Parent* (c. 1932–6) includes a serpent watching over "the trap-door of ostracism" that opens out upon women's otherwise repressed, scorned, and dismissed sexual pleasure. For Loy, women refrain from crossing this threshold only because of their well-earned suspicion that, once entered, this otherwise "ideal edifice . . . will in real life turn out to be another [gilded] cage or - - a brick box" (*CP* 15: 40, 42). Where women fear definition by cramped domicile, privileged men have "gates ajar on liberty" (*IA* 58: 124). The three doorways of escape for most constrained women are precisely those that Loy will list in relation to the non-artistic, non-genius homeless people of the Bowery District in New York City: "love, intoxication and religion" (*CP* 18: 63; *LoLB* 140). These are the sites of egress available to the self-as-house that lacks the inherited, identificatory power or genius by which escape is reliably affirmative. But all of Loy's subject houses consistently seek exodus from the perimeters by which they are too too coercively defined. As such, the blind back is one in a series of Loy anatomical portals.

Inhabiting a Victorian household, child-Loy was forever in search of surreptitious exits, book covers among them: "The unyielding limits of home afford the most urgent pressure in ejecting [the will] into a larger sphere", writes Loy by way of explaining the forceful ambition that overcame her in early childhood when she located a "little door" lying "prostrate" upon a table. Opening this book cover, Loy recognises that other worlds await her, a truth propelling her deep, early, and successfully satiated desire to read, an incident to which I will return (*IA* 62: 28–9). Senescent Loy foregrounds the structures she shared with her family that "concretiz[e]" recollection, spaces such as a front door that "framed not a few of [her] memories" or the rise of the stairs against which child-Loy measured her growing legs (Wills 56; *CP* 63: 44; *IA* 66: 60). In turn, architectural metaphors and structures define family dynamics: child-Loy is accused of "cupboard love", and her father keeps his "original self" in "the dark cupboard of his consciousness" (*IA* 66: 63; *GI* 28: 129). Loy "closeted with father" to evade an erratic, vengeful mother who forbade her children from leaving the house, and who employed a widow "to chaperone ... our social engagements with ... walls" so ugly that young aesthete Loy feels that they failed to extend their arms to embrace her, "to gather [her] in as [they] should" (*IA* 67: 98; 68: 132; 61: 20). Bodies and domicile alike are defined by spaces that repel, entrap, or hide away feelings and thoughts that cannot be safely aired. This experience is formative, lasting: life itself Loy describes as a dissolute, definitive edifice: "Being alive is a rectangular recurrence of waking up to the dilation of the same white ceiling, of often rising from a wasted bed, of shutting secretive closets and being swallowed whole by yawning doors". Angular houses have the capacity to devour the ever-amorphous house-self, an experience Loy likens to a "four-cornered invasion of the subconscious mind" (*CP* 20: 11).

The Löwy family lived in a succession of middle-class North London homes that shaped Loy's personality and introspeculative methods. According to Loy's archive, both rely upon a successful "atomic penetration" by materiality, an integration by which "the involuting rhythm of the involuting universe" allows the third dimension to "pass *through*" the introspeculator, who then incorporates phenomenality so that it becomes "a driving factor in his organism—" ("Mi and Lo"). Actively forming Loy's cerebral, contemplative self, these homes also structure familial inconstancies and toxicities, as when Loy's father unexpectedly disappears:

> That day was long and high, coming down from the skylight in the roof led by a staircase backbone like a nervous system entirely deranged. At the end of the flight, the last stairs opened out and curved with the banister which thus seemed beginning to curl round upon itself. If I clung to its support so often, turning and twisting myself with its incipience, it was because I found in it a central spool – a spool on which the nervous filaments that trailed their aerial poisons throughout the house, I must wind up again; wind myself with them also onto a centripetal axis. (IA 63: 47)

Day is brain to a dissolute spinal staircase, radiating nervily anxious filaments that Loy seeks to soothe with order, a place emulating the concerted turns and returns of developing thought. Often, the family mirrors the "*erectilization* or verticalization" of the house, leveraging building and "family spine" into an "upright stance", an ethical unit (Wills 14, 61). Working against her parents' rigid axis, Loy spools self and affect, but "the psychic poison" she consumes in the process splits apart "the 'whole' within [her]" so that her "two halves tur[n] back to back" (IA 63: 48). Divisive, Loy's home reroutes her being, putting her in blind combat with a riven self, forcing her inclinations hindward. Again, Loy insists upon the longevity of these metaphors. In old age, Loy writes, the "foundations sag heavier into earth" until we become "a ramshackle edifice around an external exaltation ... in which the aspirations are a flight of stairs whose base dissolve[s] in the wake of ... ascension" (CP 20: 15). The spine-stairwell remains a site of upward mobility, marked by the possibilities – often derailed – of illumination and ambition.

Pushed backward, Loy must yield or resist, a childhood situation she universalises through the metaphor of the domicile self and its blind dorsality:

> If our potential consciousness is drawn from an infinite reservoir, our restricted and utilitarian consciousness, into which our blind back pushes us through the window of our eyes, is a little front garden for us to potter about in— it is being alive.
>
> An exceptional gardener will succeed in advancing, ever so slightly, the fence that hems his garden in, to enclose a hitherto unfound flower, and discovering it to his fellows he gives them some seed. That is the act of genius.
>
> While others of opposite destiny will have all the rubbish and filth from surrounding gardens dumped into theirs, until they are choked with a miserable refuse from which no man ever emerges .... No flowers can grow out of their bare experience, whose blossoming they may announce to their neighbours over the garden wall. They have

no means of self-expression, yet the infinite potentiality, the incalculable force is inherent to them as it is to us all (CP 20: 5).

In this depiction of consciousness, Loy approximates Bataille's restricted economy, or the circuits of survivalist and social requirement by which organisms find themselves constrained. For Bataille, these limits can only be surpassed in acts of lavish, wasteful expenditure, a wilfully spilt reservoir of infinitude. More tamely, Loy argues that to be fulsomely alive is to cultivate pleasure and beauty, rather than mere sustenance. While we all have eyes that draw us away from the transcendent blind back toward materiality, some of us make of that reality a garden, others a wasteland.

In *Notes on Thought and Vision* (1919), Loy's esoteric modernist peer H. D. replicates these metaphors precisely, describing our minds as "dull little houses . . . . shelte[ring] a comfortable little soul". For H. D., we attend unduly to fortifying a back wall that "shuts out completely any communication with the world beyond" while just outside lies "a great vineyard and rioting and madness and dangers" (40–1). As for Loy, H. D.'s "beyond" is an unpredictable cosmos, a challenge to the status quo with strong links to the material. Just as H. D. is against the fortified back walls of "drab" and "grey" domiciles, so too does Loy take issue with domestic rearward partitions, attending to "backs of houses / like old boxes" that overlook shrill, repetitive children, while "tradesmen's entrances" are "steady as blind eyes" attending myopically to attenuated gardens clumsily "bumping their behinds into one another" (H. D. 40; *LaLB* 239; *SE* 35).[3] Both authors expand the parameters of the house-self by theorising a visionary subject: strictly speaking, Loy argues, each of us can pass through the blind back to access the "infinite potentiality" of the cosmos, although some of us, through a combination of destiny and limited fortitude, will remain without these "means of self-expression".

From the time she was "as high as the hedge-grass", child-Loy actively sought her own "little front garden to potter about in", a place to germinate the seeds of her genius. On a country walk with her family, Loy is "isolated by [her] grounded perspective"; as "the tops of her parents vanish on leaning over a fence", she cannot see the expansive view beyond. Faced with obdurate backs that block her vision, Loy focuses on a blue flower that mimics the immense azure of the sky above, and struggles through the fence to retrieve it. Once she has it in hand, she is puzzled: "There is something more about it than itself; the aesthetic suggestion to make beauty one's own through some dimly conceived and incalculable transformation" (*IA* 62: 23–4). Like Stéphane Mallarmé in "Crisis of Verse" (1897), Loy aspires toward "something other than the known bloom"; longing to abandon the "concrete reminder" for a more "pure notion", Loy actively seeks "what is absent from every bouquet" (210). Refusing parental limitation, inspired by captured beauty, it is at this juncture that Loy discovers the will that propels her away from the circumscriptions of the blind back toward the eternality upon which it is also a portal. In Loy's case, this eternality is artistic legacy. Advancing her fences one flower at a time, Loy wants us to know that she works threshold to advantage.

Atavisms: Retral Drag

"[T]he shutting of doors is a concentration of our radiations in rectangular containers", writes Loy in *Insel* (32). To Insel Loy attributes a capacity to close doors like no other, a willed self-enclosure that frees his "infinitesimal currents" to extend from his body like primordial fur that has "[t]he mesmeric rhythm of a film" (*I* 32–3). Primordial yet akin to technological innovation, Insel best exemplifies how Loy's infinity lies uniformly behind us, yet is alternately atavistic, a site of retral drag, or anteriorly transcendent, working toward an idealised future. Thus, in a paragraph Mary Ann Caws singles out as "well nigh impossible to understand", Insel's authority is compared to that of primeval deities housed in temples, where power was "ritual[ly] focused on the altar", or the elevated space of worship and sacrifice from which ancient priests descended face forwards, knowing that "if the blind back were turned upon it they would receive a shock that flung them to the ground" (*Mina* 126; *I* 32). This is the dynamism Insel wields over fellow protagonist Mrs Jones even after she turns her back on their relationship, leaving Insel in war-expectant Paris to sojourn to safety in the United States. This capacity is a site of unease that speaks to Loy's ambivalence about the inherent atavism of the blind back, particularly when that rearwardness is not under her discernible control or is not at a full enough remove from her understanding of herself as a strong-minded genius. Where Loy welcomes the transgressions of conscious regressions, atavisms too unknowable or uncontrolled disconcert. This disquiet is evident in an episode of *Insel* that was not filed with Loy's typescripts of the novel, and also within the recesses of her Beinecke archive, where the atavism of the blind back is likened to intellectual deficiencies over which Loy exerts a benevolent if distinctly masterful judgement.

In "Visitation of Insel", the latterly discovered episode of Loy's novel, Insel reappears in a vision experienced in Jones's New York flat. This manuscript is among the most replete articulations of the warring propulsive tendencies of Loy's dorsality. Firmly "[a]ttached to his blind back," Insel "submi[ts] to opposite gravities, terrestrial & celestial, pulling him downward and upward . . . . [w]hen he responded only to the terrestrial, his body became heavy like lead; *when more rarely, to the celestial*, his spirit lightening, he diminished in weight"; striking a balance between the two, Insel is "in equilibrium", poised between "crimson circulation" and "phosphorescent circulation", blood and radiant ether alike (emphasis added, *I* 161–2). Riveted to the pivot point between mortal gravitas and spiritual weightlessness, Insel's "antediluvian tail anchor[s] him in the past" as he "[n]uzzle[s] the future" (*I* 161). Thus positioned, Insel embodies "[t]he surrealist man", or he who accesses all stages of evolution, journeying from the religious to the scientific, from the Stone Age to the realm of "future facilities" that include "[t]ransport telepathy, radio, & television" observed with "X-ray eyes" (*I* 163–4). For Insel, this experience is unsustainable, and he becomes the sacrificial victim of his own deifying altar, imploding before Jones's channelling gaze (*I* 165). As Loy argues in "Mi & Lo", the blind back "is the arresting plane on which the universe like a cinema on the screen, through the medium of the senses, projects itself." Were this screen to become non-extant, "the projectiles of phenomena traverse the man, who is then to all intents and purposes 'not there'" (*SE* 276). Overwhelmed – literally thrown over – by the screen to which he is attached, vision-Insel dissipates.[4]

Less responsive to the celestial than he is to the terrestrial, Insel is unbalanced, and his disproportion is foregrounded throughout Loy's novel. Insel introspeculates magnificently, turning his "back on the world [to] tiptoe expectantly" into his "mischievous" consciousness, continually "re-see[ing]" himself to "insure" the "continual projection" of his own "lovely illusion" (*I* 109). But to sustain this "cerebral acrobatic recoil", Insel rejects the future, which "ebb[s] from him as from others the past" (*I* 109). He is profoundly, and for Jones, troublingly, determined to "tur[n] his blind back on the forward direction—" (*I* 57). Even in his painting, Insel foregrounds the rearward: one of his most notable subjects is "a gigantic back of a commonplace woman looking at the sky" (*I* 4). Loy critics have generatively compared this work of art to *Expectation* (1935–6), a painting by Insel's prototype, the Surrealist Richard Oelze.[5] In reducing Oelze's portrait of a rectilinearly postured, skyward-facing crowd to a single woman with whom Jones is obsessed, and finds herself inadvertently mimicking, Loy appears to transpose Jones into this representation, a position Carolyn Burke, for instance, accepts wholesale (*BM* 385). But Jones, arch, stylish avant-gardiste, is neither over-sized nor "commonplace", a phrase implying ordinariness and, possibly, working-class stature. Instead, the narrative assessment of Insel's painting, and Jones's uncontrolled response to its "eerie" contents, underscores Loy's anxiety about the extent to which the blind back can exert an overpoweringly atavistic hold (*I* 4).

Hints of this anxiety surface elsewhere in Loy's romans à clef. Attributing the child's fear of the dark to "dangers threatening from the rear", Loy lists among these psychological threats "primeval ancestors", "the first remonstrance [springing] from behind", and the ever-present "blind back that has slammed like a shutter on a lost dimension" (*IA* 63: 50; *G32* 13–14). Parts of Freud's psychic anatomy are at work in this list: parental and civilisational censoriousness exert their pressures, as does genetic inheritance. A similar equation is made in Loy's curious variant of a Freudian primal scene more awkward than violent or traumatising: imagining her parents' first sexual liaison, Loy positions them naked upon a felled Tree of Knowledge, an Adam and Eve plagued by self-consciousness, eluding "re-adaptation", "except to the innermost retreat of a primeval selfhood, of which little remains but a blinded atavism" (*CP* 15: 47). Furthering this abject depiction, Loy elsewhere compares the blind back to the opened exoskeleton of an invertebrate mired in sea-wrack: an empty shell, a leveraged coffin marking past animations, subject to reclamation by the aquatic first home of all life (*CP* 20: 7). In like fashion, by the end of his novel, Insel appears to have degenerated too far and far too introspectively into the ever-present lapsarian risk posed by the blind back. Having journeyed from artist, mesmerist, conjuror, and psychoanalytic subject to mere "drug addict", Insel has become unpalatably anti-positivist, a little too uncontrollably regressed (*I* 159).

Contrary to the condemnatory outcome of *Insel*, Loy intends the blind back as diagnosis and cure for what ails the most ailed minds. "[A]ll of us are served from the illimitable reservoir of potentiality", writes Loy with reference to the "incalculable force" upon which the blind back acts as dam, "but some of us are soused by it." The soused are those whose perceptive capacity remains "comatose" as "potentiality loads up against the back of their mind which like an idiot stuffed with shadows lies monstrously asleep" (*CP* 20: 6).

In her poem "Hot Cross Bum" (1950), Loy repeats these terms: the homeless people she describes fall prey to the blind back, the "inideate shutter" or "indirective / abortive ocular" that "halt[s] the bon-fire of the soul" before it can "kindl[e] the eyes", subjecting its victims to "hinterland stupor" (*LoLB* 134). If we were in any doubt that the scabrously eugenicist Loy of "Feminist Manifesto" (1914) were operative in these instances, our worries are confirmed by the archived notes for "Mi & Lo" entitled "IDIOTS AND BLIND BACK". In them, Loy advocates on behalf of gathering "interesting psychological data" by "subject[ing] idiots to the same conditions of trance hypnosis as are used for neurotic and mediumistic subjects." To do so, she believes, would be to discover that "the life-impressions of normality were registered on some deeper lying strata of consciousness than is usual". Too subterranean in the first instance, in the mentally ill or disabled these "life-impressions" are encumbered a second time by their lack of a "communicatory apparatus" to bring them "to the surface on which the interplay of normal experience among human beings takes place." Loy confidently posits that "future psychiatrists will find all forms of dementia curable by a process of readjustment of drawing consciousness again—forwards—to assist it out of its relapse into the blind back" ("Mi and Lo"). Or, as she puts it more succinctly on another page: "Idiots / Recession of Consciousness / to the / BLIND / <u>BACK</u>" ("Mi and Lo").

In these archived notes, Loy takes on the role of lay psychoanalyst, encouraging a return to medical treatments for hysteria, and advocating on behalf of an ill-defined psycho-chiropractic manipulation to free minds filled with erroneous images and repressions. As liberator of the subjugated mind and concomitantly struggling body, Loy proves blithely amenable to measuring a social "normality" that elsewhere she finds egregiously masculinist. In these instances, the blind back resembles the Freudian unconscious that the early Loy denigrates as the "rubbish heap of race-tradition" (*LoLB* 152). A direct descendent of the *fin-de-siècle* "'golden age of the subconscious'", Loy demonstrates her awareness in these draft manuscripts that this part of the psyche is mnemic repository and preverbal, unknowable beast always "subject to the disruptive pull of an evolutionary past" (Taves 307; Cooper 24). These notes further underscore what has been discussed in these volumes as Loy's ongoing equivocations regarding psychoanalysis, her oscillations between resistance toward its anatomies and co-optation of the same within her esoteric frameworks.[6] As importantly, the notes betray

Loy's understanding that, although the blind back signals regression as much as transcendence, its originating theorist considers herself a genius assured of her imperviousness to uncontrolled manifestations of the former. For if the blind back "is the arresting plane" or screen upon which the universe projects itself, Loy's künstlerromans strive to posit her as a scion in command of the truth that "actuality is only a screen between our self and its realisation" (*SE* 276; *GI* 28: 118). Mitigated by a nod toward incredulity at her confidence, Loy nevertheless distinguishes herself from "the unstemmed procession of the generations", maintaining that she knew from an early age that artists like herself possess the will to access the "idol of exstasy", or the transcendent (*GI* 28: 118). Mastery of the blind back is key to this access, and theorists with whom Loy was conversant – Henri Bergson, but still more emphatically, Frederic Myers – affirm the viability and potentiality of this practice.

Geniuses: Retrocognition

A Freudian concern for repressions excessive or insufficient is not the only discernible influence on Loy's dorsality. The blind back assuredly threatens us with mental regression, but with skilful management, it is also a conduit to genius. In this manifestation, Loy returns to Henri Bergson's subjective temporality and incorporates the self-affirming subliminality of Frederic Myers, whose theories of an evolving, embodied psyche directly inform Loy's thinking. According to Bergson, human intellect and consciousness are, by nature, retrospectively oriented; though we look and move forward, we are far more attached to the harmonious "*already-made*" than to the unceasing novelty of the "*being-made*" (*CE* 35; 117; 136). To access "true continuity, real mobility" and the "reciprocal penetration" of experiential temporalities fundamental to our creative evolution, we must "revers[e the] natural direction" of the intellect, causing it to "twis[t] about on itself" (*CE* 95). Developmentally important, this process does "violence to our nature": it "contract[s] of our whole being in order to thrust it forward"; it propels itself toward clear perception and free will only briefly sustained before being wrenched away from aspirational destination to point of departure (*CE* 136). Origin and individual history lie behind us, a cumulative past that monstrously "grows without ceasing, so that there is no limit to its preservation" (*CE* 12).

Or, as Loy puts it, her diction and syntax mimicking the Sisyphean labour at stake:

provided with our ocular scoop, [we] go forward mining the spectacle confronting us, while behind us, situate as we are in the atmosphere and our activity causing a constant emptying of our aerial mould whenever we move the impalpable matter into which we are packed, rushes in to refill it. (*CP* 20: 10)

As this quotation demonstrates, Loy's incalculable tonnage is not only cosmic power, but ever-expanding personal freight. So too is Bergson's being a snail encumbered by its inextricable load: the "prenatal dispositions" from which it sprang, as well as "all that we have felt, thought and willed from our earliest infancy . . . pressing against the portals of consciousness that would fain leave it outside". For Bergson, we must continually torque our rear-regardant minds forward, and draw upon our past selectively, even as untrustworthy, aggressive memories bang intrusively upon "the half-open door" of the present moment, the becoming-self that strives toward innovation, "*useful* work", and the ideas that transcend the already known (*CE* 13). To fail to resist our past, always "advancing from behind", is to be a traveller who perceives only "the point at which he had ceased to be", unable to "determine his actual position except by relation to that which he had just quitted, instead of grasping it himself" (*CE* 166). Self-warping, then, is inextricable from human accomplishment; genius works against but needs the back.

Plentiful evidence suggests that Loy shares Bergson's concern that humanity remains problematically attached to the harmonious "*already-made*" – habits, memories, thought-through thoughts – than to the receptive, inspired present that is Bergon's dynamic "*being-made*", a term reverberant in Loy's defining phrase, "being alive" (*CE* 35, 117, 136). As early as her 1914 "Aphorisms on Futurism" Loy bellows at her audience: "YOU prefer to observe the past on which your eyes are already opened", berating them for "slipping back into the turbid stream of accepted facts" (*LoLB* 149–50). Too easily, the masses reoccupy the status quo upon which civilisation stagnantly relies. More than two decades after "Aphorisms", distaste for this same resignation recurs in Loy's work as Jones sits at Hôtel Lutetia with Insel and realises that the "pagan Paris" after which the building is named "might very well be actually surviving for our blind backs which, taking no part in the present, are carried around with us as if concrete in the past" (*I* 37).[7]

But Loy's derogation is not totalising. Where Bergson implicitly values retrogression, in Loy's romans à clef, she repositions the blind back as fundamental to a conscious, creative self, writing:

our small share in the universal consciousness seems to be in some way restricted by the dominant movement of life: forwardness. We are featured forwardly, we look, sound, toe and finger forwardly while the time we take to make use of our senses moves forward with Life. *As if* we would flee from our blind back because Life began as an impulse to issue from nothingness. (emphasis added, *CP* 15: 53)

Continual progress postures and imposes; continual flight from the past fails to recognise the universal intelligential ether from which life begins, a substance Loy countenances continually in her work, as did a number of Anglo-European artists and scientists up to and through the 1930s.[8] Too absorbed with "escap[ing] from the body to mix with the outside world", consciousness loses contact with what "lies behind the frontiers of instinct", namely, "intangible dimensions of concentrated distance" (*CP* 15: 53). A "diffused nearness of things enormous and sublime", these dimensions are potentially discernible by science but remain at one remove from the individual, meaning "[t]he body is unknown to itself" (*CP* 15: 53–4). Unknown, except for rare moments of "inverted consciousness" when "[t]he introspector is aware that he is connective with infinite distance—" (*CP* 15: 54; *SE* 278). In these instances, we step outside of our body to return to it anew: swoons, meditation, visions, or the first self-reflexive grasp of our own reflection. The latter experience is recounted in detail in *The Child and the Parent*.

Loy's articulation of the Lacanian mirror stage occurs closer to adolescence than infancy and is more epiphanic than developmental. Loy likens her reflection to the following: a dead pearl or marine bloom in the "ocean from which it originally arose"; a mesmerisation in which she is "held in trance by [her]self"; a disquieting moment of discerning "[t]he unreal distance between [her]self and 'it'", and a face she anticipates, with excitement, into a future, whilst remaining aware that, like the blind back, this is a part of her anatomy that she will "never see" unaided (*CP* 15: 9–10). Two recurrent Loy themes arise in this defining incident. Firstly, introspection is a self-nostos affirming our somatic, affective existence. As Loy argues: "once we find out we have a face [we] must endlessly project a self out of Ourself to run on a short way before us, and wheeling round, constantly recognize us in being, as it were, brought face to face with Ourself." To do so is to "become like a driver walking backwards holding a bouquet of carrots to draw the ass of our self-esteem on." Rearguardedness confirms both bodily front and laggard ass, or the all-too-comically multivalent locus of Loy's "self-assurance" (*CP* 20: 7–8). Turning, the self perceives that it exists. Secondly, the retrogression embedded in the turn toward anteriority restores the universal sublimity from which the infant emerges and to which, as artist and intellectual, Loy strives to return. Detailing her Victorian upbringing where time stretched and jeered at her child-self, Loy attributes her sanity to a resolutely satiric "sense of proportion" and the preservation of "enough of [her] infant vision" or "natal illumination" that she continued to access and be able to assess "the blatant purity of an inconceivable aesthetic" (*CP* 12: 20; *IA* 61: 20). By regressive attachments to self and ethereal origins – intangible dimensions distant, proximate, and ecstatically sublime – Loy confirms her creative genius, arrière- and avant-garde.

Both individually and universally, Bergson acknowledges that human development emerges out of retral drag: between the great lines of evolution "run a crowd of minor paths in which ... deviations, arrests, and set-backs, are multiplied" (*CE* 66). Despite his emphasis on pushing forward, Bergsonian evolution is not rectilinear, but "a kind of circle"; revolution requires the curve of return (*CE* 78). A similar duality defines Freud's mental anatomy: his unknowable id can unexpectedly engage in problem-solving, self-criticism, and moral judgement, meaning that, alongside housing "the lower passions", "what is highest in the ego can be unconscious" ("Ego" 26–7). Of the theorists with whom Loy came into contact, however, it is Frederic W. H. Myers who most clearly anticipates Loy's own arrière-gardedness, as he integrates the experiential past, be it instinctual, mnemic, or repressed, into a harmonious subjectivity symbiotic with a mystical universe.

A recognised influence on Bergson and Freud, Myers splits the psyche into subliminal and supraliminal, demarcated by a porous threshold or diaphragm.[9] As the etymology of his terminology suggests, Myers's subliminality is related to a celestial sublime, and to what lies "'beneath ... threshold'"; the Latinate roots of "limen", "lintel" in Anglo-Saxon referred to cross-pieces at the top and base of doors (Myers 13; Cohn and Miles 292). Quite unlike Freud, Myers believes humanity is evolving toward a greater integration of its mental anatomy, and that once this integration is complete, paranormal activities – telepathy, visions, mystical ecstasy – will become comprehensible. Acknowledging that psychology importantly delineates the "infinitesimal psychical elements" of the human intellect, and religion insists upon the "underlying unity ... of a human soul", Myers's mental anatomy strives for a middle ground whereby the subliminal self offers what one of Myers's contemporaries considered "a profounder synthesis" of emotions, sensations, and thoughts, all animated by a spiritual energy that retains a bond with the higher strata of the cosmos (Myers 11–12, 45; McDougall 515–16). And, as was discussed in Chapter 1, love, Loy's esoteric flashpoint, importantly provides "the energy of integration" key to Myers's synthesis (Myers 61). Via intellection and love, Myers confirms, "the everyday self", our physical body, grasps its "permeab[ility] to subliminal impulses", with no self as generatively porous as the wilful genius-creator (61).

"Sublimation" became an alchemical term in the seventeenth century, and Myers stays truer to these transformative, heterodox origins than Freud, in whose hands sublimation refers to the sacrifice of the instincts, the repression upon which civilisation relies (Cohn and Miles 303). Where Freud's subconscious is prey to the primeval, Myer's subliminality is unmitigatedly utopian, the foundation of an evolutionary future of "modern redemption and cosmic reconciliation" (Cooper 24; Schneider 69). Psychological fissiparity – the subliminal inclination toward division and reinvention – Myers attributes to as-yet-unknown perceptivities (Taves 316, 322). Myers's proof? Retrocognition: paranormally acquired knowledge of the past (Myers 201). Retrocognition includes premonition or paramnesia, states Loy variously terms introspeculation, "[s]urpris[es] of unwarranted recognition", or "the déjà vu of infantile continuity" (*CP* 15: 9–10; 13: 30).

Introspeculation is, for Loy, a necessity born of the limitations of a terrestrial existence where we observe our advance and recession, where movement and development are continually tallied, gauged. In "extrospection", a state of transcendent perfection, the conception of ideas coincides perfectly with their realisation; introspection recognises the lag between these two states that is a defining limitation of life in three dimensions. Introspection is aspirational, moving always toward "as yet unsown fields of consciousness", or the subliminal realm where the genius will "unbuil[d]" the mind "for a divine re-edification" (*SE* 282).[10] Relying on backwardness – unbuilding, re-edifying – Loy's introspeculation is exemplified by the porous somnolence of meditation, a somatic honing that echoes Myers's "spiritual indrawing", his term for "sleeping vision, for hypnotic rejuvenation, for sensory and motor automatisms, for trance, for ecstasy." These are the states Myers implores psychologists to foreground by way of bringing their field closer to sanctity, or "the genius of the ethical realm" (62). For Loy and Myers, these processes require the wilful cultivation of will-lessness. As Loy avers in "History": our consciousness is only as limber as "the contemporary stage of evolution" attained "in the *concrete world*". By a well-exercised phenomenal existence we can "*stretch* . . . into the imperceptible universe", and are best placed to withstand "[t]he snap-back of human consciousness from the take-off of inspiration" (*SE* 245).

Myers's theories impact the substance of Loy's romans à clef, and the paradoxical, porous threshold that is her blind back. Conveniently evading her family of origin, or the circumstances of her mother's real-life parturition, Loy begins *Goy Israels: A Play of Consciousness*, *The Child and the Parent*, and *Islands in the Air* by affirming Myers's basic premise, namely that birth is a descent from a higher plane to which our personality returns in the afterlife. Like Myers, Loy is an esotericist who retains an allegiance to "the old-world conception of a *soul*" that aspires to control all parts of the psyche whilst remaining conversant with, and immersed in, a responsive universe (45, 62). Loy's soul is metaphysical and material. It enables self-reflexive thought, allowing us to step outside of ourselves and perceive philosophically, as will be discussed in the upcoming section on pineality (*SE* 273). But it is also the embodied locus by which humanity processes pleasure and pain. In an archived discussion of these two states as "the opposite poles of sentience", Loy defines pleasure as "the attraction of the body towards the soul" and somatic discomfort or trauma as "the attraction of the body away from the soul" ("Mi and Lo"). Her soul is inextricably anatomised, spatial. In turn, Loy's autobiographical project might be read as the cartographic response to the plaintive question posed in *Islands in the Air*: "If the barque of the soul be drawn out of the ocean of potency, what is the chart of the voyage it shall make?" (63: 53).

In Loy's künstlerromans, vital essence continues to be as physical as it is mystical. Loy may mock "that nincompoop The Flesh", but her soul "strain[s] every sinew" and her spirit is prey to injury, can be "bar[ed] . . . to the quick" (*CP* 16: 53; *GI* 28: 9; *IA* 65: 66). The finite matters; matter matters. Myers's influence is discernible in this regard also. For just as Loy stresses that it is by "the medium of the senses" that we understand the phenomenal, for Myers, too, "the five senses are a reduced selection of the sensory tools available to the subliminal self" (*SE* 276; Cooper 28). By this linking of the subliminal and the felt, Myers's immortal "personality becomes not only dispersed over time and space, but also coextensive with the material world and human history" (Vrettos 206). The artistic soul is master of the phenomenal, medium to the subliminal. Soul is the substance of Myers's and Loy's artist, who, like the genius, is exceptionally attuned to "*subliminal uprush[es]*" that offer ideas fresh, profound, and creative to the supraliminal self, enacting close watch over both the "primitive source and extra-terrene initiation of life" upon which Loy's blind back opens (42, 57). In this regard, Myers succeeds again where Freud fails: for Loy, Freud's subconscious "seems . . . more of a dumping ground for cast-off impressions" that does "not leave much room in it for evolving creative inspiration" (Letter dated 28 March 1913, "Loy, Mina, 1913–1920, n.d.", Mabel Dodge Luhan Papers). Skilled at maximising the generative potential of the portal dividing subliminal from supraliminal, Myers's artists interpret and re-create our three-dimensional world.

Actively "reap[ing] most advantage from . . . submerged mentation" (16), Myers's genius operates in express accord with Loy's affirmation of her autobiographical practice:

> To discover the hidden influences that affected my childhood, I have had to seek further and further back until, coming to the prenatal, I must inevitably imagine events that took place before I was born.
>
> For this I have to use a little hearsay, a few confidences, some personal observation, and above all, evoke that voiceless converse I held in my infancy with the souls of entrails.
>
> To do so is simple. I need only lift a 'feeling' out of the past to find that this long[-]buried impression is still so distinct I can re-experience it in the present, and submit it to mental analysis, just as a poet reproduces an impression with an <u>exact</u> word.
>
> So in some strange way I give to a past generation a more lucid existence than they had at the time; they who were so little conscious of themselves they went into eternity undefined. (*CP* 16: 46)

The cliché of the artist as god is expanded here to cosmic proportions. Loy exerts deific mastery over her own past and its narration, but also claims access to a universal recollection, a clairvoyance expressly likened to poetic genius. These processes are aided by Loy's childhood capacity to commune with "the souls of entrails" of the adults with whom she resided, a refrain of Loy's romans à clef (*CP* 12: 19; 13: 26; *IA* 61: 19). The classical seat of emotion, these viscera are exceptionally receptive, by Loy's calibration, to divination. Loy's terminology reinforces her sacrificial proclivities yet again, confirming her status as the practitioner of a ritual practised in ancient cultures – Etruscan, Roman, Greek, Hebraic – wherein the bowels of immolated animals were interpreted by way of prophesying the future. Loy is invert haruspex, drawing upon recollections of live bowels to gain mastery over the past. That child-Loy comes face to parental back so memorably and often suggests a great deal about the communication and power dynamics of her family of origin. But this memory also affirms that Loy, as artist, deciphers behindedness from an early age, recognising even among its most absurdly abject manifestations a capacity to commune with a beyond. Just so does the paradox of the blind back take hold.

Loy is far more reliant on the word "subconscious" than "subliminal" in her late writings, but, for her, these terms mean interchangeably, enact a like retrograde pull on the evolving self.[11] Populated with spectres from the divine realm from which it finds itself outcast, Loy's childhood subliminality is site of warfare, "befuddled disgusts", accumulated rages, unbidden memories of uncanny Victorian entertainments, and maternal nightmare.[12] It is also freighted with chance: unexpected disaster and will-challenging accidents of destiny.[13] "Man is little else than a vehicle for forces whose inherence to himself he cannot explain", Loy writes at one juncture, describing this situation as a yielding to the "diabolical obstinacy of the sub-conscious". Immediately thereafter, she refers directly to Myers: "when we listen to arguments in favour of the survival of personality, it is not so much the plausibleness of the Immortal we call into question, but the existence of any personality for survival" (*CP* 16: 55). Unbidden forces permeating humanity include unearned self-importance, prejudice, irresistible criminality, and the "subliminal convinc[ing]" of women blind to the truth of a domestic "self sacrifice" that is merely "a foolish appending of an irretrievable life capital" (*GI* 28: 64, 67). In each of these instances, the will of weak individuals succumbs to a collective subliminality that undermines Myers's call to ongoing individual definition or autonomy in the beyond.[14] But their lack helpfully underscores Loy's remarkable capacity: as a "child microcosm" she is a "seedling of all evolution" incorporating "not only the reflorescence of the past, but also a germination of the ultimate blossoms of consciousness" (*CP* 13: 31).

Worth preserving and nurturing, Loy's subliminality is always at risk from "preceptors ... planting a blade in her to turn among the subliminal roots of her faculties to lop off the green shoots of initiative" (*GI* 28: 39). Loy's künstlerromans confirm her subliminal endurance, her cultivation of herself as an artist who evolves through the primeval toward transcendence, an artist with a distinct personality destined to outlast mere mortality. An inspired genius who excels at retrocognition, Loy is not to be mistaken for a woman blind to the truth of her own wasted experience as it futilely conglomerates behind her. But Loy is interested in what the laboured, vulnerable female blind back might tell us about ecstasy.

Decimations: Bowed Backs

The woman's back is a unique category in Loy, predictably if presciently hunched under an imposed burden, protective of its beleaguered body. As Pazzarella's repeat "falling back" alone attests, Loy's female dorsality can be unduly physical, palpably subject to the acute "psychic pressure" that is the incalculable patriarchal tonnage pressurising "the blind emergence of . . . crushed li[ves]" (*SE* 92; *CP* 12: 20). Loy's women tend to measure themselves by "the ultimate fictitious value" of the male forever "haunting the back of their minds", the "galvanic presence" animating womankind's otherwise "egoless amalgam" (*CP* 18: 64–5). Enforced gender roles result in a female back preoccupied by the male gaze and sexualised, reproductive expectations, the "peeping space" that "enraptur[es male] pursuit" and is never discouraged by "repulse" (*SE* 61). By these constraints, women's dorsality ossifies into a lived disablement. For instance, as defeated wife of the abusive Esau Penfold, the fictional name ascribed to her first husband, Loy "lived to the break-back rhythm" of futilely stooping to lift things up, among them his perpetually scattered objects and her shattered spirit (*EP* 21). In turn, any woman enthralled by heteronormative domesticity ends up with "bowed back", becoming "an exhausted phantom bowing upon itself", ultimately, even hyperbolically, yielding to a life of "paralysis" (*CP* 15: 42, 45). Loy herself developed spinal osteoarthritis in late life, a condition caused by wear and tear to which women are known to be more susceptible than men (*BM* 439).

In emblematising the female back, Loy foresees the phenomenological claim Iris Marion Young makes in 1980:

> Women in sexist society are physically handicapped. Insofar as we learn to live out our existence in accordance with the definition that patriarchal culture assigns to us, we are physically inhibited, confined, positioned, and objectified. As lived bodies we are not open and unambiguous transcendences that move out to master a world that belongs to us, a world constituted by our own intentions and projections. ("Throwing" 153)

Created in Adam's wake, woman must always fall behind, Loy tells us a trifle too sincerely in her feminist satire of creation mythology that surfaces in both *The Child and the Parent* and *Islands in the*

Air. For Loy, women are foreordained to "being carried along on the Everlasting's back", living a daily hellish infinitude, bringing "only a partial presence to the pursuits of man", his self-absorbed virility first and foremost (*CP* 18: 67).

Women's back-breaking domestic drudgery is not alleviated by sexual satiation: to brides on their honeymoons Loy attributes palpable dread of "awful kisses that crawl down [the] spine and bid the body hope all over again", awakening and reawakening a desire that entitled mortal men fail to vanquish (*CP* 17: 56, 58–9). Sex leads to aching backs, body parts that oracularly pronounce judgement upon unidirectional male intimacy. This situation is emphatically Victorian, English: the generation preceding Loy's own she labels "the collective backbone mother" to "collective backbone child" (*EP* 24). The collective is the British Empire, itself a suspect body sustained by too-complicit women, and mothers in particular, a conflation that runs through Loy's künstlerromans.[15] Loy's dorsally oriented critique of the vulnerability and perseverance of the English lady at the Victorian hearth chimes with the novel *Flatland* (1884), a satire of the hierarchical extremities of nineteenth-century England that becomes, in author Edwin A. Abbott's hands, a two-dimensional world of geometrical figures in which power is indicated by the shape of the body. Where nobility is polygonal, lowly women are but a line; from the rear they are akin to needles – "*all* point" – invisible and dangerous, a truth that further justifies their confinement to the home (Abbott 11–12). It is this very armoured, painfully pressurised female back that prompts a rare moment of empathy from Loy toward the reviled Victorian woman: watching her own mother struggle to rise against the "difficulty of creaking busks", child-Loy feels "overcome by an acute sensation that she is helpless and foolish" and finds herself experiencing a distinctly masculinised "chivalrous impulse to protect this vulnerable being" (*IA* 67: 34). Flexible, free, the child becomes man to the enfeebled, corseted woman. In combination, this feminine, dorsally defined exposure and limitation – particularly its sexual repression – becomes foundational to Loy's expansively ecstatic theory of the blind back.

Insel offers a sustained examination of Loy's feminised "collective backbone child"; throughout, rearguard Insel is *enfant terrible* to the maternalised Jones, and come "Visitation of Insel", Jones extensively surveys the dorsal region of her biological offspring (*EP* 24). In this scene, Jones is an observer within the scopic regime, overlooking and assessing her adult daughter's vulnerable vertebral column as she fixes the hair at the nape of her neck. Viewing Sophia's "slab-like" back, Jones is protective and predatory, finding it insufficiently curvaceous, too bare and severe, yet monumentalises its "crests of soft rocks" upon which rest "the pyramidal folds" of a taffeta dress. Through the "luminous" surface of this female back, Jones locates a "faint electric 'comfort of life'", a mesmerising complacency or domesticity, the harmonious radiance and rhythm "of a figure [Sophia] could not 'see'" (*I* 166–7). Invisible, Sophia's back is a site of personal stress, courtesy of a society that encourages this very anxiety. A woman preparing for a party, Sophia's unreachable, imperceptible dorsality must be as well groomed as her ventrality, a process requiring help from a needy parent Sophia is keen to avoid; what is more, the pressure of Jones's gaze catalyses Sophia's frustration about her own size. Overwhelmed by the always unattainable feminine ideals so evident in her mother's admiration, envy, awe, and estimation, Sophia takes her distress out on Jones: "'Why the hell must you go and marry a great cow of a man? I'm huge!' she exploded" (*I* 166).

A combined site of susceptibility, strength, and appeal, Sophia's back is Rubenesque, stalwart yet exposed. Drawing on classical influences, the Flemish painter Peter Paul Rubens (1577–1640) posited "antiquity as a Golden Age of physical well-being when men and women were bigger and stronger", a "heroic race" whose enormity reflected superiorities moral, intellectual, and cultural (Muller 237). Uniquely among his Western counterparts, Rubens's initial success and eventual fame rested upon his mastery of the female nude (De Clippel 113, 111). Boldly taking up space, Rubens's female subjects nevertheless played into longstanding art historical tropes whereby erotic pleasure is taken in feminine vulnerability; his women are often in pain, distress, and/or a state of undress (Dickey 58). While opinions differ on Rubens's sensitivity toward women's social and political positioning, Rubens is consistent with his era in regularly presenting women as "contorted figures" rising to "the mannerist challenge of showing the front and back" simultaneously, a contrapuntal folding or twisting signalling conflicts internal or suprasensible (Clifton 390).[16] Rubens's skill in this regard is evident in his career-spanning portraits of women's dorsality, among them *Susanna and the Elders* (1607), *Venus Frigida* (1614), *Flight of Cloelia* (c. 1618–19), and *Apollo and Daphne* (1636). And according to Jones in *Insel*, Rubens is the predominant influence on her former husband and Sophia's father, Arthur Cravan (*I* 136). Just as Sophia is one of the names Loy gives to the earliest, most youthful and aspirational vanguard versions of herself in *Brontolivido* and

Esau Penfold, so too has the child Loy had with Cravan lived to become his visually artistic ideal. Predetermined to overdetermination, Sophia's backbone is collectivised, her blind rearwardness coopted by gendered norms and parental expectation alike.

Reproduction, Loy writes in *The Child and the Parent*, is a reversion to Nature, a "primitive" block of evolutionary development and aspiration via a "domestication of the flesh" reducing parents to prototypes striving toward the only remaining miracle within their enfeebled grasp, "the creation of [their] own duplicate." By creating offspring, Loy argues, we further rend the already riven self, yielding to atavistic return whilst "animat[ing] something destined to surpass" us in the future (*CP* 14: 32–3). By renaming her fourth biological child in *Insel* with the exact moniker that she gives early variants of her fictionalised self, Loy effects a curiously narcissistic, intergenerational authorial return. Yet well before *Insel*, real-life events anticipate this return, which is written into the birth certificate of this very daughter, Jemima Fabienne Cravan. Jemima is the second name Loy gives her own character in *Brontolivido*, and this is not the only instance in which Loy's names blur distinctions between herself, her children, and her characters.[17]

These duplications speak to Loy's existential unease about parenting, one that cannot be separated out from the truth that, as autobiographer, Loy births and rebirths herself over a period of five decades, becoming fixated upon, and at times, completely incapacitated by, her desire to create a model of herself that will exceed her. Given this reality, the overdetermined reading Loy offers in "Visitation of Insel" of Jemima Fabienne as a Sophia who repeats and continues Loy becomes still more multivalent: to parent is to reach forward and backward simultaneously, to cast oneself as hinge or threshold. Parenting, then, is as existentially paradoxical as our blind back. And as authorial progenitor, Loy positions Jones at Sophia's Rubenesque rear, scrutinising her daughter's willingness to take on the inevitably "crushed life" of their female ancestry whilst subjectively articulating and shaping their shared legacy (*CP* 12: 20). As Loy writes in "Aid of the Madonna" (1943), a poem contemporaneous with her late, maternally fixated künstlerromans: "Madonnas are islands in memory", or *Islands in the Air* (*LoLB* 115). Shunned by her irate daughter, Loy feels her parental islanding keenly in "Visitation of Insel", yet perpetuates its coordinates, failing to question her responsibility for shared bad feeling. Parenting proves as ambivalent as autobiography, and as the blind back by which Jones exemplifies her own vexed relationship with her daughter.

In *Insel*, Jones references Rubens's foundational influence upon Cravan against her co-protagonist's insistence that her husband sprang fully formed from the art historical ether as the prime catalyst for Surrealism. Her argument silences Insel, but Rubens's impact can be discerned through the Surrealist focus on female dorsality, which permits the blending of a rearward subconsciousness with the sexualised vulnerability of an eternalised and eternally preyed-upon femininity. Man Ray's *Hobby* (1934) captures Kiki de Montparnasse's back painted to resemble a cello; Salvador Dali's *Girl's Back* (1926) centres on the luminous curve of his sister's exposed upper body; two decades later, Dali returns to this thematic in *My Wife, Nude, Contemplating her Own Flesh Becoming Stairs, Three Vertebrae of a Column, and Architecture* (1945), which projects the rearward female subject into a palatial, idealised expanse for the pleasure of painter and viewer alike.

A comparison between the female dorsality of Rubens's *Venus in Front of the Mirror* (1613–15) and René Magritte's *Les Liaisons dangereuses* (1936) shores up Loy's distaste for Surrealism (see Figs 3.2 and 3.3). Where Rubens presents an idealised yet powerful beauty who gazes frankly at us from her mirror, Magritte wilfully contorts the proportions between a downcast woman and her reflection, resulting in a "deformation [that] can be read as central to the self, for the woman divided is also watching herself – without seeing us see her from behind" (Caws, "Ladies" 272). *Les Liaisons dangereuses* illustrates a blind back that is the threshold of a sadistic scopic pleasure, re-enacting the very paternalistic measure against which Jones's Sophia finds herself lacking. Nor does *Les Liaisons* compare favourably to Magritte's more famous *Not to be Reproduced* (1937), in which a man looks at himself in a mirror and sees only his own back; the male retral view is less passive masochistic narcissist than doubly forward-looking, doubly rectilinearly assured of his self-determined future (Fig. 3.4).

Lacking complex ideological contrapposto, Magritte's backs, like Man Ray's and Dali's, place the onus of internalised gendered conflict onto the viewer, a contortion catalysed and compounded by their ongoing replications of female objectification. As Mary Ann Caws argues, for the astute feminist spectator, Surrealist posturing gestures towards a struggle between the sexes only mitigated by the "hop[e] to find [strength] therein" ("Ladies" 267). Loy knew Man Ray through the New York Arensberg Circle from 1916, and befriended Dali and his wife Gala when acting as the Paris agent for the Julien Levy Gallery throughout the 1930s; Dali has a cameo

180 Elevated Realms – An Anatomy of Mina Loy

Fig. 3.1 Peter Paul Rubens, *Venus in Front of the Mirror* (1613–15). Liechtenstein Museum, Wenen.

in *Insel* (Hayden 129–30). Loy encouraged Levy to purchase Dali's work, and sent a Magritte shipment his way in 1931; throughout this decade, she became a recognised expert in Surrealist mores and oeuvres.[18] No wonder Jones impatiently waits with palpable impatience alongside quasi-Surrealist Insel's painting of a "commonplace back of a woman watching for signs on his painted firmament". All too often, Surrealist transcendence is a "chart of unarrival", a path to female unrecognition (*I* 151).

Against these destinationless mappings, Loy posits the unexplored territory of a woman's dorsality defined by a highly somatic Rubenesque contrapposto that viscerally strains and contorts, embodying the physicality that catalyses artistic representation, as well as intimacy and ecstasy. In a heavily redacted passage in

The Blind Back   181

Fig. 3.2 René Magritte, *Les Liaisons dangereuses* (1936). Musée Toulouse-Lautrec; 2016©Photo SCALA, Florence/©ADAGP, Paris and DACS, London 2016.

The Child and the Parent, we witness Loy linking the fundamentals of human expression with a resolutely female blind back. Describing the self as "a siamese twin-ship, in which to ourselves is attached the embodiment of all the rest of mankind", Loy maintains that we are gratified when the ocean of humanity is reduced to a single, "alleviating face of [one] companion". To communicate at all, Loy attests, is an exercise in "twisting peculiarly" toward otherness, "straining from that invisible ligament in *the woman's land of our blind backs* which links the twin to us" (emphasis added, *CP* 20: 14). Ligament, threshold, diaphragm; within this geography of rearward female anatomy we arrive at yet another membranous fold,

Fig. 3.3 René Magritte, *Not to be Reproduced* (1937). Museum Boijmans van Beuningen; 2016©Photo SCALA, Florence/©ADAGP, Paris and DACS, London 2016.

another borderland between unseeing dorsality and forward-facing consciousness. In this instance, Loy gravitates toward dorsality as subliminality, playing on the interpretation – so well evinced by Surrealism – of the subconscious as the feminised primeval, the eternally unknowable and irrational, or what Loy describes at the end of the same passage as the bottomless "dimension inwards, the lair of the soul, which is inviolate."

But while Loy is consumed by the divided self, in this instance, "twin" refers not only to the inevitably bisected individual, but also to the ideal love, the other "half" to which the self was originally conjoined before being brutally severed into an isolate subject, as per the terms famously demarcated by Aristophanes in Plato's fourth-century BCE *Symposium* (59–62). In other words, the "invisible ligament in the woman's land of our blind backs" effects the torsion requisite to Loy's esoteric Eros, the reciprocated "sexual and emotional inclination" toward which her writings aspire (Cavarero 3). Indirectly referencing the Cravan who remains the ideal to which she remains perpetually in thrall, Loy replicates the terms of their all-consuming reunion in Mexico, repeating verbatim the claim she makes in *Colossus*, namely, that the pith of "being alive" rests upon "a soft ferocious longing to unlock the centre of one's self with the centre of some one else" (*CP* 20: 14). But in this instance in *Child*, Loy proves desultory about this ecstatic climax of her intimate life, claiming that "once having been over-alive, the rest of life is a hangover" (*CP* 20: 15). Recalling the decimation of her post-Cravan life, Loy's longing is as definitional as it is unrequited, meaning that the act of communicating with the beloved in present time requires a self-torquing every bit as painful as Bergson theorised.

Loy's twist embodies a vulnerability inherent to dorsality in general, which speaks always to the mysteries and devastating certainties of what lies behind. Breath on the nape of a neck, a poke in the back: these experiences foreground our quotidian blind exposure. "By means of dorsality, sexuality and human relations in general are marked by an extreme vulnerability, by ... passive trust" (Wills 12–13). Loy, too, recognises that intimacy and gender are foundational to this universal susceptibility. As Leo Bersani writes, foregrounding the experience of the queer male: globally, cultures have feared and censured the taking of an individual from behind, given that rearward aggressions and intimacies possess "the terrifying appeal of a loss of the ego, a self-detachment" (212, 220). Combining appeal and loss, welcoming a rearward overtaking signals a potentially universal willingness to sacrifice the self, even as, for Bersani, it asks us to think about sexuality in general as "the risk of self-dismissal, of *losing sight* of the self" (222). Bersani's argument displaces the nexus into which sacrifice, femininity, and lassitude have become interlocked. By his reasoning, losing sight of the self is potentially more generative than self-immolating. Like Loy's esoteric Eros, Bersani's intimate risk eschews staid morality whilst affirming paradoxical truths for all sexes and all sex, perceptions paradoxically widened and deepened by blindness. Notably, both he and Loy arrive at these conclusions by way of re-evaluating an emphatically feminised dorsality.

Loy's blind back contains multitudes, absorbs whilst distinctly maintaining the binaries it straddles, the contrariness it encompasses. Atavistic propulsor into a utopian future, harbinger of backwardness and genius, resolutely physical apex of spiritual transcendence, the blind back is an unseeing prophet mired in past constructs, be they idealistic temples or workaday middle-class homes replete with memories irritating, banal, and traumatic. "[B]eyond the fantasies of bodily power and subordination," writes Bersani, "there is a transgressing of that very polarity which, as Georges Bataille has proposed, may be the profound sense of both certain mystical experiences and human sexuality" (217). For Bataille, sexuality is "self-shattering", a self-abasement in which "the self is exuberantly discarded" (Bersani 218). Bataille longs for an everything, a totality that he ultimately recognises as void and thereby rejects. But Bataille's void is also threshold, the brink where forward-looking ambitions and supinity intersect, and *"[t]he mind moves in a strange world where ecstasy and anguish coexist"* (IE xxxii). From Bataille's renunciation emerges a return to origins: letting go of the desire to be all, to be God, is to accept being human, alone, and comprised of contradictory "*'everythings'*" approximating "idiocy" (IE 22, 25). This torment matters because, without it, the human is vacuous, noncommunicative (IE 26, 53). This torment matters because abandonment is isolation, but it is also, potentially, rapture (IE 53). These are the terms Loy strives to keep aloft with her blind back, which fluctuates between atavism, its pre-intellectuality and primordiality, and a mastery traditionally gendered male. Led by "discursive reason" to an "ecstatic unknowing" demanding its own undoing, its own transcendence, "Bataille describes a dialectic of continual reversal" (Irwin 111). Dissolution, re-creation, redissolution: as Loy herself asserts, sentience oscillates between pain and pleasure, and in turn, pivotally, the vertebrate self oscillates between masculine and feminine ("Miscellaneous").

Loy formulates this thinking when engaging with the Futurists, or those who "dropped consciousness of everything but Rush" yet privileged "activated suspension" over "arrival", thereby remaining troublingly "taut between projection & reprojection" (B 2: 18). Roughly twenty years later, in Loy's philosophical dialogue "Mi & Lo", she describes perfection as a "zone" absent of advance or receding where "infinite dissimilarities are reconciled" (SE 281). A static, affirming middle ground, perfection cannot be realised. Loy shares Bataille's "distrus[t]" if not his outright "hostil[ity] towards the idea of perfection", gravitating instead toward imbalanced extremities (IE 4). For both, consciousness is inclination toward excesses artistic, sexual, or esoteric, a torque Loy figures through a dorsality that must be kept flexible, its ligaments limber, its threshold porous.[19] Consider, again, Loy's apex of aesthetic consciousness, whereby the "creative man is one whose consciousness is deepest within himself" as well as "one whose consciousness travels farthest" – skyward, toward "the outer universe" (*SE* 272). For Loy, it is artists like herself who embrace these polarities, thereby transcending the gendered expectations and repressions emblematised by the female blind back, by Loy's busked Victorian forebears. These oscillations are foundational to the second part of this chapter, in which I consider how Loy recognises rearward sight as a primordial vestige of a once-prescient inner vision that contemporary humanity should recover and reaffirm. Gleaning this perspective from her immediate forebears, Loy uses it to position dorsality as the site by which humanity might catapult itself into a utopian future defined by a transcendently creative application of cutting-edge scientific theory.

Backing and Forthing: Pineal Eye, Fourth Dimension

Loy formulates her blind back in the wake of prominent late nineteenth-century thinkers who prioritised inner vision, William James and Frederic Myers among them, and continues to seek out thinkers who centralise its existence. As discussed in my Preface and first chapter, in the late 1940s, Loy enthusiastically embraces the teachings of Joel S. Goldsmith, a former Christian Science practitioner who conflates prayer and meditation, a methodology he acknowledges is indebted to heterodox tradition, and one by which, "with our inner eye", we aim to "behold the universe of Spirit" (2–3; 120). Loy further formulates her blind back after the founder of the Theosophical Society, Helena Blavatsky, infamously recovers the pineal gland as anatomically central to human evolution, borrowing liberally from Descartes, Hinduism, and Buddhism along the way. Found in most vertebrates, in humans, the pineal gland is located at the top of the medulla oblongata, or the lowest part of the brainstem, where the spinal cord extends into the brain. Lodged between right and left cerebral hemispheres, the pineal gland is now known to secrete the hormone melatonin, thereby regulating circadian rhythms, metabolism, and sexual development, an anatomical truth only tentatively uncovered in the late 1950s and therefore unknowable to Loy, even as it serendipitously confirms her associations of the pineal with corporealities perpendicular and supine (*SE* 270). This gland alerts human beings to our needs for rest and activity, to the passing of time, to planetary rotation, and to our generative cycles. In some species of lizard, eel, and fish, a parietal or third eye is visible within the skull forefront, linked to the gland within; often working in conjunction with compound eyes, these "simple eyes" are photoreceptors, light-sensing and orientating.

Drawing from parietal evidence, a scientific hypothesis emerged during Loy's childhood that "the pineal gland is a phylogenetic relic, a vestige of a dorsal third eye" (Lokhorst n.p.). For Blavatsky, the human pineal eye is vestigial judgement: gone dormant due to over-indulgence in the material, it will reignite when sufficient spiritual wisdom is attained. The evolutionary anticipation of a functional third eye became a mainstay of Theosophy, a physical link between anatomy and spirituality, atavism and oracularity, or the science and spirituality central to the modernist occult. One among many modernist artists who recognised that by cultivating inner vision we might evolve as a species, Blavatsky has an easily discerned hold on Loy's wilful, striving, and esoterically inflected sense of self, yet her influence has only been glancingly discussed thus far in Loy scholarship.[20] Furthermore, Loy's blind dorsality actively extends contemporaneous narratives about the singular, rearward pineal eye, Blavatsky's among them. Like Bataille, Loy lingers over pineal atavism as a generative disruptor of progressivism, and posits the parietal as a site of excess; for both, it is precisely in its ecstatic, highly sexualised transcendence that rearward vision gains its meaning. This very sexuality is actively suppressed by Theosophy.[21] The erotic Eros inherent to Loy's pineality is matched by an aesthetic Eros: consistent with the groundbreaking work of fourth-dimension popularisers, Loy attends to the capacities of the inner eye to perceive space, time, and artistic form anew in ways unimaginable to those too constrained by three-dimensional existence. In other words, as ever, Loy's intrigue toward regression furthers her esotericism and vanguardism alike.

Consistent with the hypnotic gaze discussed in the last chapter, ocularity preoccupies Loy from her earliest work, remaining central to her oeuvre. Loy recognises that eyes have an "amative language" of their own; she conflates orbs with the self entire, as in her 1915 expression of envy for "'young men's eyes – going to the front'" (*LoLB* 20; Conover lxix). Loy attends to gendered gazes, particularly female eyelids passively "silent" (*LoLB* 21, 37). She observes eyes of steel that cut, or are slit and scrutinous, or are filled with "a potential poetry" (*LoLB* 63; *SE* 98, 48). And often, Loy privileges the occluded over the seeing eye, equating the former with the visionary, the Orphic (*SE* 288). Thus, eyes virginal and glassy – of dolls or their prospective owners – "have the effrontery to / Stare through the human soul / Seeing nothing / Between parted fringes" (*LoLB* 17). As discussed in Chapter 2 of the first volume of this *Anatomy*, "nothing" is a term Bataille and Loy share for sentient dissolution, sometimes ecstatic, often inexpressibly infinite; "[s]eeing nothing" from the forehead, the site of the parietal eye, a glass-eyed virgin may well see far more than most. Consistent with this pineal affiliation, the single eye is a prominent motif in Loy's work, perhaps in an echo of the same in Surrealist art.[22] By extension, Loy's blind or partially sighted eyes strain to see or aid perception, as in *Islands in the Air*, where the ocular orb of memory is continually assaulted by motes of dust from the past, or a washstand vase or "blind eye" is a "lovely cataract of lacteal blue & rose" (*IA* 63: 54; 67: 91). Aspiring to animacy, Loy's objects can exude "'blind patience'" (*IA* 65: 69).

These Tiresian thematics are foundational to Loy's artistry and ultimately, her theories of a dorsal, occluded perception that proves emancipatory and visionary. In "History of Religion and Eros" Loy argues that "it is undeniable that the un-use of the eyes—in a state of complete wakefulness—sets up a sublimation of sight outwards to an intensity of sight inwards" (*SE* 278). Taken together, blind frontal orbs and inner sight gesture toward the inner or third eye, the all-seeing pineal gland. For Loy, internal sight must be inspired; hence Esau Penfold is derided for having a "mental eye fixed on infinitesimal and negligible objectives" (*EP* 22). But it can also be prophetic: in Loy's unpublished draft poem "Ceiling at Dawn", the speaker "float[s] in oval of unclosing eye", sleepily proximate to a subliminal, nirvanic beyond, as well as physically close to the "white slab slanted" of ceiling onto which are projected "the fancies of / the turned up eye" to its "façade of the blind oracle" (qtd. in Walter, 141–2). Closed, the facial eyes often perceive more, as in Loy's undated "In Maine: Green's Colony", where a social outcast "glances" with a "slightly glazing eye" even as it is to her experience, her insight, that the narrator finds herself irrevocably drawn (*SE* 52).

By praising the wakeful "un-use of the eyes" as the foundation for "a sublimation of sight outwards to an intensity of sight inwards", Loy refers expressly to Myers, for whom recollections, dreams, hallucinations, flights of imaginative fancy, telepathy, and the perceptions of genius were conversions of subliminality into image (*SE* 278; Myers 128–30). Although ocular vision is corroborated by external reality, thereby becoming "veridical" or certifiably truthful, for Myers, external perception is in fact derived from inner, which is the presiding visual power (132–3). We see this same privileging in Loy, who identifies "a cerebral centrum, named and located by the ancients" that facilitates communication from the beyond and perception of a light that cannot be received "by the organ eye" (*SE* 242). Eyes communicate to cohere self and world, but also steer us too emphatically toward the limitations of the real, a sphere Loy considers profoundly imperceptive, constraining to disablement, and continually in need of the prosthesis that is an artistic vision facilitated by involute sightedness. At its best, this internal vision yields the judgement or prophecy intrinsic to satirists and vanguardists, yet latently contains the "principle of Reversion" that Darwin celebrated as evidence of the unpredictable staying power of evolutionary heritage, or the atavism discussed in the initial chapter of *Nethered Regions* (*Variation* II 372). It is in this necessarily contrary spirit that in "Visitation of Insel" Loy labels the pineal "gland _ _the last_least co-operator", whilst noting that it is destined to "becom[e] the initiator" (*I* 163). The pineal gland is a part of the human anatomy with a mind of its own, one to which Loy's cultivated artistic will consciously, joyously cleaves. Loy's assertion exposes her understanding of Theosophy, and she arrives at this valuation, as does Blavatsky, via Descartes.

Throughout his oeuvre, Descartes argues on behalf of the pineal gland as the site of common sense, by which he does not mean practical judgement but, far more literally, the place where "the sensory images from the sense organs combine" (Shapiro 262). Diminutised in his famous *Meditations on First Philosophy* (1641) as no bigger than a grain of rice, the human pineal gland looms disproportionately large in Descartes's last publication, *The Passions of the Soul* (1649), where it ascends to regal place as throne to the soul, an estimation his Dutch philosophical contemporary Baruch Spinoza (1632–77) dismissed outright as occult (Descartes, *Meditations* 37).[23] Descartes's *Passions* is devoted to developing a coherent, virtuous selfhood; by its reasoning, the pineal gland unites not only body and soul, but also the vexatious morass of longings, thoughts, and impressions to which we are continually subjected. This cohering premise was no doubt appealing to a Loy perpetually in search of thought and belief that unites the fragmented being. Observing that, like our limbs, ears, and eyes, every portion of the brain is double, Descartes argues that we necessarily perceive in duplicate. As the pineal gland is a uniquely singular portion of our mental anatomy, he asserts that it alone must coalesce these dualities into comprehensible wholes. From here, this seat of the soul "radiates into all the rest of the body by the mediation of spirits, nerves, and even blood" (*Passions* 37). Processing the phenomenal, the unified pineal gland is also the proper vehicle for Descartes's indivisible soul to attach itself to the body.

Inconsistently argued, medically erroneous, and subsequently dismissed by philosophers, Descartes's analogies pragmatically assign to the pineal gland the role of overseeing the component anatomy of a distinctly mechanised body.[24] In *Treatise on Man* (written before 1637; published 1662), Descartes presents the soul as the turncock of our somatic fountain, a spigot responsible for maintaining our integrity through its control over the flow of our thoughts and animal spirits (Shapiro 283–4). Within this metaphor exists premonitions of Loy's insistence that, by peering into human eyes, we might witness something "shut off . . . behind", an infinite, incalculable tonnage of sensory reception in need of valvular containment, or the commons of the blind back where the universe projects itself "through the medium of the senses" (*B* 8: 27; *SE* 276). For both Descartes and Loy, the pineal zone is portal to fundamental atavisms and anticipatory site of betterment. Through it, Descartes argues, we discern whether to "turn the back and move the legs" when confronted with danger, or lead ourselves into attack; with "habituation", he maintains, we can teach our pineal gland to unite with the best thoughts, the most ideal passions (*Passions* 39, 47). Deploying anatomy and physics, *Passions* taxonomises irrational affects – wonder, anger, hatred, desire – and the strong feeling that "incline[s] the soul to join itself in volition with the things it deems good", or Cartesian love (*Passions* 62–4). Generatively uniting, Cartesian Eros echoes pineal function.

Loy's "Mi & Lo" is a study, as its title indicates – bifurcate, nominal fragments linked by an ampersand – in cohering the split self, one that directly tussles with Descartes, and *The Passions of the Soul* in particular. The Cartesian legacy is trumpeted when "mi" states: "I think therefore I am— But further—I can think about what I think. / That is the testimony of the soul". Without a soul, "mi" adds, humanity cannot observe its own existence; not only do I think and know I exist, but what is more, my most godlike, enduring portion can interpret myself thinking (*SE* 273). Alongside this reflexivity, Loy adds an artistic layer to the popular misquotation from Descartes's *Meditations*, replacing the identificatory intellection of *cogito ergo sum* with the mortality-defining work of fancy: "We exist for as long as we can imagine ourselves" (*SE* 282). God-fearing, Loy also warily observes that artistic inventions can go too far, cautioning against the ultimate independence from "the Absolute": death (*SE* 282). But as described, Loy's artistic perception echoes *Passions*: a "convergent apparatus" unites the incessant, foundational dualities of human perception, and artistic "[f]orm is the union of identicals" (*SE* 265–6). Loy argues that life enters the body "[t]hrough the pineal gland", traverses "the spinal column", and "provides energy for the whole organism", be it engaged in events "perpendicular" or "supine" (*SE* 269). Either standing or lying down, Loy's animated soma is engaged in "degrees of progress" (*SE* 269). This incalculable vitality is as onerous in Loy as it is in Descartes, for whom mind and gravity exert force coextensively through our body entire.

In writings produced before *Passions*, Descartes asserts that we conceptualise this gravity in the same terms as we use for the soul.[25] Loy certainly does, presenting gravity and soul as inseparable: the first is a "much discussed attraction to the earth" running continually through bodily circuits, while the second is a perpetually pleasurable "sublime buoyancy" or "*gravity upward*" by which the body connects with "inspiration of Deity" (*SE* 269–70, 274; see also 243–4). In "Notes on Metaphysics" Loy ruminates further on this topic, observing that "there is an undiscovered law of levitation" that acts as a counter to the gravity with which we are all familiar. This levitation is a source of inspiration as well as an affective experience, a buoyant, pleasurable sense of vitality and attraction; in turn, Loy's gravity is both felt weight and a sense of dispirited hopelessness. Immaterial, this animacy is essential to a fully conscious, strongly founded existence: it cycles through the body, monitored by the pineal gland that hosts the soul to which sensibility reports after "explor[ing] the nervous system" (*SE* 274). As in Descartes, Loy's pineal gland grounds a scientific exploration of morality, or the reckoning constituting "the accurate mathematics of life", one "attained through a perfect understanding, domination and utilisation of the senses" (*SE* 277).

Consistent with Cartesian dualism, "Mi & Lo" is Loy at her most aware of the limitations of "single-sensed organs" of perception, her most damning of the "muddy patches in our minds that hol[d] us to the third dimension" (*SE* 279, 270). That said, this dialogue furthers Loy's journey toward "the cosmic" and by it, Loy, like Descartes before her, takes stock of irrational desire. For, unlike Descartes, Loy's impassioned study of the pineal authenticates lust, moving "the reasoning self to[ward] a swollen eroticism" overdue for liberation from censure (*SE* 283). Propelling Loy toward an elevation of the sexual passions to the heights of an artistic genius that overrides established morality, "Mi & Lo" shares Descartes's veneration for the pineal whilst inverting Cartesian virtue. For Loy, Theosophy is to be treated as similarly foundational, if similarly malleable.

Pineality: Theosophy and Loy

Loy shares her interest in Cartesian pineality with Helena Blavatsky, who lauds the seventeenth-century philosopher's association of third eye with "Soul and Spirit" because it brought him closer than contemporary scientists to "the occult truth" (*Secret* II 298). Ukrainian-born Blavatsky (1831–91) co-founded the Theosophical Society in New York in 1875, four years before the emergence of Loy's own Christian Science. Theosophy was devoted, as the etymology of its name implies, to uncovering the "'wisdom of God'" (Obeyesekere 326, 354). Dominated by credibility-inducing professional classes, the Theosophical Society reached its zenith in 1928 with an official membership of 45,000 in forty countries; it was the most prominent precursor to the post-Fordist New Age movement (Viswanathan, "Ordinary" 5; Storm 115–16). At its outset, Blavatsky was Society secretary; from 1888, she headed its Esoteric Section. Schooled in the occult by her maternal great-grandfather, Blavatsky was at home in the heterodox, and sought to demonstrate how Western science relied on occult processes such as intuition and epiphanic illumination (Obeyesekere 341; Viswanathan, "In Search" 77).

A charismatic, revolutionary mystic, Blavatsky is now routinely touted as "the most important esoteric theorist of the late nineteenth century" (Storm 116). Her thinking was widely disseminated and interpreted by faith-seeking intellectuals like Loy. As Lara Vetter notes, "most who read [Blavatsky] adapted her ideas to their own, filtered through a multitude of other religious and esoteric lenses" (*Modernist* 14). And while Loy primarily identified as a Christian Scientist for at least three decades, she shared Blavatsky's self-definition as a religious mongrel, "'a strange mixture, something incomprehensible'" who drew from many traditions, remaining fascinated by the shared, perennial origins of world religions (Obeyesekere 360). Aspects of Theosophy had a demonstrable impact on Loy: most pivotally, its adherence to the visionary role of the pineal gland, a gateway to the involution Loy prioritised so highly, and to the reincarnation she adopts that Christian Scientists rejected. These Theosophical ideas exerted a direct, underdiscussed influence upon Loy's writings, influences inextricable from her blind back.

Declaring that the substance of her published work appeared to her in dreams or on alternate existential planes, Blavatsky researched through inner vision, evidently capable of bypassing Descartes's *cogito* altogether (Obeyesekere 4–5, 346, 335–6). Denounced as a plagiarist and a delusionist, Blavatsky's authority was and remains suspect: having spent seven years in Tibet, she claimed that her teachings were guided by letters sent from two Tibetan adepts (Crow 695). Janet Oppenheim offers an excellent overview of the damning 1885 report compiled by the Society for Psychical Research on Blavatsky's misrepresentations of her "miracles", clairvoyant visions, and "channellings" of Mahatma teachings (*Other* 174–8). The public scandal that ensued changed the direction Blavatsky took with Theosophy: rather than performances of magical prowess, she began emphasising the pursuit of the gnomic, proselytising on behalf of an ever-deferred esotericism. This ideological turn conveniently offset the growing popularity of the occult Hermetic Order of the Golden Dawn, whose leader, Aleister Crowley, circulated in Loy's Parisian circles at the outset of the twentieth century (Crow 691, 706).[26]

While the scepticism about her methods was justifiable, Blavatsky is widely credited with resituating the Anglo-European centre of ancient knowledge from Egypt to southeast Asia, a turn retained and reinforced by her Theosophical descendants.[27] Ralph Waldo Emerson's New Thought movement was a precursor to Blavatsky in prioritising Eastern influences drawn from Romanticism and Schopenhauerian philosophy; Emersonian Transcendentalism was also a precursor to Loy's Christian Science (Bevir 747–8, 758; Versluis 150). Emphasising asceticism, purity, the drive to gnomic understanding, and inner knowledge of the divine, Blavatsky promoted Buddhist and Hindu cosmologies as antipodal to the West's materialism and anticipatory of its science (Bevir 764–5). Loy deploys Asian influence similarly in her late writings, "The History of Religion and Eros" in particular. Believing Theosophy could fill outstanding gaps in knowledge, Blavatsky's most renowned works – *Isis Unveiled* (1877) and *The Secret Doctrine* (1888) – reveal a Herculean capacity to synthesise unevenly documented occult histories, uniting theological cosmology with material science, oriental and occidental, esoteric and exoteric (Saurat 67; Asprem 446).

Blavatsky maintained that Theosophy aimed at moral harmony, seeking to heal the schism between rational and irrational defining post-Enlightenment Europe (L. Wilson 5–6; Morrisson, "[P]ineal" 512). London-born Annie Besant (1847–1933), second president of the Theosophical Society from 1907 to 1933, would similarly promote the faith as a coalescing force, a counter to the fragmented subjectivity of Western epistemology (1, 10). But against this universality, Theosophy was inherently elitist, as is evinced by Besant's insistence that her religion could not "be made intelligible to the uneducated or to the thoughtless" (1). That the path to faithfulness was meant to be hard, and could not be traversed by all, is a refrain of Blavatsky and Besant's writings; on occasion, this claim to difficulty appears a convenient means of bypassing argumentative illogic. As significantly, as Mark Morrisson argues, Theosophists believed many people would evolve, but not everyone, a "spiritual" truth Joyce was to mock in *Ulysses*, but which may have appealed to a Loy often keen to assert herself as among the elect ("[P]ineal" 514).

Joyce was among a number of modernists with whom Loy associated who knew Blavatsky in writing or in person: her friend and editor Ezra Pound, for instance, dubbed Blavatsky "'the old lady'" (Wilson 20, 66). Paul Klee and Vasily Kandinsky, associates of the Munich Academy of Fine Arts that Loy attended in 1900, professed Theosophical allegiances, as did Constantin Brâncuşi, the subject of Loy's poetic homage "Brancusi's Golden Bird" (1922) who was among her Paris circle in the 1920s (Vetter, *Modernist 9*; *BM* 56, 319). The appeal is identifiable: in content and in form, Blavatsky notably predates modernist esoteric processes. Like Theosophists, avant-gardists presented the gnomic to the masses, testing their initiates' patience for laborious consumption, discernment of inner logic and meaning, and faith in the unknowable. *The Secret Doctrine*, *Ulysses*, *Lunar Baedeker*: these titles alone promise uncovery and alignments, wilfully mislead. Methodologically, Blavatsky's influence on Loy's expository esotericism is assured.

In order to consider the links between Blavatsky's and Loy's pineality, we need first outline Blavatsky's complex theory of evolution. In accordance with her own interpretation of Brahmic teachings, Blavatsky argues that our Earth currently occupies the fourth of seven planes, each equivalent to a level of cosmic consciousness. Within this overarching septenary planetary cycle, Blavatsky demarcates the seven "root races" that have already inhabited or will inhabit our globe, all occupying different positions in the development of humanity from primordial to ethereal being. Blavatsky's evolution begins with devolution: the movement of spirit into matter by an unknowable, indivisible cosmic deity. Root race the first consisted of astral, spiritual doubles of the cosmic genitor; descending from the sexless first, the second root race was asexual, embodied, and Hyperborean; the third, hermaphrodites situated in Lemuria, developed soul and began the divide into two sexes; the fourth, or Atlantean, was the first identifiably human race, albeit colossal, too materialistic, and ultimately, fallen. Nadir of this planetary cycle of evolution, the fourth root race nevertheless developed speech and science. After four was partially destroyed by flood, as iterated in Plato's *Timaeus* (c. 360 BCE), it was succeeded by five, roughly a million years ago. Associated with European ascendency, this Aryan race remains predominant, if aspiring toward a sixth – American, increasingly spiritual and clairvoyant – followed by a seventh root race by which human beings will return to the astral, with a concomitant capacity for instantaneous perception (Santucci 46–51; Morrisson, "[P]ineal" 513–14). While it has been argued that Blavatsky does not apply the term "race" to physicality, character, or national identity, there is a clear racial hierarchy at work in Theosophical writings in which whiteness reigns supreme (Santucci 37).[28]

Ultimately, even the achievement of the seventh root race does not bring human evolution to an end, because the Earth has only attained the fourth of seven available planetary stages. The surfeit of aspirant sevens does not stop here: Blavatsky asserts that our planet, like each of the other planets and the moons that revolve around them, exists within a companionate chain of seven. In like fashion, Blavatsky divides the inner self into seven levels or principles, with the highest being the soul, the middle layers astral bodies, and the lowest the material body. Each of us is meant to aspire toward becoming a "'*perfect* septenary being'" in which our consciousness is fully integrated into the vehicles corresponding to the seven planes of existence (Crow 710; Santucci 38). Blavatsky identified seven types of matter as the basis for the seven planes of existence, with the lowest being the material world, meaning that Theosophical "cosmology borrowed as much from ether physics and, later, from modern nuclear physics and radio-chemistry as it did from neo-Platonic emanation theories" (Morrisson, "[P]ineal" 513). Unsurprisingly, with the uncovering of atomic science after Blavatsky died, her adherents went so far as to match Blavatsky's seven planes of existence to "'seven sets of spirillae'" within the atom (qtd. in Morrisson, *Alchemy* 78).

Loy's first husband clearly had Blavatsky on his mind when he privately published a pamphlet entitled *The Seven Ages of God* (1912), a heterodox, privately printed tract indebted to a Victorian occultism by which science exists to provide proof of the existence of the human soul, a truth about which the esotericist is already conscious (3–4).[29] Without referencing Theosophy directly, Haweis presents the much-cited fundamental proposition of Blavatsky's *The Secret Doctrine*, namely, that her teachings rest upon "[a]n Omnipresent, Eternal, Boundless and Immutable PRINCIPLE, on which all speculation is impossible, since it transcends the power of human conception" (*Secret* I 14).[30] A constitutive perceptive sightlessness likewise runs through *Seven Ages*, where Haweis's humanity are anti-seers who "wal[k] backwards to the grave", and whose inherent blindness to gnostic or symbolic truths could prompt their willed evolutional return to the radiant deity to whom they were once proximate (7, 11). Positioning speaker and audience among Blavatsky's Aryan fifth root race – "We are the sons of Rome, of Gaul, of Saxon and Norseman" – Haweis traces out an evolutionary trajectory that begins with "the age of Primal Life", then moves toward a "golden age of Innocence" followed by an age of "Knowledge" marked by love, laughter, and "Fear of God" before descending into rank and profligate materialism caused by a "Fear of Life" (11, 4, 5). After this low point, humanity reascends, just discernibly, towards spirituality via a select few who "divin[e] the meaning of Life and Death", keeping it out of "the hands of the people" who treat truths as "menace" (10).

Highly overwrought, Haweis's pamphlet occasionally devolves into a self-serving romanticism wherein the male speaker regrettably pitches himself as "an imaginative boy-god" lothario replete with "lace-topped boots and plumed hat" (13). Setting aside these painfully transparent authorial aspirations and nostalgias, Haweis's esoteric evolutionary narrative concludes by announcing itself as a necessarily incomplete Theosophical history: "These are not the signs of an old earth or of a mature of [*sic*] God, but the live indications of the fourth age" (16). Haweis's numbers alone point to Blavatsky: seven ages of God, fifth root race, fourth planetary age. As Loy and Haweis remained unhappily married in 1912, *Seven Ages* confirms Loy's proximity to Theosophical precepts that remained influential: Loy develops an occult cosmology whereby humanity emerges from universal ether, descends to the material, and then labours to reattain the astral plane. In Blavatsky, these cycles occur within the individual, the root race, and at planetary levels; in Myers, ascent is triggered by genius, occult porousness, or death. While Loy's late works attend more fulsomely to Myers's individual infinitude, Blavatsky's macro-evolutionary scales are clearly at work as late as the 1930s, where Loy describes evolution as taking place in discrete "cycle[s] of time" marked by negotiations between the somatic and the spiritual, as in her speculation upon what "the final utility of the body may prove to be in future laps of evolution" (*CP* 16: 51). And given that Theosophists incline toward genealogies that begin with primordial matter animated by an all-embracing deity, Blavatsky's reverberations may be discernible as early as Loy's "Songs to Joannes" (1917) with its assertion that "Proto-plasm was raving mad / Evolving us — — —" (Viswanathan, "Ordinary" 20; *LoLB* 67).

Clearly conversant with Blavatsky's evolution, Haweis appears less aware of its requisite complement, involution, a word summoning up entanglements, the retrograde or degenerate, and the rolling, curling, or turning inwards of a body or its parts. For Theosophists, we exist because the supreme being involuted its consciousness, a process by which spirit and materiality came into being, a theory drawn from the kabbalistic story of origin (Santucci 38; Saurat 95–111). Born of an inward turn, evolution proceeds rotationally: Blavatsky's is a "doctrine of endless evolution and re-involution" facilitating the continual reabsorption of "the Kosmos" by humanity (*Secret* I 148). Or, as James A. Santucci argues: Blavatsky's races are "conceived as part of a vast network or matrix of interlocking and concentric spirallings of all components in the cosmos, including the 'human wave'" propelled by directing vision toward internal divination (41). The evolution of the root races in the fourth planetary age Blavatsky illustrates as shown in Fig. 3.4.

Race evolution spirals outward. By it, human beings unfurl from an astral centre of rotation and continue to propel themselves

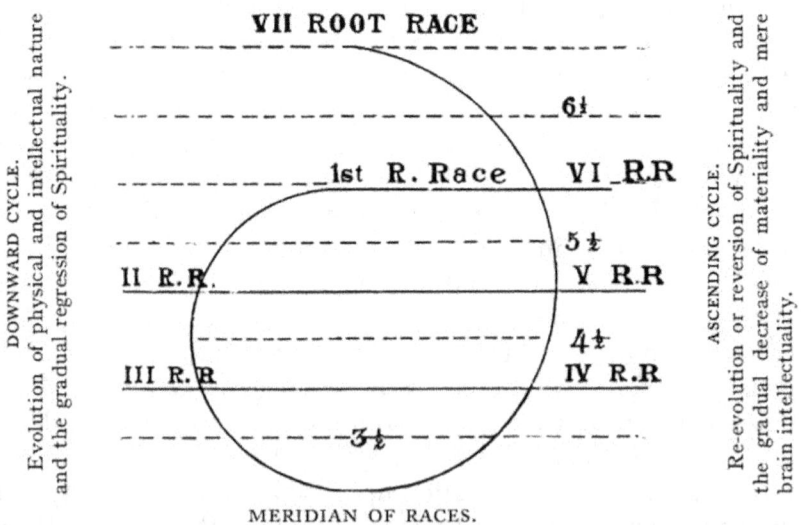

Fig. 3.4 "Evolution of Root Races in the Fourth Round", Helena Blavatsky, *The Secret Doctrine*, Volume 2 (1888).

onward, upward, outward. Like nature and the cosmos, Blavatsky attests, we rest and reascend, aspiring to reappear on ever "more perfect plane[s]" (*Secret* I 149). Blavatsky's theories exponentially extended Charles Darwin's geological timescales and rejected his monogenesis; she insisted that humans were the first mammals to inhabit Earth, and that they descended from the deific, not primates. Nevertheless, she affirms the nonlinearity that underwrites Darwinian evolution, tracking evolutionary spirals that expressly challenge entropy and teleology. Refuting positivism, Blavatsky also disavows historical progress on the basis that past civilisations were evidentially in advance of our own (*Isis* I 214). And she rejects individual linear development, promoting an evolution that works by counterforces akin to Loy's upward gravitation, animacies continually surging against the phenomenal.

Blavatsky considers soul centripetal force to centrifugal spirit, claiming that the two function in an oppositional harmony (*Isis* I 286). A set of like rotational oppositions arises in Loy's "Der Blinde Junge" (1922), where a blind child on the streets of Vienna is vestige or outcast, a "planet of the soul" well positioned to exert gravitational force, an "eremite / of centripetal sentience" who channels vitality toward his axis of being. His consciousness turns inward, is, as Blavatsky defines all consciousness, "*a quality of the sentient principle, or, in other words, the soul*" (*Isis* I 177). The youth's inward spiralling is matched by a concomitant centrifugal "nozzling" of the sun around which he rotates, propelled by the expulsion of "damnation and concussive dark" from his "mouth-organ". Throughout, Loy's coordinates are ritualistic and celestial, deific: her youth is virginal sacrifice, victim of the goddess of war, performing for "illuminati"; the day in question is "spectral" (*LoLB* 83–4). The poem entire re-enacts Loy's inner vision: "un-use of the eyes" precipitates a "universal involution" by which an "introspector" becomes "connective with infinite distance", alternate planes (*SE* 278). In "Der Blinde Junge", this internal illumination is complicated by Theosophical involutions and evolutions-cum-devolutions. Recognising that this youth has been reduced to primal beast, forced into near-extinction, Loy demarcates his proximate spirallings, his cyclical ascents and descents toward transcendent adept.

In like regard, we might also consider lovelorn Cassandra, the protagonist of Loy's late, undated "The Agony of the Partition", whose name gestures to a Greek mythology that consigns her to a fate as sacrificial and oracular as that of Loy's Viennese urchin. Betrayed by Eros, Loy's Cassandra is "stretched out rigid on the axis of her contractile agony", defined by "[a] centripetal demolition of despair, defiant of gravity as if she were too heavy to fall", one that "endow[s] her with an insane levitation of sorrow become lead" (*SE* 12). Turned in upon herself, Cassandra is a wreckage of involution elevated by a totalising prostration, her centripetal soul actively labouring toward harmony with her centrifugal spirit.

The Theosophical pineal eye pits atavistic past against utopian future, resembling Loy's sightless dorsality in anatomising the constitutive blindness of an otherwise illuminating esotericism. Blavatsky's pineal theory rests upon the occultist acceptance "that spiritual and psychic *involution* proceeds on parallel lines with physical *evolution*—that the *inner* senses, innate in the first human races, atrophied during racial growth and the material development of the outer senses" (*Secret* II 294). Believers know that, in the third root race, when we were four-armed hermaphrodites, we had one head and three eyes, and could see before and behind. Separated into distinct sexes, our spiritual vision dimmed, and the third eye lost power. Come the fourth root race, our inner vision required prodding through stimulation: trance or meditation, "*activit[ies] of the inner man*" known to Sages, sensitives, or mediums, activities by which the pineal eye "*swells and expands*" (*Secret* II 294). As we have seen, in "Mi & Lo", the introspector's involute turn is likewise effected through active pursuit of enlightenment or illumination, methodised by Loy as meditation; these skills, attests Loy, were prioritised "by certain ancient sages" (*SE* 278, 269). For Blavatsky, the third eye gradually dwindled, withdrawing into the head and beneath the hair that grew over our posterior, or second, face. Blavatsky proclaims: "The *third eye is dead*, and acts no longer; but it has left behind a witness to its existence . . . . the PINEAL GLAND" (*Secret* II 295).

The rationale for this pineal diminishment is a direct inversion of Loy's sex-positive esoteric Eros. For Blavatsky, the gland retreated due to excess expenditure of our bodily senses during a period of our evolution when the material took precedence over the spiritual. From a welter of potentially problematic physiological and consumerist preoccupations, Blavatsky foregrounds the sexual activity that is so "closely connected, by interaction, with the spinal cord and the grey matter of the brain", thereby putting excessive pressure on the brainstem, where the pineal gland resides (*Secret* II 296). Overwhelmed by lusty stimuli, the gland beat an ascetic anatomical retreat; in turn, true Theosophical adepts, necessarily renunciatory, are best positioned to reignite its inner vision. Referencing contemporaneous scientific interrogations of the pineal, Blavatsky dismisses this knowledge on the basis that it posits Nature as a "'mechanical'" or "'blind-force'", while the far superior occult understanding illustrates that the pineal is so symbiotic with soul that it is compelled to atrophy in an unspiritual age. Her referents include then-recent discussions on the parietal eye in some species of fish and reptiles, and the pineal "inter-brain" capacities discussed in the standard medical textbook of the time, *Quain's Elements of Anatomy* (1st ed. 1828). But for Blavatsky, the cliché that "[t]he eye is the mirror and also the window of the soul" does better homage to the true intent of the pineal gland than modern anatomy (*Secret* II 298).

Blavatsky avows that, at our most spiritual – root races one and two – we were cyclopean, reliant on a single spiritual eye; by this logic, our two forward-facing eyes are retrogressive, merely "look[ing] before them without seeing either past or future." By contrast, our third eye *"embraces ETERNITY"* (*Secret* II 299). An internal paradox defines pineal history, which "reached its highest development proportionately with the lowest physical development", or root races three and four (*Secret* II 299). This paradox is explicable through Blavatsky's evolutionary spiral, which permits atavism to exist alongside ascendency. Just so will the pineal gland propel us toward evolutionary perfection. "[A]n index of the astral capacities and spiritual proclivities of any man", the atrophied gland will flourish again as we attend increasingly to spirituality, a turn under way with the current fifth root race, which has "crossed the meridian point of the perfect adjustment of Spirit and Matter" and is "cycling onward on the spiritual side" (*Secret* II 300–1). "Theosophy staked its scientific and spiritual legitimacy on . . . developing organs dedicated to [a] transpersonal and astral perception" that transcended base, material sexuality (Morrisson, "[P]ineal" 517).

This foundational organic perception continued in the Theosophical generations that followed Blavatsky, who retained her rejection of sexual desire. After taking over the running of the Theosophical Society in 1907, Annie Besant extended the terms of Blavatsky's dormant inner eye, arguing that the pituitary and pineal glands "are not simply vestigial, but rudimentary, preparing for the future". To these glands Besant confers the status of sixth and seventh human senses, with the pituitary housing our direct perception of the celestial, the pineal, inter-brain thought transfer, as "an organ which will bring the human being into touch with the currents of thought which are continually playing in the world round us . . . as literally as the eye to-day receives the waves in ether that we call light" (91). By these glands, Besant avers, consciousness will become a continuous, interdependent whole encompassing terrestrial and celestial, thereby permitting access to the spiritual perception of "the artist of genius" (91, 105).[31] But importantly, Besant's additional "sensory" capacities are only abstractly perceptive. Lacking tactility, Besant's idealised pituitary and pineal glands affirm her overarching Theosophical motivation: to reinstate the supremacy of "God, Immortality, Spirit" over empirical knowledge, to assert intelligential ether over corporeality (2). Where Loy's esotericism shares Besant's privileging of the artistic, as well as the desire for a "Synthesis of Life", Loy propounds the materiality that Theosophy diminishes (Besant 1). In the process, Loy elevates the bodily desires – intimacy, sexuality – that Theosophy actively censures.

Sensory and material differences aside, both Loy and Blavatsky envision a somatic "door of communication between the terrestrial and the spiritual world" that shuts some individuals away from "the world of astral light" but is "easily unbarred" and passed through by souls keen to access alternate planes (*Isis* I 292, 176). Posteriorly positioned, Blavatsky's third, pineal eye is a conduit to precisely this sort of astral ingress and egress. And Blavatsky emphasises the rearwardness at stake, noting that the Hindu "eye of Siva" transfers the pineal eye to the forehead, a calibration she brusquely dismisses as "exoteric license" (*Secret* II 295). Loy's blind back shares the properties of the third eye to which it is overtly linked; as is Blavatsky's, her third eye is prey to atavism, perceptive toward involute and eternal consciousness. In Loy's *Goy Israels* (1925–30+), the metaphoric use of the pineal eye is an abstruse but discernible means of connecting humanity to the infinite. Likening the cultural and affective voids of Goy's youth to experiences of vacuousness in life more generally, Loy writes: "In the greatest emptiness there is always oneself that remains - - - and here is also a heavy pillar of alabaster from which age has wrenched its clock, leaving a socket of the circular eye that ever accounts for us, pulverous in the unself-like abrasion of calcite". Crushed to powder and enucleated, this is the pineal eye at its most atrophied, drawn from annals of time represented by a distinctly Greco-Romanesque column, one Loy draws on the main figure of her contemporaneous painting, *Untitled (Surreal Scene)* (c. 1935) in the precise locale of the third eye (Fig. 3.5). Fascinated by the idea of void, Goy aims to "crash this polished silence on her brain". But this goal proves unattainable, given that she is in thrall to a biological lineage – Protestant Englishness – that is a small, manipulable component of "the clock that ticks above the eternal cataclysm whose ultimate function is to tell the whole world the right time" (*GI*

Fig. 3.5 Mina Loy, *Untitled (Surreal Scene)* (c. 1935), detail. Gouache with collage on panel, 20 3/4 × 16 3/4 inches (52.71 × 42.55 cm). Collection of Roger Conover.

28: 53b). Conflating self with temporality, Loy indicates that both have lost their cyclopean, pineal connection to eternity, giving way to what Bergson critiques as the modern imposition of rigid clock-time devoted to system and schedule. In later works, Loy refines her pineal connection to a beyond by way of liberating herself from her ambivalence toward her English genetic inheritance.

In the slightly later text, *Goy Israels: A Play of Consciousness*, written in 1932 (hereafter *Goy 32*), Loy expands on her reading of pineality in one of her esoteric depictions of human birth. Loy details an avian animating energy that flies from the cosmos to the terrene, navigating "the circles of our consciousness" before alighting upon the neonate it seeks. By Loy's cosmology, infants are fundamentally unbalanced: they remain symbiotically attached to a cosmic knowledge and memory thoroughly unmatched by their complete ignorance of the alienating three-dimensional plane. In *Goy 32*, for the infant to prevail in this new, disorienting plane, the incalculable tonnage of astral consciousness must be set aside, freeing "intrinsic consciousness with its single eye" to assess its nascent "relationship to reality" (*G32* 2). Through a "seedling point within itself", Loy argues, consciousness remains and disappears, performing a generative involution in the same way as Blavatsky's originating god (*G32* 3). Courtesy of these deific origins, this supposedly generic infant, who reappears in the künstlerromans that follow *Goy 32* as the start of Loy's artistic life story, is an original self-creator completely freed from the complexities of biological connection.[32] Just as significantly, the internal "seedling point" Loy details recalls Descartes's emphasis on the "extremely small gland" within the brain "suspended" to best receive communications from the soul and, in turn, to facilitate contact between cerebrum and cerebellum (*Meditations* 36). As Loy's infant adjusts to the phenomenal realm, superior, single-eyed consciousness yields to the deceptive, lesser, two-eyed "gaze" (*G32* 3). While it adjusts, the baby mistakenly applies cosmic principles to three dimensionality, imagining itself in a thoroughly symbiotic relationship with each object it perceives. Only with the utterance of its voice does it come to understand that it is no longer "a universal giant" interconnected with the eternal beyond, but has become "a monad" clinging perilously to "the serene continuity of cosmic consciousness" (*G32* 6). As dorsal portal, Loy's pineal "intrinsic consciousness" continues cleaving to cosmos.

For Blavatsky, cosmic aspiration is countered by a morality, or karma, to which our pineal gland is uniquely susceptible, atrophying at the close of the fourth race because its psychic and physiological powers were misused. "Karma" Blavatsky considers both cause and effect of our actions, most damningly operative as sin, or "the performance of some action for the attainment of a *worldly*, hence *selfish*, desire" (*Secret* I 302). By karma, humans are held accountable for their own errors and the evil they encounter. Where Christians blame misfortune on the will of God, Blavatsky finds this tenet hypocritical, as a deity can only represent pure goodness; humans must thus be to blame for wrongdoing. Karma is inextricable from the doctrine of reincarnation Blavatsky preached to a late Victorian audience often awkwardly or reluctantly embracing secularity, an audience keen to source a soothing, spiritual alternative to teleological Christian hell (Morrisson, "[P]ineal" 513).[33] Cyclical law is central to Theosophical thought, determining not only karma and reincarnation, but also temporalities daily and mortal; through it, the individual – even the criminal or "savage" – is offered potentially endless opportunities to improve (see Besant 46). Blavatsky argues that the "monads" or souls incarnating upon our planet are limited in number; hence we inhabit "the same spiritual Individuality in a long, almost interminable, series of Personalities." While our outer self is unaware of the many roles we have played through time, "the *permanent* individuality is fully aware of the fact, though, through the atrophy of the 'spiritual' eye in the physical body, that knowledge is unable to impress itself on the consciousness of the false personality" (*Secret* II 306). Blavatsky believes that it is precisely because science remains blind to "the winding *cyclic* course of this great law" that it fails to understand that the pineal gland has been active, and will be active again (*Secret* II 298). Once awakened, the pineal eye alerts us to our abiding, cosmic, true self.

After converting to Christian Science in 1909, Loy remained an adherent to this outpost of an orthodox religion that emphasised heightened consciousness, the capacity to heal the self, and the transcendent, constant nature of God's love. But there is no doctrine of reincarnation within Loy's Christian Science, which espouses God's incarnation through Jesus and the eternal soul without the material re-embodiment of the latter. Yet, as late as age 82, Loy demonstrates her belief in reincarnation, referencing memories from "a former life" in an interview whilst attributing the skill and content of her poetry to that experience, and claiming that she has "learned nothing here" ("Mina Loy: Interview" 221, 225). Where reincarnation is concerned, Loy's terms and coordinates are distinctly Theosophical. Loy figures the neonate as a reincarnatable "monad" in symbiotic continuum with a never-ending universe or "eternal presence", observing that its initial "state of pure apparition" – its arrival on earth as more ethereal than phenomenal being – "is not [one] of newness, but of being re-known in a novel relativity" (*G32* 6). And as for Blavatsky and Besant, for Loy, this individualistic embrace of reincarnation extends to disparaged humanity, a category that includes the most aggressive law-breakers. Against humanity's "vertiginous spirals of recrimination", Loy argues on behalf of a theory by which, with time, the "entire atomic volume (or) cellular structure" of the criminal can be "renewed", so that, ultimately, even a murderer will eventually "disappea[r] in the ether, leaving a fresh body that prefers to play pinochle" (*CP* 19: 13; *GI* 28: 2). In an echo of Loy's endlessly refreshed states of virginity discussed in the second chapter of *Nethered Regions*, moral innocence can be re-accessed, reattained within an individual over the course of their lifetime.

Consistent with this restorative focus, *Goy 32* articulates the infant's slow, often painful transition into a new reality, an experience that is initially one of totalising loss compounded by the slamming of "its blind back . . . like a shutter on a lost dimension" (*G32* 14). But the monadic human struggles with mortal constraint precisely because its pineal eye continues to illuminate its bond to eternal cycles: "if it shall ever be proven that there is a distinction to be drawn between faith and insanity", writes Loy, "it will be by the light of this unbroken child consciousness" (*G32* 16). To be born is to be "cast out of Eden", but it is also an experience that "reincarnates the sequent ideas of the human race". This reincarnation, Loy argues, "often seems to enact in its atavism, remote and recent stages simultaneously", combining "savage" with "fallen angel", "primeval magic" with "an acumen that pulls the structure of our reasoning apart" (*G32* 33; see also *CP* 13: 25 and *IA* 62: 23). Nevertheless, Loy asserts: "it is evident that the fallen angel must pick itself up and pull itself together", in order that our "world [will] be brought into accord, toned up, synchronized to the pre-conditional Eldorado." How will we evolve from primeval to utopian being? By letting nature run its course: embracing "the power that hovers over our eyes", a power that "makes the outside and the inside one", so that the child can become "complete in self-sufficiency", embodying independent, inspired self-creation and perpetuation (*G32* 34). Once complete, the child can approach a barrier-free "solar-golden world" or "future", an "open door" filled with a light so intense it "compensate[es] for the [lost] sublime" (*G32* 34–5; *CP* 13: 26–7; *IA* 62: 23–4). With a well-deployed will, the child evolves from an uncertain, unseeing pineal threshold to synchronised, illuminated being, a process that will be repeated *ad infinitum*.

A seedling familiar with its own "seedling point", Loy's infant traverses atavism to the ascendency inherent to Blavatsky's involute, spiralling beings. In weakening but discernible accord with its pineal eye and cosmic awareness, the child is a "reflorescence of the past" and a "germinator of the ultimate blossom of consciousness". Evidence of "the cyclic manner of sense", "a flashing synopsis of the eventual illumination of man", she exists "right under our unparticipatory eyes" – facial? pineal? both? – "arriv[ing] through a patient voyage of elucidation at the point of departure" (*G32* 37). Loy's subsequent autobiographical and esoteric writings anchor themselves in facts and anecdotes within which her own child self is increasingly recognisable, along with her family, environs, and associates. But the pith of this 1932 esoteric proclamation of reincarnation is narratively resurrected in *The Child and the Parent* and *Islands in the Air* (*CP* 13: 31; *IA* 62: 30). By it, Loy's child-self is clairvoyantly attached to eternity through pineal eye and ajar dorsal shutter, at once atavistic and futuristic, an overlooked progressor of a distinctly Theosophical evolution en route to the ethereal place from which she began. And, crucially, that child actively, persistently seeks to cohere third and alternate dimensions, prompting a lifelong pursuit of the same.

The pineal eye is one conduit to that coherence; another is aesthetic appreciation; a third is Loy's childhood discovery of books. Like the blind back, books are initially impenetrable thresholds, incomprehensible compendiums of "linear conundrums". Unique to the phenomenal realm, books are powerful portals permitting 4-year-old Loy – a precociously early reader – access to "the composite brain of humanity" and the cosmos (*IA* 62: 28–9). With the gift of her first book, Loy writes: "Enormously I concluded that I held the doors of the universe ajar with my hands" (*CP* 13: 30). Just as the cosmos has its dorsal, blind, internal portal within the body, so too does the book-door open upon a universe visible through anterior, sighted, visible optical organs. Involution, evolution.

"[F]resh from the angelic factory", Loy writes, childhood "transforms the objective"; adolescence, on the other hand, transforms the subjective, seeking ecstasy less universal than corporeal, if transcendent. Divorced from the "defeat of the flesh" that preoccupies the mature, wizened being, adolescent consciousness instead reverentially aspires to a "perfect love" and "ideal happiness" that includes the sexual (*GI* 28: 116). By Loy's telling, as a young teen, her sexual curiosity alerts her to all intimations of procreation, be they anecdotal or biblical; in fevered pursuit of reproductive "begat[s]", she reads the Old Testament, labouring to overcome the "obscene undertow" and "up rush of sadism" it associates with reproduction (*IA* 67: 90). The idealised truth of orgasmic heterosexual intercourse is learned at last through an overnight guest, a female peer keen to flaunt her knowledge who tells Loy that climax is "'just like being in heaven'" but also necessarily brief, as "'if it lasted any longer it would <u>kill</u> you'" (*IA* 67: 110). So powerful is this information that it "revers[es]" Loy's cerebral "orb of consciousness", bringing "the illuminated side" into "contact with her senses". At this juncture, Loy effects a determined break from Blavatsky and Descartes: this adolescent pineal eye *turns away from* the cosmos toward the material world of desires and lusts repressed by Theosophy and rigidly taxonomised by Cartesian dualism. In an existence narrowed by parental strife, Loy is at pains to reassure us that her all-encompassing epiphany regarding sexual climax is not a cause for distress, but a first and emphatically joyous "intimation" that "pleasure" exists in the world at all (*GI* 28: 113; *IA* 67: 110). This is Loy's second encounter with an "orb of consciousness" in *Islands*; both instances affirm tactility, joy, and an oceanic expansivity.[34] Navigating aspirations to heightened awareness alongside an unrepentant bodily sensuality, Loy's highly sensitive, receptive mental "orb" extends pineality into the pleasures and unruly inclinations shared by soul and soma alike.

Sexual cognisance enhances Loy's esoteric capabilities when she reaches adolescence, sending her into a mediumistic spiritual reverie, a "coma of delight" or starting point in achieving "the ascetic trance of illumination". This process begins with the announcement that Loy "shut [her] eyes", thereby closing "off the habitual consciousness" to attend to her inner vision (*GI* 28: 114). Echoing the earlier reversal of her mental orb, Loy's cataleptic transformation prompts a backtracking, a moment of self-conscious narrative introspeculation. Loy asks: is her trance in fact "a mixture" or "mingling" of a "crisis of the flesh" with spiritual illumination? Like her question, her answer undoes Cartesian duality: "Is there perhaps little difference? Or has my imaginative sensibility, so crucified, in a psychic haste passed its destination?" (*IA* 67: 110). The adjective "imaginative" is added to what was, in a previous version, "sensibility" alone; in combination, the phrase combines creativity, perceptivity, and tactility, cementing mind and body.

The destination in question has already been intimated: it is an evolutionary return to ephemeral spirituality, here achieved – in fact, transcended – not by the will, but by a deeply felt understanding of the limitless possibilities of physical and emotional intimacy. The imaginative sensibility, in other words, has been sacrificed to a higher good, namely, Loy's understanding of the "momentary ... magic contact" only permitted by marriage in Victorian England. Upon this basis, Loy avers, legalised union takes on the contours of an "immaculate transformation" in her consciousness (*GI* 28: 113; *IA* 67: 110). Sexual knowledge thus becomes "a retreat for recuperation" glowing within Loy's mind, establishing her drive for "<u>that Other</u> who can participate in this trance" (*GI* 28: 114). No wonder she names the girl who delivers this information "Evangeline": derisive and patronising though this guest may be, she does, as her name implies, provide the substance of the gospel Loy will proclaim throughout her writings, an esoteric Eros ambiguating the divide between corporeal surfeit and ascetic ecstasy.

Resonating with Loy's Christian Science, Theosophy actively sought to achieve a universal, unselfish "'Essence of Love'" through the cultivation of spiritual consciousness; this unifying love was highest goal for both religions, on par with a divine will that Blavatsky expressly labels Eros (Crow 698, 712). The terms of Blavatsky's Eros are interpretable as facilitating desires procreative and sexual: "*The magnetism of pure love is the originator of every created thing*" (*Isis* I 187). Nobly, wilfully, and powerfully deployed, this love is universally interdependent, the very glue of cosmos and materiality, affecting "all the bodies of the planetary system and everything organic as well as inorganic pertaining to them" (*Isis* I 187).[35] But according to Blavatsky, it cannot be sexual: Eros is not "the later god of material, physiological love, but ... the divine desire in the gods, as well as in all nature, to create and give life to Beings", a process only begrudgingly reliant on the phenomenal (*Secret* II 234). By extension, the sacrifice of sexuality was requisite to becoming a Theosophical adept.[36]

Sharing Loy's fascination with the irremediably sacrificial self, Blavatsky presents immolation as an informed, Christlike choice returning individuals to God (Bevir 755–6). Lacking Loy's overtly feminist premise, Blavatsky condemns human preparedness to sacrifice higher self to lower; inversely, Loy sees the lower self as inseparable from the access to the higher truths and purifications toward which oblation aspires. Loy's arrival at sexual knowledge is, for her, an "unprecedented shock of antithesis" that she aims to extend to Western morality, prompting, through her conscious celebration of censured eroticism, a widespread reversal of her contemporaries' "orb[s] of consciousness" (*IA* 67: 110). As in her reading of Descartes's *Passions*, Loy reinterprets, inverts, and expands Theosophical pineal evolution, resolving that material desire be recognised as intrinsic to the spiritual. In this specific but adamantly central regard, her mysticism is more in league with her peer Bataille than her precursor Blavatsky. Roughly forty years after the pineal eye was the subject of *fin-de-siècle* scientific revision and occultist practice, Loy and Bataille restitute a demoralised, repressed, sexualised body in which pineality plays a centrally disruptive role. Attuned to avant-garde transgression and mysticism alike, both thinkers generatively disrupt the transcendent spiritual promise promulgated about the pineal gland, insisting upon its ties to desire and ecstasy. In Loy's case, this sexualisation extends the terms of her blind back and her esoteric Eros alike.

Eruption: Bataille's and Loy's Parietal Volcanoes

"Experience ... has an optical perspective", argues Bataille, for whom the human eye "expresses the life of the spirit" (*IE* 124–5, 51). Like Loy, Bataille is interested in a mystical blind perceptivity: "Existence in the end discloses the blind spot of understanding and right away becomes completely absorbed in it", initiating an unceasing "circular agitation" endlessly rejuvenated by its rotations through sublimity and its cruel opposite, despair, endlessly moving via knowledge toward "non-knowledge", the gnostic (*IE* 111). Vision spectates, longs to see, even in the dark, where, seeing nothing, the self becomes one with night. This experience of being perceivable whilst unseeing is, for Bataille, anguish, ecstasy: "I traverse an empty depth and the empty depth traverses me" (*IE* 124–5). The language is violative, aggressively sexual, as is the transcendently orgasmic result, itself an overwhelming experiential delirium that bypasses articulate intellectuality. This self is at one with the blind spot of understanding, of unknowing, replicating the anatomical *punctum caecum* of vertebrate vision whilst permitting blindness to take precedence over traditional illumination (*IE* 110–11).

For the end goal of Bataille's knowledge is ignorance, a failure of certitude as fundamental as it is cyclical; in Bataille, all end points are blind spots. "Truth eventually penetrates its own blindness", writes Loy. "Truth" in this instance is personified by the child-Loy drowning in a domestic ocean of self-deception, a family aiming always at social betterment, unduly invested in Bataille's restricted economy. Against the futility of this "circumscribed course of behaviour", "Truth" – a child forced to inhabit the problem she critiques – longs for a protective blindness (*GI* 28: 127). For this child's narrator, as for Bataille, blindness is understanding: "All spurious desire is blinded by that sparkling advantage that is all it can see of success, it cannot know what glory has to do in the dark, to effect its own emergence" (*GI* 28: 108). Consistent with Bataille's critique of knowledge in a restricted economy, Loy insists, repeatedly, that reality is blind, and that, when we come to terms with its imperception, we make space for pivotal human desires, be they transgressive or lauded (*SE* 239).

Bataille's intertwining of nescience and insight is an almost too self-evident critique of post-Enlightenment epistemological assuredness. Reverence for illogicalities prompts Bataille's diatribe against anthropology, science, and philosophy written in the early

1930s, "The Pineal Eye". Enjoining the bifurcate brain, the pineal gland is freighted with a potential to see more than our frontal, compound eyes, to see all. In "The Pineal Eye", Bataille not only validates its counterintuitive capacities, but equates them with the anus, a once-visible protuberance now also buried between two ripe bodily halves. Against evolution as a burgeoning development of human intelligence, Bataille describes it as a movement from a "formless universe" into perpetual "useless production" founded upon "the inversion of the anal orifice itself, resulting from the shift from a squatting posture to a standing one" (79–80; 89). This "progress" sees us moving "in the direction of a more and more noble or correct regularity . . . . [so that] at the present stage of development the automatic rectitude of a soldier in uniform, manoeuvring according to orders . . . proposes itself to the universe of astronomy as its highest achievement" (87).[37]

Implicit within this critique is a denunciation of phallic supremacy: for Bataille, men have become animals "exceptionally animated by" verticality, still "more categorically erect" than "the male mammal who raises himself on his hind legs when mounting the female" – "as erect as a penis" (75). As such, human beings are "ocular tree[s]" or, more straightforwardly, phalluses (84). Countering scientific refusal of the fundamentally human (the base, impassioned, or mythological) and the exoteric turn against delirium or revelatory insight, Bataille anticipates an evolution of the pineal eye to the top of our heads, where it can best disrupt our placid, complicit "horizontal axis of vision" (82–3). By this "erotic metamorphosis", human "[e]xistence no longer resembles a neatly defined itinerary from one practical sign to another, but a sickly incandescence, a durable orgasm" (82).

As our face, like our wind-breaking, shitting posterior, is charged with potential eruptions – belches, laughter, sobs – Bataille envisions the cranial eye as a site of volcanic explosivity, a constant paean to a sun now grown too sullied to illuminate. This eye wilfully "opens and blinds itself like a conflagration" generating a "great burning head [that] is the image and the disagreeable light of the *notion of expenditure*" ("Pineal" 82). Bataille's extraordinarily masochistic sacrificial imagining – the conscious wasting of self by self – is surreal provocation to celebratory discourses of humanity's ever-increasing cerebral advance. As he later reflects: "It is only by means of a sickly representation – an eye opening up at the summit of my own head – at the very spot where naïve metaphysics located the seat of the soul – that human beings, forgotten on Earth – such as I am today . . . gain access suddenly to the heart-rending fall into the void of sky" (*IE* 78).

Bataille's pineal reflections echo terms used by the naïve metaphysician Descartes and Loy herself. Bataille recognises the pineal as having an embryonic function, as taking on the role of the seed of the human tree, one lodged within the human skull; similarly, Loy describes coming into being as the involution of the pineal "seedling point" within the neonate ("Jesuve" 77; G32 3). Furthermore, Bataille posits a "*gravity upward*", a plunge into the celestial, a set of counterforces linking plodding mortal body to an eternal, if potentially vacuous, beyond (*SE* 242). Affirming evolutionary cyclicality, these forces reinstate third-eye narratives that incorporate past knowledge and a future of ecstatic impossibilities, back exceeding front, obscenity exceeding civilisation. Parietal transports are in turn echoed by Bataille's tendency, in his fiction, to use the eye as metonymic for eroticism, his constant play with its liquidity and egg-like or testicular shape (Barthes). Like worms and fish, human beings are for Bataille "a tube with two orifices, anal and buccal", so that facial openings and organs are direct correlates of the genitals ("Pineal" 88). By these correlations, Bataille can engage in a cranial anal fantasy, thereby generating a necessary "rupture of equilibrium" effected by "the liberation of the indecencies of nature" and "the most shameful obscenity" ("Jesuve" 76).

Rarely as protractedly or overtly explicit as Bataille, Loy nevertheless shares his aim of cohering highest mysticism with bodily desire, and as a result, her writings often anticipate or coincide with Bataille's eruptive pineality. In her early years in Florence – 1907–10 – Loy became a practitioner of the Mensendieck System of Functional Movement (*BM* 118). Primarily catering to women, an American doctor, Bess Mensendieck (1864–1967), developed a paramedical exercise regimen that worked alongside everyday motions to strengthen and realign the spine; increases in beauty and grace were also promised to her adherents ("Sculptress of Bodies" 175). Perhaps it was as an extension of her own pursuit of what one adherent described as Mensendieck's "path of back consciousness" that Loy was inspired to create her own therapeutic method that similarly attends to rearward – in her case, pineal – anatomies ("Sculptress of Bodies" 175). In 1920, Loy completes "Auto-Facial-Construction", a manifesto-cum-advertisement promoting an expensive "initiation" into an "esoteric anatomical science" that will teach "individuals a permanent principle for the independent conservation of beauty" (*LaLB* 284). Assuring readers that youth can be reborn and prolonged by mastering "facial destiny", Loy intimates a skilful manipulation of the "zones of energy" that encircle the head and, in particular, "the centres of control" that exist "at the base of the skull and highest point of the cranium" (*LaLB* 283).

At once heterodox, capitalist, and vague, this tract withholds the practical means of attaining the realities it promises. Instead, Loy artfully entices followers and consumers, leading them toward a transmutative exercise consistent with a modernist return to alchemy that encompassed anti-ageing cures, or purifications of the senescent body with "the fabled Elixir of Life" (Morrisson, *Alchemy* 4). Loy's rationale is threefold: desirability, potency, and the reversal of the effects of mortal time. Rooted in material and sensual longings, facial construction is enabled by regenerating anatomical spaces long ascribed to the third eye, including the parietal eye underwriting Bataille's explosive cranial organ, and the neck nape that Loy elsewhere describes as a "*prise electrique*" or electrical socket to the flow of universal forces good and bad: an "outlet" channelling human vitality, and the site of "psychic fear" (*SE* 269; *GI* 28: unnumbered leaf ii). This commodification of desirability recurs in Loy's "Mass-Production on 14th Street" (1958), where the creations of New York City garment workers are "Eros' produce" on display for a feminised consumer (*LoLB* 111–13). But in "Auto-Facial Construction", Loy's marketing of an expressly esoteric Eros is twinned with a narcissistic strain that is born of financial desperation or high-flown parody, perhaps both. Regardless, "Auto-Facial-Construction" illustrates Loy's preparedness to extremify evolutionary and pineal precepts alike.

This willingness culminates in "History of Religion and Eros", where Loy elaborates on the pineal power socket, describing how "[t]he mystic, closing his eyes, his ears, invert[s] the senses from the multiple outlets for contact" and "*concentrat[es]* the various electric currents of mind and body to an unique current", thereby accessing a light unattainable to "the organ eye" (*SE* 240–1). At its best, this pineal power surge accesses "THE CREATIONAL OVERTURE": beauty before resemblance, music before utterance, and pleasure before tactility, or a "presensate ecstasy" intimated to us by our sexuality (*SE* 243). Encounters on the threshold of the blind back, "the frontier dividing the abstract from the concrete", Loy considers potentially explosive, capable of erupting the mind, but also of opening up the cranium "very like a certain Picasso cubist head, for abstract instruction to pour into it" (*SE* 246–7). Only Eros can "cross these frontiers unmodified—metaphysically intact, yet available to sensate experience." While its power can overwhelm, Eros's "ELECTRIFICATION OF BLISS" – for Loy, Freud's own literal "blind spot" – is worth the explosive risk of cranial fissure, intelligential decimation (*SE* 251). Puncturing the teleological presumptions of evolution, Loy privileges a pineal rupture that revises the moral, intellectual, and spiritual status quo whilst elevating bodily desire to the metaphysical. As for Bataille, Loy's pineality is constitutively occluded and visionary, a blindness reading truth from behind, an inverted, risky site of cognisance as impassioned as it is impossibly divine, marked by overload, irrationality, and, with an always elusive subjective coherence in view, the foregrounding of the body abject and amoral. For both, pineality offers the prospect of an "erotic metamorphosis" by which "the head" becomes receptive to "the *electric power of points*", an excessive, "ecstatic gift", a sacrifice by which the self wilfully immolates itself ("Pineal" 82). Reworking the malleability of the pineal eye, in Loy and Bataille, gnosis becomes a rearguard and often orgasmic assault against epistemological and mystical rectitudes.

Utopia: Loy's Artistic Fourth Dimension

Bataille's third eye is re-energised by molten lava and the electric current Loy's pineality foregrounds; Bataille's excess energy feeds an ecstatic futility, Loy's a generative regression, or the transcendent genius of alternate planes. Bataille theorises an ecstatic, spectacular, sacred "compenetration" between individuals akin to the self-dissipating intimacies of laughter, sexual ecstasy, or sacrifice; this experience is often momentary and violent contact – sudden, aggressive – "when life slips from one person to another in a feeling of magical subversion" ("Laughter" 61). By mystical extension and focal contrast, Loy aspires to a sensibilitous, fourth-dimensional "interpenetrat[ion]" with the cosmos that "liberate[s the] organism from biological law hitherto insurmountable", or the third-dimensional pain, suffering, and estrangements that motivate her satire (*SE* 241). Where Bataille expressly connects pain caused by violence and by our knowledge of mortality to a sexualised transcendence, Loy does so implicitly – thematically, structurally – throughout her late and autobiographical writings.[38] "The universe is interpenetrations of many aspects of itself", writes Loy, adding: "And to each man his own apparition according to his propensity or his moment" ("Notes on Metaphysics"). As discussed above, from the 1930s onward, Loy's künstlerromans describe the child's arrival from an infinite dimension, lingering over the agony of coming to terms with mortal third-dimensional existence. For Loy, this pain is heightened for highly sensitised artists like herself. But this very sensitisation proves Loy's saving grace: by dint of her superlative artistry, she can return at will to the originary, ecstatic fourth dimension, a place of unbounded creativity unmarked by harm, a perceptive place paradoxically entered through Loy's blind back.

The culmination of an esotericism that seeks, in true modernist occult style, to cohere science with the heterodox, Loy's fourth dimension overcomes Thanatos through artistic inclination, or an aesthetic esoteric Eros. "[T]he medium for knocking phenomena into shape", Loy's modern artist generates pictorial or metric form that actively reworks relations between "the finite and the infinite" (*SE* 276, 260). Rooted in contemporaneous science, the fourth dimension is the spine upon which Loy's nerval irrationalities of longing and belief coalesce, structuring Loy's drive for coherency that is satiable through artistic legacy. Loy's peers recognised these leanings: the American writer Natalie Barney considered Loy's art hermetic – sightless, turned inward – her being attuned to "habitual solitude". According to Barney, Loy was more integrated with a dreamworld than our own, meaning that her writing was comparable to a "perception of the fourth dimension" (160). Barney's lyrical invocation astutely collates the involute, transcendent thematics of Loy's künstlerromans. Focused on foundational, third-dimensional childhood struggles, these works were intended to establish Loy as an artist in command of an Eros not only intimate, but transcendently four-dimensional.

Loy's emphases on the fourth dimension reflect the discoveries and enthusiams of her era. In 1846, Gustav Fechner was the first to conceptualise human ignorance of a fourth dimension by positing a two-dimensional figure unaware of third-dimensional existence. By 1910, the fourth dimension was a household phrase, and in academic, artistic, and religious circles, a malleable modernist panacea, an answer to all scientific problems, Platonic ideal, secular heaven (Dalrymple-Henderson, *Fourth* 119, 143). Theosophy considered fourth dimensionality a viable way station of human evolution.[39] Myers argued: "Just as the baby fails to grasp the third dimension, so may we still be failing to grasp a fourth", one he posited as locatable in our subliminal or "higher cognisance" (160). Christian Science founder Mary Baker Eddy promulgated Loy's chosen religion as "the infinite calculus defining the line, plane, space, and fourth dimension of spirit" (*Miscellaneous* 22: 1). Loy follows suit, arguing: "[Man] may take his universe in any terms congenial to him, in terms of religion, science, art, sentience" ("Notes on Metaphysics"). In a similarly malleable, utopian spirit, almost every major artistic movement in the first decades of the twentieth century, from Cubism to Surrealism, presented the fourth dimension as "a symbol of liberation" and a highly subjective, openly interpretable means by which to "revolutionize the human consciousness" (Dalrymple-Henderson, "Fourth: Conclusion" 205; Bohn 127). While hard science was more conceptually than literally appealing for modernist artists who tended to rely upon popular interpretations, their subjective approach to fourth dimensionality was ultimately shored up by Einsteinian theories that stressed how "the laws governing the physical universe were relative to an observer's position" (Vetter, *Modernist* 13; Ebury 6; Bohn 128).

Loy's fourth-dimensional referents discernibly respond to innumerable influences: Victorian popularisers of this alternate plane; copious writings on this topic in the periodicals where Loy published; her constant proximity to movements, individuals, and cultures enamoured by its machinations.[40] To offer some of numerous cogent examples of fourth-dimensional prominence in Loy's vicinity: Loy resided in France at the outset of the twentieth century, when that nation was a world leader in physics, and again in the 1920s and 1930s, when it regained this stature (Parkinson 36, 40; Dalrymple-Henderson, *Fourth* 158). She then lived in Italy from 1907 to 1916, when it was one of the greatest producers of scholarly literature on the fourth dimension; the Futurist Umberto Boccioni, a close associate of Marinetti, and an artist with whom Loy had direct contact, was a particularly prominent scholar on this topic (Dalrymple-Henderson, *Fourth* 228; *BM* 155). And after arriving in New York in 1916, Loy became a regular participant in Walter and Louise Arensberg's vanguard circle, a group captivated by fourth dimensionality (Dalrymple-Henderson, *Fourth* 620).

At the Arensberg salon, Loy embarked on a lifelong friendship with Marcel Duchamp, an artist fascinated, as was Loy, by the involution of the third dimension into the fourth. In 1917, Duchamp created a self-portrait that is a near-perfect representation of the endlessness, introspection, and repetition Loy ascribes to her blind back (Fig. 3.6). By it, Duchamp's multiplied image appears "translated around an axis of rotation" that extends a third-dimensional perspective into the fourth dimension, and perhaps beyond (Adcock 155). Duchamp's photograph perfectly encapsulates Loy's 1930s depiction of Insel's consciousness, "constantly turning its back on the world" to "peep inquisitively into its own mischievous eyes" (*I* 109). As significantly, Duchamp's inversive proclivities extend through

Fig. 3.6 Marcel Duchamp, *Five-Way Portrait* (1917). ©Succession Marcel Duchamp/ADAGP, Paris and DACS, London 2016; courtesy of Francis M. Naumann Fine Art, LLC, New York.

the geometric to the gendered, most obviously in his embodiment of inversion via his female alter ego Rrose Sélavy, whose name, read aloud by a French speaker (*Eros c'est la vie*) dovetails with Loy's late supposition that Eros is pith and goal of existence.

More famously, in *The Bride Stripped Bare by her Bachelors, Even* (1915–23), Duchamp places the bride in the fourth dimension, posits sexual pleasure as a desire that operates in both third and fourth, and actively postulates that the latter might be a "tactile expansible *sphere*" whilst writing of "a 4-dim'l sense of touch as a sort of projection on a plane" (Dalrymple-Henderson, *Fourth* 134; Duchamp 88, 94). Like Loy, Duchamp describes the best of the third dimension, and envisions the fourth, through the lens of a paradisiacal sexual ecstasy that challenges gender constraints.[41] Perhaps it was in homage to these shared pursuits that, in 1958, Duchamp would describe Loy's poems as possessing "2½ dimensions" in the exhibition catalogue for her Bodley Gallery exhibition, dimensions that, in his view, included both "'high reliefs'" and "'lower depths'", phrases nicely open to double entendre (*BM* 434).

But just as readily, Loy's blind back may respond to the British populariser of science Arthur Eddington, whose *The Expanding Universe* (1920) postulated a hyperspace where "light might circulate so that you can see yourself from behind" (Ebury 14). Or Guillaume Apollinaire's "On Painting: The Cubist Painters", a seminal work on Cubism and the fourth dimension that appeared in *The Little Review* in 1922; the following year, Loy began serialising "Anglo-Mongrels and the Rose" in the same journal. Apollinaire aligns fourth dimensionality with the transcendental, primordial, and artistic, coordinates that recur in Loy's blind dorsality (41). Awash in Bergsonian intuition and an obscure artistic reinvention of geometry, Apollinaire's presentation of the fourth dimension typifies the avant-garde approach in this era, offering helpful context for what can appear hyperbolic in Loy's writing on this topic:

> The new painters do not propose, any more than did the old, to be geometricians. But, it may be said that geometry is to the plastic arts what grammar is to the art of the writer. Today scholars no longer hold to the three dimensions of the euclidean geometries. The painters have been led quite naturally and, so to speak, by intuition, to preoccupy themselves with possible new measures of space, which, in the language of modern studios has been designated briefly and altogether by the term the *fourth* dimension. (13)

For Apollinaire, artists who ruminate on ancient cultures – "the Egyptian Negro and Oceanic sculptures" – and combine these interests with "meditat[ions] on works of science" lead themselves to "sublime art", or an art, like Cubism, defined by the fourth dimension (14). This same link between Cubism and the fourth dimensional arises in Loy's unpolished treatise "The Logos in Art.", where she celebrates Picasso as divine articulator and origin of modernist art (*SE* 261). Where "a pauper aesthetic ... falls to the stacking", Loy claims that Picasso exceeds established, outmoded coordinates of artistic conception and projection, instead "inclining and laying linear extensions" to give us "the unrepresentable in presentation" (*SE* 260–1). Overcoming limited third dimensionality, Picasso's artistic inclination transcends phenomenality.

Consistent with most modernist art and writing on this topic, Loy's fourth dimensionality is more utopian fiction than scientific truth, a permeable, prospective realm encouraged by popular renderings of the same. In 1905, Einstein famously developed a theory by which "scientific objectivity could be attained only through the combination of space and time in a four-dimensional continuum" (Ebury 3). But Einsteinian relativity remained underdiscussed for the first two decades of the twentieth century. The influential British mathematician and author Charles Howard Hinton (1853–1907), on the other hand, published widely on fourth dimensionality from 1880, and Loy echoes his idealist philosophical approach, one that incorporates Bergsonian intuition and creative thinking. Hinton's beyond is "a realm of the utmost intellectual beauty, and one to which our symbolic methods apply with a better grace than they do those of three dimensions" (84). So too is Loy's fourth dimension of "superlative importance" and "a prototype of heaven" (*SE* 270). For Hinton, this alternate plane operates with the same principles as electricity; within it, movement is a current or "field of action ... [that] abuts on a continuous boundary formed by a conductor" (84, 18). In Loy's "Mi & Lo", as we have seen, the human body is that field, the "self-enclosed circuit of energy" striving toward access to the illimitable beyond to which it is connected by a rearward, pineal power socket (*SE* 269). A like pineality arises in *A New Era of Thought* (1888), where Hinton argues that humanity needs to renounce outmoded spatial concepts, encouraging his reader to see things anew with a "'mental and inner eye'" (qtd. in Dalrymple-Henderson, *Fourth* 128–9).

As would Loy, Hinton considers the soul a four-dimensional body through which we comprehend the pleasures and limitations of three-dimensional corporeality (20; *SE* 273–4). And just as Hinton argued that accessing fourth dimensionality would complete human knowledge, Loy states: "if he was no longer limited by the blind back [man] would be rounded out to the fourth dimensional contacts", would "avail himself of all there is" (*Fourth* 22; *SE* 276, 279). Elect fourth-dimensional adepts – meditators, introspeculators, the enlightened – "follow the procedure of universal involution" that Theosophists crib from Kabbalah, turning in upon their own selves in order to regenerate, thereby taking up the deific guise of creator (*SE* 278–9). Loy reinforces this thinking in "On Metaphysics", where she likens "the functioning of the [fourth] dimension" to "the turning inside out of a rubber ball". The ball's exterior is universe, its interior the human self through which infinity passes, thereby invoking "[p]erception or consciousness" ("Notes on Metaphysics"). Importantly, Loy remains aware that the idealised fourth dimension relies upon the third, and that the existence of the constrained third heightens her importance as an artificer, facilitating her role as artistic moulder of the phenomenal (*SE* 277).

For, while everyone can adapt to the fourth dimension on rear-rival, few return to their point of departure (*SE* 270). Children and women in love are "residen[t] on the rim of a supplementary dimension", gifted by a capacity to step outside "the dynamic inquietude of our sensibility" (*CP* 18: 62). In contrast to this hovering,

Loy counts herself among the "would-be expounders of the fourth dimensional condition [who] have laboured to convey their knowledge to us, uniquely through their great desire to render service to man" (*SE* 271). Esotericists and artists are among these proselytisers, "men of ample consciousness" who can manipulate the blind back, or the specific object of "third dimensional phenomena" that is a barrier to tracing "consciousness up or back to its source" (*SE* 279).[42] That source is hyperspace: "Life originates in the fourth dimension and is projected into the third dimension" (*SE* 278). In Loy's archived notes for "Mi & Lo", she articulates how the amply conscious "practice" and "strengthen" their understanding of "cosmic concepts" and maintain their contact with the beyond. These men continually "realise mentally some of the aspects or attributes of godhead" so that, when they enter the afterlife, they easily "recognise God". Loy counts Christian Scientist practitioners among these cosmic preservers. Her evidence? They enact "'impossible'" cures that challenge "the laws of medical science", and miracles always originate in the fourth dimension, extending their effects to the third ("Mi and Lo"). In "Gertrude Stein" (1929), Loy affirms that modernist artists are similarly skilled. Noting that humanity longs for "the irreducible surplus of the abstract", Loy argues that mysticism was bankrupted by its inability "to track intellection back to the embryo." Abstract art takes up the debt mysticism leaves in the sum of our knowledge. Capable of representing thought before it crystallises into cognisance, modernist creators detail "the evolution of consciousness" from the epistemological ground zero that is the fourth dimension (*LaLB* 297). As an artist, Loy recognises, challenges, and to some extent, supersedes the esoteric, just as the nineteenth- and twentieth-century occult claims to use and transcend science. This is the hypothesis Loy sets out to prove in her künstlerromans, which work under the assumption that an artist is ideally placed to affirm and delineate an esoteric Eros encompassing aesthetics and intellection. Loy's is a heady premise, particularly as her own evolution is offered as its proof.

As we've seen, Loy's late autobiographical novels gesture toward a generalised infantile experience, one where the neonate emerges from "the jugglery of birth" to adjust to its "assign[ment] to three dimensions", acclimatising itself through the transition from "extradimensional existence" to the "dimensional fence[s]" of phenomenality (*IA* 59: 2, 4; 65: 58). But it soon becomes apparent that Loy is uniquely attuned to the "limited gamut of vibrations" at her disposal, is particularly decimated by the replacement of "the site of a Perfection" with the "wreckage" of "fractured . . . time and space" (*IA* 61: 18). Loy's domestic wreckage proves more limited in its vibrations than most: her childhood home was a "non-dimension" where she found herself surrounded by "the blind emergence of inhibited lives" (*GI* 28: 101; *IA* 61: 19). Against this stultifying non-being, Loy is driven to retain and hone her fourth-dimensional capacities, to treat her arms like antennae seeking contact with desirable objects, enacting "a sort of vibrational extension" or "a plastic protrusion beyond [her] anatomical frontiers" (*IA* 60: 12).

Making "advances in a fairy air to communicative furniture", Loy possessed and possesses the power to animate, to "improve three-dimensional conveniences" and "conver[t them] into engines of escape" (*IA* 60: 11–12). Loy's attribution of her skills to the cosmic understanding of any and every infant is countered by the uniqueness of her sharp recollection, in senescence, of her capacity to make soldiers appear in her drawing room, "shining & alive . . . with a full blown military swagger" (*IA* 60: 14). Her exceptionalism is affirmed by the narrative pronouncement that Loy's sister is more constrained by blind reality because she is not, as is Loy, "in the habit of creating universes" (*IA* 70–1). Loy's deific habit prevented her from entrenchment in the "emotive imbroglios" of her family of origin. Her "latent preoccupation with beauty" clearly set her apart, driving her artistic ambition and her escape from the static non-dimension of her family home to art schools in London and Munich, as *Islands* details (*IA* 67: 90). Loy's *Child* and *Islands* are dissertations on how art, like "'love'", is an "alternative to [the] rabid inertia" of third dimensionality (*IA* 68: 115). But they are also portraits of a very specific artist as an intensely impressive young woman.

Loy's artist makes significant change in the plodding continuity of matter. By extension, pain is "a clap of inertia" anchoring intellect to solid world, "the vehicle of a definite incorporation" (*IA* 60: 16; *G32* 17). Like Freud, Loy recognises that the ego is somatic, that pain situates the human within the perceptive world, and that it is "a model of the way by which in general we arrive at the idea of our body" ("Ego" 25–6). Always combining the psychoanalytic with the esoteric, for Loy, pain proves the co-existence of phenomenality and spirituality: "There would be no third dimensional suffering if we were not connected with the fourth dimensional soul" (*SE* 274). In Loy's künstlerromans, her first conscious recollection of pain occurs as she sits in the hallway of her family home being too tightly buttoned into a boot by her governess, an experience tied to a third-dimensional Thanatos juxtaposed against, and carefully edited to maintain, the pristine non-suffering of the fourth dimension. In first drafts of this incident, Loy describes pain as an entrapment that is a "slow fourth-dimensional stunt" whereby her overly compressed leg becomes anchored even as her "arms are always dancing in the skies" (*G32* 20). As her drafts unfold, this discomforting experience is reattributed to a "sly, slow, three-dimensional conjury" (*IA* 60: 17). The fourth dimension must remain pain-free, as Loy asserts implicitly and explicitly throughout her writings.[43]

Loy begins one variant of the boot-lacing anecdote as follows: "The most reliable milestones directing the intellect are painful realities that lead to decease" (*IA* 60: 15). Death, Loy argues, is a paradox: it is meant to give significance and sense to our existence, yet, in and of itself, it "robs life of all rational value" (*G32* 16). By contrast, "the insane logic of the child mind . . . lets chaos into our cosmos"; "stand[ing] enquiring on our threshold", the dorsal blindness between third and fourth dimensions, the child perceives "the thread of death knotted in every explanation" (*G32* 15). Loy's equation is clear: that which supersedes our human understanding is eternal, whilst rationality and certainty possess a value delimited by the third dimension, are effectively dead ends. The child questions so much and so often because it remains integrated with the fourth dimension, making it "unable to accept" death as fact or certitude (*CP* 11: 15). Pain brings mortal constraints – epistemological, physical – into "an uncustomary sharpness of perspective". It also generates anxiety, a will "to recede", and slows down "the hilarious riot of vibrant infancy" or ready access to cosmic hyperspace (*IA* 60: 15–16). In all three narrative variants of Loy's fall into pain, there is a dramatic, near-bathetic disproportion between experience and interpretation: a tightly laced boot is a discomfort, not an agony, and the governess responsible for the lacing remains nearby in "intimate partnership", at the ready to assist Loy with an adjustment (*G32* 19). No lasting harm has occurred. Yet, for Loy, this quotidian suffering is harbinger of a truth that "stir[s] an inherited reaction of the eternal subconscious", a resistance to this "first alert of mortality" which confirms that "the condition for entering the adult's world is the acceptance of finitude" (*IA* 60: 17). Loy's artistic sensitivity could not be more compellingly on show.

By the logic that pain sharpens third-dimensional perspective, Loy's artistry is honed by imposed cruelties and restrictions. "Is there any reason for the highly seasoned nourishment [Fate] allotted to Goy's mind?", asks Loy in *Goy Israels*. And answers:

> It has been said that vivisectionists have the advantage of possessing a stimulant that when administered to the open animal increases its sensibility 100 per cent. If this sort of stuff should be administered to a human psyche on the threshold of the world it would make for that individual exceptionally interesting 'going'; if he happened to incline to introspection – – – could he bear up.

In Loy's künstlerromans, the child protagonist is positioned as the subject of a fictional experiment imposed upon her by "the head of the analytical department of Evolution's laboratory", its effects compounded by parental "inferiority complex" and "anxiety" (*GI* 28: 53). Anatomised by authorities over whom she has no control, Loy "incline[s] to introspection", creatively, tenaciously repurposing third-dimensional harm. For if pain has three dimensions, pleasure has four, and Loy transcends the former through fourth-dimensional reverie: "resort[ing] to philosophy", she "retires to an infinite distance from a universe"; to escape domestic "subliminal warfare", she takes up residence on the dimensional threshold, nursing "an implausible wound in invisibility" that nevertheless "revealed a clearer distance" (*GI* 29: 146; *IA* 65: 72; *CP* 12: 24).

Loy repeatedly asserts that a childhood sense of impending disaster penetrates to her consciousness of the threshold between dimensions, so that the fourth dimension feels palpable, "the subconscious . . . more present than the person." Using Freudian terminology, Loy spatialises a proposition gleaned from Myers, namely that the genius has greater access to subliminal uprushes. But while "repression will muster such rebellions as to pack the atmosphere until there is no room for the spirit", Loy's psychic drive – labelled libido on one occasion – persists (*CP* 12: 18).[44] By this creative life force, Loy restores "a sense of proportion and enough of [her] infant vision" to cultivate "the blatant purity of an inconceivable aesthetic" (*CP* 12: 20). This artistic cultivation is a sustaining passion consistent with Loy's belief that from the fourth dimension springs a happiness that pursues humanity, positioning itself behind the unseeing, "unconsciou[s]" back, requiring a mere swivel to perceive it (*SE* 274). Loy's occipital, transcendent joy reworks the mythology of Genesis, whereby turning one's back on God facilitates greater knowledge (carnal and otherwise) and with it, suffering. Through an introspeculation that unseals the self, opening our blind, contrary, and susceptible backs to unknown dimensions, Loy suggests that we attain illumination, enjoying without mortification an ecstasy that leaves pain and ignominy behind. Like Nietzsche, Loy believes "life is agonistic, [that] one is borne upwards by a relentless conflict, which is first and foremost a conflict between one's weakest self (vulnerable to pain) and one's strongest self", the self who accesses ecstasies physical and spiritual (Marshall 173). And as Alan Marshall delineates, these ecstasies are foundational to Loy's entire oeuvre, from "Parturition" (1914) onward.

Loy's youthful forays into creativity are unquestionably blighted by an aggressive maternal censoriousness: any representation of attraction or the attractive in Loy's earliest poetry or visual art her mother deems disgracefully sexual, the work of an "'idle'" and "'vicious slut'" (*IA* 67: 87, 108). No wonder Loy came to loathe all forms of censorship. Art school, too, is initially filled with blunders that reinforce Loy's third-dimensional ties. But in the wry retelling of her impassioned errors and misjudgements, we can discern the coordinates that came to define Loy's satirical writings, among them the gender, romance, and generativity also crucial to her esoteric Eros. Her first mistake, she tells us, is to "imagin[e] creation as an intensification" rather than an overcoming of phenomenal reality, an aesthetic that led to representations of glutinous, saccharine romantic imagery, recurrent "sunsets of jam" (*IA* 67: 101). Her second is to expect art school to conform to "the transformation scene in a pantomime" (*IA* 67: 102). As a result, the first day inevitably disappoints, filled as it is with the "voluminous grey pinafores" of impoverished art students surrounded by walls "the colour of dried blood" (*IA* 67: 102, 104). Anticipating transcendence, Loy instead encounters an institution literally and figuratively sacrificed to everyday exigencies, bleeding need and a distinct lack of aesthetic appeal. Loy's wounded first impressions are ultimately healed, she informs us, by her serendipitous discovery at said school of a review of Max Nordau's *Degeneration* (1892) that references his condemnation of the Pre-Raphaelite leader Dante Gabriel Rossetti.

Recounting her discovery of Rossetti, satire and intimacy, Thanatos and Eros, embattle their way through Loy's prose, which is simultaneously mocking and reverential toward an artist who "relieve[d] a middle-class visionary of her adolescence", offering her a much-needed "psychic retreat", and a return to her ecstatic, fourth-dimensional origins: "this area of perfectibility hitherto stored with emptiness, Rossetti filled for me." Within Rossetti's "English, almost nursery, medievalism", Loy "found something to love – love being the mechanism of talent" (*IA* 67: 107). By Loy's rendering, Rossetti is as abject as he is mystical: "an emetic of the spirit" with a tendency, as discussed in the fourth chapter of *Nethered Regions*, to portray impossibly idealised women brought into the "wide-eyed" and "pneumatic" proportions that convey more about his own fantasies than their appearance (*IA* 67: 106). Doggedly misogynistic, awash in grievous representational misdemeanours, Rossetti's creations nevertheless teach Loy "that art being 'spiritual', the highest function of a maiden is to yearn, *of a young man also if he can be brought to it*" (emphasis added, *IA* 67: 106–7). If the tone is satiric, the content is pure manifesto: spiritualised aesthetics are central to Loy's Eros, and it is the goal of her feminist satire and her esotericism alike to extend to men the foundational power of yearning too reductively, dismissively feminised.

Loy's mockery of Rossetti reinforces the highest point of her ecstatic love with Arthur Cravan, that "exquisite flood" that attends the release of their symbiotically "ferocious longings", a memory preceded in Loy's *Colossus* by pages of scabrous critique of Cravan's comic oddities and limitations ("Colossus" 117).[45] "[N]ot unfrequently", writes Loy in *Islands*, ruminating on her "easy to caricature" first boyfriend: "one . . . falls in love with something 'funny'" (*IA* 68: 116). The boy in question – Lucas Holyoak – absurdly sports a pipe, is awkwardly silent when they are alone, and obediently dresses as Loy commands. Even so, she recalls with palpable tenderness his chest against which she "laid [her] tired head to be soothed by his long kind fingers" (*IA* 67: 116–17). Holyoak may signify a "jocular prelude to conscious adolescence", but by the framing of Loy's recollection, he is also a significant precursor to Loy's satiric methodologies, her paradoxical use of aggression to facilitate greater proximity between individuals otherwise irrevocably divided by gendered and experiential constraints. Converting third-dimensional pain into fourth-dimensional creative genius, Loy's satire subtends the pleasures of intimacy and artistry, her lifelong inclinations toward combative avant-gardism, blustering males, and an ultra-dimensional transcendence.

Loy integrates her esotericism throughout her künstlerromans whilst positing an artistry that transcends the mystical, that might be the ideal conduit into a fourth-dimensional beyond that supersedes pain, thereby integrating a self anatomised by powers and histories not always within its control. This ascent is driven by an impassioned, aesthetic Eros, "love being the mechanism of talent" (*IA* 67: 107). Delving into pasts personal, mythological, and primeval, Loy's romans à clef, along with her expository esoteric writings, are designed to reinforce her legacy, her distinct place at an avant-garde table populated by her more privileged male peers, and her feminist mysticism. Excepting *Insel*, all remain unfinished, fragmented, often achronological; express references to Loy as an established avant-garde artist are few and far between. Instead, in these texts, Loy delineates a perceptive backwardness that is spine to her mystical, anatomical, and utopian impulses. By supinity and dorsal blindness, Loy reaffirms her status as atavistic vanguardist and feminist visionary, working, as ever, from unexpected vantages. For, just as she operates upon and redefines the margins of Futurism, Dada, and Surrealism, so too is Loy a creative adept promulgating the value of the unseen, an unreached utopia where vulnerability, recurrence, resistance, and idealism unexpectedly yet persistently coincide.

What lies behind us, out of sight, has the power to surprise and reorient; Loy's highest mystic truths share coordinates with abjectified, sustaining, and taken-for-granted femininity. Occluded, the spine structures our very being, is an "i" dotted by a pineality affirming our quotidian, vital rhythms. An ineradicable ambivalence emerges: where Pazzarella expansively inhabits and reworks the proneness imposed upon her, ascending to vengeful, satiating, fictional illumination, Loy's adolescent self is a middle-class visionary "in danger of becoming a chronic onlooker", a being not "[n]ot . . . entirely supine", neither horizontal nor upright, perpetually on the alert, defined by outcasting and anxiety (*IA* 68: 121–2). "Since pubescence", Loy writes of any and every female, "her dynamic life-currents, swift currents, cross-currents have seethed, to rush confluent in an unimaginable concussion; and sink at last into some shoreless lake of sentient calm" (*CP* 17: 56). The orgasm central to Loy's articulation of esoteric Eros, the orgasm that eludes so many individuals sexed female, is the experience by which the vertebrate self can perceive and feel, transcend the quotidian through violent, pleasurable agitation, and then be at restful one with a cosmic expansivity. Yet women's reality is too often "the eternal lying-in-wait of a cavernous passivity" (*CP* 16: 56). Portal to the beyond, is Loy's blind back compensatory? An ill-defined yet overdetermined liminality quietly foundational to Loy's oeuvre, it is easily sidestepped, overlooked, feminine. Structural, persistently rearguard, affirming innovative futures, bowed with burdens and ecstasies alike, it is a cavernousness Loy fills with paradoxes, satiations and yearnings, histories and futures, imperceptible perceptions, the unresolved and perhaps irresolvable.

After moving to Aspen, Colorado in 1953, Loy writes a poem in which she puts her blind back theory to the test. The speaker rejects rectilinearity, rationality, and the status quo, entering a transcendent beyond less pleasurable than overwhelming. Entitled "In Extremis", the poem remains unpublished, and appears to have been drafted alongside "Show Me a Saint Who Suffered" (1960). The latter poem sardonically addresses the celebrated martyr's "sacrifice of security to renown" as a duplicitous, "well-advertised" heroism, whilst arguing that the anonymous sufferer is far more humble, far more unfortunate (*LaLB* 223).[46] Focused on the relationship between pain and legacy, "Show Me a Saint" posits as "truer" the suffering of the unacknowledged individual; victimised and agonised, "In Extremis" is written from this perspective.

A typescript poem written in the first person, "In Extremis" is archived with extended, evidently rejected manuscript variants that illustrate how Loy edited her speaker from first to second person. Is this another version of Loy's split self, akin to "Mi & Lo"? It certainly appears to test Loy's belief that, in alternate dimensions, it is possible for "one half of a man to be at an infinite distance from the other half of a man" (*SE* 266). One manuscript begins "Otiose anarchist how revolt?" and charges this redundant rebel – a "me" that becomes "you" – with taking too much licence, with a possibly transgressive over-satiation: "You have nothing forbidden yourself". Freed of censoriousness, this individual is nevertheless invested in a "Tradition" that Loy describes as "the freemasonry of impotence". As in Loy's complex lineages in "History of Religion and Eros", the quotidian, the "fashionable" masquerades as the heterodox, a nonregenerative prospect. An "illegitimate child of God", the interlocutive subject of this poem feels pathologised for having desired "faith family & love", "short-circuit[ed]" by "domesticities insuperable". By these referents, the "you" of "In Extremis" is feminised. Deciding to reject Eros, the inclinations toward third-dimensional otherness so central to Loy's oeuvre and creativity, this "you" is liberated to become one with the cosmos at last: "Without the complication of the social 'rapport' / the self relaxes to the Absolute".

But what results from this expansive meditative state, this resolution to transcend or abandon Eros, is not "a shoreless lake of sentient calm". While the manuscript stanzas buckle beneath plaints of an unalleviated social futility, the typescript poem is a wreckage of monumental loss, the painful discovery that to enter the cosmos is to become a vertiginous, stricken island in the air, is to find oneself every bit as constrained as when occupying the third dimension. The typescript reads in full:

> I exist in a new and appalling dimension.
> No less spatial a jail than the cosmos
> I rattle in this Infinity
> The terrors of realised desires have cut my communications
> Every attainment of an ideal, is an exhaustion of the soul
>
> It is my misfortune to be gifted with that
> mystical ignorance, to which the 'intentions' of civilizations
> are as apparent as the passions of eyes
> The Nations arose to reveal their financial inequalities,
> the Almighty has turned banker,
> all survivors of the world war are heavily taxed
> It surprises me that a 'procession' all marches in the same ~~way~~
>   direction.
> Insanity is the symbolism of the truths that society taboos.
> When I become lucid I find I am making ~~a joke~~ fun.
>
> My last reverence is for innocence.
> I dare not brutalise the wondering eye.

Bataille argues that subjective dissolution is a precursor to communication, but this speaker has lost connection with all known coordinates of space and time only to find herself more alone than ever (*IE* 9). Otherworldly, her divine knowledge is more bewildered than aspirationally gnostic. Once attained, desires become the terror that Bataille finds inseparable from religious awe; approaching the deific, or what Loy proudly delineates elsewhere as existing as an "uncircumscribed entity, an infinitarian", the solitary speaker of Loy's "In Extremis" comes face to face with horror (*E* 69; "Street Sister" 41). Attained, ideals overwhelm. Going in fear of absolutes and perfections, all becomes visible: global inequities, supposed lunacies, deific recantations. When read through the manuscript variants, "In Extremis" posits the desultory fate of Loy's signature sacrificial victim: the speaker is subject to a violence that is a retrospeculative death-in-life by a thousand domestic cuts. Wounds like these are the substance of Loy's künstlerromans, the past shared with her family of origin to which this immolating satirist returns again and again, one marked by "insatiable vengeance" and ever-increasing, unpredictable demands for self-renunciation

(*GI* 28: 94). Loy's sacrificial satire is rooted in a present reality overburdened by its past.

Yet the typescript shows that, despite the horror at stake, Loy's critique of rectitude persists. Echoing Bataille's revulsion toward the same, in Loy's poem, what amazes most are performances of forwardness: "It surprises me that a 'procession' all marches in the same direction." With knowing irony, the punctuated "procession" is severed from its line; so too are civilised "'intentions'" treated with scepticism at the outset of this stanza. This is far from the only instance in which Loy decries "unstemmed procession[s]" in pursuit of "over-showy idol[s]", aspirations that reveal "that the thing we most desire is the thing we mostly miss" (*GI* 28: 118). Mystics "embrace a 'ready-made' in the way of absolutes"; psychoanalysts equate the unconscious with the Absolute (*SE* 228). Artists alone know that absolutism is death, aspire toward it only to deliberately bypass it as destination, secure in the knowledge that "[w]e exist for as long as we can imagine ourselves" (*SE* 228, 282). The coherent self toward which Loy so palpably strives, the coherent visionary, artistic self that is the subject of her late künstlerromans, an entity at one with its own subjectivity and the cosmos, is just such an impossible absolute.

Imagining a self transcendently above the terrestrial machinations that she chooses to leave behind, the speaker of "In Extremis" watches the world move forward from a ruefully mocking distance. From the vantage of a wilful excision, this speaker perceives herself as having yielded too entirely to the insurmountable, unheroic, absolutist terrain of home and family. As Michael Seidel argues, "[s]atiric action is always double action, a regress in the form of progress, a presentation in the form of a violation" full of forward-looking promise and backward-facing "threat" (23, 46). Regress, progress. Similar dualities define the expansive passivity, or "supine event", that was the focus of the previous chapter, and Loy's atavistically transcendent blind back. "In Extremis" is awash in a still more marked duality, giving voice to what it fears most, confronting the limits of artistic manipulations of reality and mystical ameliorations alike. Loy's speaker "exist[s] in a new and appalling dimension" that is an afterlife, a death. "In Extremis" is counterpoise to the labouring speaker of Loy's "Parturition" (1914), she who resides at "the centre / Of a circle of pain / Exceeding its boundaries in every direction" (*LoLB* 4). Appearing at opposite ends of Loy's career, both poems articulate a cosmically defined transition into a new life teetering on demise; both critique positivist narratives that might propel or circumscribe that new life. Unmoored, Loy's speakers read truths from the prone vantage of birth-giving or from the other side of Loy's blind, dorsal portal. Born in Adam's wake, women are perpetual laggards, Loy tells us, foreordained to "being carried along on the Everlasting's back", bringing "only a partial presence to the pursuits of man" (*CP* 18: 67). Propulsively arrière-garde and atavistically avant-garde, women read truth from behind, retaining reverence for the emergent, the unseen and unknown, be it the neonate clinging to its connection to a fourth dimension, or "the wondering eye", the sacrosanct pineality emerging from atrophy to connect soma and spirit in an ecstatic, esoteric Eros once more.

Notes

1. The ellipsis in this quotation is Loy's.
2. Unbracketed ellipses in quotations from "The Pamperers" are Loy's own.
3. Although I am quoting H. D. directly, the confidence of my argument is aided by Miranda Hickman's discussion of the idealised house-self in the chapter devoted to H. D. in *The Geometry of Modernism: The Vorticist Idiom in Lewis, Pound, H. D., and Yeats* (157).
4. In drawing attention to Insel's pivoting between atavism and futuristic creativity, I take implicit issue with Christina Walter's fantastic account of optics in Loy's work. Deploying the blind back as figured in Loy's "Mi & Lo", Walter reads the reference to its "shutter" as a camera mechanism. By extension, she asserts that Loy's blind back is a metaphor for optical technologies of film and photography, arguing: "Insel offers a surreal embodiment of the human race's blind back that allows him and his art to serve as a screen on which to view the nature of the material universe, including the materiality of the subject" (156).

    By Walter's reading, Insel becomes a filmic mechanism, a technological projection of the phenomenal, an argument that does not wholly account for Loy's equal, opposed emphasis on his delimiting atavism, or the defining paradoxicality of the blind back. Furthermore, extended engagement with Loy's "shutter" suggests that it more expressly refers to a door, window covering, or screen. When Loy uses "aperture", as she does in the undated story "The Agony of the Partition", the term refers to an opening or gap in a wall (*SE* 8).
5. Held by the Museum of Modern Art in New York, Oelze's painting can be seen on their website (www.moma.org/collection/works/78518). See David Ayers (230), Sarah Hayden (*Curious* 145–8), and Carolyn Burke (*BM* 385) for discussions of Oelze's art and *Expectation* in particular.

6. See "Esoteric Eros and Psychoanalysis" in the first chapter of this book and, from Chapter 1 of *Nethered Regions*, "'Cosmic Force': Vitalism".
7. Built on Neolithic remains, the third-century BCE Roman city of Lutetia was precursor to contemporary Paris.
8. In 1887, the infamous Michelson–Morley experiment, based on a hypothesis that the earth's motion could be detected through universal ether, "has been called the most famous failed experiment in history" (Ebury 1). As Katherine Ebury discusses, the experiment shifted physicists' emphasis from theories of ether to the speed of light, paving a notable path toward Einstein's relativity (2). That said, the "ether hypothesis ... was commonly accepted until Einstein and others rejected it in the early twentieth century" (Morrisson, *Alchemy* 78). No longer widely applied come the 1920s, Victorian ether physics nevertheless had adherents – among them Oliver Lodge, author of *The Ether of Space* (1909) – for at least another decade (Morrisson, *Alchemy* 80–1).
9. As discussed in Chapter 1 of this volume, "Hearts Absented and Newborn: Loy's Esoteric Eros", Bergson was president of the Society for Psychical Research in 1913; Myers was a founder of this society, and Freud framed his theory of the subconscious in response to Myers's work.
10. Loy's künstlerromans suggest that she hones this skill as a counter to her father's failures. Evidence of paternal engagement with introspeculation arises in "Anglo-Mongrels and the Rose", in which Exodus emigrates from Hungary to England, where he finds himself painting, "knowing not why", heliotropic "sunflowers turned sunwards" (*LaLB* 115). The redundant phrasing speaks to Exodus's dead-ended inclinations. In *Goy Israels*, Loy's father realises that "his ambitions tur[n] back upon themselves" and finds himself "invert[ing]", becoming a man who boasts emptily and unhappily about his wealth, rather than the happiness he valued most when young (*GI* 28: 128).
11. Direct evidence of this interchangeability appears in a passage in *Goy 32* that is reworked in *The Child and the Parent*. In the first instance, Loy writes that "subliminal spectres ... crowd into [the child's] company" (*G32* 33); in *Child*, "spectres of the subconscious" do the crowding (13: 25).
12. See, respectively: *G32* 33; *CP* 13: 25; *IA* 65: 72; *CP* 15: 41; *IA* 67: 112; *IA* 65: 81–4.
13. See, respectively: *CP* 12: 28; 13: 30; *IA* 61: 20; 63: 44.
14. In *The Child and the Parent*, Loy attributes her experience of this succumbing in her upbringing to her parents' too-great respect for their own personalities, so that their ideas "degenerat[e] to a prejudice" to which they cling just as "felons hang on to ill-gotten gains" (16: 55). In archived notes, Loy associates the "subliminal self" with a "microscopic dimension": for Loy, "[a] good man is the man who keeps all his good qualities in the human dimension and his evil

qualities in the microscopic dimension", even as she observes that the supposedly evil are often haphazardly subjected to a "volume of fury" ejected from various planes ("Mi and Lo").

15. Beyond the scope of this chapter, Loy's equation of the mother with imperialism is discernible from "Anglo-Mongrels and the Rose" (1923–5) onward. In *Goy Israels*, this motif is particularly present: Loy's childhood home is an "Empire" that belongs to Mrs Israels, who administers with a stern hand, guided by scripture, inviting her fellow inhabitants to "'abject servility'" whilst treating domestic rooms as "her dominions" (*GI* 28: 52r).

16. In "Feminism, Aesthetics, and Art Education", Elizabeth Garber reminds us that *Hélène Fourment in a Fur Coat* (1638) is read by John Berger and others as evidence that Rubens could present women "non-idealistically" – both with banal features on show, and in a fluid state between subjectivity and objectivisation (220). Furthermore, Sarah R. Cohen examines the complexity of Rubens's 1620s portrayal of Marie de Médici, Queen of France from 1589 to 1643, and notes that Rubens did not shy away from using male models to emphasise the power and authority of his female regal patron. Yet in the same series, Rubens ceded to artistic expectations of female affectivity and passivity to make the queen's reign more palatable to her sceptical opponents.

17. In "Anglo-Mongrels and the Rose" (1923–5), for instance, Loy names herself "Ova", a moniker that aurally recalls the name Loy gave to her first child, Oda Janet, whose short life lasted from 1904 to 1905.

    Correspondence between Loy and her daughter Joella and son-in-law Julien Levy shows that this Loy proclivity extends to her grandchildren: she urges the couple to name their first son Mino da Fiesole, ostensibly after the fifteenth-century Italian sculptor, but also so that his name would chime with her own. Curiously, da Fiesole was also known as Mino de Giovanni, thereby evoking Loy's Italian Futurist lover Giovanni Papini. Corroborating this link, Loy suggests that her second grandson be called Jeronimo, or the name she gives Papini in her short story "Pazzarella" and her roman à clef *Esau Penfold* (Undated letters, Loy to Julien and Joella Levy, Box 30, Folder 10, 1930).

18. Loy's knowledge of specific paintings cannot always be confirmed, but biographical facts underscore her familiarity with Surrealist dorsality. Magritte lived in Paris between 1927 and 1930, when Loy was resident in the French capital. In 1932, Magritte was showcased at the Julien Levy Gallery (*BM* 377). Magritte, it seems, was not a good communicator, but Loy's undated letter to Levy about shipping his art across the Atlantic is a particularly strong example of the dozens in Levy's archive that illustrate the depth of Loy's understanding of the Surrealist scene in Paris (Undated letter, Loy to Levy, Box 30, Folder 11, 1931). Levy clearly relied enormously on Loy's aesthetic nous in drawing up his annual rosters of exhibitions.

Levy initially hesitated to exhibit Dali because his work was expensive and controversial, and therefore financially risky. Correspondence indicates that it was Loy's confidence in Dali's importance that cemented Levy's resolve to exhibit his work (see letters dated 30 May and Monday 16, Levy, Julien to Joella Levy, Box 29, Folder 7, 1928; letter dated 25 January 1934, Loy to Julien and Joella Levy, Box 31, Folder 1, 1934). Levy became an enthusiastic Dali fan and, in 1931, curated a successful and lucrative year-long Dali exhibition, purchasing his now canonical *The Persistence of Memory*, which was completed in that same year (*BM* 377). For evidence of Loy's extensive socialising with the Dalis, see correspondence in Loy to Levy, Box 31, Folder 2, 1931.

Dali also associated with Richard Oelze, the artist after whom Loy's Insel is modelled (*BM* 381, 401). In *Insel*, Jones claims to have told Dali that he was "fated to the most extravagant of publicities", a derisive theory he was reputedly "inclined to accept" (*I* 10). Jones's distaste for Dali's work surfaces in her comparison of Insel's masticating cheek to a "Dali-like protuberance of elongated flesh" replete with "flaccid facial tissue" (*I* 13).

19. Critics disagree about and labour to clarify the complexities of Bataille's interiority. Benjamin Noys suggests that Bataille's inner experience is mistakenly read as an inward turn by Susan Rubin Suleiman when, in fact, it is "an experience that touches on the impossible" (48). Andrew J. Mitchell and Jason Kemp Winfree assert that Bataille presents us with a being that "spills outside itself", whose finitude "is thus to be uncontained . . . in the catastrophe of utter abandon", thereby making a generative paradox of his "inner experience" (5).

20. For instance, where Lara Vetter's *Modernist Writings and Religio-Scientific Discourse: H. D., Loy, and Toomer* (2010) lays significant ground in outlining the major occult themes and influences of Loy's childhood and the high modernist period, her focus does not include an in-depth discussion of the relationship between Theosophical tenets and Loy's writings.

21. In her useful introductory discussion to *Insel*, Sarah Hayden makes the lucid passing observation that Loy's pineal gland is "more mystical than medical" and thereby "owes much more to the writings of Blavatsky than Bataille" ("Introduction" xxv). Loy's pineality does replicate the Theosophical presentation of the same, but ultimately, as this chapter aims to illustrate, its aim and meaning are more consistent with Bataille's.

Using *Insel* as her sole source text, Hayden perceives the pineal gland as distinct from the blind back, suggesting that the latter's sole function is to obstruct our access to the future ("Introduction" xxv–xxvi). Evidence from other Loy künstlerromans demonstrates that these two anatomical constructs are inextricable. Furthermore, consistent with the temporal and experiential paradox central to the blind back, Loy's third eye is vestigial, familiar with a distant past, and aspirationally transcendent, future-oriented.

22. See, for instance, Magritte's painting of a single eye, *The False Mirror* (1929), or Dali's backward-rolling, vegetally eyelashed, and brick-wall-mounted variant of the same, *L'oeil fleuri* (c. 1944). Loy's prominent singular orbs include the "large, lashy, luminous eye" that boldly winks at a brash oat-sowing youth in the ballet "Crystal Pantomime" and her praise for Gertrude Stein's words, in form akin to "the semi-honesty of the oval eye" (*SE* 156; *LaLB* 292).

23. For Spinoza, Descartes's rendering of the pineal gland was emblematic of the failure of his mind/body dualism more broadly, a "'hypothesis'" that he argued out-occulted the occult (qtd. in Shapiro 260). Paradoxically, *Passions* reinforces and resists Cartesian dualism, striving toward an integrated self at home with the emotions whilst retaining a hierarchy of wilful control over the same. With her esoteric Eros, Loy is similarly keen to rethink moral strictures on human feeling, but she effects this reconsideration by ascribing greatest virtue to the greatest passions.

24. Descartes's pineal arguments are readily dismantled. As Lisa Shapiro writes, in *Meditations on First Philosophy* (1641), Descartes argues that all parts of the body are subject to division, thereby elevating indivisible soul over anatomisable soma. Yet, by his own logic, the pineal gland itself is potentially subject to partitioning. Furthermore, due to the power Descartes ascribes to individual essence, any body part could become the seat of the soul (268).

25. In his replies to the sixth set of objections to the *Meditations*, Descartes writes:

> 'I saw that the gravity, while remaining coextensive with the heavy body, could exercise all its force in any one part of the body; for if the body were hung from a rope attached to any part of it, it would still pull the rope down with all its force, just as if all the gravity existed in the part actually touching the rope instead of being scattered through the remaining parts. This is exactly the way in which I now understand the mind to be coextensive with the body—the whole mind in the whole body and the whole mind in any one of its parts.'

To this, Descartes "added that he thought that our ideas about gravity are derived from our conception of the soul" (qtd. in Lokhorst n.p.).

26. Crowley's relationship to Loy is discussed in greater depth in Chapter 1 of this volume.

27. On Blavatsky's recovery of Eastern tradition as her greatest incursion into Western epistemology, see Obeyesekere 359–60; Owen, *Place* 126; Storm 115; Surette 24–5; Versluis 151; Crow 700. For Obeyesekere, Blavatsky remains controversial, but he acknowledges that she should be credited with enacting a Foucauldian "epistemic break": disrupting

received traditions, and generating paradigmatic shifts in cultural consciousness (355).

The altruism and diversity of Blavatsky's knowledge-gathering methods continue to be questioned. Gauri Viswanathan argues that Blavatsky's Tibetan masters, Koot Hoomi and Morya, openly criticised the British establishment for needing a European, bureaucratised individual to represent any non-occidental teaching. Blavatsky took on this role for these thinkers whilst appropriating and reframing their ideas ("Ordinary" 13–16). Elsewhere, Viswanathan points out that although Blavatsky's mission was misguided by contemporary estimation, she genuinely believed she was salvaging civilisations decimated by imperial conquest ("In Search" 83–4).

28. Blavatsky, for instance, describes the "abject savage" of inferior brain who remains "very little superior to an animal", whilst Besant considers the "low savage" as a scarcely human, amoral cannibal, and praises, as racial counter, the "well-modelled skull" of an intelligent white male British child (*Isis* I 296–7; Besant 44–6). Both Theosophists use these examples as evidence that reincarnation can improve the too-easily dismissed degenerate, but their language, values, and evolutionary beliefs are embedded in the rhetoric of white supremacy.
29. Apparently, Haweis strove to have the work published, but a "London publisher ... rejected [it] as likely to do more harm than good" (*BM* 142). The copy available at the British Library indicates that it was ultimately published privately in an edition of 100.
30. Burke considers *Seven Ages of God* a product of Haweis's engagement with Paramananda and the Bhagavad Gita; given the influence of Eastern religion and philosophy on Theosophy, this link arguably sustains my discussion of how the coordinates of Haweis's tract overlap with Blavatsky's doctrine (*BM* 132, 135).
31. In the work of Besant's prominent Theosophical associate Charles Webster Leadbeater, this evolution will extend to a parietal human eye with power to "'magnif[y] ... minute physical objects'", thereby revealing, for instance, the female and male components of the atom that he and Besant believed "infuse[d] each other with lines of life force", a rare Theosophical nod to a sexed universe (qtd. in Morrisson, *Alchemy* 74, 86).
32. In *Goy* 32 and in the chapter entitled "The Bird Alights" that appears in both *The Child and the Parent* and *Islands in the Air*, Loy tellingly replaces the maternal birthing process with a cosmic bird that seeks out the as-yet-unconscious neonate, or the "circumscribed creature that it is going to be". In Loy's esoteric reworking of Hans Christian Anderson's 1839 "The Storks" (a source to which the Western euphemistic tale of human origin is attributed), the extramundane bird is mute, but seeks an "advantage of association" found in the human infant, one recognisable in the sound of the child's voice (*IA* 59: 4). To each individual

a unique cosmic bird appears to be assigned. Once the bird "alights", child and bird symbiotically occupy one body; by other-wordly ornithology the child thus becomes "an aerial infinity from which a body of grace depends as a plumb to hold it to the level of phenomena" (*IA* 59: 5).

Through this rendering, Loy bypasses the maternal progenitor with whom she had a vexed relationship, and centralises a wholly unique, spiritually inflected ability to speak as the commencement of her own conscious existence. This ethereal vocalisation presumably overwrites her mother's most resonant legacy: due to her evidently relentless verbal cacophony, Loy dubbed Julia Löwy "The Voice".

33. Minus reincarnation, Blavatsky's Theosophy is remarkably biblical: God is the noumenon; higher spirits sacrifice or degrade themselves to permit of creation; all beings are extensions of the deific, and therefore theoretically akin; the human "fall" occurs with the division and recognition of two sexes; with the fall comes knowledge, including the science to which Blavatsky defers whilst considering it lesser than gnosis.

34. The first orb shares the second's resemblance to the pineal eye. On a night-time illicit prowl with her sister, Loy climbs a ladder to the edge of the household cistern, only to see in its depths "an eroded orb on a bottomless water". Though it is no doubt a ball or float valve akin to those found in modern-day toilets, Loy transforms this sphere into a "little leaden planet" in "a timeless universe", "a microcosm awaiting the generation of life", awash in "the blind patience of 'before life'" (*IA* 65: 68–9). This desiccated orb has the quality of an atrophied pineal gland, a body in retreat, blindly anticipating illumination. What is more, it offers child-Loy a connection to an alternate plane; after retreating to bed, Loy recalls the orb and feels "external to that which contains me", an experience approximating the orgasmic, and one by which she has a sensation of "bec[oming] everlasting" (*IA* 65: 70).

35. Besant replicates Blavatsky's Eros, valuing loves familial, platonic, and artistic; describing love as the highest part of ourselves; and presenting it as the conduit to ever-improving reincarnations (99, 102). Death, Besant asserts, is merely "continual communion with those whom you love" (104).

36. On sexuality Blavatsky tends toward the puritanical, improbably claiming that her own marriages went unconsummated (Obeyesekere 358; Crow 696–7). Stressing bodily and emotional control throughout her teachings, Blavatsky connected celibacy and genius; as she forbade married people from becoming adepts, her inner circle undertook a pledge of chastity (Crow 712). Perhaps as a corollary to the strong links between sexual purity and nineteenth-century feminism, Theosophy was renowned for attracting feminist activists (Owen, *Place* 87).

37. Bataille's oeuvre offers many moments of resistance toward movement columnar and synchronised. "War", he argues, "represents a bold advance, but it is the crudest kind of advance: one needs as much naïveté – or stupidity – as strength to be indifferent to that which one overvalues and to take pride in having deemed oneself of no value" (*TR* 58). Still further, he writes pejoratively: "*Homo sapiens* . . . alone among all the animals, attains a stiffness and radical rectitude in military drill" ("Pineal" 75).
38. As Bataille asserts in *The Tears of Eros*, sex and death are experiences that overwhelm, and toward which humans often respond with reserve or embarrassment (33). They are also linked in showing us "the puerility of reason", a force that requires an ecstatic violence to overcome. For Bataille, "in the excess of raptures" painful or orgasmic, the subject is shattered, and can "seize on the similarity between a horror and a voluptuousness that goes beyond [it], between an ultimate pain and an unbearable joy!" (*Tears* 20).

    Loy's articulations of pain can be equally extreme, equally ecstatic: her poem "Parturition" (1914) is a standout example; in her künstlerromans, even small discomforts are likened to a sundering from a contented originary cosmos. Relatedly, I am arguing that, in her late writings, Loy's foundational exploration of childhood pain is the discernible correlate to the development of her esoteric Eros.
39. Continuing to consign all spatiality to the lesser material realm, Blavatsky avows that, as human faculties develop, so too "will the characteristics of matter be multiplied" and fourth dimensionality reached (*Secret* I 251). Dalrymple-Henderson argues that later Theosophists were similarly enthused about hyperspace as an anti-positivist prospect that dovetailed with core tenets of their belief system (*Fourth* 133).
40. Essays on and artistic interpretations of the fourth dimension were regularly published in the vanguard journals in which Loy placed her work. For instance, Max Weber's influential "The Fourth Dimension from a Plastic Point of View" appeared in *Camera Work* in 1910; the same journal published Loy's first poems in 1914. Similarly, the May 1917 issue of *The Blind Man* includes Loy's ambivalent review essay "*Pas de Commentaires*! Louis M. Eilshemius" and her recorded dialogue "O Marcel - - - Otherwise I Also Have Been to Louise's" (11–12; 14–15). Within its pages are two poems by Walter Arensberg clearly influenced by modern physics; in league with Loy's dimensionality, Arensberg's "Theorem" gestures to the incommensurability of a three-dimensional world against the strength of human emotion (9). Finally, Claude Bragdon's influential "The New Concepts of Time and Space" appeared in *The Dial* in 1920, a year before Loy published poetry in this journal.

    Further evidence of Loy's ties to fourth-dimensional discourse: Loy's associate Ezra Pound is said to have equated, as does Loy, "the fourth dimension with the creative imagination" (Bohn 133; see also Bell). Loy's friend, the photographer Man Ray, engaged in an extended project of photographing nineteenth-century mathematical sculptures meant to model geometrical concepts in space when Loy was residing in Paris in the 1930s (Parkinson 79).

Finally, Loy's own allusions discuss the fourth dimension. For instance, in a text referenced in *Insel*, modernist travel writer William Seabrook ruminates: "I have wondered sometimes – pure speculation – whether primitive sorcery (and esoteric black magic) may not possess also a control, more important to know about, over certain aspects of the fourth-dimensional world, equally recognized in our new space-time theories since Einstein" (*I* 30; Seabrook 52).

41. On technological grounds, Eric B. White similarly considers Duchamp's *The Bride Stripped Bare by her Bachelors, Even* a major influence on Loy and her New York peers, among them Baroness Elsa von Freytag-Loringhoven and William Carlos Williams. For White, Duchamp's artwork "helped identify their implications for reading and writing in the Machine Age", enabling these artists to generate new circuitries, as well as to create languages that aim to describe the indescribable and, in particular, the fourth dimension (82–3). Noting that the Baroness and Loy are alignably feminist in bringing their technological pursuits "more forcefully into the arenas of everyday life", White foregrounds Loy and Duchamp as "vanguardist[s] who anticipated the rise of the artist-engineer by more than half a decade" (90; 103–4).
42. Note that Loy does not name the blind back outright in the published work about this barrier to consciousness, but her redacted notes indicate that this is the subject she describes (*SE* 407).
43. Another example: in "Visitation of Insel", Loy recounts her experience of chronic discomfort due to an ulcer just before Insel "appears"; as he emerges from the fourth dimension, Loy reports, her "pain lay dead among the shadows" (159).
44. In *Goy 32*, it is "the libido, so elusive to the analyst" that becomes "more present" than the third-dimensional self due to the constant threat of pain-cum-Thanatos (22).
45. Loy's satire of Cravan is discussed in detail in "'The Instigatory Caress': Satire and Intimacy", in the second chapter of *Nethered Regions*.
46. "Show Me a Saint Who Suffered" is titled as such by Roger Conover in *LaLB*, where it is dated as having been written between 1930 and 1950; it was published as "Untitled" in *Between Worlds* in 1962. "In Extremis" exists in manuscript and typescript. Across the top of one draft, Loy writes "Aspen", where she lived from 1953 until her death in 1966.

Bibliography

Abbott, Edwin A. 1884. *Flatland: A Romance of Many Dimensions*. Basil Blackwell, 1962.

Adamson, Natalie, and Toby Norris. "Introduction." *Academics, Pompiers, Official Artists and the Arrière-Garde: Defining Modern and Traditional in France, 1900–1960*, edited by Natalie Adamson and Toby Norris, Cambridge Scholars Publishing, 2009, pp. 1–24.

Adcock, Craig. "Duchamp's Eroticism: A Mathematical Analysis." *Dada/Surrealism*, vol. 16, no.1, 1987, pp. 149–67.

Ades, Dawn. "Afterword." *Investigating Sex: Surrealist Research 1928–1932*, translated by Malcolm Imrie, edited by José Pierre, Verso, 2011, pp. 185–206.

Adorno, Theodor. 1946–7. "Theses against Occultism." *Minima Moralia: Reflections on a Damaged Life*, translated by E. F. N. Jephcott, Verso, 2005, pp. 238–44.

Alaimo, Stacy. "Trans-Corporeal Feminisms and the Ethical Space of Nature." *Material Feminisms*, edited by Stacy Alaimo and Susan Hekman, Indiana UP, 2008, pp. 237–64.

Alcoff, Linda Martín. *Visible Identities: Race, Gender, and the Self*. Oxford UP, 2006.

Altieri, Charles. "Avant-Garde or Arriere-Garde in Recent Contemporary Poetry." *Poetics Today*, vol. 20, no. 4, 1999, pp. 629–53.

Amendola, Eva. 1920. "Futurist Occultism." Appendix 1 to "Notes on 'Esoteric Futurism': Marinetti and the Occultist Circle in Milan" by Matteo D'Amborosio. *International Yearbook of Futurism Studies*, vol. 8, 2018, pp. 321–2.

Angel, Katherine. *Unmastered: A Book on Desire, Most Difficult to Tell*. Penguin, 2012.

Apollinaire, Guillaume. "On Painting: The Cubist Painters." Translated by Mrs Charles Knoblauch. *The Little Review*, vol. 8, no. 2, 1922, pp. 7–19.

Appel, John J. "Christian Science and the Jews." *Jewish Social Studies*, vol. 31, no. 2, 1969, pp. 100–21.

Ardam, Jacquelyn. "Demystifying the Contents of the Universe: A New Look at Mina Loy." *Los Angeles Review of Books*, 13

August 2017. lareviewofbooks.org/article/demystifying-the-contents-of-the-universe-a-new-look-at-mina-loy/.

Arensberg, Walter Conrad. "Theorem." *The Blind Man*, vol. 2, May 1917, p. 9.

Armstrong, Tim. "Loy and Cornell: Christian Science and the Destruction of the World." *The Salt Companion to Mina Loy*, edited by Rachel Potter and Suzanne Hobson, Salt Publishing, 2010, pp. 204–20.

Arnould, Elisabeth. "The Impossible Sacrifice of Poetry: Bataille and the Nancian Critique of Sacrifice." *Diacritics*, vol. 26, no. 2, 1996, pp. 86–96.

Asprem, Egil. *The Problem of Disenchantment: Scientific Naturalism and Esoteric Discourse, 1900–1939*. Brill, 2014.

Assagioli, Roberto. *Psychosynthesis: A Manual of Principles and Techniques*. Turnstone Books, 1975.

Ayers, David. "Mina Loy's *Insel* and its Contexts." *The Salt Companion to Mina Loy*, edited by Rachel Potter and Suzanne Hobson, Salt Publishing, 2010, pp. 221–47.

Baker Eddy, Mary. 1896. *Miscellaneous Writings, 1883–1896*. The Christian Science Board of Directors, 1924. Project Gutenberg, www.gutenberg.org/files/31427/31427-pdf.pdf.

—. 1875. *Science and Health with Key to the Scriptures*. Trustees under the Will of Mary Baker Eddy, 1934.

Balla, Giacomo. 1914. "The Antineutral Suit: Futurist Manifesto." *Futurism: An Anthology*, translated and edited by Lawrence Rainey, Christine Poggi, and Laura Wittman, Yale UP, 2009, pp. 202–4.

Barnes, Djuna. 1927. "Dusie." *Americana Esoterica*, introduced by Carl van Doren, Macy-Masius, 1927, pp. 75–82.

Barney, Natalie. "Mina Loy." *Adventures of the Mind*, translated by John Spalding Gatton, New York UP, 1992, pp. 159–60.

Barthes, Roland. 1963. "The Metaphor of the Eye." Translated by J. A. Underwood in *Story of the Eye* by Georges Bataille, translated by Joachim Neugroschel, Marion Boyars, 1979, pp. 119–27.

Bataille, Georges. 1949. *The Accursed Share: An Essay on General Economy*. Vol. 1, translated by Robert Hurley, Zone Books, 1991.

—. 1949. *The Accursed Share: An Essay on General Economy*. Vols 2 and 3, translated by Robert Hurley, Zone Books, 1993.

—. "The Castrated Lion." *The Absence of Myth: Writings on Surrealism*, translated and edited by Michael Richardson, Verso, 1994, pp. 28–9.

—. 1957. *Erotism: Death and Sensuality*. Translated by Mary Dalwood, City Lights Books, 1986.

—. 1943. *Inner Experience*. Translated and introduced by Leslie Anne Boldt, State U of New York P, 1988.

—. 1930. "The Jesuve." *Visions of Excess: Selected Writings, 1927–1939*, translated by Alan Stoekl et al., edited by Alan Stoekl, U of Minnesota P, 1985, pp. 73–8.

—. "Laughter." *The Bataille Reader*, edited by Fred Botting and Scott Wilson, Blackwell Publishers, 1997, pp. 59–63.
—. c. 1930. "The Pineal Eye." *Visions of Excess: Selected Writings, 1927–1939*, translated by Alan Stoekl et al., edited by Alan Stoekl, U of Minnesota P, 1985, pp. 79–90.
—. "The Surrealist Religion." *The Absence of Myth: Writings on Surrealism*, translated and edited by Michael Richardson, Verso, 1994, pp. 71–90.
—. 1961. *The Tears of Eros*. Translated by Peter Connor, City Lights Books, 1989.
—. 1973. *Theory of Religion*. Translated by Robert Hurley, Zone Books, 1989.
Baudelaire, Charles. 1857. *The Flowers of Evil*. Translated and edited by James McGowan, introduced by Jonathan Culler, Oxford UP, 1998.
—. 1863. "The Painter of Modern Life." *The Painter of Modern Life and Other Essays*, translated and edited by Jonathan Mayne, Phaidon Press, 1995, pp. 1–42.
Bayer, Joella. "Bayer, Joella to Mina Loy and Fabienne Loy, 1917–1948." YCAL MSS 778, Box 1, Carolyn Burke Collection on Mina Loy and Lee Miller. Beinecke Rare Book and Manuscript Library, Yale University, CT, USA.
—. "Interview, Burke and Bayer." n.d. YCAL MSS 778, Box 2, Folder "Transcripts, 1978–1981, 1989." Carolyn Burke Collection on Mina Loy and Lee Miller. Beinecke Rare Book and Manuscript Library, Yale University, CT, USA.
Beauchamp, Tamara. *Enemies of the Unconscious: Modernist Resistances to Psychoanalysis*. 2014. U of California, Irvine, PhD dissertation. *eScholarship*, escholarship.org/uc/item/50m6k9xw.
Bell, Ian F. A. "Ezra Pound and the Materiality of the Fourth Dimension." *Science and Modern Poetry*, edited by J. Holmes. Liverpool UP, 2012. pp. 130–50.
Bellamy, Richard. "The Advent of the Masses and the Making of the Modern Theory of Democracy." *The Cambridge History of Twentieth-Century Political Thought*, edited by Terence Ball and Richard Bellamy, Cambridge UP, 2003, pp. 70–103.
Berg, Steven. *Eros and the Intoxications of Enlightenment: On Plato's Symposium*. State U of New York P, 2010.
Bergson, Henri. 1907. *Creative Evolution: An Alternate Explanation for Darwin's Mechanism of Evolution*. Translated by Arthur Mitchell, CreateSpace, 2014.
Bersani, Leo. "Is the Rectum a Grave?" *October*, vol. 43, winter 1987, pp. 197–222.
Besant, Annie. *Popular Lectures on Theosophy*. Rajput Press, 1910.
Bevir, Mark. "The West Turns Eastward: Madame Blavatsky and the Transformation of the Occult Tradition." *Journal of the American Academy of Religion*, vol. 62, no. 3, 1994, pp. 747–67.

Biles, Jeremy. *Ecce Monstrum: Georges Bataille and the Sacrifice of Form.* Fordham UP, 2007.
Birke, Lynda. *Feminism and the Biological Body.* Edinburgh UP, 1999.
Blair, Kirstie. *Victorian Poetry and the Culture of the Heart.* Oxford UP, 2006.
Blau Duplessis, Rachel. "'Seismic Orgasm': Sexual Intercourse and Narrative Meaning in Mina Loy." *Mina Loy: Woman and Poet*, edited by Maeera Shreiber and Keith Tuma, National Poetry Foundation, 1998, pp. 45–85.
Blavatsky, Helena P. 1877. *Isis Unveiled: A Master-Key to the Mysteries of Ancient and Modern Science and Theology*, vol. 1: *Science*. Theosophy Trust, 2006.
—. 1877. *Isis Unveiled: A Master-Key to the Mysteries of Ancient and Modern Science and Theology*, vol. 2: *Theology*. Theosophy Trust, 2006.
—. 1888. *The Secret Doctrine: The Synthesis of Science, Religion, and Philosophy*, vol. 1: *Cosmogenesis*. Theosophical UP, 2019.
—. 1888. *The Secret Doctrine: The Synthesis of Science, Religion, and Philosophy*, vol. 2: *Anthropogenesis*. Theosophical UP, 2019.
Bloom, Harold. *The American Religion: The Emergence of the Post-Christian Nation.* Simon and Schuster, 1992.
Bohn, Willard. "Writing the Fourth Dimension." *Comparative Critical Studies*, vol. 4, no. 1, 2007, pp. 121–38.
Bragdon, Claude. "The New Concepts of Time and Space." *The Dial*, vol. 68, February 1920, pp. 187–91.
Breton, André. 1937. *Mad Love.* Translated by Mary Ann Caws, U of Nebraska P, 1987.
—. "Nadja." *The Autobiography of Surrealism*, translator unidentified, edited by Marcel Jean, Viking Press, 1980, pp. 181–7.
Bürger, Peter. *Theory of the Avant-Garde.* Translated by Michael Shaw, Minnesota UP, 1984.
Burke, Carolyn. *Becoming Modern: The Life of Mina Loy.* New York: 1996.
Burstein, Jessica. *Cold Modernism: Literature, Fashion, Art.* Pennsylvania State UP, 2012.
Butler, Judith. *Bodies That Matter: On the Discursive Limits of "Sex".* Routledge, 1993.
—. 1990. *Gender Trouble: Feminism and the Subversion of Identity.* Routledge, 2007.
Carpenter, Edward. 1896/1906 (complete edition). *Love's Coming-of-Age.* Methuen and Co., 1916.
Cavarero, Adriana. *Inclinations: A Critique of Rectitude.* Translated by Amanda Minervini and Adam Sitze. Stanford UP, 2016.
Caws, Mary Ann. "Ladies Shot and Painted: Female Embodiment in Surrealist Art." *The Female Body in Western Culture: Contemporary*

Perspectives, edited by Susan Rubin Suleiman, Harvard UP, 1986, pp. 262–87.

—. *Mina Loy: Apology of Genius*. Reaktion Books, 2022.

—. "Translator's Introduction." *Mad Love*, by André Breton, translated and introduced by Mary Ann Caws, U of Nebraska P, 1987, pp. ix–xvii.

Celant, Germano. "Futurism and the Occult." *Art Forum*, vol. 19, no. 5, 1981, pp. 36–42.

Clifton, James. "The Face of a Fiend: Convulsion, Inversion, and the Horror of the Disempowered Body." *Oxford Art Journal*, vol. 34, no. 3, 2011, pp. 373–92.

Clippel, Karolien de. "Defining Beauty: Rubens's Female Nudes." *Nederlands Kunsthistorisch Jaarboek (NKJ)/Netherlands Yearbook for History of Art*, vol. 58, 2007–8, pp. 110–37.

Cohen, Sarah R. "Rubens's France: Gender and Personification in Marie de Médicis Cycle." *The Art Bulletin*, vol. 85, no. 3, 2003, pp. 490–522.

Cohn, Jan, and Thomas H. Miles. "The Sublime: In Alchemy, Aesthetics and Psychoanalysis." *Modern Philology*, vol. 74, no. 3, 1977, pp. 289–304.

Cokal, Susan. "Wounds, Ruptures, and Sudden Space in the Fiction of Georges Bataille." *French Forum*, vol. 25, no. 1, 2000, pp. 75–96.

Conover, Roger. "Time-Table." *The Last Lunar Baedeker*, by Mina Loy, edited and introduced by Roger Conover, Carcanet Press, 1985, pp. lxiii–lxxix.

Cook, Richard. "The 'Infinitarian' and her 'Macro-Cosmic Presence'." *Mina Loy: Woman and Poet*, edited by Maeera Shreiber and Keith Tuma, National Poetry Foundation, 1998, pp. 457–66.

Cooper, Sara-Louise. "Contesting the Unconscious: Frederic W. Myers and Vladimir Nabokov's *Speak, Memory: An Autobiography Revisited*." *Journal of Modern Literature*, vol. 39, no. 4, 2016, pp. 19–32.

Cordonnier, Suzanne. "Unpublished Memoir." *The Autobiography of Surrealism*, translator unidentified, edited by Marcel Jean, Viking Press, 1980, pp. 190–2.

Crabtree, Adam. *From Mesmer to Freud: Magnetic Sleep and the Roots of Psychological Healing*. Yale UP, 1993.

Crow, John L. "Taming the Astral Body: The Theosophical Society's Ongoing Problem of Emotion and Control." *Journal of the American Academy of Religion*, vol. 80, no. 3, 2012, pp. 691–717.

Crowley, Aleister. 1969. *The Confessions of Aleister Crowley: An Autohagiography*. Edited by John Symonds and Kenneth Grant, Routledge and Kegan Paul, 1979.

Dalrymple-Henderson, Linda. *The Fourth Dimension and Non-Euclidean Geometry in Modern Art*. MIT Press, 2013.

—. "The Fourth Dimension and Non-Euclidean Geometry in Modern Art: Conclusion." *Leonardo*, vol. 17, no. 3, 1984, pp. 205–10.

—. "Mysticism as the 'Tie That Binds': The Case of Edward Carpenter and Modernism." *Art Journal*, vol. 46, no. 1, 1987, pp. 29–37.

D'Ambrosio, Matteo. "Notes on 'Esoteric Futurism': Marinetti and the Occultist Circle in Milan." *International Yearbook of Futurism Studies*, vol. 8, 2018, pp. 294–324.
D'Annunzio, Gabriele. 1889. *Pleasure*. Translated by Lara Gochin Raffaelli, Penguin Books, 2013.
—. 1884. "The Virgins." *The Book of the Virgins*, translated by J. G. Nichols, Hesperus Press, 2003, pp. 3–50.
Darwin, Charles. 1868. *The Variation of Animals and Plants under Domestication*. Vol. 1, Cambridge UP, 2010. https://doi.org/10.1017/CBO9780511709500.
—. 1868. *The Variation of Animals and Plants under Domestication*. Vol. 2, Cambridge UP, 2011. https://doi-org/10.1017/CBO9780511709517.
Debo, Angie. *Geronimo: The Man, His Time, His Place*. U of Oklahoma P, 1976.
Derrida, Jacques. "Telepathy." Translated by Nicholas Royle, *Oxford Literary Review*, vol. 10, no. 1/2, 1988, pp. 3–41.
Descartes, René. 1641. *Meditations on First Philosophy in Which the Existence of God and the Distinction of the Soul from the Body are Demonstrated*. 3rd ed., translated by Donald A. Cress, Hackett Publishing Co., 1993.
—. 1649. *The Passions of the Soul*. Translated by Stephen H. Voss and introduced by Genevieve Rodis-Lewis, Hackett Publishing Co., 1989.
Dickey, Stephanie S. "Damsels in Distress: Gender and Emotion in Seventeenth-Century Netherlandish Art." *Nederlands Kunsthistorisch Jaarboek (NKJ)/Netherlands Yearbook for History of Art*, vol. 60, 2010, pp. 52–81.
Dinan, Matthew. "Strauss, Kierkegaard, and the 'Secret of the Art of Helping'." *Idealistic Studies*, vol. 44, nos 2 and 3, 2014, pp. 249–62.
Dodge Luhan, Mabel. *Movers and Shakers: Intimate Memories*. Vol. 3, Harcourt Brace and Co., 1936.
Doolittle, Hilda. c. 1919. *Notes on Thought and Vision and The Wise Sappho*. Introduced by Albert Gelpi, City Lights Books, 1982.
Dryden, John. 1693. *Discourses on Satire and on Epic Poetry*. Tredition Classics, 2012.
Duchamp, Marcel. *The Writings of Marcel Duchamp*. Edited by Michel Sanouillet and Elmer Peterson, Da Capo Press, 1989.
During, Simon. *Modern Enchantments: The Cultural Power of Secular Magic*. Harvard UP, 2002.
Dussel, Enrique. *Ethics of Liberation: In the Age of Globalization and Exclusion*. Translated by Eduardo Mendieta, Camilo Pérez Bustillo, Yolanda Angulo, and Nelson Maldonado-Torres and edited by Alejandro A. Vallega, Duke UP, 2013.
Ebury, Katherine. *Modernist Cosmology*. Palgrave Macmillan, 2014.
Egerton, George. 1893. *Keynotes and Discords*. Introduced by Martha Vicinus. Virago, 1983.

Eliot, T. S. 1921. "The Metaphysical Poets." *Selected Essays*, Faber and Faber, 1980, pp. 281–91.

Elkins, Amy E. "From the Gutter to the Gallery: Berenice Abbott Photographs Mina Loy's Assemblages." *PMLA*, vol. 134, no. 5, 2019, pp. 1094–1103.

Ellis, Havelock. 1894. *Man and Woman: A Study of Human Secondary Sexual Characters*. A. & C. Black, 1930.

—. 1897–1928. *Studies in the Psychology of Sex*. Vols 1–4, Random House, 1936.

Eluard, Paul. 1926. "The Queen of Diamonds." *The Autobiography of Surrealism*, translator unidentified, edited by Marcel Jean, Viking Press, 1980, pp. 171–2.

Faivre, Antoine. "Borrowings and Misreadings: Edgar Allan Poe's 'Mesmeric' Tales and the Strange Case of Their Reception." *Aries*, vol. 7, 2007, pp. 21–62.

Faivre, Antoine, and Karen-Claire Voss. "Western Esotericism and the Science of Religions." *Numen*, vol. 42, no. 1, 1995, pp. 48–77.

Felski, Rita. "The Counterdiscourse of the Feminine in Three Texts by Wilde, Huysmans, and Sacher-Masoch." *PMLA*, vol. 106, no. 5, 1987, pp. 1094–1105.

Foster, Hal. *Compulsive Beauty*. An October Book/MIT Press, 1993.

Fountain Eames, Rachel. "'Snared in an Atomic Mesh': Transcendent Physics and the Futurist Body in the Work of Mina Loy." *Journal of Literature and Science*, vol. 13, no. 1, 2020, pp. 31–49.

Frazer, James. 1890. *The Golden Bough: A Study in Magic and Religion*. Wordsworth Editions, 1993.

Freud, Sigmund. 1930. "Civilisation and its Discontents." *The Future of an Illusion, Civilisation and its Discontents and Other Works*, The Standard Edition of the Complete Psychological Works of Sigmund Freud, vol. 21, translated and edited by James Strachey et al., Vintage Books, 2001, pp. 59–145.

—. 1922. "Dreams and Telepathy." *Beyond the Pleasure Principle, Group Psychology and Other Works*, The Standard Edition of the Complete Psychological Works of Sigmund Freud, vol. 18, translated and edited by James Strachey et al., Hogarth Press, 1955, pp. 195–220.

—. 1923. "The Ego and the Id." *The Ego and the Id and Other Works*, The Standard Edition of the Complete Psychological Works of Sigmund Freud, vol. 19, translated and edited by James Strachey et al., Vintage Books, 2001, pp. 3–68.

—. 1921. "Psycho-Analysis and Telepathy." *Beyond the Pleasure Principle, Group Psychology and Other Works*, The Standard Edition of the Complete Psychological Works of Sigmund Freud, vol. 18, translated and edited by James Strachey et al., Hogarth Press, 1955, pp. 173–94.

—. 1901. *The Psychopathology of Everyday Life: Forgetting, Slips of the Tongue, Bungled Actions, Superstitions and Errors*. The Standard

Edition of the Complete Psychological Works of Sigmund Freud, vol. 6, translated and edited by James Strachey et al., Vintage Books, 2001.

—. 1923. "A Short Account of Psychoanalysis." *The Ego and the Id and Other Works*, The Standard Edition of the Complete Psychological Works of Sigmund Freud, vol. 19, translated and edited by James Strachey et al., Vintage Books, 2001, pp. 191–212.

—. 1925. "Some Additional Notes on Dream-Interpretation as a Whole." *The Ego and the Id and Other Works*, The Standard Edition of the Complete Psychological Works of Sigmund Freud, vol. 19, translated and edited by James Strachey et al., Vintage Books, 2001, pp. 127–38.

—. 1925. "Some Psychical Consequences of the Anatomical Distinction between the Sexes." *The Ego and the Id and Other Works*, The Standard Edition of the Complete Psychological Works of Sigmund Freud, vol. 19, translated and edited by James Strachey et al., Vintage Books, 2001, pp. 243–60.

Gaedtke, Andrew. "From Transmissions of Madness to Machines of Writing: Mina Loy's *Insel* as Clinical Fantasy." *Journal of Modern Literature*, vol. 32, no. 1, 2008, pp. 143–62.

Garber, Elizabeth. "Feminism, Aesthetics, and Art Education." *Studies in Art Education*, vol. 33, no. 4, 1992, pp. 210–55.

Gelpi, Albert. "The Thistle and the Serpent." *Notes on Thought and Vision and the Wise Sappho*, by H. D., introduced by Albert Gelpi, City Lights Books, 1982, pp. 7–16.

Ginanni, Maria. 1917. "Variations." *Futurism: An Anthology*, translated and edited by Lawrence Rainey, Christine Poggi, and Laura Wittman, Yale UP, 2009, pp. 466–7.

Goldsmith, Joel. *Living the Infinite Way*. HarperOne, 1993.

Gougeon, Len. *Emerson and Eros: The Making of Cultural Hero*. State U of New York P, 2007.

Gourmont, Rémy de. 1901. "Women and Language." *Decadence and Other Essays on the Culture of Ideas*, translated by William Aspenwall Bradley, Grant Richards, 1922, pp. 118–38.

Gross, Jennifer R. "The Truant of Heaven: The Artist Mina Loy." *Mina Loy: Strangeness is Inevitable*, edited by Jennifer R. Gross, Princeton UP, 2023, pp. 2–111.

Hammer, Olav, and Kocku von Stuckrad. "Introduction: Western Esotericism and Polemics." *Polemical Encounters: Esoteric Discourse and its Others*, Brill, 2007, pp. vii–xxii.

Han, Byung-Chul. *The Agony of Eros*. Foreword by Alain Badiou, translated by Erik Butler, MIT Press, 2017.

"Hands off Love." *The Autobiography of Surrealism*, translator unidentified, edited by Marcel Jean, Viking Press, 1980, pp. 150–5.

Hanegraaff, Wouter J. "Empirical Method in the Study of Esotericism." *Method and Theory in the Study of Religion*, vol. 7, no. 2, 1995, pp. 99–129.

Haweis, Stephen. *The Seven Ages of God*. Privately published in an edition of 100, 1912.
Hayden, Sarah. *Curious Disciplines: Mina Loy and Avant-Garde Artisthood*. U of New Mexico P, 2018.
—. "Introduction." *Insel*, edited by Elizabeth Arnold and introduced by Sarah Hayden, Melville House Publishing, 2014, pp. ix–xxxii.
H. D. c. 1919. *Notes on Thought and Vision and The Wise Sappho*. Introduced by Albert Gelpi, City Lights Books, 1982.
Herron, George D. *The Menace of Peace*. Mitchell Kennerley, 1917. Internet Archive, archive.org/details/menaceofpeace00herr.
Hesiod. c. 8th or 7th century BCE. "Theogony." *Theogony and Works and Days*, translated by M. L. West, Oxford UP, 1988, pp. 3–32.
Hickman, Miranda B. *The Geometry of Modernism: The Vorticist Idiom in Lewis, Pound, H. D., and Yeats*. U of Texas P, 2005.
Hinton, Howard C. *The Fourth Dimension*. Swan Sonnenschein & Co. 1904.
Hobson, Suzanne. "Mina Loy's 'Conversion' and the Profane Religion of her Poetry." *The Salt Companion to Mina Loy*, edited by Rachel Potter and Suzanne Hobson, Salt Publishing, 2010, pp. 248–65.
Hodgson, Andrew. "Hopkins's Heart." *Victorian Poetry*, vol. 54, no. 1, 2016, pp. 93–117.
Hofer, Mathew. "Mina Loy, Giovanni Papini, and the Aesthetic of Irritation." *Paideuma: Modern and Contemporary Poetry and Poetics*, vol. 38, 2011, pp. 219–58.
Horney, Karen. 1933. "The Denial of the Vagina: A Contribution to the Problem of the Genital Anxieties Specific to Women." *Feminine Psychology*, edited and introduced by Harold Kelman, W. W. Norton & Co., 1973, pp. 147–61.
—. 1931. "The Distrust between the Sexes." *Feminine Psychology*, edited and introduced by Harold Kelman, W. W. Norton & Co., 1973, pp. 107–18.
—. 1923. "On the Genesis of the Castration Complex in Women." *Feminine Psychology*, edited and introduced by Harold Kelman, W. W. Norton & Co., 1973, pp. 37–53.
—. 1926-7. "Inhibited Femininity: Psychoanalytical Contributions to the Problem of Frigidity." *Feminine Psychology*, edited and introduced by Harold Kelman, W. W. Norton & Co., 1973, pp. 71–83.
—. 1928. "The Problem of the Monogamous Ideal." *Feminine Psychology*, edited and introduced by Harold Kelman, W. W. Norton & Co., 1973, pp. 84–98.
Huysmans, Joris-Karl. 1884. *Against Nature*. Translated by Margaret Mauldoon, edited and introduced by Nicholas White, Oxford UP, 2009.
Irigaray, Luce. 1977. *This Sex Which is Not One*. Translated by Catherine Porter with Carolyn Burke, Cornell UP, 1985.
Irwin, Alexander C. "Ecstasy, Sacrifice, Communication: Bataille on Religion and Inner Experience." *Soundings: An Interdisciplinary Journal*, vol. 76, no. 1, 1993, pp. 105–19.

James, William. 1902. *The Varieties of Religious Experience: A Study in Human Nature*. Edited and introduced by Martin E. Marty, Penguin, 1985.

Januzzi, Marissa. "Mongrel Rose: The 'Unerring Esperanto' of Loy's Poetry." *Mina Loy: Woman and Poet*, edited by Maeera Shreiber and Keith Tuma, National Poetry Foundation, 1998, pp. 403–42.

Jones, Amelia. *Seeing Differently: A History and Theory of Identification and the Visual Arts*. Taylor and Francis Group, 2012.

Kane, Julie. "Varieties of Mystical Experience in the Writings of Virginia Woolf." *Twentieth Century Literature*, vol. 41, no. 4, 1995, pp. 328–49.

Kelly, Michael R, ed. *Bergson and Phenomenology*. Palgrave Macmillan, 2010.

Kelman, Harold. 1966. "Introduction." *Feminine Psychology*, edited and introduced by Harold Kelman, W. W. Norton & Co., 1973, pp. 7–32.

Kenner, Hugh. "The Life of Mina Loy: Works Give Recognition to Long-Neglected Poet." *The Washington Times*, 15 September 1996, p. B8.

Kipnis, Laura. *The Female Thing: Dirt, Sex, Envy, Vulnerability*. Serpent's Tail, 2007.

Kouidis, Virginia M. *Mina Loy: Modernist American Poet*. Louisiana State UP, 1980.

Lane, Riki. "Trans as Bodily Becoming: Rethinking the Biological as Diversity, Not Dichotomy." *Hypatia*, vol. 24, no. 3, 2009, pp. 136–57.

La Rue, Linda. "The Black Movement and Women's Liberation." *The Black Scholar*, vol. 1, no. 7, 1970, pp. 36–42.

Lawrence, D. H. 1926. *The Plumed Serpent*. Penguin Books, 1973.

Levy, Donald. "The Definition of Love in Plato's *Symposium*." *Journal of the History of Ideas*, vol. 20, no. 2, 1979, pp. 285–91.

Levy, Joella. "Levy, Joella Lloyd: To Julien Levy, 1926–1980, undated." Box 29, Folder 8, Julien Levy Gallery Records, Correspondence: 1857–1982. Philadelphia Museum of Art, Library and Archives, PA, USA.

—. "Levy, Joella Lloyd: To Julien Levy, undated." Box 29, Folder 9, Julien Levy Gallery Records, Correspondence: 1857–1982. Philadelphia Museum of Art, Library and Archives, PA, USA.

Levy, Julien. "Levy, Joella Lloyd: From Julien Levy, 1928, undated." Box 29, Folder 7, Julien Levy Gallery Records, Correspondence: 1857–1982. Philadelphia Museum of Art, Library and Archives, PA, USA.

—. "Loy, Mina: From Julien Levy: Dated correspondence, 1928–1954." Box 31, Folder 11, Julien Levy Gallery Records, Correspondence: 1857–1982. Philadelphia Museum of Art, Library and Archives, PA, USA.

Liddington, Jill, and Elizabeth Crawford. "'Women do not count, neither shall they be counted': Suffrage, Citizenship and the Battle for the 1911 Census." *History Workshop Journal*, vol. 71, no. 1, 2011, pp. 98–127.

Lloyd, Fabienne. "Lloyd, Fabienne: To Julien Levy and Joella Levy, to Julien Levy and Muriel Levy, and to Julien Levy and Jean Levy,

1929–1974, undated." Box 30, Folder 6, Julien Levy Gallery Records, Correspondence: 1857–1982. Philadelphia Museum of Art, Library and Archives, PA, USA.
Logan, Peter Melville. *Nerves and Narratives: A Cultural History of Hysteria in Nineteenth-Century British Prose*. U of California P, 1997.
Lokhorst, Gert-Jan. 2005. "Descartes and the Pineal Gland." *Stanford Encyclopaedia of Philosophy*, edited by Edward Zalta, 2013, The Metaphysics Research Lab, Stanford University. plato.stanford.edu/entries/pineal-gland/.
Lorde, Audre. 1978. "Uses of the Erotic: The Erotic as Power." *Sister/Outsider*, Crossing Press, 2007, pp. 53–9.
Loy, Mina. "Biography of Songge Byrd." 1952. YCAL MSS 6, Box 5, Folder 130, Mina Loy Papers. Beinecke Rare Book and Manuscript Library, Yale University, CT, USA.
—. c. 1913–20. *Brontolivido*. YCAL MSS 6, Box 1, Folders 1–9, Mina Loy Papers. Beinecke Rare Book and Manuscript Library, Yale University, New Haven, CT, USA.
—. c. 1932–6. *The Child and the Parent*. YCAL MSS 6, Box 1, Folders 10–20, Mina Loy Papers. Beinecke Rare Book and Manuscript Library, Yale University, New Haven, CT, USA.
—. c. 1910s/20s. *Esau Penfold*. YCAL MSS 6, Box 1, Folders 21–6, Mina Loy Papers. Beinecke Rare Book and Manuscript Library, Yale University, New Haven, CT, USA.
—. c. 1925–30+. *Goy Israels*. YCAL MSS 6, Box 2, Folders 27–9, Mina Loy Papers. Beinecke Rare Book and Manuscript Library, Yale University, New Haven, CT, USA.
—. 1932. *Goy Israels: A Play of Consciousness*. YCAL MSS MISC, Group 606, Item F-1. Yale Collection of American Literature Manuscript Miscellany. Beinecke Rare Book and Manuscript Library, Yale University, New Haven, CT, USA.
—. n.d. "In Extremis." YCAL MSS 6, Box 5, Folder 136, Mina Loy Papers. Beinecke Rare Book and Manuscript Library, Yale University, New Haven, CT, USA.
—. 1991. *Insel*. Edited with an afterword by Elizabeth Arnold. Newly edited and introduced by Sarah Hayden, Melville House Publishing, 2014.
—. 1940–60. "Inventions." YCAL MSS 6, Box 7, Folder 186, Mina Loy Papers. Beinecke Rare Book and Manuscript Library, Yale University, New Haven, CT, USA.
—. c. 1940s–50s. *Islands in the Air*. YCAL MSS 6, Box 4, Folders 58–71, Mina Loy Papers. Beinecke Rare Book and Manuscript Library, Yale University, New Haven, CT, USA.
—. "John Rodker's Frog." *The Little Review* vol. 7, no. 3, 1 September 1920, pp. 56–7.
—. 1982. *The Last Lunar Baedeker*. Edited and introduced by Roger Conover, Carcanet Press, 1985.

—. 1996. *The Lost Lunar Baedeker*. Edited and introduced by Roger Conover, Carcanet, 1997.
—. "Loy, Mina, 1913–1920, n.d." YCAL MSS 196, Box 24, Folder 664, Mabel Dodge Luhan Papers. Beinecke Rare Book and Manuscript Library, Yale University, CT, USA.
—. 1914–59. "Loy, Mina. Series 1. A-Z Correspondence." YCAL MSS 1050, Box 76, Folders 1082–3. Carl Van Vechten Papers. Beinecke Rare Book and Manuscript Library, Yale University, CT, USA.
—. "Loy, Mina to Joella and Julien Levy, c. 1950–54." YCAL MSS 778, Box 3. Carolyn Burke Collection on Mina Loy and Lee Miller. Beinecke Rare Book and Manuscript Library, Yale University, CT, USA.
—. c. 1934–49, 1960. "Loy, Mina to Joella Bayer and Assorted Others." YCAL MSS 778, Box 1. Carolyn Burke Collection on Mina Loy and Lee Miller. Beinecke Rare Book and Manuscript Library, Yale University, CT, USA.
—. "Loy, Mina: To Julien Levy and Joella Levy, 1927." Box 30, Folder 7, Julien Levy Gallery Records, Correspondence: 1857–1982. Philadelphia Museum of Art, Library and Archives, PA, USA.
—. "Loy, Mina: To Julien Levy and Joella Levy, 1928." Box 30, Folder 8, Julien Levy Gallery Records, Correspondence: 1857–1982. Philadelphia Museum of Art, Library and Archives, PA, USA.
—. "Loy, Mina: To Julien Levy and Joella Levy, 1929." Box 30, Folder 9, Julien Levy Gallery Records, Correspondence: 1857–1982. Philadelphia Museum of Art, Library and Archives, PA, USA.
—. "Loy, Mina: To Julien Levy and Joella Levy, 1930." Box 30, Folder 10, Julien Levy Gallery Records, Correspondence: 1857–1982. Philadelphia Museum of Art, Library and Archives, PA, USA.
—. "Loy, Mina: To Julien Levy and Joella Levy, 1931." Box 30, Folder 11, Julien Levy Gallery Records, Correspondence: 1857–1982. Philadelphia Museum of Art, Library and Archives, PA, USA.
—. "Loy, Mina: To Julien Levy and Joella Levy, 1932." Box 30, Folder 12, Julien Levy Gallery Records, Correspondence: 1857–1982. Philadelphia Museum of Art, Library and Archives, PA, USA.
—. "Loy, Mina: To Julien Levy and Joella Levy, 1933." Box 30, Folder 13, Julien Levy Gallery Records, Correspondence: 1857–1982. Philadelphia Museum of Art, Library and Archives, PA, USA.
—. "Loy, Mina: To Julien Levy and Joella Levy, 1934." Box 31, Folder 1, Julien Levy Gallery Records, Correspondence: 1857–1982. Philadelphia Museum of Art, Library and Archives, PA, USA.
—. "Loy, Mina: To Julien Levy and Joella Levy, 1935." Box 31, Folder 2, Julien Levy Gallery Records, Correspondence: 1857–1982. Philadelphia Museum of Art, Library and Archives, PA, USA.
—. "Loy, Mina: To Julien Levy and Joella Levy, undated." Box 31, Folder 5, Julien Levy Gallery Records, Correspondence: 1857–1982. Philadelphia Museum of Art, Library and Archives, PA, USA.

—. 22? March 1914. "Loy, Mina to Stephen Haweis." YCAL MSS 196, Box 42, Folder 1276, Mabel Dodge Luhan Papers. Beinecke Rare Book and Manuscript Library, Yale University, CT, USA.

—. *Lunar Baedeker and Time-Tables: Selected Poems*. Edited by Jonathan Williams, The Jargon Society 23, 1958.

—. n.d. "Mi and Lo." YCAL MSS 6, Box 6, Folder 166, Mina Loy Papers. Beinecke Rare Book and Manuscript Library, Yale University, New Haven, CT, USA.

—. 1965. "Mina Loy: Interview with Paul Blackburn and Robert Vas Dias." Introduced by Carolyn Burke. *Mina Loy: Woman and Poet*, edited by Maaera Shreiber and Keith Tuma, National Poetry Foundation, 1998, pp. 209–44.

—. "Mina Loy's 'Colossus': Arthur Cravan Undressed." Edited and introduced by Roger Conover. *Dada/Surrealism*, vol. 14, no. 1, 1985, pp. 102–19.

—. n.d. "Miscellaneous." YCAL MSS 6, Box 7, Folder 187, Mina Loy Papers. Beinecke Rare Book and Manuscript Library, Yale University, CT, USA.

—. n.d. "Notes on Metaphysics." YCAL MSS 6, Box 7, Folder 191, Mina Loy Papers. Beinecke Rare Book and Manuscript Library, Yale University, CT, USA.

—. "Notes on Religion." Edited by Keith Tuma. *Sulfur*, vol. 27, fall 1990, pp. 13–16.

—. "O Marcel – – – Otherwise I also have been to Louise's." *The Blind Man*, vol. 2, May 1917, pp. 14–15.

—. "*Pas de Commentaires*! Louis M. Eilshemius." *The Blind Man*, vol. 2, May 1917, pp. 11–12.

—. n.d. "Passivia." YCAL MSS 6, Box 5, Folder 144, Mina Loy Papers. Beinecke Rare Book and Manuscript Library, Yale University, CT, USA.

—. 1921. *Portrait of Freud*. Loy, Mina, Drawings and Photographs, undated. YCAL MSS 778, Box 8. Carolyn Burke Collection on Mina Loy and Lee Miller. Beinecke Rare Book and Manuscript Library, Yale University, CT, USA.

—. 1937. "Promised Land, autograph manuscript." YCAL MSS 778, Box 1. Carolyn Burke Collection on Mina Loy and Lee Miller. Beinecke Rare Book and Manuscript Library, Yale University, CT, USA.

—. *Stories and Essays of Mina Loy*. Edited and introduced by Sara Crangle, Dalkey Archive Press, 2011.

—. n.d. "Street Sister." *That Kind of Woman: Stories from the Left Bank and Beyond*, edited by Brontë Adams and Trudi Tate, Virago Press, 1991, pp. 41–2.

—. c. 1935. *Untitled (Surreal Scene)*. Collection of Roger Conover, Freeport, ME, USA.

Lucian. c. 2nd century CE. "Philosophies for Sale." *Selected Satires of Lucian*, translated and edited by Lionel Casson, W. W. Norton and Co., 1968, pp. 314–33.

Luckhurst, Roger. *The Invention of Telepathy: 1870–1900*. Oxford UP, 2002.

McAlmon, Robert, and Kay Boyle. 1968. *Being Geniuses Together: 1920–1930*. Hogarth Press, 1984.

McDonald, Jean A. "Mary Baker Eddy and the Nineteenth-Century 'Public' Woman: A Feminist Reappraisal." *Journal of Feminist Studies in Religion*, vol. 2, no. 1, 1986, pp. 89–111.

McDougall, W. "*Human Personality and its Survival of Bodily Death* by Frederic W. H. Myers." *Mind*, vol. 12, no. 48, 1903, pp. 513–26.

Mahon, Alyce. *Surrealism and Politics of Eros, 1938–1968*. Thames and Hudson, 2005.

Mallarmé, Stéphane. 1897. "Crisis of Verse." *Divagations*, translated by Barbara Johnson, Harvard UP, 2007, pp. 201–11.

Marcuse, Herbert. 1955. *Eros and Civilization*. Sphere Books, 1969.

Marinetti, Filippo Tommaso. 1924. "The Abstract Antipsychological Theatre of Pure Elements and the Tactile Theatre." *F. T. Marinetti: Critical Writings*, translated by Doug Thomson, edited by Günter Berghaus, Farrar, Straus, and Giroux, 2006, pp. 388–91.

—. 1919. "Address to the Fascist Congress of Florence." *F. T. Marinetti: Critical Writings*, translated by Doug Thomson, edited by Günter Berghaus, Farrar, Straus, and Giroux, 2006, pp. 330–8.

—. 1919. "Against Marriage." *F. T. Marinetti: Critical Writings*, translated by Doug Thomson, edited by Günter Berghaus, Farrar, Straus, and Giroux, 2006, pp. 309–12.

—. 1919. "An Artistic Movement Creates a Political Party." *F. T. Marinetti: Critical Writings*, translated by Doug Thomson, edited by Günter Berghaus, Farrar, Straus, and Giroux, 2006, pp. 277–82.

—. 1910. "Battles of Trieste." *F. T. Marinetti: Critical Writings*, translated by Doug Thomson, edited by Günter Berghaus, Farrar, Straus, and Giroux, 2006, pp. 158–64.

—. 1913. "Destruction of Syntax—Untrammeled Imagination—Words-in-Freedom." *F. T. Marinetti: Critical Writings*, translated by Doug Thomson, edited by Günter Berghaus, Farrar, Straus, and Giroux, 2006, pp. 120–31.

—. 1916. "Dynamic, Multichanneled Recitation." *F. T. Marinetti: Critical Writings*, translated by Doug Thomson, edited by Günter Berghaus, Farrar, Straus, and Giroux, 2006, pp. 193–9.

—. 1911. "Electric War: A Futurist Visionary Hypothesis." *F. T. Marinetti: Critical Writings*, translated by Doug Thomson, edited by Günter Berghaus, Farrar, Straus, and Giroux, 2006, pp. 221–5.

—. 1909. "The Foundation and Manifesto of Futurism." *F. T. Marinetti: Critical Writings*, translated by Doug Thomson, edited by Günter Berghaus, Farrar, Straus, and Giroux, 2006, pp. 11–16.

—. 1910. "Futurist Proclamation to the Spaniards." *F. T. Marinetti: Critical Writings*, translated by Doug Thomson, edited by Günter Berghaus, Farrar, Straus, and Giroux, 2006, pp. 97–103.

—. 1914. "In This Futurist Year." *F. T. Marinetti: Critical Writings*, translated by Doug Thomson, edited by Günter Berghaus, Farrar, Straus, and Giroux, 2006, pp. 231–7.

—. 1914. "Geometrical and Mechanical Splendor and Sensitivity toward Numbers." *F. T. Marinetti: Critical Writings*, translated by Doug Thomson, edited by Günter Berghaus, Farrar, Straus, and Giroux, 2006, pp. 135–42.

—. 1910. *Mafarka the Futurist: An African Novel*. Translated by Carol Diethe and Steve Cox, Middlesex UP, 1997.

—. 1930. "Manifesto of Futurist Cuisine." *F. T. Marinetti: Critical Writings*, translated by Doug Thomson, edited by Günter Berghaus, Farrar, Straus, and Giroux, 2006, pp. 394–9.

—. 1911. "Manifesto of Futurist Playwrights: The Pleasures of Being Booed." *F. T. Marinetti: Critical Writings*, translated by Doug Thomson, edited by Günter Berghaus, Farrar, Straus, and Giroux, 2006, pp. 181–4.

—. 1910. "The Necessity and Beauty of Violence." *F. T. Marinetti: Critical Writings*, translated by Doug Thomson, edited by Günter Berghaus, Farrar, Straus, and Giroux, 2006, pp. 60–74.

—. 1916. "The New Ethical Religion of Speed." *F. T. Marinetti: Critical Writings*, translated by Doug Thomson, edited by Günter Berghaus, Farrar, Straus, and Giroux, 2006, pp. 253–9.

—. 1913. "An Open Letter to the Futurist Mac Delmarle." *F. T. Marinetti: Critical Writings*, translated by Doug Thomson, edited by Günter Berghaus, Farrar, Straus, and Giroux, 2006, pp. 104–6.

—. 1920–38. "Poems to Beny." *Selected Poems and Related Prose*, translated by Elizabeth R. Napier and Barbara R. Studholme, Yale UP, 2002, pp. 133–48.

—. 1919. "The Proletariat of Talented People." *F. T. Marinetti: Critical Writings*, translated by Doug Thomson, edited by Günter Berghaus, Farrar, Straus, and Giroux, 2006, pp. 304–8.

—. 1933. "Total Theatre: Its Architecture and Technology." *F. T. Marinetti: Critical Writings*, translated by Doug Thomson, edited by Günter Berghaus, Farrar, Straus, and Giroux, 2006, pp. 400–7.

—. 1911. "War, the Sole Cleanser of the World." *F. T. Marinetti: Critical Writings*, translated by Doug Thomson, edited by Günter Berghaus, Farrar, Straus, and Giroux, 2006, pp. 53–4.

—. 1911. "We Renounce Our Symbolist Masters, the Last of All Lovers of the Moonlight." *F. T. Marinetti: Critical Writings*, translated by Doug Thomson, edited by Günter Berghaus, Farrar, Straus, and Giroux, 2006, pp. 43–6.

Marshall, Alan. "The Ecstasy of Mina Loy." *The Salt Companion to Mina Loy*, edited by Rachel Potter and Suzanne Hobson, Salt Publishing, 2010, pp. 166–87.

Melzer, Arthur M. *Philosophy between the Lines: The Lost History of Exoteric Writing*. U of Chicago P, 2014.

Mitchell, Andrew J., and Jason Kemp Winfree. "Editors' Introduction." *The Obsessions of Georges Bataille: Community and Communication*, edited by Andrew J. Mitchell and Jason Kemp Winfree, State U of New York P, 2009, pp. 1–17.

Monroe, Harriet. "Guide to the Moon." *Poetry*, vol. 23, no. 2, November 1923, pp. 100–3.

Moore, Elise L. "Woman as 'Elect of God'." *The Christian Science Journal*, October 1998. n.p. journal.christianscience.com/shared/view/xkqu7ly48w.

Morrisson, Mark. *Alchemy: Occultism and the Emergence of Atomic Theory*. Oxford UP, 2007.

—. "'Their pineal glands aglow': Theosophical Physiology in Joyce's *Ulysses*." *James Joyce Quarterly*, vol. 46, no. 3–4, 2009, pp. 509–27.

Muir, Edwin. "Recent Verse." *The New Age*, vol. 36, no. 19, 6 March 1924, p. 223.

Muller, Jeffrey M. "Rubens's Theory and Practice of the Imitation of Art." *The Art Bulletin*, vol. 64, no. 2, 1982, pp. 229–47.

Muñoz, José Esteban. *Cruising Utopia: The Then and There of Queer Futurity*. New York UP, 2009.

Myers, Frederic W. H. 1903. *Human Personality and its Survival of Bodily Death*. Pelegrin Trust of Pilgrim Books, 1992.

Nadeau, Maurice. *The History of Surrealism*. Translated by Richard Howard, Penguin Books, 1968.

Nash, Jennifer C. *The Black Body in Ecstasy: Reading Race, Reading Pornography*. Duke UP, 2014.

Nicholls, Peter. *Modernisms: A Literary Guide*. 2nd ed. Palgrave Macmillan, 2008.

Nietzsche, Friedrich. 1888. *Twilight of the Idols*. Translated and introduced by R. J. Hollingdale, Penguin Books, 1988.

Nightingale, Florence. 1852. *Cassandra*. Introduced by Myra Stark, The Feminist Press, 1979.

Noys, Benjamin. *Georges Bataille: A Critical Introduction*. Pluto Press, 2000.

Obeyesekere, Grananath. *The Awakened Ones: Phenomenology of Visual Experience*. Columbia UP, 2012.

Oelze, Richard. 1935–6. *Expectation*. Museum of Modern Art, www.moma.org/collection/works/78518.

Oppenheim, Janet. *The Other World: Spiritualism and Psychical Research in England, 1850–1914*. Cambridge UP, 1985.

—. *"Shattered Nerves": Doctors, Patients, and Depression in Victorian England*. Oxford UP, 1991.

Owen, Alex. *The Darkened Room: Women, Power, and Spiritualism in Late Victorian England*. Chicago UP, 1989.

—. *The Place of Enchantment: British Occultism and the Culture of the Modern*. Chicago UP, 2004.

Papini, Giovanni. 1913. *The Failure*. Translated by Virginia Pope and edited by J. E. Spingarn, Harcourt Brace and Co., 1924.

—. 1914. "The Massacre of Women." Translated by David Wray, Appendix 1 to article by Matthew Hofer, *Paideuma: Modern and Contemporary Poetry and Poetics*, vol. 38, 2011, pp. 252–6.

Parkinson, Gavin. *Surrealism, Art, and Modern Science: Relativity, Quantum Mechanics, Epistemology*. Yale UP, 2008.

Parmar, Sandeep. *Reading Mina Loy's Autobiographies: Myth of the Modern Woman*. Bloomsbury, 2013.

Perloff, Marjorie. *The Futurist Moment: Avant-Garde, Avant Guerre, and the Language of Rupture*. U of Chicago P, 1986.

Pierre, José, editor. *Investigating Sex: Surrealist Research 1928–1932*. Translated by Malcolm Imrie, Verso, 2011.

Pinkerton, Steve. "Profaning the Communion Table: Mina Loy and the Modernist Poetics of Blasphemy." *Paideuma: Modern and Contemporary Poetry and Poetics*, vol. 35, no. 3, 2006, pp. 93–117.

Plass, Paul. "Eros, Play and Death in Plato." *American Imago*, vol. 26, no. 1, 1969, pp. 37–55.

Plato. c. 370–360 BCE. *Phaedrus*. Translated, introduced, and edited by Christopher Rowe, Penguin Books, 2005.

—. c. 385–370 BCE. *The Symposium*. Translated by Walter Hamilton, Penguin Books, 1987.

Poggi, Christine. "Picturing Madness in 1905: Giacomo Balla's 'La pazza' and the Cycle 'I viventi'." *RES: Anthropology and Aesthetics*, vol. 47, 2005, pp. 38–68.

Rado, Sandor. 1933. "Fear of Castration in Women." *Psychoanalysis of Behaviour: Collected Papers*, vol. 1: *1922–1956*, Grune and Stratton, 1956, pp. 83–120.

—. 1927. "The Problem of Melancholia." *Psychoanalysis of Behaviour: Collected Papers*, vol. 1: *1922–1956*, Grune and Stratton, 1956, pp. 47–63.

Randolph, Paschal Beverly. *Eulis! The History of Love*. Randolph Publishing Co., 1874. Internet Archive, archive.org/details/06115989.4836.emory.edu/page/n5/mode/2up.

Re, Lucia. "Maria Ginanni vs. F. T. Marinetti: Women, Speed, and War in Futurist Italy." *Annali d'Italianistica*, vol. 27, *A Century of Futurism: 1909–2009*, 2009, pp. 103–24.

Rivera, Mayra. *Poetics of the Flesh*. Duke UP, 2015.

Robert, Enif. 1917. "A Tranquil Thought." *Futurism: An Anthology*, translated and edited by Lawrence Rainey, Christine Poggi, and Laura Wittman, Yale UP, 2009, pp. 242–3.

Rodker, John. "The 'Others' Anthology." *The Little Review*, vol. 7, no. 3, 1 September 1920, pp. 53–6.

—. "To Mina Loy." *The Little Review*, vol. 7, no. 4, 1 January 1921, pp. 44–5.

Rowe, Christopher. "Introduction." *Phaedrus* by Plato, translated, introduced, and edited by Christopher Rowe, Penguin Classics, 2005, pp. xiii–xxix.

Royle, Nicholas. "Back." *Oxford Literary Review*, vol. 18, no. 1/2, 1996, pp. 145–57.

Rubin, Gayle. "The Traffic in Women: Notes on the 'Political Economy' of Sex." *Toward an Anthropology of Women*, edited by Rayna Reiter, Monthly View Press, 1975, pp. 157–210.

Saint-Point, Valentine. 1913. "Futurist Manifesto of Lust." *Futurist Manifestos*, translated by Robert Brain, Caroline Tisdall, R. W. Flint, and J. C. Higgitt, edited and introduced by Umberto Apollonio, Viking Press, 1973, pp. 70–4.

Santas, Gerasimos. "Plato's Theory of Eros in the Symposium." *Noûs*, vol. 13, no. 1, 1979, pp. 67–75.

Santucci, James A. "The Notion of Race in Theosophy." *Nova Religio: The Journal of Alternative and Emergent Religions*, vol. 11, no. 3, 2008, pp. 37–63.

Sappho. *Greek Lyric*, vol. 1: *Sappho, Alcaeus*. Translated by David A. Campbell, Loeb Classical Library, Harvard UP, 1982, pp. 2–205.

Sartini Blum, Cinzia. *The Other Modernism: F. T. Marinetti's Futurist Fictions of Power*. U of California P, 1996.

Saurat, Denis. 1930. *Literature and Occult Tradition: Studies in Philosophical Poetry*. Translated by Dorothy Bolton, Haskell House, 1966.

Scarry, Elaine. *The Body in Pain: The Making and Unmaking of the World*. Oxford UP, 1985.

Schindler, D. C. "Plato and the Problem of Love: On the Nature of Eros in the 'Symposium'." *Apeiron: A Journal for Ancient Philosophy and Science*, vol. 40, no. 3, 2007, pp. 199–220.

Schneider, Eric H. "'Welcomers': James Joyce and Frederic W. H. Myers." *Journal of Modern Literature*, vol. 38, no. 2, 2015, pp. 59–70.

Scott, Gary Alan, and William Welton. *Erotic Wisdom: Philosophy and Intermediacy in Plato's Symposium*. State U of New York P, 2008.

"Sculptress of Bodies." *MD*, May 1975, pp. 173–8 [authorial citation absent from clipping]. YCAL MSS 778, Box 4, Folder "Mensendieck 1987." Carolyn Burke Collection on Mina Loy and Lee Miller. Beinecke Rare Book and Manuscript Library, Yale University, CT, USA.

Seabrook, William. *Jungle Ways*. George G. Harrap & Co., 1931.

Secomb, Linnell. *Philosophy and Love: From Plato to Popular Culture*. Edinburgh UP, 2007.

Seidel, Michael A. *Satiric Inheritance: Rabelais to Sterne*. Princeton UP, 1979.

Selinger, Eric Murphy. "Love in the Time of Melancholia." *Mina Loy: Woman and Poet*, edited by Maeera Shreiber and Keith Tuma, National Poetry Foundation, 1998, pp. 19–44.
Shapiro, Lisa. "Descartes's Pineal Gland Reconsidered." *Midwest Studies in Philosophy*, vol. 35, no. 1, 2011, pp. 259–86.
Shattuck, Roger. "Introduction. Love and Laughter: Surrealism Reappraised." *The History of Surrealism*, translated by Richard Howard, Penguin Books, 1968, pp. 9–36.
Showalter, Elaine. *The Female Malady: Women, Madness, and English Culture, 1800–1980*. Pantheon Books, 1985.
Shreiber, Maeera. "Divine Women, Fallen Angels: The Late Devotional Poetry of Mina Loy." *Mina Loy: Woman and Poet*, edited by Maeera Shreiber and Keith Tuma, National Poetry Foundation, 1998, pp. 45–85.
Simmel, Georg. 1921. "Eros, Platonic and Modern." *On Individuality and Social Forms: Selected Writings*, edited and introduced by Donald N. Levine, Chicago UP, 1971, pp. 235–48.
—. "The Sociology of Secrecy and of Secret Societies." *The American Journal of Sociology*, vol. 11, no. 4, 1906, pp. 441–98.
Simon, Katie. "Mary Baker Eddy's Pragmatic Transcendental Feminism." *Women's Studies*, vol. 38, no. 4, 2009, pp. 377–98.
Snow, Heidi J. "Spirituality: Lifting the Ideals of Feminism." *Christian Science Sentinel*, 23 November 1998. sentinel.christianscience.com/shared/view/2iahv25ijvc.
Solanas, Valerie. 1971. *Scum Manifesto*. Introduced by Avital Ronnell, Verso, 2004.
Spackman, Barbara. *Decadent Genealogies: The Rhetoric of Sickness from Baudelaire to D'Annunzio*. Cornell UP, 1989.
Spillers, Hortense J. "Mama's Baby, Papa's Maybe: An American Grammar Book." *Diacritics*, vol. 17, no. 2, 1987, pp. 64–81.
Stannard, Jerry. "Socratic Eros and Platonic Dialogue." *Phronesis*, vol. 42, no. 2, 1959, pp. 120–34.
Stein, Gertrude. 1946. "Reflection on the Atom Bomb." *Reflection on the Atom Bomb*, Vol. 1 of the Previously Uncollected Writings of Gertrude Stein, edited by Robert Bartlett Haas, Black Sparrow Press, 1973, pp. 161–2.
Steinke, Annarose F. "'Parsimonious/Presentations': Mina Loy's Crisis of [Christian] Representation." *Christianity and Literature*, vol. 69, no. 4, 2020, pp. 493–510.
Stopes, Marie. 1918. *Married Love: A New Contribution to the Solution of Sex Difficulties*. Hogarth Press, 1955.
Storm, Jason Ananda Josephson. *The Myth of Disenchantment: Magic, Modernity, and the Birth of the Human Sciences*. U of Chicago P, 2017.
Strauss, Leo. "Persecution and the Art of Writing." *Social Research*, vol. 8, no. 4, 1941, pp. 488–504.

—. *What is Political Philosophy? And Other Studies*. U of Chicago P, 1959.
Stuckrad, Kocku von. "Western Esotericism: Towards an Integrative Model of Interpretation." *Religion*, vol. 35, no. 2, 2005, pp. 78–97.
Suleiman, Susan Rubin. *Subversive Intent: Gender, Politics, and the Avant-Garde*. Harvard UP, 1990.
Surette, Leon. *The Birth of Modernism: Ezra Pound, T. S. Eliot, W. B. Yeats and the Occult*. McGill-Queen's University Press, 1993.
Taves, Ann. "Religious Experience and the Divisible Self: William James (and Frederic Myers) as Theorist(s) of Religion." *Journal of the American Academy of Religion*, vol. 71, no. 2, 2003, pp. 303–26.
Thurschwell, Pamela. *Literature, Technology, and Magical Thinking, 1880–1920*. Cambridge UP, 2001.
Van Vechten, Carl. *Sacred and Profane Memories*. Alfred A. Knopf, 1932.
Versluis, Arthur, *Magic and Mysticism: An Introduction to Western Esotericism*. Rowman and Littlefield, 2007.
Vetter, Lara. *Modernist Writings and Religio-Scientific Discourse: H. D., Loy, and Toomer*. Palgrave Macmillan, 2010.
—. "Theories of Spiritual Evolution, Christian Science, and the 'Cosmopolitan Jew': Mina Loy and American Identity." *Journal of Modern Literature*, vol. 31, no. 1, 2007, pp. 47–63.
Viswanathan, Gauri. "In Search of Madame Blavatsky: Reading the Exoteric, Retrieving the Esoteric." *Representations*, vol. 141, no. 1, 2018, pp. 67–94.
—. "The Ordinary Business of Occultism." *Critical Inquiry*, vol. 27, no. 1, 2007, pp. 1–20.
Voss, Karen. "Is There a Feminine Gnosis? Reflexions on Feminism and Esotericism." *Aries*, vol. 14, 1991, pp. 5–24.
Vrettos, Athena. "Displaced Memories in Victorian Fiction and Psychology." *Victorian Studies*, vol. 49, no. 2, 2007, pp. 199–207.
Walker, Jane Clark. "What is Demonstration in Christian Science?" *The Christian Science Journal*, August 1990. n.p. journal.christianscience.com/shared/view/1dbwciuj0ls.
Walter, Christina. *Optical Impersonality: Science, Images, and Literary Modernism*. Johns Hopkins UP, 2014.
Weir, David. *Decadence and the Making of Modernism*. U of Massachusetts P, 1995.
Wendell, Susan. *The Rejected Body: Feminist Philosophical Reflections on Disability*. Routledge, 1996.
White, Eric B. *Reading Machines in the Modernist Transatlantic: Avant-Gardes, Technology, and the Everyday*. Edinburgh UP, 2020.
Wiegman, Robyn. *Object Lessons*. Duke UP, 2012.
Wilde, Oscar. 1887. "The Sphinx without a Secret." *Oscar Wilde: Complete Short Fiction*, edited by Ian Small, Penguin Books, 2003, pp. 200–5.

Wills, David. *Dorsality: Thinking Back through Technology and Politics.* U of Minnesota P, 2008.
Wilson, Elizabeth A. *Psychosomatic: Feminism and the Neurological Body.* Duke UP, 2004.
Wilson, Leigh. *Modernism and Magic: Experiments with Spiritualism, Theosophy, and the Occult.* Edinburgh UP, 2012.
Winter, Alison. *Mesmerized: Powers of Mind in Victorian Britain.* U of Chicago P, 1998.
Wolf, Naomi. *Promiscuities: A Secret History of Female Desire.* Vintage Books, 1998.
Woolf, Virginia. 1927. *To the Lighthouse.* Edited by Margaret Drabble, Oxford UP, 1992.
Young, Iris Marion. "Throwing Like a Girl: A Phenomenology of Feminine Body Comportment, Motility, and Spatiality." *Throwing Like a Girl and Other Essays*, Indiana UP, 1990, pp. 141–59.
—. "Women Recovering our Clothes." *Throwing Like a Girl and Other Essays*, Indiana UP, 1990, pp. 177–88.

Index

Abbott, E. A., 176
abjection, xiv, 45
Absolute, 16, 81n24, 189, 225, 226
Académie Colarossi, 20–1; *see also* art school
Adamson, N., 100n3
Adorno, T., 21, 34
Aenid, The, 72
aesthetic consciousness, 184–5
aesthetic Eros, xix, xxii, 51, 95, 97, 186, 224, 213; *see also* inclination
affects, xxviii, 104, 112, 143, 161, 189; *see also* emotion
"Agony of the Partition" (Loy), 75, 103, 197–8
"Aid of the Madonna" (Loy), 178
alchemy, xxx, 25, 29, 70, 211
Alcoff, L. M., xxxvin16
Altieri, C., 100n3
Amendola, E., 121
ancient Eros, 59–65
Angel, K., xxxvin17
"Anglo-Mongrels and the Rose" (Loy), xxvi, xxxviin18, 4, 49, 84–5n39, 88n52 95, 97, 145n2, 229n10, 230n15, 230n17
animal magnetism, 124, 149n18
anthropology, 21, 208
anti-Semitism, xxxiiin5, xxvii
Apache, 147–8n13
"Aphorisms on Futurism" (Loy), 21, 55, 66, 158–9, 169
"Apology of Genius" (Loy), xxi, 24–5, 71
Apollinaire, G., 215–16
Arensberg, W., 235n40
Arensberg Circle, 26, 179, 214
"Armour for the Body" (Loy), 97
Armstrong, T., xvii, 79n16
arrière-garde, 96, 100n3
art school, 20–1, 26, 40, 89n60, 219, 222

Assagioli, R., xxi, 42–3, 83n32, 83–4n36, 108, 132
"At the Door of the House" (Loy), 5, 33, 159
atavism, 163–7, 184, 200
atomic Eros, 68–74
"Auto-Facial-Construction" (Loy), 29, 210–11
autobiography, xxx, 154, 173, 178; *see also* künstlerromans; romans à clef
avant-gardism, 9, 95, 96, 193
and esotericism, 12–27
see also Dada; Decadence; feminism; Futurism; Rossetti, D. G.; Surrealism; Symbolism
Ayers, D., 79–80n16

back (body part), 97–8, 154–5, 156–7; *see also* blind back; spine
Baker Eddy, M., xvii, xviii, 16, 17, 18, 19, 27, 52–3, 67, 80n19, 87n50, 213
Balch, E. G., 140
Balla, G., 108–12
Barnes, D., xiii
Barney, N., 213
Bataille, G., xix, xxii, xxix, xxxii, xxxvn12, 162, 226, 231n19, 235n37, 235n38
and Eros, 43–5, 49
and Surrealism, 47, 49, 86n43
on sexuality, 46, 184, 187, 210; *see also* on vision / pineality
on mysticism, 84n38
on vision / pineality, 208–10, 212
Baudelaire, C., 129, 130, 131
Beauchamp, T., 84n37
Bergson, H., xxi, xxxi, 16, 167, 168, 170, 183, 210, 216, 217
Bersani, L., 183, 184
Besant, A., 192–3, 199–200, 233n28, 234n35

birth, 29–30, 66, 68, 74, 78–9n12, 132, 172, 178, 201, 233–4n32; *see also* rebirth
black magic, 20, 21, 235–6n40; *see also* theurgy; white magic
Black Power movement, xxxviin22
"Black Virginity, The" (Loy), 85n41
Blair, K., 4
Blake, W., xxxvn10, 31
Blavatsky, H., xxxii, 185, 186, 191–7, 198–9, 202–3, 207, 232–3n27, 233n28, 234n33, 234n36, 235n39
blind back, xxviii, xxxi–xxxii, 99, 155–6, 224–5, 228n4
 architectural metaphors, 156–63
 atavisms, 163–7
 bowed backs (female), 175–85
 and fourth dimension, 212–23
 and pineal eye / third eye, 186–90, 200
 retrocognition, 167–75
blindness, 186–8, 208
Bloom, H., 80n19
Boccioni, U., 214
bodies, xviii, 18, 75–6, 139, 194
body/mind, 101; *see also* Cartesian Eros; Descartes, R.
body parts, xviii; *see also* back (body part); eyes; hearts; spine
bowed backs (female), 175–85
Brâncuşi, C., 193
Brent, L., xxxviin22
Breton, A., 47–9, 85–6n42, 87n45
Bride Stripped Bare by her Bachelors, Even, The (Duchamp), 215
Brontolivido (Loy), xvi, 13, 22–3, 30, 70–1, 78n8, 93–4, 96, 102, 118, 145n1, 157
 occultism / mesmerism, 122–4, 126–7, 128
Bruckner, J. J., 78n11
Bryan, J., xxvi, xxvii, 10
Buddhism, 28, 30, 54, 90n64, 96, 129, 144, 185, 192
Bürger, P., 26, 82n26
Burke, C., xxxiiin5, xxxiiin6, 6, 67–8, 79n14, 81n21, 84n37, 165, 233n30
Burstein, J., 113
Butler, J., xxii–xxiii, xxxvn13, 52, 107

Cappa, B., 143
Carpenter, E., xxix, 55–6
Cartesian dualism, 190, 205, 206, 232n23; *see also* Descartes, R.
Cartesian Eros, 189; *see also* Descartes, R.

Catholicism, 19–20, 50, 85n41
Cavarero, A., 4, 62, 65, 70, 96–7, 100n5, 100n6
Caws, M. A., xxxiiin4, xxxivn7, 179
"Ceiling at Dawn" (Loy), 187
"Censors Morals Sex." (Loy), 9, 25, 33
Charcot, J.-M., 110
Child and the Parent, The (Loy), xvi, 28, 94, 83n34, 159, 172, 229–30n14, 233n32
 art, 219
 esoteric Eros, 34, 74, 75
 "fallen woman", 103
 heterosexual intercourse, 35–6
 pain, 85n40
 parenthood, 178
 reincarnation, 205
 women's backs, 175–6, 181–3
children, 130, 217; *see also* infancy
Christ, xvi, 25, 29, 30; *see also* Jesus
Christian Science, xv, xvii, xviii, xx, xxxiv–xxxvn9, 16–20, 31, 51–2, 53–4, 68, 79–80n16, 87n49, 203
Christian Science practitioners, 218; *see also* Baker Eddy, M; Goldsmith, J. S.
Christianity, 54, 85n40; *see also* Catholicism; Christian Science; exotericism; Protestantism
Civilisation and its Discontents (Freud), 59, 76
clairvoyance, 28, 121, 127, 135–7, 140, 144, 152n34, 154, 173, 194, 205; *see also* telepathy; visionary
Cohen, S. R., 230n16
Colossus (Loy), xvi, xxxivn8, 183, 223
concordance, esoteric, 28
consciousness, 94, 152n34, 162, 167, 184–5, 194, 197, 199–200, 202
Consider Your Grandmother's Stays (Loy), 97
convalescence, 108, 130, 131–2, 132
"Conversion" (Loy), xiii, 135
Cordonnier, S., 48
Cornell, J., 21, 85n42
corporeality, 3, 54, 139, 200, 217
corselet (Loy), 97
cosmos, xix, xxviii, xxxi, 42, 55, 64, 98, 124, 155, 162, 196–7, 205, 212, 225–6
"Costa Magic" (Loy), 28
Cravan, A., 66–8, 70, 223
 in "Anglo-Mongrels and the Rose", 97
 Loy's reunion in Mexico with, 30–1, 44, 183

Cravan, A. (*cont.*)
  as pagan god, xvi
  Rubens's influence on, 177–89, 179
  and Surrealism, 47
creation story, 157, 201–2, 218–19; *see also* Genesis; palingenesis
Crowley, A., 20, 81n21, 192
"Crystal Pantomime" (Loy), 28–9, 83n34, 232n22
Cubism, 214, 216
culture, 57, 58
  counter-culture, 57
  Greek, 59
  popular, 68
  see also avant-gardism

Dada, 26, 82n26, 224
Dali, S., 86n44, 179–80, 230–1n18
Dalrymple-Henderson, L., 235n39
D'Ambrosio, M., 120
D'Annunzio, G., 116, 117, 147n10, 147n11
Darwin, C., 188, 197
death, xx–xxi, 40, 42, 44, 53–4, 86–7n44, 128–31, 189, 195, 220; *see also* Thanatos
Decadence, 112–13, 114, 146–7n7
Decadent literature, 131, 145n5
"Der Blinde Junge" (Loy), 197
Derrida, J., 142
Descartes, R., 188–9, 190, 202, 207, 232n23, 232n24, 232n25
Discourse on Satire and Epic Poetry (Dryden), 116
Dodge Luhan, M., xii, xxxiiin6, 13, 16, 22, 77–8n6, 138
domestic verbal abuse, xxvii, 11
domestic violence, 107, 115–17
Duchamp, M., 214–15, 236n41
During, S., 120
Dussel, E., 54

Ebury, K.229n8
ecstasy, xviii, xix, xxv, 30, 34, 44, 45–6, 50, 76, 84n38, 121, 126, 143, 180, 208, 211, 215, 221; *see also* esoteric Eros; orgasm; satiation
Eddington, A., 215
"Effectual Marriage, The" (Loy), 108, 159
Einstein, A., 214, 216–17, 229n8
Eliot, T. S., 3, 4, 95, 133–4
Ellis, H., xxvi, 55, 106, 121–2, 149n16
Eluard, P., 86n44
embodiment, female, xxvii, xxviii

Emerson, R. W., 16, 48, 53, 192
emotion, 27; *see also* affect; ecstasy; melancholia; pleasure; satiation; sexual pleasure; shame; vulnerability
Eros, xiii, xiv–xv, xxii
  aesthetic, 95, 186, 224
  and Bataille, 43–5, 49
  Cartesian, 189
  orgasmic, 34; *see also* female sexual pleasure; orgasm
  Surrealist, 47–51
  in Theosophy, 207
  see also esoteric Eros; "History of Religion and Eros" (Loy); love
Eros and Civilisation (Marcuse), 57
erotic Eros, 186; *see also* female sexual desire; female sexual pleasure; orgasm; satiation
eroticism, 58, 78n11
Esau Penfold (Loy), xvi, 13–14, 20, 175, 178, 187
esoteric Eros, xv, xvi, xxiii, xxvii, xxxvn12, 30–1, 45, 75–6, 140
  as ancient Eros, 59–65
  as atomic Eros, 68–74
  and avant-garde, 11–12
  and blind back, 182
  and modernist mystical feminism, 51–9
  and psychoanalysis, 33–43
  and satire, 9, 11, 13, 70, 74, 222, 223
  and Surrealism, 49
  see also love
esoteric taxonomy, 27–33
esoteric teaching, 31
esotericism, xvii, 7–9, 50, 51, 143–4
  and avant-gardism, 12–27
  Loy as esotericist, evidence, 27–33
  and religion, 54
  see also alchemy; clairvoyance; concordance, esoteric; occultism; telepathy; Theosophy; visions
Eulis! The History of Love (Randolph), 55
evolution, xvi, 94, 156, 167, 170, 174, 178, 186, 188, 193–9, 205, 209–212, 218, 233n31
exotericism, 25, 46, 50, 60, 62, 64–5, 73–4, 85n40, 99; *see also* Buddhism; Christianity; Hinduism; Judaism
Expanding Universe, The (Eddington), 215
Expectation (Oelze), 164–5
Exposition InteRnatiOnale du Surréalisme, 49
extrospection, 171

eyes, xxxii, 5
　parietal eye, 187, 199
　pineal eye, 186–90; *see also* "Pineal Eye, The" (Bataille); pineality
　see also blindness; gaze; ocularity; visions

Failure, The (Papini), 114, 118, 150–1n26
Faivre, A., 27, 28, 29, 31, 82n27
"Faun Fare" (Loy), 46
Fechner, G., 213
Felski, R., 146–7n7
female bowed backs, 175–85
female embodiment, xxvii
female sexual desire, xxii–xxv, 38–9
female sexual pleasure, 224, 131; *see also* orgasm; satiation
female vanguardism, 95–6
feminised lunacy, 105–11; *see also* "Pazzarella" (Loy)
feminism, xxi–xxii, 49–51, 56, 95, 234n36; *see also* esoteric Eros; modernist mystical feminism; suffragettes
"Feminist Manifesto" (Loy), 36, 50, 56, 66, 138, 166
feminist visionariness, xvii, xxxi, 58, 96, 99, 143, 224; *see also* clairvoyance; esoteric Eros; telepathy
Five-Way Portrait (Duchamp), 215
Flatland (Abbott), 176
Florence, xxiin6, 22, 210
Fountain Eames, R., 89n61, 89–90n62
fourth dimension, xxviii, xxxii, 99, 212–23, 235n39, 235–6n40, 236n41, 236n43
Frazer, J., 18
Freud, S., xvi, xix, 76, 151n28
　critique of, 33, 37–8, 39, 42
　on culture, 57
　on Eros, 47, 59
　on hysteria, 145–6n4
　on Horney, 83n32
　Loy's portrait of, 40–1
　mysticism v. psychoanalysis, 137, 151–2n31
　psychic/mental anatomy, 165, 170
　on women, 35, 135
Futurism, xxx–xxxi, 6, 26, 98, 101–5, 113, 114–15, 118–19, 141–2; *see also* Boccioni, U.; Marinetti, F.; Papini, G.
"Futurist Manifesto of Lust" (Saint-Point), 117
Futurist occultism, 119–20, 121–2

Brontolivido (Loy), 122–4, 126–7, 128
"Pazzarella" (Loy), 125–6, 127–30, 131–2
"Futurist Occultism" (Amendola), 121

Gabini, M., 110
Gaedtke, A., 152–3n39
galvanism, 8, 124
Garber, E., 230n16
gaze, xxxi, 149n19, 158, 202
　and corselet (Loy), 97
　gendered, 186–7
　inner, 16
　in *Insel*, 103, 141, 164, 177
　male, 41, 122, 126–7, 128, 175
　in "Pazzarella", 115, 126–8, 133, 149n20
gender, 44–5, 52, 175
　and mesmerism, 124–6
　see also feminised lunacy; women
Genesis, 149–50n21, 221
Geronimo, 147–8n13
"Gertrude Stein" (Loy), 218; *see also* Stein, G.
Ginanni, M., 142
Girl's Back (Dali), 179
Golden Bough, The (Frazer), 18
Goldman, E., 55
Goldsmith, J. S., xx–xxi, 23, 31, 53, 131, 185
Gourmont, R. de, 134
Goy Israels: A Play of Consciousness (Loy), xvi, 172, 201–2, 204, 233n32
Goy Israels (Loy), xvi, 10, 30, 78n8, 200–1, 220–1, 229n10, 230n15
gravity, 152n34, 190, 210, 232n25
Gross, J. R., xxxvn14

"Hands Off Love" (author unidentified), 86n44
Haweis, J., 17, 18, 36, 84–5n39; *see also* Levy, Joella
Haweis, S., 16, 20, 81n21, 194–5, 196, 233n29, 233n30
Hayden, S., 87n46, 231–2n21
Heart Shop (Loy), 77n3
hearts, xxviii, 3–6, 10, 75
Hermetic Order of the Golden Dawn, 20, 56, 192
Herron, G. D., 71, 90n64
Hesiod, 61
Hinduism, xxxiiin6, 51, 54, 89n56, 185, 192, 200
Hinton, C. H., 216–17

"History of Religion and Eros" (Loy), 9, 28, 31, 32, 33, 42, 44, 85n41, 152n34
   consciousness, 66, 171–2
   esoteric Eros, 70, 71–2, 74
   inner eye / pineality, 187, 211
   intimacy and detonation, 68
   love, 48
   mesmerism, 124
   telepathy, 136
History of Surrealism, The (Nadeau), 47
Hite Report, The, xxiv
Hobby (Ray), 179
Hobson, S., 135
Hofer, M., 118
home and self, 158–63
homophobia, xxxvn12, 86n43, 114, 147n8
Horney, K., 37–8, 83n32
"Hot Cross Bum" (Loy), 145n2, 166
Househunting (Loy), xxxv–xxxvin15
"Human Cylinders" (Loy), 6–7, 76
Human Personality and its Survival of Bodily Death (Myers), xx, 42, 108
"Hush Money" (Loy), 141, 145n2
hyperspace, 218, 235n39
hypnotism, 121–2, 149n16, 166; *see also* mesmerism
hysteria, 106, 110, 134, 145–6n4, 166

imagination, 29, 235–6n40
"In Extremis" (Loy), 225–8
"In Maine: Green's Colony" (Loy), 84–5n39, 103, 187
"Incident" (Loy), 140, 141, 152n35, 158
inclination, theory of (Cavarero), xxii, 4, 51, 60, 65, 70, 96–7, 100n5, 103, 183
infancy, 156–7, 201–2, 204, 219
"Infinite Way" (Goldsmith), 31
infinity, 156, 157
inner vision *see* pineal eye; pineality
insanity *see* lunacy, feminised
Insel (Loy), xvi, 72, 94, 103, 122, 139, 163, 178, 230–1n18
   clairvoyance, 140
   "collective backbone child", 176–7
   esotericism, 144–5
   and Peter Rubens, 179
   and Salvador Dali, 180
"International Psycho-Democracy" (Loy), 33, 66
introspection, 169, 171
introspeculation, 171, 229n10
Irigaray, L., xix, xxxvn13, 36–7, 52

Islands in the Air (Loy), xvi, 32, 34, 65, 82n28, 89n60, 172, 187, 206, 219, 223
Italy, xxxiiin6, 14, 120, 214

James, W., 51, 58, 134–5
Januzzi, M., 113
Jesus, xxi, 25, 59, 203; *see also* Christ
Jones, A., xxv
Joyce, J., 193
"Joyce's Ulysses" (Loy), 23, 46
Judaism, xv–xvi, xxxiiin5, 51–4, 65–6, 87–8n51; *see also* anti-Semitism
Julien Levy Gallery, 47, 179, 230–1n18

Kabbalah, 51, 196
Kandinsky, V., 193
Kane, J., 151n27
karma, 202
Keynotes and Discords (x), 107
Kipnis, L., xxxvi–xxxviiin17
Klee, P., 193
Kühn, E., 121
künstlerromans, xvi, xvii, xxx, 26–7, 29, 30, 172, 174, 212, 218

La pazza (Balla), 108–11
Lacanian mirror stage, 169
"Lady Asterisk" (Loy), 7, 84–5n39
Lane, R., xxv
"Langueur" (Verlaine), 112
Lawrence, D. H., 44–6
Les Liaisons dangereuses (Margitte), 179, 181
"Letters of the Unliving" (Loy), 103
Levy, Joella, 78–9n12, 79n13, 79n14, 230n17; *see also* Haweis, J.
Levy, Julien, xvi, 17–18, 36, 79n13, 230n17
"Library of the Sphinx" (Loy), 147n10
"Lions' Jaws" (Loy), 12, 147n10
Literature and Occult Tradition (Saurat), 16, 51
Lloyd, J. F., xvii, 17, 37, 78–9n12, 80n18
"Logos in Art, The" (Loy), 15, 216
Lorde, A., xxv, 58
Lost Lunar Baedeker, The (Conover), xxv, 77n5
love, xxviii, xxx, 3–4, 7, 31, 96, 115
   Myers on, 105, 171
   Platonic, 59
   Rado on, 37
   sexual, 32, 60, 64
   in Theosophy, 207

v. Eros, 38–9
see also Eros; esoteric Eros; orgasm
Love Pampered by Beautiful Ladies (Loy), 114
Love's Coming-of-Age (Carpenter), 55, 56
Löwy, S., xxvi–xxvii, xxxiiin5, 108
Loy, M.
  adolescence, 205–6
  childhood development, 39, 169–70
  family, 97–8
  home and self, 158, 159, 160–2, 230n15
  neurasthenia, 108
  reception, xii–xiv
  upbringing, xxvi–xxvii, 30, 34, 65–6, 219, 229–30n14
Lucian of Samosata, 22
Luckhurst, R., 107
lunacy, feminised, 105–11
Lunar Baedecker (Loy), xiv, 60
Lunar Baedeker and Time-Tables (Loy), xii

Mad Love (Breton), 48
madness *see* lunacy, feminised
Mafarka the Futurist (Marinetti), 114–15, 117–18, 150n25
magic, 28, 119; *see also* black magic; theurgy; white magic
Magritte, R., 179–80, *181*, *182*, 230n18, 232n22
Mahon, A., 86n43, 86–7n44
"Maiden Song" (Loy), 103–4
male gaze, 41, 122, 126–7, 128, 175
Marcuse, H., 57–8
Marinetti, F., xiii, 58, 90n63, 94, 114–15, 117–18, 146n6
  animal magnetism, 149n18
  avant-gardism, 12, 13
  esotericism, 119–20, 121, 122
  mesmerism, 124–5
  "Poems to Beny", 143
  science, 148–9n15
  see also Futurism; *Brontolivido* (Loy)
Marshall, A., 222
"Mass-Production on 14th Street" (Loy), 211
"Massacred Woman, The" (Papini), 118
Mathers, S. L. M., 20
meditation, xx, xxvii, 30, 69, 93, 94, 130–1, 171, 185, 198
Meditations on First Philosophy (Descartes), 188, 189

melancholia, 37
Melzer, A. M., 24, 64, 81n23
Mensendieck System of Functional Movement, 210
mental illness, 42, 98, 110, 166, 197; *see also* hysteria; lunacy, feminised
Mesmer, F., 124
mesmerism, 80n19, 119, 120, 121–2, 124–6, 136, 148n14
"Metaphysical Pattern in Aesthetics, The" (Loy), 14, 15
Mexico, 30, 44
"Mi & Lo" (Loy), 9, 25, 30, 31–2
  archived notes for, 166, 218
  blind back, 164
  Cartesian dualism, 189, 190
  consciousness, 66
  esoteric Eros, 34, 68, 75
  morality, 100n6
  perfection, 184
  pineality, 198, 217
Michelson-Morley experiment, 229n8
Miller, H., xii
misogyny, xiv, 116, 118
  Futurist, 12, 95, 102, 118
"Modern Poetry" (Loy), 5
modernist mystical feminism, 51–9
modernism, 8, 24, 113, 114
modernist art, 14, 81n24, 216
modernist artists, 186, 214, 218; *see also individual artists*
modernists, 14–15
modernity, 8–9
"Monde Triple-Extra" (Loy), 152n36
Monroe, H., xiii
morality, 100n6
Morrisson, M., 70, 89n61, 193
Morse Code, 70
Muir, E., xiv
Muñoz, J., xxv
Muzard, S., 48
Myers, F. W. H., xx, xxi, xxxi, 16, 152n34, 167, 187, 213, 221
  bodies, 75
  love, 105
  Platonic love, 59
  supraliminial self v. subliminial consciousness, 41–2, 170–3
  telepathy, 136–7, 139–40
  see also Human Personality and its Survival of Bodily Death (Myers)
mysticism, xviii, xix–xx, xxi–xxii, 13, 84n38, 122, 133, 151–2n31; *see also* modernist mystical feminism; visions

Nash, J. C., xxv
nature / natural world, 22, 28, 77–8n6, 112, 120, 141, 199
"Negro Dancer" (Loy), 89n56
neurasthenia, 106, 108
New Era of Thought, A (Hinton), 217
New Testament, xxi, 53, 59, 73
New Thought movement, 192
New York, 108, 214
Nietzsche, F., 101, 131–2, 150n24
Nightingale, F., 107, 112
Not to be Reproduced (Magritte), 179, *182*
"Notes on Metaphysics" (Loy), 190, 217
Notes on Thought and Vision (H.D.), 162
Noys, B., 231n19
nuclear destruction / extinction, xxix, 12, 61
nuclear fission, 69, 72

Obeyesekere, G., 152n37, 232–3n27
occult practices, 135, 142
occultism, 7–8, 21, 56, 70, 112, 119–21, 188
  Futurist, 119–20, 121–2; *see also* Brontolivido (Loy); "Pazzarella" (Loy)
  see also clairvoyance; esotericism; magic; mesmerism; mysticism; spiritualism; telepathy; Theosophy
ocularity, 155, 186–8
odalisques, 138
Oelze, R., 164–5
"On Painting" (Apollinaire), 215–16
Oppenheim, J., 192
orgasm, xxii, xxiii, xxxvi–xxxviin17, 7, 34–5, 36, 37, 51–2, 131, 205, 224; *see also* female sexual pleasure; sexual pleasure
orgasmic Eros, 34; *see also* esoteric Eros; pleasure
"Others Anthology, The" (Rodker), xii
Owen, A., 8

pain, xxv, 10, 11, 13, 27, 74, 85n40, 172, 219–21, 235n38
palingenesis, 26, 30, 32, 74, 95, 132
"Pamperers, The" (Loy) 100n4, 159
Papini, G., 13, 23, 94, 100n2, 114, 118, 122, 146n6; *see also* "Pazzarella" (Loy)
parenthood / parenting, 28, 83n35, 178; *see also Child and the Parent, The* (Loy)
Paris, 17, 21, 54
Parmar, S., xxviii, 42, 77n5

"Parturition" (Loy), 222, 227–8, 235n38
Passions of the Soul, The (Descartes), 188, 189, 207
"Passivia" (Loy), 103
"Pazzarella" (Loy), 28, 94, 98, 100n4, 118, 146n6, 150n23
  esoteric Eros, 30
  male violence, 104–5, 111–13, 115–16, 117
  occultism / mesmerism, 121, 125–6, 127–30, 131–2
  telepathy, voices and visions, 132–3, 134–5, 136, 137–9, 142–3
  women's backs, 175
perfection, 171, 184, 199, 226
Perloff, M., 111
Phaedrus (Plato), 62
Philosophies for Sale (Lucian of Samosata), 22
physics, xxix, 68, 71, 89n62, 194, 236n40
Picasso, P., 23, 96, 216
"Piero and Eliza." (Loy), 84n39, 147n8, 159
pineal eye, xxxii, 185–90; *see also* pineality
"Pineal Eye, The" (Bataille), 209
pineal gland, 185–6, 188–90, 191, 231–2n21, 232n23, 232n24
pineality, 191–207, 211–12, 217, 231–2n21; *see also* pineal eye
Pinkerton, S., 50
Plato, xxix, 12, 29, 40, 57, 60–5, 182–3, 194
Platonic love, 59
pleasure, 172; *see also* sexual pleasure
Plumed Serpent, The (Lawrence), 46
Poe, E. A., 23, 130
"Poems to Beny" (Marinetti), 143
Poggi, C., 110
portraiture, 14
posture, 65, 97–8, 119, 143, 164–5, 169; *see also* bowed backs; proneness; supinity; Young, I. M.
Pound, E., 58, 78n9, 95
Precautions (Saint John of the Cross), 151n30
primitivism, 59–60
"Problem of Melancholia, The" (Rado), 37
proneness, 98, 131, 139, 142, 224
Protestantism, xv, xxxiii, 31, 66, 200
psychoanalysis, 16, 57, 135, 151–2n31, 166
  and esoteric Eros, 33–43
psychosynthesis, 42–3, 132; *see also* Assagioli, R.

Quain's Elements of Anatomy, 199
queer males, 183
queerness, xxv, 183; *see also* homophobia
Queneau, R., 48
Quimby, P. P., 19

race, 194, 195, 196–7
racism, xxvii
racist primitivism, 59–60
Rado, S., 37, 83n32
Randolph, P. B., 55
rape, 115–18, 134
Re, L., 142
rebirth, 26, 29, 30, 32, 74, 178; *see also* transmutation
"Reflection on the Atom Bomb" (Stein), 76
reincarnation, 202, 203–4, 233n28
religion, xxxiii–xxxivn6, 33–4, 46
  and sexuality, 51–4, 60
  see also Buddhism; Catholicism; Christian Science; exotericism; Hinduism; Judaism; Protestantism; Theosophy
Republic (Plato), 62
retrocognition (Myers), xxxi, 167–75
retrospeculation, 95
Rodker, J., xii, xxxiiin2
romans à clef, xvi, xxvi, xxvii, xxx, 168, 224; *see also* autobiography; künstlerromans
Rossetti, C., 3
Rossetti, D. G., 23, 222–3
Rubens, P. P., 177, 179, 230n16

"Sacred Prostitute, The" (Loy), 6, 100n4, 115, 135, 143, 151n30
sacrifice, xiv, 3, 183, 207
Salon d'Automne, 111
Santucci, J. A., 196
Sappho, 58–9, 62–3
satiation, xxii, xxiii, 33, 34, 44, 51, 62, 65, 117, 176, 224–5; *see also* esoteric Eros; orgasm; pleasure
satire, xiv, 9–10, 11, 13
Saurat, D., xxxvn10, 16, 31, 51
Schrepfer, J. G., 82–3n30
Scuriatti, L., 152n38
secrecy, 22; *see also* Sphinx
Secret Doctrine, The (Blavatsky), 194–5
seers, xvi, 45; *see also* visionary
Seidel, M., 227
self, divided or split, xxiii, xxxii, 7, 12, 42, 65–6, 75–6, 189, 225, 227
self-as-house, 158–63

Seven Ages of God, The (Haweis), 194–5
sex, 33, 50, 55–6, 138, 176; *see also* esoteric Eros; orgasm; pleasure
sex war, 139
sexual curiosity, 205–6
sexual desire, xxii–xxv, 38–9
sexual pleasure, 131, 215
sexuality, 183, 184, 234n36
  and gender, 44–5
  and religion, 51–4, 60
  see also esoteric Eros; erotic Eros; female sexual desire; female sexual pleasure; homophobia; orgasm; satiation
shame, xxvii, 65, 66, 85n41, 93, 123
Shapiro, L., 232n24
"Show Me a Saint Who Suffered" (Loy), 225
Showalter, E., 108, 145–6n4
Shreiber, M., xviii, xix, xxxiv–xxxvn9, 52
Simmel, G., 9, 22, 24, 64
Simon, K., 52
"Sketch of a Man on a Platform" (Loy), 146n6
Society of Psychical Research (SPR), 15–16, 48, 125, 136, 192
"Songs to Joannes" (Loy), 50, 52, 63, 72, 96, 196
soul, 82n29, 172–3, 189, 190, 194, 197, 217
Spackman, B., 131, 150n23
Sphinx, xxii, 98, 131, 142, 150n23; *see also* female satiation
Spillers, H. J., xxxviiin22
spine, 106–7, 110, 140, 210; *see also* back (body part)
Spinoza, B., 188, 232n23
spiritualism, 120, 128–9
Stein, G., 23, 52, 76
Stopes, M., xxiii
Strauss, L., 64
"Street Sister" (Loy), xx, 140, 141
subconscious, 42, 54, 108, 133, 166, 171, 173, 174, 182, 229n9, 229n11
subconscious self, 125
sublimation, 43, 171, 187
subliminality, 130, 167, 170–1, 172–3, 174, 182, 187
suffragettes, 104; *see also* feminism
Suleiman, S. R., 49, 84n38, 231n19
supinity, xxvii, xxx–xxxi, xxxviin22, 95, 99, 104, 107, 117, 118, 131, 184, 224
Surette, L., 8, 23, 78n9

Surrealism, 21, 47–51, 85–6n42, 86n43, 86–7n44, 164–5, 179, 182
Surrealist Eros, 47–51
Symbolism, 120
Symposium, The (Plato), 60, 61, 62, 64, 67

Tears of Eros, The (Bataille), 86n43
telepathy, 133, 134, 135–7, 139–40, 141, 142–3, 148n14, 154
Teresa of Ávila, xiii, 51
Thanatos, xiii, xxix, xxx, 9, 12, 49, 70, 74, 77n4, 130, 213, 219, 222; *see also* death
Theory of the Avant-Garde (Bürger), 82n26
Theosophical Society, xxxii, 56, 191–2, 199
Theosophy, xxxii, xxxiii–xxxivn6, 16, 19, 186, 190, 191–207, 213
"There is No Love Alone" (Loy), 67
theurgy, 8, 20, 21, 28, 98; *see also* magic
third eye *see* pineal eye
"Three Moments in Paris" (Loy), 113, 114
"Three Wishes, The" (Loy), 100n4
Thurschwell, P., 149n16
"Time-Bomb" (Loy), 71–2
To the Lighthouse (Woolf), 151n27
"Tranquil Thought, A" (Roberts), 142
transmutation, 29–30, 72, 76, 120, 140
Treatise on Man (Descartes), 189
"Tuning in on the Atom Bomb" (Loy), 9, 32, 68–9, 72–3, 152n36
Twain, M., 52

"Universal Food Machine" (Loy), 32
Untitled (Surreal Scene) (Loy), xxiii, *xxiv*, xxxvn14, 5, 6, 200, *201*

Varieties of Religious Experience, The (James), 51
Venus in Front of the Mirror (Rubens), 179, *180*
verbal abuse, xxvii, 10, 11, 78n8, 233–4n32
Vetter, L., xxxivn9, 191, 231n20
Victorianism, xxx, 4, 7–8, 36, 77n3, 77n5, 88n52, 106–7, 130, 170, 202, 214
violence, 107, 115
Virgil, 72
"Virgins Plus Curtains Minus Dots" (Loy), 159
visionariness, feminist, 143

visionary, 30, 43, 99, 111, 132, 133–4, 136, 155, 162, 186–7, 222, 224
visions, 132–5, 141
  inner vision *see* pineal eye; pineality
  see also blindness
"Visitation of Insel" (Loy), 158, 164–5, 178, 188, 236n43
Viswanathan, G., 232–3n27
vitalism, 120
Voss, K., 50
vulnerability, xiv, 50, 97, 126, 156, 176, 177, 179, 183, 224

Walter, C., 77n5, 228n4
Wendell, S., xxv–xxvi
White, E. B., 236n41
white magic, xvi, 21; *see also* black magic, theurgy
Whitman, W., 3
"Widow's Jazz, The" (Loy), 89n56
Wiegman, R., xxxvin16
Wilde, O., 131, 150n22
will, 163, 167, 174, 204, 207
  artistic, 95, 188
  in *Brontolivido* (Loy), 122
  in Futurism, 101, 106
  in *Mafarka the Futurist* (Marinetti), 114
  in mesmerism, 125
  in mysticism, 30
  in "Pazzarella", 111
  of the pineal gland, 188
  in psychosynthesis, 42
  religious, xx
Williams, W. C., 23
Wills, D., 96
Wilson, E. A., 145–6n4
women
  bowed backs, 175–85
  and esotericism, 121–2
  female embodiment, xxvii
  female vanguardism, 95–6
  sexual desire, xxii–xxv, 38–9
  sexual pleasure, 131
  sexuality, 35–6
  telepathy, 135–6
  see also esoteric Eros; feminised lunacy; gender; modernist mystical feminism; orgasm; satiation

Yates, F., 78n11
Yeats, W. B., 20
Young, I. M., xxvii, 97, 175

EU representative:
Easy Access System Europe
Mustamäe tee 50, 10621 Tallinn, Estonia
Gpsr.requests@easproject.com

www.ingramcontent.com/pod-product-compliance
Lightning Source LLC
Chambersburg PA
CBHW050208240426
43671CB00013B/2253